The
American Paradox

The American Paradox

A History of the United States Since 1945

Third Edition

Steven M. Gillon
University of Oklahoma
and The History Channel

WADSWORTH
CENGAGE Learning·

Australia · Brazil · Japan · Korea · Mexico · Singapore · Spain · United Kingdom · United States

**The American Paradox:
A History of the United States
Since 1945, Third Edition**
Steven M. Gillon

Senior Publisher: Suzanne Jeans

Senior Sponsoring Editor: Ann
West

Development Manager: Jeff
Greene

Assistant Editor: Megan
Chrisman

Editorial Assistant: Patrick
Roach

Managing Media Editor: Lisa
Ciccolo

Senior Art Director: Cate
Rickard Barr

Manufacturing Planner: Sandee
Milewski

Marketing Program Manager:
Caitlin Green

Design Direction, Production
Management, and Composition:
PreMediaGlobal

Rights Acquisition Specialist:
Jennifer Meyer Dare

Cover Images:
Political campaign buttons,
close-up © Ed Honowitz/
Stone/Getty Images Social
issues buttons © Ed Honowitz/
Stone/Getty Images

For product information and
technology assistance, contact us at **Cengage Learning
Customer & Sales Support, 1-800-354-9706**

For permission to use material from this text or product,
submit all requests online at **www.cengage.com/permissions**.
Further permissions questions can be emailed to
permissionrequest@cengage.com.

Library of Congress Control Number: 2011941100

ISBN-13: 978-1-133-30985-7

ISBN-10: 1-133-30985-2

Wadsworth
20 Channel Center Street
Boston, MA 02210
USA

Cengage Learning is a leading provider of customized learning
solutions with office locations around the globe, including
Singapore, the United Kingdom, Australia, Mexico, Brazil and Japan.
Locate your local office at **international.cengage.com/region**

Cengage Learning products are represented in Canada by
Nelson Education, Ltd.

For your course and learning solutions, visit
www.cengage.com.

Purchase any of our products at your local college store or at our
preferred online store **www.cengagebrain.com.**

Instructors: Please visit **login.cengage.com** and log in to access
instructor-specific resources.

Contents

6 | American Ideals and Social Realities, 1952–1960   109

7 | The Kennedy Presidency, 1961–1963   133

10 | Richard Nixon and the New Republican Majority, 1969–1974   212

11 | The Clash of Cultures, 1969–1980   237

15 | The End of the Cold War, 1988–1992   338

16 | The Clinton Presidency, 1993–2001   355

17 | The Prosperous Nineties   376

18 | The Challenges of the New Century, 2001 to the Present   402

Maps and Graphs

Preface

My approach to the study of modern America grows out of my experience growing up in suburban Philadelphia in the late 1970s. As an undergraduate at Widener University (class of 1978), I was introduced to many of the classics in modern American history, and I was often struck by how many of these books, and the authors who wrote them, used the 1930s and the New Deal as their reference point. They emphasized the success of major reform movements and the achievements of progressive presidents to chart the steady triumph of liberal values in America. In many of these accounts, the expanding power of the federal government represented the clearest evidence of the triumph of liberal values.

But these books made little sense of the political events that I was witnessing all around me. My racially divided local community revolted against large-scale busing initiatives. My neighbors, mainly working-class Irish and Italians who had once worshiped Roosevelt, now voted Republican. By the time I entered graduate school at Brown University in 1980, the conservative movement was at high tide: Jerry Falwell was a national celebrity, Ronald Reagan was president, tax revolts were spreading like wildfire across the country, and the once powerful New Deal coalition was in full retreat. But of course the story was not that simple. The decade also witnessed the emergence of a number of important empowerment movements, which fed off the momentum created by the civil-rights movement of the 1960s. Women were demanding the Equal Rights Amendment, post-Stonewall gays were fighting against discrimination, and other racial minorities—especially Asians and Hispanics, whose numbers had swelled because of massive immigration—were raising their voices in protest. Nothing I was reading was making sense of this polarized, confused, and contentious national environment.

It was around that time that I came across an observation by the British journalist Godfrey Hodgson, who said that "Americans love change, but they hate to be changed." We change our clothing style, our homes, and our hairstyles more than any other people on earth, but we resist altering our attitudes about the way we view the world. He was simply recasting a question that Robert Kennedy had asked in the months before his death in 1968: "How do we seek to change a society that yields so painfully to change?" That question captured for me the central contradiction of postwar politics and society: Americans had come to expect government to solve most major social problems, but they retained a traditional fear of federal power. Americans, as two political scientists noted in the 1950s, are philosophically conservative and operationally liberal. In the abstract, Americans believe in equal rights and oppose discrimination of any kind, but they cling tenaciously to deeply held values about limited government, self-help, and racial and gender stereotypes. Especially in the years since the 1960s, the tension between rising expectations of government and deep-seated fear of federal power has shaped public debate in America. Hence the title of this book: *The American Paradox*.

It is important that a book of this nature expose students to the many different subfields that make up the study of history—social, cultural, political, and intellectual. While all fields are represented here, the emphasis is on culture and politics. Students today have no connection to the old and tired debates between social and political historians. They are forging a new paradigm that views history through the prism of culture. Social surveys also reveal that this generation of students is the most politically engaged in recent memory. The results of the most recent presidential elections, which have shown a dramatic increase in voter turnout among young people, prove that students today care about politics. For that reason, politics and culture will serve as the building blocks for the narrative and help distinguish the book from others in the market. At its core, this book recognizes the need for synthesis in historical writing, and for weaving together the threads of individual experiences into the broader fabric of American history.

This book also includes a number of stylistic and pedagogical devices that are designed to make it both practical and readable. I have integrated into the narrative important primary documents that are designed to provoke debate and discussion. Especially in upper-division courses, students need to develop the skill to analyze and interpret evidence. Students have under one cover some of the key documents in modern America: from George Kennan's famous Mr. X article, to the Supreme Court's decision *in Brown* v. *Board of Education* (1956), to Phyllis Schlafly's attack on the Equal Rights Amendment. Ample graphs, charts, and photographs provide visual support for some of the important points raised in the text.

In an effort to animate the narrative, I included lots of colorful quotations, personality sketches, and anecdotes. I also chose to omit the names of people who appear only once in the narrative. As a result, there are references to "a congressman said" or "a journalist noted." The important players and figures, however, are all properly identified. In addition, although the narrative makes reference to key historical debates, specific references to historians are usually confined to the selected bibliography at the end of each chapter. The bibliography contains both standard works and, when appropriate, the most recent books on major issues raised in the chapter.

New to the Third Edition

In response to feedback from reviewers, I have made changes throughout the book. These changes are designed to make this third edition easier to teach from and more accessible to students. There are new sections on the Cold War, Martin Luther King and Malcolm X, the politics of the 1990s, globalization, and the wars in Iraq and Afghanistan. Most significantly, the theme of "American Identity" is woven into the fabric of the narrative. "American Identity" has been contested terrain throughout American history where various groups—religious, ethnic, class, racial—have fought for dominance. The objective is to help students understand that many of the issues that dominate the headlines today—immigration reform, race relations, gay rights, fear of global terrorism, and tax policy—are part of a longer conversation that is deeply rooted in competing notions of American identity. The conversation continues today, and students have a voice in the debate.

Acknowledgments

A number of people helped make this book possible. My first debt is to the scholars of modern America whose work provides the intellectual foundation for this book. I am grateful to Douglas Miller, a talented graduate student at the University of Oklahoma, who read every chapter and offered a number of constructive suggestions. I would also like to thank the colleagues who reviewed the book: Phil McCaskey, Cape Fear Community College; Rick Moniz, Chabot College; Jacqueline Moore, Austin College; Pam Pennock, University of Michigan–Dearborn; Emilie Raymond, Virginia Commonwealth University; Patrick Reagan, Tennessee Tech University; Howard Smead, University of Maryland; Jason Sokol, Cornell University; and Karin Zipf, East Carolina University.

At Cengage Learning, I would like to thank Ann West and Megan Chrisman for skillfully overseeing the revisions for this edition, and Margaret Bridges and Joseph Malcolm for seeing it through to publication. I thank also Sandee Mileski, manufacturing planner.

The book is dedicated to the Ryan family. Jim and Kate Ryan have welcomed me into their lives, providing me with an endless supply of affection, support, and guidance. They have also allowed me to experience the joy of spending time with their wonderful children. When I first wrote this book there were three—Will, Sam, and Ben. Since the last edition of this book they have welcomed a fourth child—Phebe—who has added a touch of feminine grace to the Ryan family.

Steven M. Gillon
Norman, Oklahoma

Introduction: The American Paradox

At 7:00 P.M. on Tuesday, August 14, 1945, President Harry S. Truman invited reporters to the Oval Office for a brief, informal press conference. For weeks rumors had circulated about an imminent Japanese surrender. As the horde of reporters rushed into the room, a solemn Truman rose from his desk to greet them. Reading from a prepared text, he announced that he had received a message of surrender from the Japanese government. "Arrangements are now being made," he said, "for the formal signing of surrender terms at the earliest possible moment." The president then smiled and sat down.

The nation erupted in celebration. Across the country church bells rang, air-raid sirens screeched, horns honked, and bands played. The celebrations, however, were clouded by fears about America's role in the postwar world and Truman's ability to shift America to a peacetime economy. Perhaps most of all, Americans brooded about the legacy of the atomic bomb, which had produced such a swift and dramatic end to the war. "For all we know," warned popular radio host H. V. Kaltenborn, "we have created a Frankenstein." The bomb, which President Truman hailed as "the greatest achievement of organized science in history," also possessed the power to destroy the world. A few weeks after the United States dropped the first bomb on Hiroshima on August 6, the *Washington Post* editorialized that the life expectancy of the human race had "dwindled immeasurably."

Despite these worries, most Americans had high hopes for the postwar world. In 1945 the influential columnist Walter Lippmann predicted that "what Rome was to the ancient world, what Great Britain has been to the modern world, America is to be to the world of tomorrow." There were many reasons for such optimism. The nation, which had been mired in depression during the 1930s, was experiencing an unprecedented economic expansion. Unemployment, which stood at 17 percent when Japanese planes attacked Pearl Harbor, later dropped to nearly unmeasurable levels. National income more than doubled from $81 billion in 1940 to $181 billion five years later. The war also improved the distribution of income—an accomplishment that had eluded New Deal planners. The share of income owned by the richest 5 percent declined from 23.7 to 16.8 percent, while the average wages of workers employed full-time in manufacturing rose from $28 per week in 1940 to $48 in 1944.

An expansion of federal power played a central role in the new prosperity. A growing centralization of power in Washington, begun during the New Deal, accelerated during World War II. Between 1940 and 1945, the number of civilian employees in government posts rose from 1 million to 3.8 million. Federal expenditures from 1940 to 1945 rose from $9 billion to $98.4 billion. The final bill for the war came to more than $251 billion, a sum greater than the total of all government spending in the history of the United States to that point. By comparison, Roosevelt's New Deal responded to the 1938 recession by spending $3 billion on public works.

The spending was matched by regulations that made the federal government a part of the fabric of life for most Americans. Congress dramatically expanded the federal income tax during the war. Most Americans had never filed an income-tax return before World War II because the income tax, on the books since 1913, had been a small tax on upper-income families. Starting with 1942, anyone earning $600 or more annually had to file a return. Income-tax withholding from paychecks went into effect in 1943. But it was the draft that brought the federal government into the homes of millions of Americans. Following the Japanese attack on Pearl Harbor, Congress ordered the registration of all men between the ages of twenty (lowered to eighteen in 1942) and forty-four for war service. During the war the nation peacefully registered 49 million men, selected 19 million, and inducted 10 million, twice the number who volunteered.

World War II also refigured social relations in America, providing African Americans and other racial minorities with new opportunities. The war lured millions of blacks into war plants and labor unions in the North and West. Wartime experience raised the expectations of African American veterans, who had risked their lives to guarantee freedom in Europe and were unwilling to accept second-class citizenship in their own country. "I spent four years in the army to free a bunch of Dutchmen and Frenchmen, and I'm danged if I'm going to let the

Alabama version of the Germans kick me around when I get home," a discharged army corporal from Alabama exclaimed. "No siree-bob! I went into the Army a nigger; I'm comin' out a man." World War II also inspired a drive for equal rights among Asian American, Native American, and Hispanic American veterans who returned home to their communities determined to secure full access to American life.

The war also expanded opportunities for women. With men being drafted for the service, employers looked to women to maintain industrial production at home. "Rosie the Riveter," who, according to a popular song of the time, was "making history working for victory," became the media symbol of the woman at work. She could do a man's job without compromising her feminine qualities. Over the next four years nearly 6 million women responded to the call. By the end of the war almost 19 million women (or 36 percent) were working, many at jobs from which they had previously been excluded. Nearly 2 million women—about 10 percent of female workers—took up jobs in defense plants. For many women, working in the factories was "the first time we got a chance to show that we could do a lot of things that only men had done before."

Above all else, the war was responsible for producing the striking paradox that would define postwar America: World War II revolutionized American society, but it did not produce a corresponding change in public attitudes. The war may have transformed America's relationship with Washington, producing a dramatic expansion of federal power, but it did little to challenge deeply rooted fears of centralized power. At the same time that the war contributed to the growth of big government, it reaffirmed Americans' faith in limited government and individualism. In all of the major initiatives of the war—building an army, mobilizing industry, controlling wages and prices—Americans tried to balance the needs of war with the values of democracy. In fact, the brutality of Adolf Hitler's regime made Americans more skeptical of state power. In a war depicted as a struggle between good and evil, the victory over fascism seemed to confirm the continuing relevance of America's democratic experiment.

Although social relations had been transformed by war, American attitudes about race and gender remained remarkably resilient in the wake of extraordinary changes. Women, African Americans, and other racial minorities may have emerged from the war with expanded expectations, but the majority of Americans showed little interest in questioning old stereotypes or changing past practices. Though Rosie the Riveter became a popular symbol of working women during the war, polls showed that majorities of men and women disapproved of working wives, and most women of traditional child-bearing age (twenty through thirty-four) remained at home. As a result, the war did little, in the short run, to challenge traditional notions that a women's proper place was in the home raising the children. "The housewife, not the WAC or the riveter, was the model woman," observed the historian D'Ann Campbell.

The war gave African Americans a glimpse of a better life, but it did little to change deeply embedded racial attitudes or undermine the structure of

segregation. The army, which in 1940 counted ust five African American officers, three of them chaplains, remained rigidly segregated. Black soldiers had to
watch the army segregate the blood plasma of whites and blacks. Regulations restricted blacks to their own barracks, movie houses, and commissaries. Conditions on the home front were not much better. Management and labor joined
forces to limit black access to the war boom. "We will not employ Negroes," declared the president of North American Aviation. "It is against company policy."

This tension between American ideals and social realities, which had roots deep
in the nation's past, was sharpened in the years following World War II by what the
historian James T. Patterson has described as America's "grand expectations." These
expectations touched on nearly every aspect of American society: economists believed they had discovered the tools to guarantee growth, promising a better life for
all Americans; marginalized groups—especially African Americans and women—
gained new wartime opportunities, which they hoped would translate into tangible
peacetime gains; and victory convinced policymakers of the universal appeal of
American values and the need to project U.S. power abroad.

While Americans entered the postwar world with high hopes about the possibilities of change, they remained deeply ambivalent about the consequences of
change. The British journalist Godfrey Hodgson once observed that "Americans
love change, but they hate to be changed." This paradox is essential to understanding the dynamics of American history since 1945. Franklin Roosevelt's leadership during the Great Depression and World War II had altered America's
relationship with the federal government. Once the war ended, Americans
continued to look to Washington, especially the president, to satisfy their expectations of a better life. The result was a dramatic and sustained expansion of
federal power. By the end of the century Washington played a role in the daily
lives of most Americans. This expansion of government power, however, did not
produce a corresponding change in attitudes toward government power. The tension between expectations of government as a vehicle of change and traditional
fears of encroaching state power provides the central narrative of this book.

This paradox has its roots in the nation's revolutionary past. The Founders
rebelled against the imperial designs of a distant and impersonal British government. Believing that "power" was antithetical to "liberty," they created a system of
government that made it difficult for power to concentrate in any one branch of
government. "The constant aim," James Madison explained in *The Federalist
Papers,* "is to divide and arrange the several offices in such a manner that they
may be a check on the other—that the private interest of every individual may be
a sentinel over the public rights."

Despite these inhibitions, Americans have witnessed a dramatic increase in
the size and scope of government power. This trend was especially pronounced in
the years after World War II when Americans, their expectations whetted by
prosperity and rising expectations of the "good life," placed enormous pressure
on government to increase services and benefits. By the 1990s, 48 percent of all
American households, including many with high incomes, received some form of

federal entitlement check—unemployment compensation, Medicare, social security, food stamps, pension, veteran's benefits, or welfare allotment. (The *Federal Register,* which lists government rules and regulations, grew from 5,307 pages in 1940 to 68,101 in 1995.)

The irony is that Americans have come to accept the benefits of a modern welfare state without accepting the legitimacy of federal power. Polls, for example, show overwhelming support for the large entitlement programs that make up a significant portion of domestic spending. Yet the same surveys show a clamoring for cuts in government spending, a reduction in Washington's power, and a demand for local control. A bellwether poll conducted by Princeton Survey Associates in 1995 found that by a margin of 61 to 24 percent Americans trusted state government to "do a better job running things" than the federal government. The poll results confirm the historian Arthur Schlesinger Jr.'s assertion that America is "operationally liberal and philosophically conservative." Americans are against big government but they want Washington to provide for social security, Medicare, Medicaid, clean air and water, and safe streets.

The same paradox of grand expectations shaped America's postwar foreign policy. The American victory in the fight against Hitler shattered the myth of isolationism that had dominated thinking during the 1930s and introduced a new consensus in favor of internationalism. America emerged from the struggle as the leading economic and military power in the world. Flush with victory, the United States prepared to launch a new crusade against communism armed with enormous military might and confidence in the universal relevance of American values. But the experience of total war against absolute evil did little to prepare Americans for the prospect of limited war or for the moral ambiguity of many Third World conflicts. The Cold War raised troubling new questions: How could the United States balance its support for democracy with its fear of communism? Did the expansion of the national security state, and the fear of subversion, threaten democracy and liberty at home? It would take a tragic war in Vietnam to expose the tension between American expectations of the postwar world and the realities of international power. The end of the Cold War in the 1990s only heightened the tension. The absence of an international rival left many Americans questioning whether the nation needed to maintain a strong presence in the world. The emergence of new threats from amorphous terrorist groups forced the nation to rethink its global interests and the best ways to protect them.

A further dimension of the paradox of expectations and social realities shaped many of the cultural assumptions of postwar America. The war reinforced the image of the melting pot, a singular American identity that transcended racial and class differences. Most Americans emerged from the war with a renewed faith in consensus, a belief in a common American identity and culture. But the war also sowed the seeds of cultural pluralism—a belief in many different American identities based on racial, gender, religious, and cultural differences—by promoting racial consciousness and by raising the expectations of groups that had been excluded from the nation's political and economic life. The clash between these competing notions of American identity culminated with the social and political struggles of the 1960s and 1970s. As the historian Daniel T. Rodgers has noted, the last decades of the twentieth century represented an "age of fracture" as a far more complicated and diverse sense of American identity emerged from the remnants of consensus.

The war forged the foundation of postwar America, but it was an ambiguous legacy that rested on a paradox. The war, and the prosperity that came with it, stimulated America's appetite for a better life, producing an ever-widening cycle of expectations about the possibility of change. But the war also produced a celebration of American values that emphasized national unity, limited government, and traditional ideas about race relations and gender roles. The tension between rising expectations and traditional attitudes would define the nature of social and political conflict in America for the remainder of the century.

SELECTED READINGS

▌ John Morton Blum's *V Was for Victory* (1976) is a colorful analysis of American culture and society during World War II. William O'Neill's *A Democracy at War* (1993) is a fascinating look at the impact of American political ideology on the mobilization of the country for war. David M. Kennedy's lucid *Freedom from Fear* (1999) provides the best overview of the war at home and abroad. For the theme of paradox in American history, see Michael Kammen's insightful *People of Paradox* (1975).

▌ I relied heavily on Gary Gerstle's *American Crucible* (2001) for his insight into American identity and the problem of race. David Kryder's *Divided Arsenal* (2000) explores the government's dealings with the race issue as a whole. Mario T. Garcia's *Mexican-Americans* (1989) examines the Hispanic experience during the war. Kenneth Townsend addresses the impact of the war on Native Americans in World War Two and the American Indian (2000). Sherna Berger Gluck's *Rosie the Riveter Revisited* (1987) is a compelling oral history of women workers during World War II. Ronald Takaki's *Double Victory* (2000) is a general history of the wartime experiences of Asians in America.

▌ The starting point for understanding America's attitudes toward government is Gordon Wood, *The Radicalism of the American Revolution* (1992). Also useful in understanding the contradictions in American views of government are Joseph Nye, "In Government We Don't Trust," *Foreign Policy* 108 (September 22, 1997); James Morone, *The Democratic Wish: Popular Participation and the Limits of American Government* (1990); Michael Kazin, *The Populist Persuasion* (1995); and Samuel P. Huntington, *American Politics: The Promise of Disharmony* (1981).

▌ James T. Patterson's *Grand Expectations* is the finest synthesis of the gap between postwar hopes and reality. Also valuable is the very readable Robert J. Samuelson, *The Good Life and Its Discontents: The American Dream in the Age of Entitlement, 1945–1995* (1995). Daniel T. Rodgers analyzes the breakup of consensus in *Age of Fracture* (2011).

1

The Specter of Appeasement: The Cold War, 1945–1949

On February 22, 1946, the State Department's telex machine began clattering with a secret eight-thousand-word telegram from Moscow. The cable, written by George Frost Kennan, a forty-two-year-old Soviet specialist in the U.S. embassy, tried to explain Soviet aggression to puzzled officials in Washington. Since the end of World War II, U.S. policymakers had grown increasingly alarmed as the Soviets violated wartime agreements and tightened their military grip over Eastern Europe. Worried officials were all asking the same questions: What were Soviet intentions? And how should the United States respond to them? They turned to Kennan for the answers.

Kennan laid out a frightening picture of an aggressive Soviet Union intent upon world domination. The Soviets, he wired, were driven by a "neurotic view of world affairs" that emerged from an "instinctive Russian sense of insecurity." They compensated for their insecurity by going on the attack "in patient but deadly struggle for total destruction of rival power, never in compacts and compromises with it." Moscow, he suggested, was "highly sensitive to logic of force. For this reason it can easily withdraw—and usually does—when strong resistance is encountered at any point." According to

Kennan's analysis, the Soviets were solely to blame for international tensions, negotiations and compromise had reached an impasse, and only military and economic pressure could tame the Russian bear.

Kennan's telegram caused a sensation in Washington. "Splendid analysis," exclaimed Secretary of State James Byrnes. The following year Kennan published an expanded public version of the telegram in an article written under the pseudonym "Mr. X." The Soviets, he argued, saw the world divided into hostile capitalist and communist camps, between which there could be no peace. He recommended a U.S. foreign policy based on the "long-term, patient but firm and vigilant containment of Russian expansive tendencies." From Kennan's essay a word emerged to characterize a new experiment in American foreign policy: *containment.*

PRIMARY SOURCE

1.1 | *The Sources of Soviet Conduct*

GEORGE KENNAN

George Kennan, a student of Russian language and history, served in the American embassy in Moscow from 1933 to 1937 and again from 1944 to 1946. His understanding of Soviet policy led to his warning in the July 1947 issue of *Foreign Affairs* under the pseudonym "Mr. X."

The political personality of Soviet power as we know it today is the product of ideology and circumstances: Ideology inherited by the present Soviet leaders from the movement in which they had their political origin, and circumstances of the power which they have now exercised for nearly three decades in Russia. . . .

5   It is difficult to summarize the set of ideological concepts with which the Soviet leaders came into power. Marxian ideology . . . has always been in process of subtle evolution. . . . But the outstanding features of Communist thought as it existed in 1916 may perhaps be summarized as follows: (a) that the central factor in the life of man, the fact which determines the character of public life and the

10   "physiognomy of society," is the system by which material goods are produced and exchanged; (b) that the capitalist system of production is a nefarious one which inevitably leads to the exploitation of the working class by the capital-owning class and is incapable of developing adequately the economic resources of society or of distributing fairly the material goods produced by human labor; (c)

15   that capitalism contains the seeds of its own destruction and must, in view of the

inability of the capital-owning class to adjust itself to economic change, result eventually and inescapably in a revolutionary transfer of power to the working class; and (d) that imperialism, the final phase of capitalism, leads directly to war and revolution. . . .

20   These considerations make Soviet diplomacy at once easier and more difficult to deal with than the diplomacy of individual aggressive leaders like Napoleon and Hitler. On the one hand it is more sensitive to contrary force. . . . On the other hand it cannot be easily defeated or discouraged by a single victory on the part of its opponents. And the patient persistence by which it is animated means that it

25 can be effectively countered not by sporadic acts which represent the momentary whims of democratic opinion but only by intelligent long-range policies on the part of Russia's adversaries—policies no less steady in their purpose, and no less variegated and resourceful in their application, than those of the Soviet Union itself.

30   In these circumstances it is clear that the main element of any United States policy toward the Soviet Union must be that of a long-term, patient but firm and vigilant containment of Russian expansive tendencies. It is important to note, however, that such a policy has nothing to do with outward histrionics: with threats or blustering or superfluous gestures of outward "toughness." While the

35 Kremlin is basically flexible in its reaction to political realities, it is by no means unamenable to considerations of prestige. Like almost any other government, it can be placed by tactless and threatening gestures in a position where it cannot afford to yield even though this might be dictated by its sense of realism. The Russian leaders are keen judges of human psychology, and as such they are highly

40 conscious that loss of temper and of self-control is never a source of strength in political affairs. They are quick to exploit such evidences of weakness. . . .

    In the light of the above, it will be clearly seen that the Soviet pressure against the free institutions of the Western world is something that can be contained by the adroit and vigilant application of counter-force at a series of constantly shift-

45 ing geographical and political points, corresponding to the shifts and maneuvers of Soviet policy, but which cannot be charmed or talked out of existence. The Russians look forward to a duel of infinite duration, and they see that already they have scored great successes.

Source: Reprinted by permission of *Foreign Affairs* (July 1947). Copyright 1947 by the Council on Foreign Relations, Inc.   ■ ■ ■

The "Long Telegram" and the "Mr. X" article provided the ideological justification for a new "get-tough" approach with the Soviets. The strategy of containment fundamentally transformed American foreign policy. It ripped the United States from its isolationist roots, imposed new international obligations on the American people, and created a massive national security state. World War II had reconfigured the international environment and America's place in it, but it had failed to produce a corresponding change in American attitudes toward the world. Once the war ended, most American soldiers planned to return home and most policymakers planned to reduce the nation's military commitments abroad. At the same time, victory raised expectations of a peaceful postwar world shaped by American commerce and influenced by American values. As a result, the Cold War confronted America with a paradox: How could the nation assume its new position of world power, and justify the dramatic enlargement of the national security state, while also being true to its democratic faith in limited government?

Roots of the Cold War

Who started the Cold War? This question has inspired years of passionate debate among historians. Some scholars place most of the blame on the Soviet Union, charging that its aggressive foreign policy was the logical outgrowth of an ideological commitment to world revolution. Other scholars contend that Russian aggression reflected a legitimate fear of American economic imperialism. In recent years historians studying the origins of the Cold War have emphasized that both nations shared responsibility for the conflict, though these same historians differ greatly on how much responsibility to assign each side. Rather than seeing the Cold War as the product of conspiracies hatched in the Kremlin or in Washington, post–Cold War historians stress how history, ideology, and national interest created serious misperceptions, limited the range of options on both sides, and made confrontation nearly inevitable.

The Cold War between the Soviet Union and the United States had its genesis in the past. In 1917, relations between the two nations plummeted into a deep freeze when the Bolsheviks seized control of the Russian government. Under V. I. Lenin, the Soviets pulled out of World War I, leaving the West to fight the Central Powers alone. More importantly, the Soviets committed the new state to the goal of world revolution and the destruction of capitalism. Communism challenged the basic tenets of the American dream: it threatened democratic government, supported state power over individual freedom, and cut off free markets.

The brutality of the Soviet regime further inflamed American hostility. Joseph Stalin, who seized control of the Soviet Union following Lenin's death in 1924, consolidated his power through a series of bloody purges that killed nearly 3 million citizens. He initiated a massive effort to collectivize agriculture that led to the deaths of 14 million peasants. In 1939, after Stalin signed a prewar non-aggression treaty with Adolf Hitler, he sent troops pouring into Finland, Estonia, Latvia, and Lithuania. By then most Americans agreed with the *Wall Street Journal* that "the principal difference between Mr. Hitler and Mr. Stalin is the size of their respective mustaches."

Likewise, the Soviets had reason to distrust the United States. The rhetoric and actions of American policymakers appeared to support one of the principal teachings of Marxist-Leninist doctrine: the incompatibility of capitalism and communism. Western leaders, including President Woodrow Wilson, made no secret of their contempt for Lenin or their desire to see him ousted. Wilson's decision to send American troops on a confused mission to north Russia in 1918 confirmed the Soviets' suspicion of a Western conspiracy to topple their government. Indeed, the United States did not extend diplomatic relations to the Soviets until 1933—sixteen years after the new government came to power.

Hitler's invasion of Russia in 1941 forced the United States and the Soviet Union into a brief alliance to defeat Germany. Wartime cooperation greatly improved the Soviet Union's image in America. Confronted with evidence that the Russian people were willing to fight to defend their country, many Americans jumped to the conclusion that the Soviet Union had suddenly become a democracy. In the best-selling book *Mission to Moscow* (1943), former Ambassador Joseph E. Davies proclaimed that "the Russia of Lenin and Trotsky—the Russia of the Bolshevik Revolution—no longer exists." *Life* magazine declared in 1943 that Russians "look like Americans, dress like Americans and think like Americans."

The war may have softened American public opinion, but it did little to ease the mistrust between leaders. Franklin Roosevelt, though hopeful about a postwar settlement, recognized that "a dictatorship as absolute as any . . . in the world" ruled Moscow. At the same time, Roosevelt's agreement with Winston Churchill in delaying a second front in Europe, and his refusal to share information about the development and testing of the atomic bomb, convinced Stalin that the Western Allies could not be trusted.

The Legacy of World War II

The brutality and destructiveness of World War II set the stage for the Cold War. The conflict devastated nations, crippled societies, and shattered the international system beyond recognition. The war left 60 million people dead; more than half of those—36 million—were Europeans. The Soviet Union lost 24 million people, or 14 percent of its population. An estimated 1.3 million Chinese soldiers died, along with as many as 15 million civilians. Japan lost 3 million people.

With typically vivid prose, British Prime Minister Winston Churchill described postwar Europe as "a rubble heap, a charnel house, a breeding ground of pestilence and hate." Allied bombing had leveled entire cities. The Germans had destroyed many of the cities they occupied. "The odor of death," recalled an American diplomat, "was everywhere." Tens of millions of people had no shelter. Everywhere farmlands had been despoiled, animals slaughtered. In Poland almost three-fourths of all horses and two-thirds of all cattle were gone.

The war produced the most sweeping changes in the international power structure in history. For the previous 500 years, Europe had dominated the international system. Not anymore. European nations that had been among the most powerful in the world before the war—Germany, Britain, Italy, and France—were either defeated and occupied, or crippled and nearly bankrupt. Unable to feed their own people, these nations could no longer preside over colonial empires, providing an opportunity for nationalist movements in the Middle East and in Asia to break away from their former masters.

As a result, the next few decades witnessed the creation of hundreds of new, independent nations. In 1947, after years of struggle, Britain gave up control of India and Pakistan. Other European powers followed suit, relinquishing control of many of their colonies in Africa and Indonesia.

Only two nations emerged with the ability to project power beyond their borders: the United States and the Soviet Union. Both nations agreed that a new international order needed to be created; otherwise anarchy and chaos would follow. They, however, had very different ideas about the structure of the new order and their role in it. Their visions of the future were shaped by memories of the recent past.

The Japanese attack on Pearl Harbor on December 7, 1941, shaped American views of the postwar world. Before the attack, many policymakers were convinced that geographical distance protected the United States from foreign threats. The surprise Japanese offensive made American military planners recognize that advances in technology, especially air power, meant that the two oceans no longer guaranteed security from potential adversaries. "If you imagine two or three hundred Pearl Harbors occurring all over the United States," an official warned in 1944, "you will have a rough picture of what the next war might look like."

Technology made the world smaller. For the first time, American planners believed the nation needed a network of defense bases around the world to respond quickly to potential trouble spots. Instability anywhere in the world posed a potential threat to American security. "We are now concerned with the peace of the entire world," General George C. Marshall warned.

Many American officials were also convinced that the policy of trying to appease Hitler during the 1930s had only produced greater suffering and sacrifice. Never again would the United States allow a potential adversary to gain control of such a large part of Europe. Hitler used the captured manpower and factories of Europe to unleash his war machine against the United States. The United States needed to guarantee that no future adversary would have access to the same resources.

The key was to maintain open markets and free trade to sustain the global economy. The belief in free trade and open markets meshed with American faith in individual rights and democracy. Policymakers assumed that open markets would produce prosperity, and a more prosperous world would also be more stable and peaceful.

In the immediate aftermath of World War II, no American policymakers worried about a direct Soviet assault on the United States, and few believed the Soviets could muster the resources—military, financial, or psychological—for an invasion of Western Europe. The danger was that the Soviets would extend their influence politically by capitalizing on social and economic chaos in Europe, which created a fertile breeding ground for communism.

Americans also emerged from the war with a newfound optimism, not only in the righteousness of their ideals but also in their ability to impose them on the rest of the world. On V-J day the United States had 12.5 million people serving in the armed forces. Its navy was larger than the combined fleets of all the nations in the world. Washington, not London, was now the capital of finance and power.

Power bred grand expectations. In 1945, the influential publisher Henry R. Luce coined the term "The American Century," to describe the heightened expectations for the postwar period. "America," he proclaimed, "must be the elder brother of the nations in the brotherhood of man."

There was one obstacle to this American vision of the future. In 1945, *Life* Magazine cautioned that the Soviet Union "is the number one problem for Americans because it is the only country in the world with the dynamic power to challenge our own conceptions of truth, justice, and the good life."

At the end of the war the Soviets had one overriding goal: to secure their borders from foreign invaders. They had been as shocked by Hitler's surprise attack in June 1941 as Americans were by the Japanese assault on Pearl Harbor a few months later.

The German attack revived old memories of past invasions. In 1812, Napoleon's armies reached the gates of Moscow. Twice in the twentieth century German armies swept over Russia like hungry locusts. The Soviets, determined to head off another attack, insisted on defensible borders and friendly regimes on their western flank. The sheer size of the Soviet Union—three times larger than the United States and covering one-sixth of the world's landmass—made that task more difficult. Blocking the Poland invasion route, or "gateway," was the top Soviet priority. Poland, Stalin declared, was "a matter of life or death" to his country. To minimize the potential threat, Stalin insisted that pro-Soviet governments be installed in Poland and other key Eastern European states, that Soviet borders be expanded as far as possible, and that Germany be permanently crippled with severe reparations. With its army in control of most of Eastern Europe, the Soviets were in a position to enforce their will.

The deeply-rooted hostility and suspicion between the United States and the Soviet Union proved too much to overcome. By 1945, the battle lines were clearly drawn. Stalin interpreted U.S. calls for free elections and democratic reform in Eastern Europe as part of a capitalist plot to surround the Soviet Union. The Americans viewed the Soviet Union's effort to consolidate its control over Eastern Europe as the first step of a larger plan of global conquest. Moscow and Washington became ensnarled in a "security dilemma": each step taken by one side to enhance its security appeared an act of provocation to the other.

The Yalta Conference

In February 1945, flush from his electoral victory at home, Roosevelt traveled to Yalta, a resort on the Black Sea coast, to meet with Churchill and Stalin. He hoped the leaders could resolve a number of thorny questions. The leaders reached compromises on many issues. Stalin promised to declare war on Japan "two or three months" after Germany's surrender. In return, Roosevelt accepted Soviet claims to the Kurile Islands in the Far East. Stalin dropped his demands for $20 billion in reparations from Germany, agreeing to discuss the issue further. Roosevelt, who made establishment of a postwar organization a major diplomatic goal, succeeded in gaining Stalin's support for the creation of the United Nations. All three leaders approved plans for a United Nations Conference in San Francisco in April 1945.

The postwar political status of Poland, which Churchill counted as "the most urgent reason for the Yalta Conference," caused the most controversy at the conference. Two Polish governments demanded recognition. The British and Americans supported the exiled government living in London. Stalin recognized a communist-led provisional government based in Lublin. Roosevelt proposed a government comprising representatives of Poland's five major political parties. The Soviets rejected the proposal, but Stalin agreed to add "democratic elements" to the Lublin regime. To avoid letting arguments over Poland undermine conference harmony, the Allies worked out an agreement that papered over significant

Cold War Europe With the end of World War II, political ideologies divided Europe. While Eastern Europe received its orders from the Soviet Union, the United States worked to maintain noncommunist governments in the West by means of the Marshall Plan and the North Atlantic Treaty Organization.

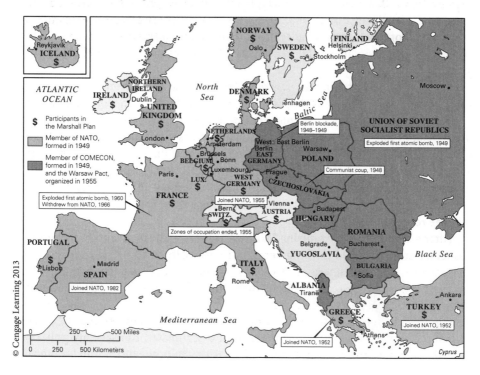

differences with vague, elastic language. Stalin agreed to "free and unfettered elections," but at an unspecified time in the future.

Roosevelt left Yalta convinced that he had laid the foundation for a peaceful postwar. Years later, critics would charge Roosevelt with selling out to the Russians by acquiescing to Soviet domination of Eastern Europe. But military and political realities had weakened Roosevelt's bargaining position. By the time of the Yalta Conference, the powerful Red Army already dominated most of Poland, Czechoslovakia, and Hungary, and Roosevelt desperately wanted Russian assistance in defeating the Japanese. Knowing that most Americans wanted an end to the hostilities and a return of U.S. servicemen, the president had little choice but to accept Soviet control and focus on building trust between the two nations.

Roosevelt returned home from Yalta a very ill man. On March 1, the president told Congress that Yalta had been "a great success," and he asked the American people to support the agreements reached there. On April 12, Roosevelt retreated to his vacation home in Warm Springs, Georgia to try and recoup his energy. Around noon, he slumped in his chair. "I have a terrific headache," he muttered. A few hours later, he died of a cerebral hemorrhage.

Harry Truman Takes Charge

Roosevelt's sudden death thrust Harry Truman into the presidency. Although he faced one of the most dangerous and complicated international predicaments ever to confront an American president, Truman had little experience in foreign affairs. His views of the world were shaped by his temperament and his background.

Truman, the last American president who had not been to college, was born in 1884 in Lamar, Missouri. He spent most of his early years on the farms and in the small towns of western Missouri. His poor eyesight—doctors called his condition "flat eyeballs"—forced him to wear thick glasses and prevented him from playing sports. It also gave him lots of time to spend at the local library, where he absorbed books about great leaders, especially political and military leaders. His reading of history taught him to see the world in terms of black and white, good versus evil. This very clear moral framework during these early years would guide him the rest of his life.

After a stint in the army during World War I, Truman set up and ran a haberdashery, a store that sold clothing items, in Kansas City until a steep recession in 1921 destroyed the business. A few years shy of his fortieth birthday, Truman confronted a bleak future: he presided over a failed business, faced the real threat of bankruptcy, and had few career options.

His luck changed one day in the summer of 1921 when a representative of the notorious Pendergast political machine, which dominated Kansas City politics, invited Truman to run for county judge. He seized the opportunity, ran for office, and won election in 1922. Truman served on the court for most of the next twelve years. In 1934, he won election to the U.S. Senate. With the nation mired in depression, Truman supported most of Franklin Roosevelt's New Deal agenda. In 1944, FDR selected him as his new running mate.

Truman had barely had time to settle into his new job when FDR died. He was clearly unprepared for the problems that confronted him. The new president knew little about Roosevelt's growing doubts about Soviet international intentions. He learned quickly when he sought the recommendations of Roosevelt's advisors, most of whom favored a tougher policy toward the Soviets.

A combative posture fit Truman's temperament. Impulsive and decisive, he lacked Roosevelt's talent for ambiguity and compromise. "When I say I'm going

Atomic Detonation at Bikini Atoll, July 1, 1946   In December 1945, Truman issued a directive to the military, ordering them to determine the impact of atomic bombs on the nation's warships. The military chose Bikini Atoll, located in the Marshall Islands at some distance from regular air and sea routes, as the place to conduct their tests. After removing the 167 residents of the island, the navy moved more than 200 ships into the area, along with thousands of goats, pigs, and rats, to determine the bomb's effect on living beings. The military conducted two tests, one detonation above the surface and one underwater. *(Source: Harry S. Truman Library)*

to do something, I do it," he once wrote. On his desk he displayed a sign: "The Buck Stops Here." Truman viewed the Yalta Accords as contracts between East and West. He was committed to seeing that Stalin honored the agreement.

The new President, emboldened by America's monopoly of atomic bombs and eager to show critics and the nation that he was in charge, matched Stalin's intransigence with calls for self-determination and free elections in Eastern Europe. It was, he declared, time to "stand up to the Russians."

In reality, Truman had not completely abandoned hope of reaching some settlement with Moscow. In July 1945, he traveled to Potsdam, outside Berlin, for the final meeting of the Grand Alliance. Truman and Stalin squabbled over the sensitive issues of reparations and implementation of the Yalta Accords. By the end of the meeting, the leaders had reached tentative agreements. Russia agreed to permit Anglo-American observers in Eastern Europe and to withdraw its troops from oil-rich Azerbaijan in Iran. In return, the West reluctantly accepted Soviet occupation of German territory and approved Russian annexation of eastern Poland. "I can deal with Stalin," Truman wrote in his diary. "He is honest—but smart as hell."

Truman's optimism proved unfounded. With the 10-million strong Red Army occupying half of Europe at the end of the war, Stalin installed governments subservient to Moscow in Bulgaria, Hungary, and Rumania. Refusing to abide by his agreement at Potsdam, he denied Western observers access to Eastern Europe and continued his occupation of Azerbaijan. Stalin's actions in Poland and Germany were especially troubling to Truman. The Soviet dictator ignored the Yalta Accords and brutally suppressed Polish democratic parties.

Stalin's words added to the American anxiety. On February 9, 1946, Stalin delivered a rare public speech in which he explained the fundamental incompatibility of communism and capitalism. The American system, he stressed, needed war for raw materials and markets. *Time* magazine concluded that the remarks were "the most warlike pronouncement uttered by any top-rank statesman since V-J Day."

Truman struggled with how to respond to Stalin's provocative actions and words. It was not clear to him why the Soviets were being so intransigent. Why would they oppose reasonable American demands for open trade and free elections? Was Stalin another Hitler? If the United States appeased his demands the way the West had given into Hitler, would it lead inevitably to another protracted war? What could the United States do to protect its interests without provoking a confrontation?

Truman turned for advice to the certified members of the American Establishment dubbed "The Wise Men." Most grew up in the northeastern United States, attending elite prep schools and Ivy League universities. They worked in New York's big banking houses and law firms and joined the same social clubs. Tied by culture and traditions to Europe, they tended to be patronizing to "lesser" peoples. They detested Marxist dogma and Soviet repression, but were usually pragmatic, nonpartisan, and nonideological in their worldview.

Secretary of State Dean Gooderham Acheson was perhaps the most influential of the Wise Men. Educated at Groton, Yale, and the Harvard Law School, Acheson worked at a prestigious Washington law firm before joining the State

Department in 1941. With his heavy eyebrows, carefully waxed moustache, and perfectly tailored suits, he symbolized the American establishment. Acheson was certain of his own convictions, and he was determined that the United States assume its proper role as leader of the world. America, he said, was the "locomotive at the head of mankind" and "the rest of the world is the caboose."

Another of the "Wise Men" was George Kennan, a forty-two-year-old Soviet specialist in the U.S. Embassy in Moscow. In February 1946, he sent his 8,000-word telegram to Washington that would profoundly shape American foreign policy for decades to come.

The Truman Doctrine and Marshall Plan

The "Wise Men" believed it was necessary for the United States to take a tough new stance against the Soviets. They got their chance in February 1947, when the British ambassador informed the U.S. State Department that his country could no longer afford to support Greece and Turkey with economic and military aid.

Both countries were under threat from the Soviets. The U.S. administration, fearful that Soviet-backed insurgents might gain the upper hand, wanted to fill the vacuum. First, it needed to overcome deep-seated American fears of getting involved in European affairs. One influential senator suggested that the White House build support by "scaring hell out of the country."

The Truman administration accepted the challenge. On March 12, 1947, Truman stood before a joint session of Congress to make his case for American aid to Greece and Turkey. The speech echoed many of Dean Acheson's warnings about a world divided between the free and unfree. "I believe that it must be the policy of the United States to support free peoples who are resisting attempted subjugation by armed minorities or by outside pressures," he declared. The future of the "free world," he insisted, rested in America's hands. After setting the stage, Truman requested that Congress appropriate $400 million for Greek and Turkish military and economic aid. The American people rallied around the cause of freedom.

PRIMARY SOURCE

1.2 | *The Truman Doctrine*
Harry Truman

Looking to hinder the growth of Soviet-supported insurgency in Greece and Turkey, President Truman wanted to provide American military and economic aid, but many Americans wanted to stay out of European affairs. To garner support, Truman spoke before a joint session of Congress on March 12, 1947, and explained why Americans should assist the free peoples of the world.

M r. President, Mr. Speaker, Members of the Congress of the United States:

The gravity of the situation which confronts the world today necessitates my appearance before a joint session of the Congress. The foreign policy and the national security of this country are involved. . . .

5   The United States has received from the Greek Government an urgent appeal for financial and economic assistance. Preliminary reports from the American Economic Mission now in Greece and reports from the American Ambassador in Greece corroborate the statement of the Greek Government that assistance is imperative if Greece is to survive as a free nation.

10   I do not believe that the American people and the Congress wish to turn a deaf ear to the appeal of the Greek Government. . . .

The very existence of the Greek state is today threatened by the terrorist activities of several thousand armed men, led by Communists, who defy the government's authority at a number of points, particularly along the northern

15   boundaries. A Commission appointed by the United Nations Security Council is at present investigating disturbed conditions in northern Greece and alleged border violations along the frontier between Greece on the one hand and Albania, Bulgaria, and Yugoslavia on the other.

Meanwhile, the Greek Government is unable to cope with the situation. The

20   Greek army is small and poorly equipped. It needs supplies and equipment if it is to restore the authority of the government throughout Greek territory. Greece must have assistance if it is to become a self-supporting and self-respecting democracy.

The United States must supply that assistance. We have already extended to Greece certain types of relief and economic aid but these are inadequate.

25   There is no other country to which democratic Greece can turn. . . .

Greece's neighbor, Turkey, also deserves our attention.

The future of Turkey as an independent and economically sound state is clearly no less important to the freedom-loving peoples of the world than the future of Greece. The circumstances in which Turkey finds itself today are consider-

30   ably different from those of Greece. Turkey has been spared the disasters that have beset Greece. And during the war, the United States and Great Britain furnished Turkey with material aid.

Nevertheless, Turkey now needs our support.

Since the war Turkey has sought financial assistance from Great Britain and

35   the United States for the purpose of effecting that modernization necessary for the maintenance of its national integrity.

That integrity is essential to the preservation of order in the Middle East. . . .

At the present moment in world history nearly every nation must choose between alternative ways of life. The choice is too often not a free one.

40   One way of life is based upon the will of the majority, and is distinguished by free institutions, representative government, free elections, guarantees of individual liberty, freedom of speech and religion, and freedom from political oppression.

The second way of life is based upon the will of a minority forcibly imposed upon the majority. It relies upon terror and oppression, a controlled press and radio, fixed elections, and the suppression of personal freedoms.

I believe that it must be the policy of the United States to support free peoples who are resisting attempted subjugation by armed minorities or by outside pressures.

I believe that we must assist free peoples to work out their own destinies in their own way.

I believe that our help should be primarily through economic and financial aid which is essential to economic stability and orderly political processes. . . .

It is necessary only to glance at a map to realize that the survival and integrity of the Greek nation are of grave importance in a much wider situation. If Greece should fall under the control of an armed minority, the effect upon its neighbor, Turkey, would be immediate and serious. Confusion and disorder might well spread throughout the entire Middle East.

Should we fail to aid Greece and Turkey in this fateful hour, the effect will be far reaching to the West as well as to the East.

We must take immediate and resolute action. . . .

If we falter in our leadership, we may endanger the peace of the world—and we shall surely endanger the welfare of our own nation.

Great responsibilities have been placed upon us by the swift movement of events.

I am confident that the Congress will face these responsibilities squarely.

Source: Courtesy of the U.S. Historical Documents Archive.   ■ ■ ■

The Truman Doctrine represented a turning point in American foreign policy. For the first time, the United States intervened in the peacetime affairs of nations outside the Western Hemisphere. The moralistic rhetoric Truman used to justify U.S. involvement reflected America's penchant to view the world as divided between the forces of good and evil. The experiment in "nation-building" in Greece and Turkey assumed the superiority of American values and the universal appeal of democracy. By rooting America's response to a local conflict in universal language, Truman hoped to prepare the American people for their responsibility as a world power. Presidential aide Clark Clifford called it "the opening gun in a campaign to bring the people up to [the] realization that the war isn't over by any means."

The administration realized that military assistance might deter the Soviets in Greece and Turkey, but it would not save war-torn Western Europe from economic disaster. Worried that Russia might take advantage of the situation, administration officials moved to shore up Europe's battered economy. As new Secretary of State George C. Marshall observed: "The patient is sinking while the doctors deliberate."

On June 5, 1947, the "doctor" offered his prescription for recovery. Marshall chose the Harvard University commencement ceremony to announce a bold new plan of economic assistance to Europe. Marshall explained that the aid program was "directed not against any country or doctrine but against hunger, poverty, desperation, and chaos." Marshall invited the participation of any country, including the Soviet Union, that was "willing to assist in the task of recovery." Truman realized that Stalin would never accept a plan that required him to share vital economic information with the United States and leave in Western hands control of how funds would be distributed.

In December 1947, Truman submitted the plan to Congress, with a recommendation that the U.S. spend $17 billion over four years. At first, congressional leaders were cool to the idea. Critics condemned the plan as "a bold Socialist blueprint." While Congress held hearings during the fall, Europe sank deeper into its economic abyss. England announced it was cutting individual meat rations to twenty cents' worth per week.

Inadvertently, the Soviet Union provided the Marshall Plan with the boost it needed. During the summer of 1947, an increasingly paranoid Stalin established the Communist Information Bureau (Cominform) to coordinate Communist party activity around the globe. The Cominform tightened Stalin's control in the Eastern bloc and within Russia at the same time that it called upon communists in the underdeveloped world to accelerate "their struggle" for liberation. A U.S. diplomat called the creation of the Cominform "a declaration of political and economic war against the U.S. and everything the U.S. stands for in world affairs."

In February 1948, communists staged a coup in Czechoslovakia, overthrowing a freely elected coalition government. Western leaders interpreted the coup as part of an aggressive Soviet plan to conquer Europe before it could be revived. According to Kennan, a "real war scare" swept Washington. Once again, top policymakers were aware that the hysteria was exaggerated and war was unlikely. But they were not above using fear to help sell their new approach to the Soviets. Sometimes, said Dean Acheson, "it is necessary to make things clearer than the truth."

Opposition to the Marshall Plan wilted in the heated atmosphere. On April 2 the House approved the plan by the lopsided vote of 318 to 75. The Senate roared its approval by an overwhelming voice vote. In April the SS *John H. Quick* sailed from its port in Galveston, Texas, with 19,000 tons of wheat for starving Europeans. Within months it was joined by 150 ships carrying food and fuel to Europe every day. Between 1948 and 1951 American aid to Europe amounted to a staggering $12.5 billion. Thanks in part to the plan, European industrial production increased 200 percent between 1948 and 1952. Perhaps the Marshall Plan's greatest export was hope. British foreign secretary Ernest Bevin called the plan "a lifeline to a sinking man."

The Marshall Plan also added to the mutual misperception that contributed to the Cold War. The plan reassured America's European allies but worried Stalin, who was convinced that the United States designed the aid program to lure Eastern European nations out of the Soviet orbit and to rebuild Germany. In response,

The Marshall Plan at Work in Austria World War II devastated the European landscape and economy, making it difficult for citizens to acquire even basic necessities. The United States feared the Soviet Union would exploit the anxiety, spreading communist ideology across the continent. Marshall and other policymakers believed that massive aid would enable European nations to resist communism and would build loyalty to the United States. They certainly won a friend in this little boy, who is obviously thrilled with his new shoes, brought by American planes and distributed by Red Cross workers. (Source: *Courtesy of the American Red Cross, all rights reserved in all countries*)

the Kremlin cracked down on dissent in Poland, Rumania, and Bulgaria; encouraged the coup in Czechoslovakia; and blockaded Berlin. "For Stalin," concluded two scholars familiar with new archival information in Moscow and Eastern Europe, "the Marshall Plan was a watershed."

The Soviet moves in turn magnified the sense of threat in Washington, leading to a massive expansion of federal power in the traditionally antistatist United States. By approving the Truman Doctrine and the Marshall Plan, Congress institutionalized the Cold War. In 1947, it passed the National Security Act, which has been called the "Magna Charta of the national security state." The act created the skeleton of what would become an overpowering national security apparatus; it expanded executive power by centralizing previously dispersed responsibilities in the White House. It established the Department of Defense to oversee all branches of the armed services and formed the Joint Chiefs of Staff, which included the generals of the three services and the Marines. The act also created the National Security Council (NSC), a cabinet-level body to coordinate military and foreign policy for the president. In addition, it created the Central Intelligence Agency (CIA), which carried out espionage operations directly under the authority of the National Security Council.

Berlin Blockade

The hardening of positions on both sides produced the first major crisis of the Cold War. Yalta had divided Germany into four zones (U.S., USSR, British, and French) and Berlin into four sectors. The Soviets were determined to prevent Germany from reemerging as an industrial power. But America, wanting to rebuild the world economy for the benfit of U.S. markets, initiated financial reforms that produced a remarkable economic revival in its sector.

The Russians retaliated on June 24 by clamping a tight blockade around West Berlin, which lay 110 miles within the Soviet occupation zone. West Berlin was in essence a small Western enclave deep inside the Soviet zone. Using his geographical advantage, Stalin blocked all surface transportation into West Berlin, depriving some 2.5 million people of food and fuel.

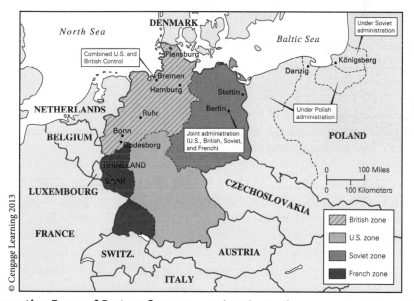

Occupation Zones of Postwar Germany   At the Yalta Conference in early 1945, the Allied powers decided that after Germany surrendered unconditionally the Allies would dismember the enemy, dividing Germany and its capital, Berlin, into zones of occupation. After Germany's official surrender May 8, the Soviet Union, Great Britain, the United States, and France established control over their zones, with the hope of keeping their policies relatively uniform so that Germany could remain a single nation once disarmament and demilitarization took place. However, as the Cold War intensified, conflicting political and economic systems made compatible zone standards impossible. In December 1946, the American and British zones merged and in 1948 France agreed to join them, resulting in the Soviet Union's blockade of West Berlin. (Source: *Melvyn P. Leffler,* A Preponderance of Power: National Security, the Truman Administration, and the Cold War *[Palo Alto, Calif.: Stanford University Press], p. 66. Copyright © 1992.)*

The situation was full of danger and Truman searched for a response that would demonstrate American resolve without forcing a direct confrontation. Treading a careful middle path, Truman decided to counter the Russian move by ordering a massive airlift operation. For the next 324 days, American and British planes dropped 2.5 million tons of provisions to sustain the 10,000 troops and the 2 million civilians in Berlin. Truman threatened to use "the bomb" if the Soviets shot down the relief planes. "We are very close to war," he wrote in his diary. On May 12, 1949, the Russians accepted defeat and ended the blockade.

The Berlin crisis catalyzed western leaders to present a unified front to the Soviets. In January 1949, Truman proposed committing the United States to the defense of Europe. In April, he pledged American involvement in the North Atlantic Treaty Organization (NATO), a mutual defense pact that bound twelve signatories (Britain, France, Canada, Italy, the Benelux countries, Ireland, Denmark, Norway, and Portugal) to fight against aggression. Article 5 provided "that an armed attack against one or more . . . shall be considered an attack against them all."

While challenging the Soviets' claim to a "sphere of influence" in Europe, the United States consolidated its own sphere in the Western Hemisphere. In 1947, Secretary of State Marshall led a delegation of American officials to Brazil where, on September 2, he signed the Rio Treaty. The signatories agreed that "any armed attack by any state against an American state shall be considered an attack against all the American states." The following year, North and Latin American countries created the Organization of American States (OAS).

The Soviets matched the Western initiatives by intensifying their domination of Eastern Europe. In October 1949, Stalin created a separate government in East Germany, the German Democratic Republic. Moscow sponsored an economic association, the Council for Mutual Economic Assistance or COMECON (1949), and a military alliance for Eastern Europe, the Warsaw Pact (1955). The Soviets poured massive amounts of aid into Poland, Czechoslovakia, and Bulgaria to accelerate industrialization and increase Russian control. The only exception to Soviet control was Yugoslavia, which managed to develop as an independent socialist state.

The Birth of Israel

The Cold War also shaped American policy in the Middle East. After World War II, many Jews who had survived Nazi concentration camps resettled in British-controlled Palestine. In 1947 the British, weakened by World War II, turned over control of Palestine to the United Nations, which voted to partition the region into separate Jewish and Arab states. Violence between Arabs and Jews escalated as each side tried to maximize their territorial position in advance of the British partition.

The president's military advisors feared recognition of the Jewish state of Israel would anger Arab oil-producing nations. Other factors weighed in Truman's mind. Since Stalin had already announced his support of Israel, Truman worried about the possibility of a close Soviet-Israel relationship that would exclude the United States. On an emotional level, the president empathized with the suffering of Jews during World War II. Political considerations supported recognition. "In all of my political experience," Truman during the campaign of 1948, "I don't ever recall the Arab vote swinging a close election."

On May 14, 1948, Israel declared its independence. Eleven minutes later, the United States recognized the new state. Less than a week later, five Arab neighbors invaded Israel, which beat back the attack and expanded its control over territory designated for the Palestinian Arab State. Jordan and Egypt occupied the other parts of the territory. Over half the Palestinian population fled or were expelled. Between six hundred and seven hundred thousand Palestinians became refugees, forced to live in squalid conditions in the West Bank and along the Gaza Strip. The "Palestinian Issue" would remain a source of anger and frustration in the Middle East for years to come.

Debating Containment

The adoption of the containment policy thrust upon the United States political and military responsibilities as a "world policeman" that went far beyond anything ever contemplated by the American people. It also raised new and troubling questions that went to the heart of American identity. The Cold War, and the need for an expanded military, presented the American people with a conundrum: Could the nation adapt to the demands of total war without losing its democratic identity? Or, as the *New York Times* asked in 1947, "how can we prepare for total war without becoming a 'garrison state' and destroying the very qualities and virtues and principles we originally set out to save?"

Many conservatives believed it was impossible to reconcile the administration's new national security goals with the nation's democratic traditions. The new military bureaucracy, built on the foundation of the New Deal's expansion of federal power, threatened to regiment American life and take the nation down the same road as Nazi Germany. "We are having our initial experience with the garrison state," complained a congressman, "in which the conduct of our lives is made secondary to the demands of the Military Establishment." Concentration of power in the hands of the executive would inevitably lead to higher levels of taxation and an erosion of the traditional American commitment to fiscal responsibility and a balanced budget. "We must not let our fear of Communism blind us to the danger of military domination," warned a Republican congressman.

Many conservatives feared that an expansive foreign policy would distort national and international priorities. Powerful Republican senator Robert Taft of Ohio observed that the traditional purpose of U.S. involvement in the world was "to maintain the liberty of our people" rather than "reform the entire world or spread sweetness and light and economic prosperity to peoples who have lived and worked out their own salvation for centuries." The country should expand the national security state only "as far toward preparing for war as we can go in time of peace without weakening ourselves . . . and destroying forever the very liberty which war is designed to protect."

A few voices on the Left joined the chorus of criticism, though often for different reasons. In a series of newspaper columns, later published in book form as *The Cold War,* the journalist Walter Lippmann charged that containment would increase executive power at the expense of the other branches of government and divert energy and resources away from domestic needs. The policy of containment, he wrote, "can be implemented only by recruiting, subsidizing and supporting a heterogeneous array of satellites, clients, dependents, and puppets." Most of all, he argued, containment would militarize American foreign policy and force the United States to support corrupt dictators. Unlike many conservatives, however, Lippmann supported the administration's effort to strengthen the Western alliance and criticized conservatives as outdated isolationists.

PRIMARY SOURCE

1.3 | *The Last Chance for Peace*
HENRY WALLACE

President Truman's postwar get-tough policy with the Soviet Union troubled many Americans, including liberal members of his own party. Former Vice President and current Secretary of Commerce Henry Wallace sent Truman a twelve-page, single-spaced letter in July 1946 expressing his opposition to Truman's aggressive stand against the Soviets.

I should list the factors which make for Russian distrust of the United States and of the Western world as follows. The first is Russian history, which we must take into account because it is the setting in which Russians see all actions and policies of the rest of the world. Russian history for over a thousand years has been a suc-
5   cession of attempts, often unsuccessful, to resist invasion and conquest. . . . The Russians, therefore, obviously see themselves as fighting for their existence in a hostile world.

Second, it follows that to the Russians all of the defense and security measures of the Western powers seem to have an aggressive intent. Our actions to expand

10 our military security system . . . appear to them as going far beyond the require-
ments of defense. I think we might feel the same if the United States were the only
capitalistic country in the world, and the principal socialistic countries were creating a level of armed strength far exceeding anything in their previous history.

Finally, our resistance to her attempts to obtain warm-water ports and her
15 own security system in the form of "friendly" neighboring states seems, from the
Russian point of view, to clinch the case. After twenty-five years of isolation and
after having achieved the status of a major power, Russia believes that she is entitled to recognition of her new status. Our interest in establishing democracy in
Eastern Europe, where democracy by and large has never existed, seems to her an
20 attempt to reestablish the encirclement of unfriendly neighbors which was created after the last war, and which might serve as a springboard of still another effort to destroy her.

If this analysis is correct, and there is ample evidence to support it, the action
to improve the situation is clearly indicated. The fundamental objective of such
25 action should be to allay any reasonable Russian grounds for fear, suspicion and
distrust. . . .

We should make an effort to counteract the irrational fear of Russia which is
being systematically built up in the American people by certain individuals and
publications. The slogan that communism and capitalism, regimentation and de-
30 mocracy, cannot continue to exist in the same world is, from a historical point of
view, pure propaganda.

Source: Steven M. Gillon and Cathy D. Matson, *The American Experiment: A History of the
United States,* 2nd ed., (Boston: Houghton Mifflin) 1092–1093. ■ ■ ■

The administration argued that a new era of total war required the country to
take unprecedented steps to defend its interests. "Total war" could not be confined to the battlefield; it required the full participation of the home front as well.
All of the nation's resources had to be mobilized to defeat the enemy, blurring the
line between civilian and military. Every citizen was a soldier, responsible for
defending the American way of life. In an age of total war, Americans had to
abandon traditional objections to a standing army and enlarged federal power.
"Wars are no longer fought solely by armed forces," explained navy Admiral
Ernest J. King. "Directly or indirectly, the whole citizenry and the entire resources
of the nation go to war."

Supporters of containment won the argument by claiming that Americans
faced a new situation that required unprecedented steps. "A drastic departure
from the antimilitaristic tradition of our peace-loving America is now necessary,"
argued a congressman. The greatest threat to American liberty came not from the
expansion of state power produced by national security needs, but from the threat
from abroad. "The loss of Europe, Asia, and Africa," claimed Democratic senator
Paul Douglas of Illinois, "would bring an irresistible drive toward isolationism in
the United States and the consequent erection of a garrison state. The effort to
build an unconquerable bastion while surrounded by a Communist world would
bring in its train the suppression of many of our precious liberties."

SELECTED READINGS

▪ Robert J. McMahon provides a concise, brief overview of the period in *The Cold War: A Very Short Introduction* (2003). Two books by Melvyn P. Leffler are essential: *A Preponderance of Power* (1992) and *For the Soul of Mankind* (2008). John L. Gaddis provides the most up-to-date synthesis in *The Cold War: A New History* (2006). The Cold War from the Soviet Union's perspective, using recently declassified materials, is contained in *Inside the Kremlin's Cold War* (1996), by Vladislav Zubok and Constantine Pleshakov. Robert Dallek offers an alternative view of missed opportunities in *The Lost Peace* (2010). Odd Arne Westad documents the impact of the U.S.-Soviet competition on the Third World in his Bancroft Prize–winning book, *The Global Cold War* (2007).

▪ Derek Leebaert, *The Fifty-Year Wound* (2002) is a good account of the immediate postwar period. John L. Gaddis, in his Bancroft Prize–winning book, *The United States and the Origins of the Cold War* (1972), illuminates the many factors—domestic, political, and bureaucratic—that influenced American foreign policy regarding the Soviet Union. In *Debating the Origins of the Cold War* (2002), Ralph Levering examines the beginnings of the conflict from both the Soviet and American perspectives. Lloyd C. Gardner's *Architects of Illusion* (1970) has biographical vignettes of America's leading foreign policymakers and explores mistakes that contributed to the Cold War.

▪ George Mazuzan and J. Samuel Walker collected a wealth of information for their book on nuclear regulation and the Atomic Energy Commission, *Controlling the Atom* (1985). The part played by the Soviet military in maintaining control of the Eastern bloc nations is the focus of Christopher Jones's *Soviet Influence in Eastern Europe* (1981), and Peter Grose's *Operation Rollback* (2000) discusses America's secret programs to encourage resistance behind the Iron Curtain.

▪ Lawrence Wittner focuses on the Greek civil war in *American Intervention in Greece* (1982). Howard Jones examines the reasons for the development of the Truman Doctrine, its application in the Greek civil war, and its long-lasting effect on American foreign policy in *A New Kind of War* (1989). Michael Hogan's *The Marshall Plan* (1987) is a good one-volume history of that ambitious initiative. Imanuel Wexler's *The Marshall Plan Revisited* (1983) offers a more critical analysis of the plan. Timothy P. Ireland examines the formation of NATO in *Creating the Entangling Alliance* (1981). A 1989 conference at the Truman Library on the birth of NATO and its first decade of operation served as the basis for editors Francis Heller and John Gillingham's work, *NATO* (1992).

▪ Bruce R. Kuniholm's *The Origins of the Cold War in the Near East* (1980) has good material on the formation of Israel, as does Paul Merkley's *American Presidents, Religion, and Israel* (2004). The division of Germany is the subject of Carolyn Eisenberg's *Drawing the Line* (1996), while W. R. Smyser's *From Yalta to Berlin* (2000) traces the history of the German question from the division to the collapse of communism. A detailed history of the Berlin blockade can be found in Thomas Parrish's *Berlin in the Balance* (1998). The history of the National Security Council, from its inception by Truman as a channel for collective advice to its massive expansion as an institution that dictates foreign policy, can be found in John Prados's *Keeper of the Keys* (1991).

▎ George Kennan's *American Diplomacy* (exp. ed., 1985) and Dean Acheson's *Present at the Creation* (1970) offer intriguing insider accounts of the early Cold War, while John L. Harper compares these two men to FDR in *American Visions of Europe* (1994). Walter Isaacson and Evan Thomas's *The Wise Men* (1986) provides incisive profiles of Truman's advisors and their impact on American foreign policy.

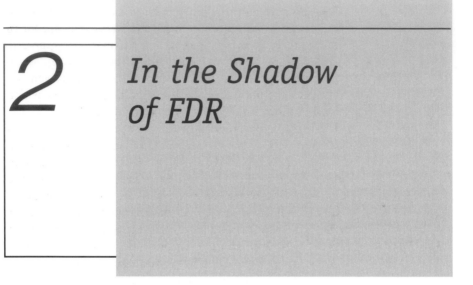

2 In the Shadow of FDR

It was nearly 2:00 A.M. before Harry Truman and his running mate, Alben Barkley, made their way to the podium at the Democratic National Convention in Philadelphia. An accidental president, Truman presided over a deeply divided party convinced that it had no chance of defeating the Republicans in November. "We are here to honor the honored dead," a Democratic official declared, reflecting on the party's chances in the 1948 presidential contest. Wearing a double-breasted white suit and black tie, Truman nevertheless appeared cool and confident despite the oppressive July heat. He understood the deep sense of loyalty many Americans felt toward Franklin Roosevelt and the New Deal. Truman's task was to convince his party, and the countless Americans who were seeing him on television for the first time, that he was the true heir of the Roosevelt legacy.

Instead of highlighting his own agenda, Truman attacked the hypocrisy of a Republican Party that talked like FDR but acted like Herbert Hoover. "The Republican platform is for extending and increasing social security benefits. . . . I wonder if they think they can fool the people of the United States with such poppycock as that," he thundered. Truman decided to call his opponents' bluff. "On the 26th day of July, which out in Missouri we call 'Turnip Day,' I am going to call Congress back and ask them to pass laws to halt rising prices, to meet the housing crisis—which they say they are for in their platform." How the Republican Congress responded, he said, "will be the test," and "the American people . . . will decide on the record." The speech electrified convention delegates and put the Republicans on the defensive—which is where they would stay through election day.

Truman managed to pull together the New Deal coalition to score a surprising victory in the 1948 election. But the icy winds of the Cold War froze Truman's drive to expand Roosevelt's agenda. Many liberals hoped that the postwar world would see a revival of the New Deal at home. But a host of new problems—the emerging Cold War, labor unrest, inflation, and a powerful conservative coalition in Congress—dimmed many of these aspirations. These new issues divided the once-powerful Democratic coalition, which had carried Roosevelt to four successive victories.

In an effort to institutionalize and expand the New Deal, Truman confronted the central paradox of American postwar politics: Americans had come to expect the president to offer solutions to pressing social problems, but they also feared the expansion of federal power. During the 1948 campaign Truman successfully managed the tension between expectations of government and fear of Washington by tying his administration to the legacy of Roosevelt. After the election, however, growing fear of the Cold War made Truman's balancing act even more precarious.

From War to Peace

Truman could not match his success in winning support for his Cold War policies abroad with similar achievements in domestic policy. World War II ended so quickly that the American economy did not have time to adjust. Many people worried that the end of wartime spending would cripple the economy and lead to another depression. "We are completely unprepared for a Japanese collapse," the journalist I. F. Stone wrote a few weeks before the war ended, "and unless we act quickly and wisely [we] may face an economic collapse ourselves."

As Stone predicted, the sudden end of the war sent shock waves through the American economy. Within a month the government canceled $35 billion in war contracts and slashed war-related production by 60 percent. The cuts produced massive layoffs. Within ten days of the Japanese surrender, 2.7 million men and women lost their jobs. Economists predicted that more than 10 million Americans would be thrown out of work by peace.

At the same time, a flood of servicemen returned home looking for civilian jobs. Both Roosevelt and Truman planned to maintain a strong American military presence overseas at the end of the war. The public, however, demanded immediate demobilization. "We are getting 10,000 letters a day" about the slow pace of demobilization, complained a senator. An Oklahoma constituent made his threat explicit in a letter to his representative: "You put us in the army, and you can get us out. Either demobilize us, or, when given the next shot at the ballot box, we will demobilize you." Truman gave in to the public pressure, releasing almost 7 million men and women from the armed forces by April 1946.

Inflation added to the economic anxiety. During the war speculation had pushed property values and stock prices to new highs. People made lots of money during the war, but there were few consumer products to purchase. Once the war ended, people rushed to spend their savings. The sudden increase in demand produced soaring inflation.

The problem was compounded when Congress decided to abandon wartime price controls. The first week controls ended, prices increased 16 percent. Steak increased in price from fifty-five cents to one dollar a pound. A headline in the *New York Daily News* screamed: "Prices Soar, Buyers Sore, Steers Jump over the Moon."

High prices and job losses squeezed American workers. During the war labor unions honored a voluntary no-strike pledge. With the war ended and prices rising, labor demanded steep wage increases. When their demands were not met, they went on strike. By October 1945, half a million workers were walking the picket line. In April 1946, when John L. Lewis led 400,000 coal miners out of the pits, a furious Truman ordered government troops to take over the mines. When railway workers threatened to join the strikers and potentially cripple the economy, Truman went before Congress to ask for the authority to draft strikers into the army. The threat was effective: the strike ended after only a few days. But the president's tough talk did little to assure liberals that he would continue FDR's legacy. *The New Republic* called Truman's congressional message the "most vicious piece of antiunion legislation ever introduced by an American President."

With liberals carping and labor–management disputes sweeping the nation, Truman's approval rating dipped below 50 percent. Republicans, capitalizing on the pervasive dissatisfaction with rising prices, labor strikes, and the anxieties aroused by the Cold War, pounced on the hapless Democrats in the 1946 congressional elections. Their campaign slogan was as simple as it was effective: "Had enough?" The Republicans gained control of both Houses of Congress for the first time since 1930. Among the new members of the class of '46 were Representative Richard Nixon of California, Representative John F. Kennedy of Massachusetts, and Senator Joseph McCarthy of Wisconsin.

John L. Lewis Interviewed by the Press   President of the United Mine Workers from 1920 to 1960 and leading organizer of the CIO, John Lewis often defied the wishes of Washington and other labor unions in his efforts to improve conditions for the nation's miners, including conducting a strike during World War II, which led to accusations that Lewis was disloyal. By 1948, Lewis and his coal miners had won significantly higher wages, but their combative tactics brought down the wrath of Congress on all labor unions. *(© United Mine Workers Archive)*

The Splintering of the Roosevelt Coalition

Truman's plunging popularity and the Republican success in the 1946 election left liberals sour and disillusioned. Cold War with the USSR and conservative resurgence at home frustrated their hopes for the postwar world. Most blamed Truman for their plight, agreeing with the liberal *Nation*'s characterization of the president as a "weak, baffled, angry man." The columnists Joseph and Stewart Alsop, looking toward the 1948 election, predicted that "if Truman is nominated, he will be forced to wage the loneliest campaign in history."

Truman lacked the grace and magnetism liberals had come to expect from the White House. Many New Dealers distrusted Truman, believing he lacked FDR's grace, dignity, and patrician vision. Many viewed the new president as a provincial man incapable of transcending his modest roots. In September 1945, Truman tried to put to rest doubts about his leadership by announcing his support for a range of new domestic initiatives, including laws to increase the minimum wage, broaden social security, and establish a national health program. The House Republican leader fumed, "Not even President Roosevelt ever asked so much at one sitting." Even many Democrats grumbled that the president was asking Congress to move too quickly on too many different fronts. As a result, over the next few years Congress frustrated most of Truman's domestic agenda.

Most significantly, Congress passed, over Truman's veto, the Labor–Management Relations Act of 1947, better known as the Taft-Hartley Act. The measure, a major blow to organized labor, outlawed the closed shop, which had required that all hiring be done through a union hall; permitted states to pass so-called right-to-work laws allowing nonunion members to work in unionized plants; empowered authorities to issue federal injunctions against strikes that jeopardized public health or safety; and gave the president power to stave off strikes by proclaiming a "cooling-off" period of up to eighty days. The legislation also required union leaders to swear that they were not communists. "We have got to break with the corrupting idea that we can legislate prosperity, legislate equality, legislate opportunity," declared Senator Robert Taft (R-Ohio), the chief spokesman for economic conservatism.

These political setbacks further frustrated liberals, who were unanimous in their disaffection with Truman's domestic leadership but divided over how to respond to Cold War tensions. Many liberals, who called themselves "progressives," believed that American–Soviet cooperation was essential to the preservation of the wartime antifascist alliance. Believing that legitimate security needs inspired Joseph Stalin's actions in Eastern Europe, they opposed Truman's growing hard line with the Soviets. Progressives looked to former Vice President Henry Wallace for leadership. Born on a small farm in 1888, Wallace served first as secretary of agriculture from 1933 to 1940, then as vice president until January 1945, and finally as secretary of commerce under Truman. While Truman seemed to be moving away from Roosevelt's domestic and international policies, Wallace lifted liberal hopes with calls for economic development, full employment, and cooperation with the Soviet Union. In September 1946 Wallace criticized both U.S. and Soviet policy at a labor rally in New York. Under pressure from Secretary of State James Byrnes and Republican Senator Arthur Vandenberg, Truman fired Wallace. In December 1947 Wallace announced that he would run for president on a third-party progressive ticket. Few people believed Wallace could win the election, but many Democrats feared that he could siphon liberal votes away from Truman in key states.

By then Stalin's repressive regime and Soviet aggression in Eastern Europe were making any coalition with communists at home less attractive to many on the left. Liberals, who had worked together with communists on domestic issues as part of the wartime Popular Front, now distanced themselves from their former allies. Labor organizations led the way. In 1946 Walter Reuther purged communists from the United Auto Workers. Following his lead, in 1949 the Congress of Industrial Organizations expelled nine unions, representing nine hundred thousand workers, for refusing to purge themselves of communist leaders. Liberal politicians joined the drive to purge communists from Democratic Party organizations. In Minnesota the young Democratic mayor of Minneapolis, Hubert Humphrey, gained control of the Minnesota Farmer-Labor Party and purged communists from its ranks. In 1947 many leading anticommunist liberals met in Washington and created the Americans for Democratic Action, an independent political organization.

Truman sided with the anticommunist left, but he tried to diffuse the debate over foreign policy issues by highlighting his support for liberal domestic programs. The president championed an aggressive liberal reform agenda, calling for a far-reaching housing program, stronger rent control, a sweeping enlargement of social security coverage, and federal aid to education. Before Congress had a chance to act, he went on the offensive, blaming Republicans for not supporting his program.

The Struggle for Civil Rights

Truman made support for civil rights a centerpiece of his fighting liberal program. In 1946 Truman had established the President's Committee on Civil Rights, the first presidential committee ever created to investigate race relations in America. The following year the committee released its report, *To Secure These Rights,* which called for an end to segregation and discrimination and advocated legislation to abolish lynching and the poll tax. In February 1948 Truman hailed the report as "an American charter of human freedom" and asked Congress to support the committee's recommendations.

In July Truman signed Executive Order 9981, which set up procedures for ending racial discrimination in the military. Top military leaders opposed the measure, claiming that it would undermine morale and discipline. "The Army is not out to make any social reform," complained army chief of staff Omar Bradley. Organized resistance from within the ranks of the military prevented implementation until the Korean War, when the army had to scramble to find troops. For many African Americans, however, the order symbolized Truman's commitment to civil rights. The *Chicago Defender,* a black newspaper, called the order "unprecedented since the time of Lincoln."

Truman's advocacy of civil rights in 1948 exposed the deep ideological and sectional strains in his party. The New Deal coalition consisted of groups that shared a common sense of class solidarity but were deeply divided on social issues such as race relations. During the 1930s, fearing the potential of a white backlash, Roosevelt avoided tackling sensitive civil-rights issues. But the war elevated racial tension, both in the North and the South, and increased white anxiety about the future of race relations. In the North industrial expansion lured African Americans there to fill a desperate labor shortage. In Detroit, where Ford, Chrysler, and General Motors served as the "arsenal of democracy," the African American population doubled. To preserve the whiteness of their neighborhoods, many locals refused to sell goods to blacks, established restrictive covenants, and used intimidation to discourage their movement away from black enclaves. In June 1943 race riots in Harlem and Detroit devastated swaths of the urban landscape.

African Americans—many of whom anticipated a "double victory" over fascism abroad and racism at home—grew less patient with rhetorical and symbolic actions. The National Association for the Advancement of Colored People (NAACP) railed against lynching while seeking a federal law making it illegal. At the same time, black veterans began to challenge the disfranchisement of African Americans. In 1944, the Supreme Court in *Smith v. Allwright* struck down the white primary. Signs of growing black activism, combined with indications that the federal government would support civil rights for blacks, produced a wave of anxiety and fear across the white South.

As early as 1948 the civil-rights issue was revealing its potential for unraveling the New Deal coalition. In July when Democrats assembled in sultry Philadelphia for their convention, Truman was feeling the southern heat on civil rights. Fearful of a revolt, he backtracked, endorsing a weak plank that made no mention of his own proposals. Northern liberals, however, whom Truman needed to ward off the threat from Henry Wallace, made civil rights the litmus test of their support for the president. Only if the president included a strong civil-rights plan in the Democratic platform would they endorse him.

When Truman hedged, liberals took their fight to the floor. In a dramatic and emotional speech Hubert Humphrey, who was seeking a Senate seat, called upon the party to enact a "new emancipation proclamation." "The time has come," he declared, "to walk out of the shadow of states' rights and into the sunlight of human rights." Humphrey's emotional appeal carried the day. Convention delegates rejected Truman's compromise measure and approved a strong civil-rights plank.

Rejected by the national party, southern delegates stormed out of the convention. They formed the States' Rights Democratic, or "Dixiecrat," Party, and nominated J. Strom Thurmond, governor of South Carolina, for the presidency. "We stand for the segregation of the races and the racial integrity of each race," the party's platform declared. For his part, Thurmond avoided direct racial appeals and instead focused on states' rights. The civil-rights program, Thurmond declared, and the expansion of federal power that it required, had their "origin in communist ideology" and sought "to excite race and class hatred," thereby "creat[ing] the chaos and confusion which leads to communism." Thurmond's bolt from the Democratic Party represented the first major crack in the once-solid Democratic South and set the stage for the massive movement of southern whites to the Republican Party in the 1970s and 1980s.

2.1 | *Hubert Humphrey Inspires the Democrats*

When it became clear that President Truman planned to retract his support for a strong civil rights plank at the 1948 Democratic convention, Hubert Humphrey took to the floor to rally liberals. His fiery speech swayed delegates and forced Truman to accept the liberal civil rights position.

From the time of Thomas Jefferson, the time when that immortal American doctrine of individual rights, under just and fairly administered laws, the Democratic Party has tried hard to secure expanding freedoms for all citizens. Oh, yes, I know, other political parties may have talked more about civil rights,
5 but the Democratic Party has surely done more about civil rights.

We have made progress. We've made great progress in every part of this country. We've made great progress in the South; we've made it in the West, in the North, and in the East.

But we must now focus the direction of that progress towards the realization
10 of a full program of civil rights to all. This convention must set out more specifically the direction in which our Party efforts are to go.

We can be proud that we can be guided by the courageous trail blazing of two great Democratic Presidents. We can be proud of the fact that our great and beloved immortal leader Franklin Roosevelt gave us guidance. And we be proud of
15 the fact that Harry Truman has had the courage to give to the people of America the new emancipation proclamation.

It seems to me that the Democratic Party needs to make definite pledges of the kinds suggested in the minority report, to maintain the trust and the confidence placed in it by the people of all races and all sections of this country. Sure, we're
20 here as Democrats. But my good friends, we're here as Americans; we're here as the believers in the principle and the ideology of democracy, and I firmly believe that as men concerned with our country's future, we must specify in our platform the guarantees which we have mentioned in the minority report.

Yes, this is far more than a Party matter. Every citizen in this country has
25 a stake in the emergence of the United States as a leader in the free world. That world is being challenged by the world of slavery. For us to play our part effectively, we must be in a morally sound position.

We can't use a double standard. There's no room for double standards in American politics for measuring our own and other people's policies. Our
30 demands for democratic practices in other lands will be no more effective than the guarantee of those practices in our own country.

Friends, delegates, I do not believe that there can be any compromise on the guarantees of the civil rights which we have mentioned in the minority report. In spite of my desire for unanimous agreement on the entire platform, in spite

35 of my desire to see everybody here in honest and unanimous agreement, there are some matters which I think must be stated clearly and without qualification. There can be no hedging—the newspaper headlines are wrong. There will be no hedging, and there will be no watering down—if you please—of the instruments and the principles of the civil rights program.

40   My friends, to those who say that we are rushing this issue of civil rights, I say to them we are 172 years late. To those who say that this civil rights program is an infringement on states' rights, I say this: The time has arrived in America for the Democratic Party to get out of the shadow of states' rights and to walk forthrightly into the bright sunshine of human rights.

45   People—human beings—this is the issue of the 20th century. People of all kinds—all sorts of people—and these people are looking to America for leadership, and they're looking to America for precept and example.

    My good friends, my fellow Democrats, I ask you for a calm consideration of our historic opportunity. Let us do forget the evil passions and the blindness of 50 the past. In these times of world economic, political, and spiritual—above all spiritual crisis, we cannot and we must not turn from the path so plainly before us. That path has already led us through many valleys of the shadow of death. And now is the time to recall those who were left on that path of American freedom.

    For all of us here, for the millions who have sent us, for the whole two billion 55 members of the human family, our land is now, more than ever before, the last best hope on earth. And I know that we can, and I know that we shall begin here the fuller and richer realization of that hope, that promise of a land where all men are truly free and equal, and each man uses his freedom and equality wisely well.

    My good friends, I ask my Party, I ask the Democratic Party, to march down 60 the high road of progressive democracy. I ask this convention to say in unmistakable terms that we proudly hail, and we courageously support, our President and leader Harry Truman in his great fight for civil rights in America!

Source: "Civil Rights Speech 1948," Box 25, Mayor's Political Files, Hubert H. Humphrey Papers, Minnesota Historical Society, St. Paul, Minnesota.   ■ ■ ■

Truman selected the seventy-five-year-old Senator Alben Barkley of Kentucky as his running mate, but he could do little to lift the spirits of Democratic leaders who feared that defections of Democratic voters to Wallace and Thurmond spelled doom in November. At a nearby convention hotel, a group of Democratic leaders called for room service. "Send up a bottle of embalming fluid," they said. "If we're going to hold a wake, we might as well do it right."

The 1948 Election

The 1948 election was one of the most exciting in American history. Rarely has a campaign revealed such a wide range of opinions on issues that were crucial to America's future.

The confident Republicans nominated New York governor Thomas E. Dewey, who had run a strong race against Roosevelt in 1944 and seemed certain to beat Truman. The convention, which was the first ever televised, picked California Governor Earl Warren for the second place on the ticket. Ignoring Truman and avoiding specific issues, Dewey concentrated on convincing voters that he was an efficient administrator who could bring unity to the country and effectiveness to its foreign policy.

While Dewey tried to stay above the partisan fray, Truman waged a tough, bare-knuckled campaign. Criss-crossing the country by train, Truman reminded voters that the Democratic Party had led the nation through depression and world war. His speeches pictured politics as a struggle between the "people," represented by the Democrats, and the "special interests," represented by Republicans. Enthusiastic crowds shouted "Give 'em hell, Harry!" Truman responded: "I don't give 'em hell. I just tell the truth and they think it's hell."

The two other candidates in the race raised basic questions about the direction in which the nation was headed. Running on the Progressive ticket, Henry Wallace challenged the evolving Cold War consensus. He advocated compromise with the Soviet Union while championing an expansive liberal program at home. Strom Thurmond, the States-Rights' nominee, galvanized white southern support by attacking civil-rights legislation and defending the system of Jim Crow that defined race relations in the South.

Truman on the Campaign Trail   Considered the underdog in 1948, President Truman ran an aggressive campaign, touring the country on a train called the *Ferdinand Magellan.* Truman covered 31,000 miles, gave 351 speeches, and spread his message to an estimated 12 million Americans. Surrounded by the press, Harry and Bess Truman prepare to pull out of Washington's Union Station. *(© Bettmann/CORBIS)*

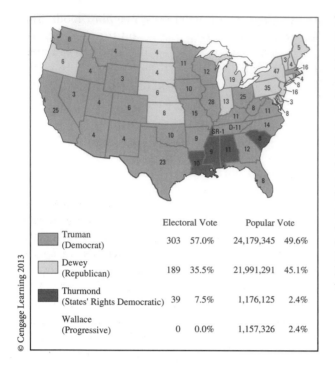

	Electoral Vote		Popular Vote	
Truman (Democrat)	303	57.0%	24,179,345	49.6%
Dewey (Republican)	189	35.5%	21,991,291	45.1%
Thurmond (States' Rights Democratic)	39	7.5%	1,176,125	2.4%
Wallace (Progressive)	0	0.0%	1,157,326	2.4%

The Election of 1948 Thomas Dewey was the favorite in the polls, in large part due to the fracturing of the Democratic Party as Dixiecrats and Progressives rejected Truman's domestic and international policies. Several Deep South states supported J. Strom Thurmond's platform, but Progressive candidate Henry Wallace failed to win a single state. Truman's aggressive campaign, in which he castigated the "do-nothing" Republican Congress, helped him pull out the unlikely victory.

With Democrats so divided, Truman lagged behind Dewey in the polls. On election night the *Chicago Tribune* was so certain Truman would lose that it ran the headline: "DEWEY DEFEATS TRUMAN." Instead, Truman scored the most dramatic upset victory in the history of presidential elections, winning 24.1 million votes to Dewey's 22 million.

How did Truman pull off such a surprising victory? First, both Wallace and Thurmond were hurt by the public's reluctance to waste their vote on a third-party candidate with little chance of victory. At the same time, their campaigns actually helped Truman. With Wallace being openly supported by the communists, and with Truman denouncing him, the president was much less vulnerable than he might otherwise have been to charges of being "soft" on communism. The Dixiecrat rebellion against Truman's civil-rights program encouraged the loyalty of liberals and most black voters, many of whom might otherwise have been attracted to Wallace or even to Dewey.

Second, Dewey's bland campaign failed to excite voters. Dewey was vague and unclear on the issues, and he ignited little grass-roots enthusiasm. Fewer Republicans went to the polls in 1948 than in either 1940 or 1944.

Finally, the election demonstrated the enduring appeal of the New Deal. The president assembled the key groups of the New Deal coalition: urban workers, Jews, and African Americans. Like Roosevelt, Truman carried the nation's thirteen largest cities, scoring well in the poorest neighborhoods. The president's aggressive campaigning in the Great Plains and the West helped maintain the support of farmers. "I talked about voting for Dewey all summer, but when the time came I just couldn't do it," said one farmer. "I remembered the depression and all the other things that had come to me under the Democrats."

The "Fair Deal"

Liberals had high hopes that the newly elected president would use his mandate to revive the New Deal. The Democrats, by picking up nine seats in the Senate and seventy-five in the House, regained control of Congress. Truman certainly viewed his victory as a mandate for liberalism, and he outlined his ambitious social and economic agenda in his 1949 State of the Union message. "Every segment of our population and every individual," he declared, "has a right to expect from our Government a fair deal." Truman implored Congress to expand many New Deal programs while launching new initiatives in civil rights, national health insurance, and federal aid to education. The liberal *New Republic* called Truman's Fair Deal "one of the boldest reform programs ever presented by an American President."

The eighty-first Congress often complied with Truman's pleas to expand existing programs. In the most ambitious burst of reform since 1935, Congress increased the minimum wage from forty to seventy-five cents per hour, extended rent controls, and approved a displaced persons act admitting some four hundred thousand refugees to the United States. It passed the National Housing Act of 1949, which authorized the construction of 810,000 low-income housing units and provided funds for slum clearance and rural housing. In 1950 Congress increased social security benefits by an average of 80 percent, extending the system's coverage to an additional 10.5 million people.

Congress, however, showed little desire to support Truman's calls for new programs that moved beyond the New Deal. It rejected the president's proposals for federal aid to education, a crop-subsidy system, and the repeal of Taft-Hartley. When Truman proposed a system of national health insurance, the American Medical Association (AMA) hired an advertising agency to fight against the measure. "Would socialized medicine lead to socialization of other phases of American life?" asked an AMA leaflet. The answer: "Lenin thought so." Most Americans agreed, and the bill died in Congress. Congress also stymied Truman's efforts to enact civil-rights legislation. Truman proposed creating a civil-rights division in the Department of Justice to protect the right to vote, to abolish the poll tax in federal elections, and to establish a permanent fair employment practices committee. Southern Democrats and Republicans killed the bill before it reached the floor for debate.

To some extent, Truman's Fair Deal was a victim of the Cold War, which drained attention and resources away from domestic initiatives. The Cold War also strengthened the power of conservatives, whose support Truman needed to maintain his foreign and defense policies. "Any illusion that the liberal Democrats dominate either the House or the Senate has been completely blasted," Hubert Humphrey observed. The 1948 election was "not so much a victory as a reprieve."

The Vital Center

Truman may have governed in the shadow of Roosevelt, but his administration produced a limited redefinition of American liberalism and marked an important shift in the evolution of the Democratic Party. The liberalism that emerged in America after World War II rested on a foundation of shared assumptions forged during the Depression and World War II. Arthur Schlesinger Jr., in a popular book published in 1949, referred to the new liberalism as *The Vital Center,* which he defined as a middle way between the tyranny of the Left and of the Right.

Three basic assumptions undergirded the vital center. The "gospel of economic growth" formed the first pillar. By 1949 most Americans believed that economic growth would eliminate class division, guarantee social harmony, and provide a constant source of revenue for necessary social programs. This faith in capitalism marked an important shift from the New Deal. During the 1930s many liberals had been convinced that the Great Depression signaled the death of capitalism. They spent most of the decade experimenting with different plans for restructuring the economy. All included large-scale government planning and controls. But the enormous productivity during the war, which saw the gross national product double in four years, revitalized liberal faith in capitalism and fostered new confidence in government's ability to regulate the economy. Full employment was possible, liberal economists believed, and they now felt they knew how to use their tools to achieve that end.

A new consensus formed around the idea that government should continue to provide essential services not offered by the private sector—low-cost housing, medical insurance, and funds for education—but its emphasis would be on expanding the economic pie, not reslicing it. Economic growth, and the constant tax revenue that it generated, would provide the nation with the resources it needed to fund necessary social problems at home while also paying for the military needs of the Cold War. The nation, in other words, could have both guns and butter.

Foreign-policy issues had been largely absent from the New Deal agenda, but the question of America's role in the world formed the second pillar of the vital center. Since Russian aggression of the 1940s was seen as the same as the German belligerence of the 1930s, American policymakers reacted toward the Soviet Union as they believed their predecessors should have behaved toward the expansionist states of their time. "The image of Hitler," wrote the historian Gaddis Smith, "seared itself on the eye of all who fought him. When Hitler was gone, his image lingered." Between 1946 and 1948 Truman shifted liberals and the Democratic Party toward an aggressive internationalism based on fear of Soviet expansion and an enlarged definition of American interests. Truman's victory in the 1948 election signaled the triumph of liberal anticommunism.

A faith in consensus and social harmony served as the third pillar of the vital center. The contrast with Adolf Hitler's fascism and Joseph Stalin's totalitarianism convinced Americans of their common faith in the values of freedom and democracy and underscored the importance of consensus. Prosperity maintained that consensus by muting ideological differences and by blurring the lines of potential conflict based on race or gender. Everyone benefited from abundance: business reaped high profits, labor received better wages, farmers earned larger incomes, and the poor—both black and white—gained the opportunity to lead a better life.

The vital center, a blend of liberal goals and conservative means, represented an accommodation with the new political realities of postwar America. It recognized the need for an activist federal government and an internationalist foreign policy, but it rested on conservative assumptions about the power of private capital to solve social problems and to forge consensus. The vital center promised to raise the standard of living, promote social justice, and guarantee U.S. interests abroad, but with a minimum of social dislocation or sacrifice. The nation could fulfill its grand expectations of the future while remaining faithful to its conservative values.

In the end, this new liberalism created unrealistic expectations about the possibilities of change and thus intensified the American paradox. Though general prosperity increased the quality of life for most Americans, it did not produce meaningful redistribution of income. Economic growth not only failed to erase class division; it also was unable to mute ideological conflict in America. At the same time, the promise of gradual reform failed to satisfy the rising expectations of African Americans, who demanded an end to segregation in the South. The bipolar view of the world, born in the heat of the Cold War, quickly became obsolete as nationalist movements in the Third World complicated the global balance of power. America's zero-sum view of the world also failed to account for differences among communist countries or appreciate the limits of American power.

SELECTED READINGS

▌ Jack S. Ballard's *The Shock of Peace* (1983) recounts the economic trauma of demobilization at war's end. The conflict that arose between labor and government is described in George Roukis's *American Labor and the Conservative Republicans* (1988). In *Beyond the New Deal* (1973), Alonzo L.

Hamby assesses Truman's effort to preserve and expand the New Deal. Robert J. Donovan captures the 1940s feeling of upheaval in *Tumultuous Years* (1982). Susan Hartmann outlines Truman's first-term frustrations in *Truman and the 80th Congress* (1971). Monte S. Poen details the defeat of national health insurance in *Harry S. Truman Versus the Medical Lobby* (1979).

▮ Robert Dallek's *Harry S. Truman* (2008) is the best brief biography of Roosevelt's successor. David G. McCullough's *Truman* (1992) is a generally uncritical appraisal of Truman's life and policies. Alonzo L. Hamby provides the best treatment of Truman in *Man of the People* (1995). John Culver and John Hyde's *American Dreamer* (2000) examines Wallace's political career and his groundbreaking work in agricultural economics. The work of Leon Keyserling, Truman's economic policy adviser, is analyzed in W. Robert Brazelton's biography of Keyserling, *Designing U.S. Economic Policy* (2000).

▮ Zachary Karabell makes a convincing case in *The Last Campaign* (2000) that the 1948 election was the last to provide Americans with choices across the ideological spectrum. Both William C. Berman's *The Politics of Civil Rights in the Truman Administration* (1970) and Michael R. Gardner's *Harry Truman and Civil Rights* (2002) cover the controversy within the Democratic Party and Truman's civil-rights record.

▮ Arthur Schlesinger Jr. argues the virtues of Fair Deal liberalism in *The Vital Center* (1949). The tension within the liberal community in the early Cold War years is described in Jim Tuck's *The Liberal Civil War* (1998). Steven M. Gillon's *Politics and Vision* (1985) examines the new political environment that liberals of the Cold War era faced.

3 The Cold War Heats Up

On May 1, 1950, communist insurgents seized control of the small Wisconsin town of Mosinee, population 1,400. The takeover began at 6:00 A.M. when an armed group arrested the mayor at his house. "Come out with your hands on your head!" they shouted. "I represent the Council of People's Commissars and we're taking over this town." While the mayor was being arrested, another raiding party grabbed the police chief. "Well, you rat, you're under arrest," the script instructed them to say. When the chief refused, he was "shot" for failing to cooperate.

As the day wore on the vigilante bands took over newspapers, closed churches, and seized control of the telegraph and telephone offices. They forced restaurants to serve only communist culinary favorites: potato soup, black bread, and coffee.

Once their control of the town was complete, the communists outlawed the constitution, ended private property, and declared free speech and free assembly dead. They celebrated the beginning of red rule by organizing a march to the center of town for a mass rally. Over 500 townspeople—about one-third of the population—participated, carrying signs reading "Stalin is the Leader" and "Religion is the Opium of the People."

In reality, there was no "communist takeover" of Mosinee. The entire event was designed as a publicity stunt. The exercise in communist control lasted for less than 24 hours. That evening, town members marked the overthrow of communist rule with a celebration in the town square where they tossed all the evidence of Soviet occupation into a massive bonfire. The evening ended with a spirited singing of "God Bless America."

The occupation was designed to remind Americans of the freedoms they enjoy and the dangers communism presented to the American way of life. The demonstration struck a responsive chord with a nervous nation. Nearly sixty reporters showed up to cover the "Day under Communism." Three television networks sent correspondents. All the major newspapers covered the story. Two newsreel companies recorded all the events. Even the Soviet TASS news agency sent a reporter.

A string of foreign policy setbacks abroad raised fears of communist subversion at home and set the stage for demonstrations like the one in Mosinee. Charges of espionage and subversion gripped the nation. The anticommunist hysteria created a fertile breeding ground for demagogues who used fear of communism as a blunt weapon against dissent, real or imagined. Wisconsin Senator Joseph McCarthy emerged as the most talented demagogue of all.

The success of the publicity stunt in Mosinee highlighted the nation's uneasiness about the Cold War and the threat of communist subversion. America's unrealistic faith in the universal appeal of American values left it unprepared for the dramatic news in 1949 that the communists had triumphed in China's civil war. The shock led to accusations of subversion at home. The Red Scare forced Americans to confront a fundamental question of identity: What did it mean to be an American? Fears of communist subversion produced a narrow definition of Americanism, isolated potential radicals, and reinforced the postwar consensus. The Korean War intensified the debate over American identity, but it also exposed the gap between American expectations of the postwar world and the realities of international power. The war underscored the limits of American power and revealed the nation's discomfort with the demands of limited war. Meanwhile, the Cold War pressured Americans to balance their commitment to freedom and individual

communism

rights with their sense of patriotism and national security. This conflict between freedom and security, which was intensified by the Korean War, presented Americans with a painful choice.

The Cold War in Asia

During the 1930s, many Americans viewed China as America's junior partner in the Pacific. *Time* chose its Christian leader Jiang Jieshi (Chiang Kai-shek) and his American-educated wife as the magazine's "Man and Wife of the Year" in 1938. World War II enhanced China's reputation in the United States, with wartime propaganda depicting the Chinese people as democratically inclined and desirous of an American way of life. The Office of War Information asked Hollywood to portray China as "a great nation, cultured and liberal, with whom, inevitably, we will be closely bound in the world that is to come." The effort worked: by 1942, 82 percent of Americans believed that China would be a strong ally after the war.

When World War II ended, however, Jiang Jieshi's Nationalists in the south faced a serious challenge from Mao Zedong's (Mao Tse-tung) Communists in the north. At first the Nationalists had the upper hand, but Jiang's corrupt and incompetent government failed to inspire public support or stem the tide of Chinese communism. In 1945–1946 Harry Truman, anxious to work out a peaceful settlement between Jiang and Mao, sent General George C. Marshall to China in a failed attempt to negotiate a compromise. U.S. efforts continued, but by 1949 Truman had grown weary of Jiang's refusal to undertake necessary reforms or attack corruption in his government. The president wrote in his diary that Jiang's government "was one of the most corrupt and inefficient that ever made an attempt to govern a country."

Deciding there was little the United States could do to salvage the noncommunist government, Truman stopped all aid to Jiang in 1949. Shortly afterward Jiang's forces collapsed, sending the Nationalist leader scurrying to the offshore island of Formosa (Taiwan), where Nationalists set up the independent Republic of China. The Soviet Union consolidated its power in Asia by extending diplomatic recognition to Mao's government and signing a "mutual-assistance" agreement.

The communist victory precipitated a firestorm of criticism at home against those responsible for "losing China." Many Americans viewed China as the best hope for democracy in Asia. Now it had fallen into enemy hands. A widespread and false assumption took root that Truman had abandoned a cherished ally in the hopes of appeasing communist aggression. One powerful congressman called American policy "an Oriental Munich." Worse still, many people assumed that communist spies in the government had conspired to manipulate U.S. policy.

Years later John F. Kennedy and Lyndon Johnson, remembering the bruising assault Truman endured for losing China, would determine never to lose another inch to the communists.

The emotional reaction to the communist triumph in China focused U.S. attention on Asia. At the end of World War II the United States occupied Japan and, under the leadership of General Douglas MacArthur, transformed the vanquished country into a model of Western democracy where women could vote, trade unions were encouraged, and land was redistributed among the peasants. Wanting to make sure that Japan would never reemerge as a military threat, the United States wrote a Japanese constitution, adopted in 1946, that renounced war, promising that "land, sea and air forces, as well as other war potential, will never be maintained." The growing communist threat in Asia, however, forced a dramatic shift in American policy. Now, viewing Japan as a potential military counterweight against China, policymakers negotiated a new treaty in 1951 that terminated the U.S. occupation and conceded to Japan "the inherent right of individual or collective self-defense."

While debating the consequences of the "fall of China" Americans experienced another Cold War setback. On September 23, 1949, they learned that the Soviet Union had exploded its own atom bomb. The United States no longer possessed a monopoly of nuclear weapons.

Following the Soviet nuclear explosion, Truman decided to develop a hydrogen bomb, potentially a thousand times more powerful than the atomic weapon that destroyed Hiroshima and Nagasaki. On November 1, 1952, the United States exploded the first H-bomb, obliterating an uninhabited island in the Pacific. The bomb blast created a fire ball five miles high and four miles wide and left a hole in the Pacific floor a mile long and 175 feet deep. The following year the Russians exploded their first hydrogen bomb. Britain and France soon joined the nuclear club. The arms race had begun in earnest.

Together the "fall" of China and the Soviet nuclear test forced American policymakers to rethink U.S. strategic doctrine. In April, after months of deliberation, the National Security Council recommended that the president initiate a massive rebuilding of the American military to confront the new Soviet nuclear threat. The report, National Security Council Memorandum 68 (NSC-68), presented a frightening portrait of a Soviet system driven by "a new fanatic faith" that "seeks to impose its absolute authority over the rest of the world." Since the United States could no longer depend solely on nuclear weapons to deter the Russians, it needed to expand its conventional capability. To deter the Russians and inspire confidence in its allies, the report called for an extraordinary increase in the defense budget, from $13 to $50 billion a year. NSC-68, observed the historian Stephen Ambrose, "provided the justification for America's assuming the role of world policeman."

3.1 | *NSC-68*

NATIONAL SECURITY COUNCIL

After the Soviet Union detonated its first atomic bomb and China fell to communism, President Truman ordered his advisers to study America's role in world affairs and the nation's military capability. In April 1950, after months of deliberation, the National Security Council (NSC), in Memorandum 68, recommended that the president initiate a massive rebuilding of the American military, both nuclear and conventional forces, to confront the new Soviet nuclear threat.

The issues that face us are momentous, involving the fulfillment or destruction not only of this Republic but of civilization itself. They are issues which will not await our deliberations. With conscience and resolution this Government and the people it represents must now take new and fateful decisions. . . .

5   The fundamental design of those who control the Soviet Union and the international communist movement is to retain and solidify their absolute power, first in the Soviet Union and second in the areas now under their control. In the minds of the Soviet leaders, however, achievement of this design requires the dynamic extension of their authority and the ultimate elimination of any effective opposi-
10   tion to their authority.

The design, therefore, calls for the complete subversion or forcible destruction of the machinery of government and structure of society in the countries of the non-Soviet world and their replacement by an apparatus and structure subservient to and controlled from the Kremlin. To that end Soviet efforts are now
15   directed toward the domination of the Eurasian land mass. The United States, as the principal center of power in the non-Soviet world and the bulwark of opposition to Soviet expansion, is the principal enemy whose integrity and vitality must be subverted or destroyed by one means or another if the Kremlin is to achieve its fundamental design.
20   The Kremlin regards the United States as the only major threat to the achievement of its fundamental design. There is a basic conflict between the idea of freedom under a government of laws, and the idea of slavery under the grim oligarchy of the Kremlin, which has come to a crisis with the polarization of power described in Section I, and the exclusive possession of atomic weapons by the
25   two protagonists. The idea of freedom, moreover, is peculiarly and intolerably subversive of the idea of slavery. But the converse is not true. The implacable purpose of the slave state to eliminate the challenge of freedom has placed the two great powers at opposite poles. It is this fact which gives the present polarization of power the quality of crisis. . . .
30   Thus unwillingly our free society finds itself mortally challenged by the Soviet system. No other value system is so wholly irreconcilable with ours,

so implacable in its purpose to destroy ours, so capable of turning to its own uses the most dangerous and divisive trends in our own society, no other so skillfully and powerfully evokes the elements of irrationality in human nature everywhere,
35 and no other has the support of a great and growing center of military power. . . .

Our overall policy at the present time may be described as one designed to foster a world environment in which the American system can survive and flourish. It therefore rejects the concept of isolation and affirms the necessity of our positive participation in the world community. . . .

40 In summary, we must, by means of a rapid and sustained build-up of the political, economic, and military strength of the free world, and by means of an affirmative program intended to wrest the initiative from the Soviet Union, confront it with convincing evidence of the determination and ability of the free world to frustrate the Kremlin design of a world dominated by its will. Such evi-
45 dence is the only means short of war which eventually may force the Kremlin to abandon its present course of action and to negotiate acceptable agreements on issues of major importance.

The whole success of the proposed program hangs ultimately on recognition by this Government, the American people, and all free peoples, that the cold war
50 is in fact a real war in which the survival of the free world is at stake. Essential prerequisites to success are consultations with Congressional leaders designed to make the program the object of non-partisan legislative support, and a presentation to the public of a full explanation of the facts and implications of the present international situation. The prosecution of the program will require of us all the
55 ingenuity, sacrifice, and unity demanded by the vital importance of the issue and the tenacity to persevere until our national objectives have been attained.

Source: Excerpts from "NSC-68: A Report to the National Security Council," April 14, 1950, from *Foreign Relations of the United States: 1950*, I, 237–92.　■ ■ ■

The Korean War: From Invasion to Stalemate

In January 1950 Secretary of State Dean Acheson omitted any mention of Korea when he outlined the "defensive perimeter" that the United States would protect in Asia. At the end of the Second World War, the United States and the Soviets had temporarily divided the Korean peninsula, previously dominated by Japan, at the 38th parallel. Cold War tensions, however, ended any hope of unification. The Russians installed Kim Il Sung to lead the communist North, while Syngman Rhee, a conservative nationalist, emerged as the American-sponsored ruler in the South. Korea was not a top American priority, however, and the United States withdrew its troops from Korea in June 1949.

That changed on June 25, 1950, when 110,000 North Korean soldiers crossed the 38th parallel and within hours overpowered South Korean forces. The circumstances surrounding the invasion remain unclear, but documents in Soviet archives, made available to historians at the end of the Cold War, suggest that the North Koreans, not the Soviets, pushed for the invasion. Kim Il Sung pestered Joseph Stalin with forty-eight telegrams seeking his approval for an attack on the South. Stalin, fearful of a military conflict with the United States, refused many times, but he finally gave his approval in January 1950. Why the change of mind? Most historians speculate that he believed that the United States would not respond. "According to information coming from the United States, it is really so," Stalin told Kim in a Kremlin meeting in April 1950. "The prevailing mood is not to interfere." The new information included Acheson's speech excluding South Korea from the U.S. "defense perimeter" and a top-secret government document, which Soviet spies in London had stolen, that reinforced Acheson's statement.

Truman viewed the situation in a dramatically different light. He interpreted the invasion as a Soviet-engineered assault, the opening salvo in a broader Soviet attack on the American sphere of influence. Committed to avoiding the same mistake Roosevelt made in dealing with Hitler, Truman immediately ordered American air and naval forces to support the South Koreans. "If this was allowed to go unchallenged," he wrote in his memoirs, "it would mean a third world war, just as similar incidents had brought on the second world war."

Two days later, on Tuesday, June 27, 1950, Truman asked the United Nations Security Council to condemn North Korea as an aggressor and to send forces to South Korea. The resolution passed because the Russian delegate, who could have used his veto to defeat the measure, was boycotting the meetings. The defense effort was theoretically a UN venture, but in the end the United States provided half the ground troops and most of the sea and air support.

In the first few weeks it appeared that the North Korean forces might win a decisive victory. Their troops pushed the South Koreans and the entire U.S. Eighth Army down the peninsula to its tip around the port city of Pusan. Then on September 15, General Douglas MacArthur turned the war around with a daring amphibious invasion behind enemy lines at Inchon, near the South Korean capital of Seoul. At the same time the American and South Korean armies attacked in great force at Pusan. The dual tactic fooled the North Koreans, who suffered heavy losses and quickly retreated beyond the 38th parallel. On September 28 American troops liberated Seoul and reestablished Syngman Rhee's government in the South. By the end of October, MacArthur's forces had advanced within fifty miles of the Yalu River, the boundary between Korea and the Chinese province of Manchuria.

The dramatic victory on the ground raised hopes that the United States could overthrow Kim Il Sung and unite Korea under a noncommunist government. Truman was not so sure about attempting a military reunification of Korea. In October, the president flew to Wake Island in the Pacific to consult with

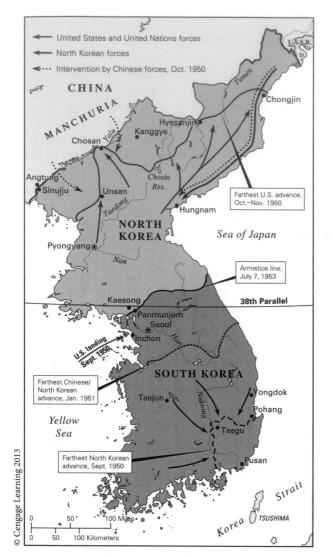

Map legend:
- United States and United Nations forces
- North Korean forces
- Intervention by Chinese forces, Oct. 1950

CHINA

MANCHURIA

U.S.S.R.

Tumen

Chongjin

Hyesanjin

Kanggye

Chosan

Yalu

Angtung

Sinuiju

Unsan

Chosin
Res.

Taedong

Hungnam

NORTH
KOREA

Sea of Japan

Pyongyang

Nan

Farthest U.S. advance,
Oct.–Nov. 1950

Armistice line,
July 7, 1953

Kaesong

Panmunjom

Seoul

Inchon

Han

38th Parallel

U.S. landing
Sept. 1950

Farthest Chinese/
North Korean
advance, Jan. 1951

SOUTH KOREA

Taejon

Naktong

Yongdok

Pohang

Yellow
Sea

Taegu

Farthest North Korean
advance, Sept. 1950

Pusan

Korea
Strait

TSUSHIMA

0   50   100 Miles
0   50   100 Kilometers

© Cengage Learning 2013

The Korean War, 1950–1953 After the initial wave of North Korean troops swept through the South in the summer of 1950, United Nations' forces under General Douglas MacArthur countered at Inchon and Pusan. By November, UN troops occupied most of Korea, but Chinese troops quickly repulsed the advance and pushed MacArthur's men south of the 38th parallel. There the fighting remained until the armistice in 1953.

MacArthur. The general assured Truman that the Chinese Communists, despite their buildup of troops on the border and their loud warnings against crossing of the 38th parallel, would not intervene in the war. The president, uplifted by MacArthur's optimistic assessment and Acheson's support, gave the general the go-ahead.

MacArthur and Acheson were wrong about the Chinese. On November 25, a Chinese army of 300,000 men, armed with Russian tanks and aircraft, swept down from the mountains and attacked the unprepared American forces in North Korea. The United States suffered one of its greatest military defeats in history. Its shattered units raced backward 120 miles in 10 days, leaving most of their weapons and equipment behind. By Christmas, the massive wave of Chinese troops had pushed MacArthur south of the 38th parallel again.

The massive Chinese invasion and the humiliating military defeat did not deter MacArthur, who asked Truman for permission to attack Chinese military bases in the North. This time Truman rejected MacArthur's strategy, fearing that direct attack on Chinese installations would antagonize the Russians and precipitate a global conflict. In January 1951, the U.S. Eighth Army halted the communist advance and, by March, pushed back to the 38th parallel. The war bogged down, with neither side able to gain the advantage.

"Old soldiers never die . . ."

When MacArthur publicly criticized the commander-in-chief for seeking a negotiated compromise, Truman fired him. It proved a very controversial decision. Sixty-six percent of Americans initially opposed Truman's action. On April 19, 1951, MacArthur gave an impassioned farewell address to a joint session of Congress. He concluded by repeating a line from a West Point ballad, "Old soldiers never die," he said, "they just fade away." The words moved many congressmen to tears.

MacArthur's critique of Washington's handling of the Korean conflict revealed the frustration and confusion of a nation struggling to adjust to the idea of a limited war. Seventy years old when the Korean War started, MacArthur had been trained in the military doctrine of total war. His experience in two world wars taught him that "In war, there is no substitute for victory." Truman and his advisors argued that the Cold War forced America to develop a new strategy for fighting limited wars. MacArthur, they argued, failed to recognize that the real enemy was not North Korea, but the Soviet Union. The fighting in Korea was a strategic diversion, a Russian maneuver to draw American strength away from Europe. Larger strategic goals, namely containing Moscow, required the United States to avoid squandering its resources on proxy wars in remote places. "Frankly, in the opinion of the Joint Chiefs of Staff," General Omar Bradley declared, "this strategy would involve us in the wrong war, at the wrong place, at the wrong time and with the wrong enemy."

The administration won the debate with MacArthur, but the questions raised by the confrontation would continue to haunt policymakers. Americans accustomed to waging total war and reaping the benefits of total victory never fully adjusted to the demands of limited war. Containment required Americans to settle for fighting limited, protracted wars, seeking diplomatic solutions rather than military victory, and enduring the hardship of an uncertain peace.

Douglas MacArthur Addresses Congress   As commander of the UN forces in Korea, General Douglas MacArthur was expected to accept the decisions made by his commander-in-chief, President Harry Truman. However, in the spring of 1951, MacArthur's public pronouncements and his letter to representative Martin led to his dismissal. MacArthur returned to the United States where he received a hero's welcome. On April 19, MacArthur addressed a joint session of Congress, announcing the end of his long, and at times controversial, military career. *(© Bettmann/CORBIS)*

Consequences of Korea

The stalemated fighting in Korea would drag on, amid cease-fire talks, for more than a year, ending soon after Truman left office. Despite the limited nature of the war, it resulted in 36,940 American deaths and left 103,284 American soldiers wounded. It also brought significant change within the United States. It produced a huge escalation of defense spending from approximately $14 billion in 1949 to $44 billion in 1953. As government spending created millions of new jobs, unemployment dropped to its lowest level in years. Federal expenditures, together with special tax incentives, encouraged industries to expand production. From 1950 to 1954 steel capacity increased by 24 percent, electrical generating capacity by 50 percent, and aluminum capacity by 100 percent.

The Korean War also accelerated the desegregation of the armed services. By mid-1950 the navy and air force had taken strides toward desegregation, but the army still maintained separate black and white units. Critics had complained that segregation, besides being morally wrong, was also wasteful and inefficient. Korea exposed another problem with segregation: assigning African Americans to noncombat duty led whites to suffer a disproportionate share of casualties. When white troops experienced heavy losses in the early days of the war, field commanders in Korea broke with existing policy and used black soldiers as replacements. In March 1951, the Pentagon announced the integration of all training facilities in the United States. By the end of the war nearly all African American soldiers were serving in integrated units.

The war continued the expansion of presidential power begun under Franklin Roosevelt. When North Korea invaded, Truman made a unilateral decision to intervene, acting with neither Congress's approval nor its declaration of war. Only after he had authorized American force did Truman meet with Congress to inform members about what he had done. This expansion of presidential power, and the consequent dramatic increase in government spending, however, produced little public debate or discussion. The war only sharpened the inconsistencies in America's attitude toward government. The structure of government expanded during the Korean War, but public fear of federal power persisted. In the short run conservatives tapped into this fear to fan the flames of anticommunism, but in the long run the tension between expectations of government and fear of government only sharpened during the 1950s.

The Politics of Fear

The Korean War intensified suspicions of communist subversion at home. It was bad enough that the Soviets were making gains around the world. What worried Americans more was the possibility that spies here at home were secretly helping their cause. Anticommunist crusaders assumed that democracy could not be trusted to fight such a determined and disciplined opponent. Americans needed to adopt aggressive new measures to identify subversives and to root them out before they destroyed the American way of life. The issues raised by the "Red Scare" went to the very core of what it meant to be an American. How do you define loyalty? How do you distinguish between legitimate dissent and subversion?

There was genuine reason for Americans to feel anxious about the threat of communist subversion. In March 1945, government agents found numerous classified documents in the Manhattan offices of the allegedly pro-Communist *Amerasia* magazine. A year later, a Canadian investigation led to the arrest of twenty-two people for passing classified U.S. documents to the Soviets. Together the cases proved that Soviet spies had successfully gained access to secret government documents. "The disloyalty of American Communists is no longer a matter of conjecture," declared FBI head J. Edgar Hoover.

Americans cried out for protection against communist influence in government. In an attempt to quell public concern, President Truman, in March 1947, issued Executive Order 9835, which established the Federal Employee Loyalty Program. The Truman program allowed for dismissal from federal employment in cases where "reasonable grounds exist for belief that the person involved is disloyal."

But what constituted disloyalty and who decided? Could the claim of "disloyalty," of being anti-American, be used as an excuse to intimidate people who had different ideas? While most people believe the Truman program was limited in scope, there were abuses. Civil rights activists, for example, came under intense scrutiny. The head of one government loyalty board noted, "The fact that a person believes in racial equality doesn't prove he's a Communist, but it certainly makes you look twice, doesn't it?" Fear of subversion also provided the backdrop to what one historian has called a Cold War "lavender scare." For 25 years, the

Bogey and Bacall Attend the Hollywood Ten Trials Anticommunist hysteria infiltrated all walks of American life, including the film industry. Actors, writers, and directors faced the difficult decision of cooperating with the investigation or risking their careers. When called before the committee, the Hollywood Ten refused to answer questions, claiming that, even if they were communists, the First Amendment gave them that right. Humphrey Bogart and Lauren Bacall, seen here going into the hearings, joined other stars to form the Committee for the First Amendment in support of those who refused to cooperate. However, most studio heads, fearing a public backlash against Hollywood, blacklisted the Ten and over two hundred others. (© *Bettmann/CORBIS*)

government automatically dismissed suspected homosexuals, claiming they were susceptible to blackmail.

The courts joined in the anticommunist crusade. In July 1948, the administration charged eleven top communists with violating the Smith Act of 1940, which made it a crime to conspire to "advocate and teach" the violent overthrow of government. After ten months of trial and deliberation, a lower court declared the Smith Act constitutional and found the communists guilty of conspiracy to advocate the overthrow of the government. The communists appealed the decision to the Supreme Court, which, in *Dennis v. U.S.* (1951), upheld the conviction. The decision cleared the way for the prosecution of other communist leaders.

Congress refused to sit on the sidelines. In 1947, using information provided by informers, the House Committee on Un-American Activities (HUAC) opened a series of investigations into the Hollywood entertainment industry. In September, the committee subpoenaed forty-one witnesses. Most cooperated with the committee by offering names of suspected communists. A small group of screenwriters, the "Hollywood Ten," served prison terms for refusing to answer questions about their ties to the Communist Party. Shaken by the hearings, the studios initiated a policy of "blacklisting" writers, directors, technicians, and actors who refused to denounce communism.

Alger Hiss and The Rosenbergs

While examining reports of communist influence in Hollywood, HUAC investigators turned their attention to potentially explosive accusations of espionage in Washington. In August 1948, Whittaker Chambers, a *Time* editor, accused Alger Hiss, who had served as a high-ranking aide to Franklin Roosevelt at Yalta, of having given him microfilm of sixty-five classified State Department documents.

To prove his charges Chambers produced microfilm of secret documents taken from a hollowed-out pumpkin on his Maryland farm. (The documents, quickly labeled the "Pumpkin papers," were later revealed to contain information on navy life rafts and fire extinguishers). Testifying before a grand jury in New York, Hiss denied Chambers's charges. Since the statute of limitations on espionage had expired, Hiss was indicted for perjury. After two trials Hiss was found guilty and sentenced to five years in jail.

More than any other event, the Hiss trial convinced many Americans that the Roosevelt and Truman administrations had been oblivious to the dangers of communist espionage. California congressman Richard Nixon, the most aggressive HUAC investigator, described the case as "the most treasonable conspiracy in American history."

Adding to the anxiety was news that spies may have stolen information that allowed the Soviets to develop the atom bomb. Two weeks after Hiss's conviction, the British government announced the arrest of Klaus Fuchs, an atomic physicist who had worked at the Los Alamos laboratory. In May the FBI arrested Julius and Ethel Rosenberg for conspiring with Fuchs to pass secrets to the Russians. The Rosenbergs denied the allegations, insisting they were the victims of anti-communist hysteria and anti-Semitism. Recent declassified documents suggest that the government knew Ethel was innocent of espionage but charged her in an effort to squeeze a confession out of her husband so that other members of the ring might be prosecuted. After a two-week trial, a jury pronounced them guilty of espionage. On April 15, Judge Irving Kaufman, arguing their crime was "worse than murder" because it furthered the goal of "godless" communism, sentenced the Rosenbergs to death. In June 1953, despite personal pleas from the Pope and worldwide protests, they were executed for their crimes.

The Culture of Fear and American Identity

Congress responded to the hysteria by passing the Internal Security Act of 1950. Among other restrictions, the act required Communist and Communist-front organizations to register with the government and to identify as Communist all their official mail and literature. The act's most severe provisions authorized the government to place all Communists in concentration camps whenever a national emergency should occur. Truman vetoed the bill denouncing it as "the greatest danger to freedom of speech, press, and assembly since the Alien and Sedition Laws of 1798." But Congress garnered enough votes to override the veto and enact the measure into law.

The government used the widespread fear of a communist takeover to expand its power to spy on its own citizens. By 1953 almost one in five Americans working in government or defense-related industries had gone through the loyalty review program. The government created millions of secret files on private citizens. HUAC alone had 1 million secret files. At the same time, the National Security Administration intercepted up to 150,000 cables a month and listened to countless phone calls.

FBI chief J. Edgar Hoover skillfully manipulated the communist issue to enhance his personal reputation as a tough crime fighter and to expand his power in Washington. Between 1947 and 1952, the number of FBI agents increased from 3,559 to 7,029. Hoover manipulated public fear in pursuit of a program of widespread political surveillance that included both government employees and many private citizens. By the mid-1950s, Hoover expanded his operations from intelligence gathering to harassment. In 1956, he created the Counterintelligence Program, or COINTELPRO, to neutralize perceived "enemies." Agents leaked damaging information to the media, falsified documents, used IRS audits to harass people, and spread rumors to produce dissension within the ranks.

Fear of communism was not limited to the federal government or the courts; it infiltrated every institution in America. Since American identity was so fluid, and not based on birth or blood, many people made loyalty the litmus test to prove their Americanism.

In the hysteria over communist subversion, many Americans went to unusual lengths to prove their loyalty. Indiana required professional boxers and wrestlers to take a non-Communist oath before entering the ring. A small town in New York required residents to take a loyalty oath before getting a permit to fish in the local reservoir. The Cincinnati Reds baseball team proved its patriotism by changing its name to the Cincinnati Redlegs.

The nation's schools and universities did not escape the ravages of the Red Scare. In June 1948, the University of California required all of its 4,000 faculty members to profess their loyalty to America. More than six hundred professors lost their jobs during the "Great Fear." Some three hundred New York City school teachers were fired as security risks. Zealots forced libraries to purge their shelves of "subversive" works. Included among the long list of banned works were copies of *National Geographic*, *Time*, *Life*, and *Look*, along with any materials critical of capitalism or American values. A librarian in Bartlesville, Oklahoma, lost her job for shelving such magazines as *The New Republic, Consumer's Research,* and *Negro Digest* and for taking part in "group discussions on race relations." A member of the Indiana State Textbook Commission tried unsuccessfully to ban from school libraries any reference to Robin Hood. The reason, he said, was that Robin Hood "robbed the rich and gave . . . to the poor. That's the Communist line. It's just a smearing of law and order."

By taking in movies, reading magazines and novels, and watching television, Americans imbibed the culture of the Cold War. Hollywood produced films such as *The Red Menace* (1949), *The Iron Curtain* (1948), and *The Steel Fist* (1952). All painted dark portraits of the Soviets, created gross stereotypes of Russians, and underscored the menace of communist espionage.

Communist subversives also became popular villains in comic books. The same company that used to produce baseball cards now introduced a set of seventy pasteboards titled "Children's Crusade against Communism." Most depicted dangerous communist agents disguised as typical Americans, while others showed the mayhem that would ensue if communists successfully infiltrated American society. Card number #21, titled "Mined harbor," showed dock workers running from an atom bomb explosion on a ship.

"I hold in my hands . . ."

In the midst of this cultural Red Scare, Joseph McCarthy became the most feared demagogue of his time. Born in 1908 to poor Irish-American farmers in northeastern Wisconsin, McCarthy earned a degree in 1935 and entered politics in 1939,

running successfully for circuit judge in Wisconsin's Tenth Circuit. With the outbreak of World War II, McCarthy decided to join the glamorous marines. For three
years he served as an intelligence officer debriefing American pilots following raids
over the Pacific. Not satisfied with his low-profile role but unwilling to risk injury
in combat, McCarthy fabricated his military record for the folks back home. He
bragged about his exploits as a tail gunner flying dangerous missions and shooting
down enemy planes. He claimed to have been injured when his plane crash-landed.
During his Senate campaigns he walked with a limp and complained about having
"ten pounds of shrapnel" in his leg. In reality, he injured his leg not while flying on
a dangerous mission, but during a hazing ceremony aboard a navy ship when he
slipped as he was running a gauntlet of paddle-wielding sailors.

In 1946, armed with phony wartime press releases, McCarthy ran for the
Senate. During his campaign to unseat sitting Republican Robert LaFollette Jr.,
McCarthy criss-crossed the state attacking the New Deal, criticizing wartime con-
trols, and pleading with voters to send a "tail gunner" to the Senate. His energetic
campaign style worked: McCarthy scored a surprising victory over LaFollette in a
GOP primary and went on to win easily against his Democratic opponent in the fall.

During his first few years in the Senate, McCarthy supported Truman's
foreign-policy initiatives but voted with the conservative wing of his party on
domestic issues. He developed a close relationship with many corporate lobbyists. His efforts to end price controls on sugar earned him the nickname "the
Pepsi-Cola kid." In Senate debates McCarthy frequently distorted facts and manipulated evidence to prove his point. He reduced political issues to personal
terms and turned Senate debates into angry brawls. "He can be the most affable
man in the world," one senator reflected, "and suddenly he will run the knife into
you—particularly if the public is going to see it."

PRIMARY SOURCE

3.2 | *Final, All-Out Battle*
JOSEPH McCARTHY

Speaking to the Republican Women's Club of Wheeling, West Virginia, at its annual luncheon honoring Abraham Lincoln, McCarthy announced that he had
uncovered the names of current government employees involved with the Communist Party. The speech, given on February 9, 1950, capitalized on the growing
fear of espionage and communist infiltration of the government.

At war's end we were physically the strongest nation on earth and, at least
potentially, the most powerful intellectually and morally. Ours could have
been the honor of being a beacon in the desert of destruction, a shining living

proof that civilization was not yet ready to destroy itself. Unfortunately, we have
5 failed miserably and tragically to rise to that opportunity.

The reason why we find ourselves in a position of impotency is not because
our only powerful potential enemy has sent men to invade our shores, but rather
because of the traitorous actions of those who have been treated so well by this
nation. It has not been the less fortunate or members of minority groups who
10 have been selling this nation out, but rather those who have had all the benefits
that the wealthiest nation on earth has had to offer—the finest homes, the finest
college education, and the finest jobs in government we can give.

This is glaringly true in the State Department. There the bright young men
who are born with silver spoons in their mouths are the ones who have been
15 worst. . . . In my opinion the State Department, which is one of the most important government departments, is thoroughly infested with communists.

I have here in my hand a list of 205—a list of names that were made known to
the secretary of state as being members of the Communist Party and who nevertheless are still working and shaping policy in the State Department.
20 One thing to remember in discussing the communists in our government is
that we are not dealing with spies who get thirty pieces of silver to steal the blue-
prints of a new weapon. We are dealing with a far more sinister type of activity
because it permits the enemy to guide and shape our policy. . . .

This brings us to the case of one Alger Hiss, who is important not as an indi-
25 vidual anymore, but rather because he is so representative of a group in the State
Department. It is unnecessary to go over the sordid events showing how he sold
out the nation which had given him so much. Those are rather fresh in all of our
minds. . . .

As you know, very recently the secretary of state proclaimed his loyalty to
30 a man guilty of what has always been considered as the most abominable of all
crimes—of being a traitor to the people who gave him a position of great trust.
The secretary of state, in attempting to justify his continued devotion to the
man who sold out the Christian world to the atheistic world, referred to Christ's
Sermon on the Mount as a justification and reason therefore, and the reaction
35 of the American people to this would have made the heart of Abraham Lincoln
happy. When this pompous diplomat in striped pants, with a phony British accent, proclaimed to the American people that Christ on the Mount endorsed
communism, high treason, and betrayal of a sacred trust, the blasphemy was so
great that it awakened the dormant indignation of the American people.

Source: 81st Congress, 2nd sess., *Congressional Record* 96 (February 12, 1950) 1954–1957.

■ ■ ■

McCarthy's speech, standard Republican rhetoric of the time, charged that traitors and spies had infiltrated the State Department. What was different about the
speech was McCarthy's claim to have proof. Though few people paid him much notice at first, he repeated, expanded, and varied his charges in succeeding speeches.
By March he was front-page news across the country. McCarthy, observed a journalist, "was a political speculator who found his oil gusher in Communism."

McCarthy shrewdly manipulated the press, which treated his sensational charges as page-one news. He held press conferences early in the morning to announce that he would soon release dramatic information on domestic spying. The nation's afternoon papers then printed banner headlines: "McCarthy's New Revelations Expected Soon." When reporters hounded him for details, McCarthy announced that he would soon produce a key witness. Headlines the following day would read, "Delay in McCarthy Revelations: Mystery Witness Sought." McCarthy never produced the evidence to support his accusations, but his tactics gained him the publicity he needed and thus fueled his attacks. The rules of objective journalism dictated that the press cover McCarthy's charges even if reporters knew they were not true. "Joe couldn't find a Communist in Red Square," reflected one journalist, "he didn't know Karl Marx from Groucho—but he was a United States Senator."

PRIMARY SOURCE

3.3 | *Declaration of Conscience*

MARGARET CHASE SMITH

Senator McCarthy's allegations promoted him to a position of political power that made opposition to his actions dangerous; McCarthy could easily make those against him the target of his next inquiry and in the process ruin political careers. Despite the risk, Senator Margaret Chase Smith (R-Maine), the only female senator at the time, questioned McCarthy's practices in a speech she gave before her colleagues on June 1, 1950.

I think that it is high time for the United States Senate and its members to do some real soul searching and to weigh our consciences as to the manner in which we are performing our duty to the people of America and the manner in which we are using or abusing our individual powers and privileges. I think
5 that it is high time that we remembered that we have sworn to uphold and defend the Constitution. I think that it is high time that we remembered that the Constitution, as amended, speaks not only of the freedom of speech but also of trial by jury instead of trial by accusation. Whether it be a criminal prosecution in court or a character prosecution in the Senate, there is little practical
10 distinction when the life of a person has been ruined.

    Those of us who shout the loudest about Americanism in making character assassinations are all too frequently those who, by our own words and acts, ignore some of the basic principles of Americanism: the right to criticize, the right to hold unpopular beliefs, the right to protest, the right of indepen-
15 dent thought. The exercise of these rights should not cost one single American

citizen his reputation or his right to a livelihood, nor should he be in danger of losing his reputation or livelihood merely because he happens to know someone who holds unpopular beliefs. Who of us does not? Otherwise none of us could call our souls our own. Otherwise thought control would have set in.

20   The American people are sick and tired of being afraid to speak their minds lest they be politically smeared as communists or fascists by their opponents. Freedom of speech is not what it used to be in America. It has been so abused by some that it is not exercised by others.

    The American people are sick and tired of seeing innocent people smeared

25 and guilty people whitewashed. But there have been enough proved cases—such as the *Amerasia* case, the Hiss case, the Coplon case, the Gold case—to cause nationwide distrust and strong suspicion that there may be something to the unproved, sensational accusations. . . .

    The nation sorely needs a Republican victory. But I do not want to see the Re-

30 publican Party ride to political victory on the Four Horsemen of Calumny—Fear, Ignorance, Bigotry, and Smear. I doubt if the Republican Party could do so, simply because I do not believe the American people will uphold any political party that puts political exploitation above the national interest. Surely we Republicans are not that desperate for victory. . . .

35   As members of the minority party, we do not have the primary authority to formulate the policy of our government. But we do have the responsibility of rendering constructive criticism, of clarifying issues, of allaying fears by acting as responsible citizens. As a woman, I wonder how the mothers, wives, sisters, and daughters feel about the way in which members of their families have been

40 politically mangled in Senate debate—and I use the word *debate* advisedly. As a United States senator, I am not proud of the way in which the Senate has been made a publicity platform for irresponsible sensationalism. I am not proud of the reckless abandon in which unproved charges have been hurled from this side of the aisle. I am not proud of the obviously staged, undignified countercharges

45 which have been attempted in retaliation from the other side of the aisle. . . .

    As an American, I condemn a Republican fascist just as much as I condemn a Democrat communist. I condemn a Democrat fascist just as much as I condemn a Republican communist. They are equally dangerous to you and me and to our country. As an American, I want to see our nation recapture the strength and

50 unity it once had when we fought the enemy instead of ourselves.

Source: 81st Congress, 2nd sess., *Congressional Record* 96 (June 1, 1950) 7894–7895.

■ ■ ■

By the fall of 1950 McCarthy was the most feared man in American politics. His face appeared on the cover of *Time* and *Newsweek*. Republican candidates begged him to make appearances on their behalf. Why did McCarthy have such appeal? His charges against the established elite tapped into a deep populist impulse in the American character. McCarthy called Dean Acheson a "pompous diplomat in striped pants, with a phony British accent." He denounced the "egg-sucking phony liberals" who defended "communists and queers." In focusing on liberal thinkers, homosexuals, and others who did not fit with Americans' traditional view of themselves, McCarthy exploited America's unease with its new international stature and its discomfort with alien ideas and lifestyles. In this sense McCarthyism was part of a recurring pattern in American history. In 1798 Federalists had tried to silence critics by introducing the Alien and Sedition Acts, targeting dissenters as traitors. Waves of prejudice against foreigners swept the country during the 1850s and again in the 1870s. Following World War I, the United States tried to drown "radical" thoughts in a Red Scare wave of "100 percent Americanism."

McCarthyism was also the product of partisan politics at midcentury. McCarthy had the support of conservative Republicans, who saw him as a useful means to reassert their authority in the country. Embittered by their stunning loss in the 1948 election, Republicans saw McCarthy as a way to undermine support for Truman and the Democrats and guarantee victory in the 1952 presidential campaign. So long as McCarthy wielded his anticommunist club against

McCarthy and His Fans   As this photograph indicates, Senator Joseph McCarthy at first enjoyed widespread support from those who viewed him as a tireless crusader for national security. *(AP/Wide World Photos, Inc.)*

Democrats, many Republicans were willing to overlook his offensive tactics. Many GOP members repeated the refrain "I don't like some of McCarthy's methods but his goal is good."

Most of all, McCarthy capitalized on Cold War anxieties. He offered simple answers to the complex questions of the time. Strong faith in the righteousness of their position left Americans ill-prepared to comprehend the foreign-policy setbacks of the immediate postwar years. McCarthy reassured a troubled nation that the string of bad news resulted from the traitorous actions of a few individuals, not from a flawed view of the world or the strengths of communist opponents. China turned communist, he explained, because "traitors" in the State Department had sold out American interests, not because of the internal weakness of the Nationalist regime. The Soviets developed the atomic bomb because spies sold them America's secrets, not because they had talented scientists capable of developing their own bomb. The paradox of demagogues like Joseph McCarthy was that they eroded individual liberty in the name of freedom and used legitimate security concerns to undermine support for the very values they claimed to be upholding.

SELECTED READINGS

▮ Akira Iriye's *The Cold War in Asia* (1974) is a good introduction for developments on that continent. Russell D. Buhite's *Soviet-American Relations in Asia* (1982) details the superpowers' conflict over the region. Michael Schaller's *The American Occupation of Japan* (1985) and John Dower's *Embracing Defeat* (1999) both study the American role in postwar Japan. Daniel Yergin's *Shattered Peace* (1977) demonstrates both the American and the Soviet motives that contributed to the arms race. Gregg Herken critiques U.S. leaders' reliance on the bomb in *The Winning Weapon* (1980), and Richard Rhodes's *Dark Sun* (1995) examines the development of the hydrogen bomb. Ernest May's *American Cold War Strategy* (1993) places NSC-68 in historical context and provides analysis of the document by over twenty former government officials and scholars.

▮ Two recent books reveal the lively debate that endures over the origins and nature of the Korean War. See David Halberstam, *The Coldest Winter* (2007) and Bruce Cummings, *The Korean War: A History* (2010). For General MacArthur, William Manchester's *American Caesar* (1979) is the classic work; Michael Schaller's *Douglas MacArthur* (1989) is also helpful.

▮ Harvey Klehr and Ronald Radosh cover the *Amerasia* controversy in *The Amerasia Spy Case* (1996). The development of Soviet spy networks in the United States before the Cold War is the focus of Katherine Sibley's *Red Spies in America* (2004). John E. Haynes and Harvey Klehr's *Venona* (1999) offers a new interpretation of the Hiss case based on declassified Soviet documents while Sam Tanenhaus examines his accuser in the biography *Whittaker*

Chambers (1997). Walter Schneir and Miriam Schneir detail the Rosenberg trial in *Invitation to an Inquest* (1983). Interviews with Ethel Rosenberg's brother, David Greenglass, are the basis of Sam Roberts's *The Brother* (2001). Victor S. Navasky surveys the world of informants and blacklists in *Naming Names* (1980). Larry Ceplair and Steven Englund's *The Inquisition in Hollywood* (1980) analyzes the Red Scare's impact on popular culture, while the story of one member of the Hollywood Ten is described in the autobiography of Edward Dmytryk, *Odd Man Out* (1995). Athan Theoharis and John S. Cox study the role of J. Edgar Hoover and the FBI in the Red Scare in *The Boss* (1988).

▌ George Lipsitz studies popular culture during the era in *Class and Culture in Cold War America* (1981). The Mosinee communist "takeover" is chronicled well in Richard Fried's *The Russians Are Coming!* (1998). Stephen J. Whitfield provides broader context in *The Culture of the Cold War* (1996). Two of the most valuable studies of Joseph McCarthy are Richard Fried's *Nightmare in Red* (1990) and Stanley Kutler's *The American Inquisition* (1982). David M. Oshinsky's *A Conspiracy So Immense* (2005 ed.) portrays Joseph McCarthy as a product of the political conditions of the era. Ellen Schrecker's *Many Are the Crimes* (1998) analyzes the birth of anticommunism and the political repression of the 1950s. David K. Johnson documents the persecution of homosexuals during the Cold War in *The Lavender Scare* (2006).

4

The Consumer Society, 1945–1960

As shocked journalists looked on, Vice President Richard Nixon and Soviet premier Nikita Khrushchev stood toe to toe in the hottest personal confrontation of the Cold War. The exchange took place in July 1959, as Nixon escorted the Soviet leader through the U.S. National Exhibition, a two-week exhibit in Moscow that celebrated American life. After playing with the new TV equipment and sipping soda from a bottle of Pepsi-Cola, they moved on to the most publicized display of American affluence: a six-room, model suburban ranch house filled with shining new furniture. "I want to show you this kitchen," Nixon said. "It is like those of our houses in California." "We have such things," Khrushchev retorted. But in the United States any worker could afford this house, Nixon replied. Later, when Nixon turned the topic to the new consumer devices making life easier in American homes, Khrushchev became enraged. "You Americans think that the Russian people will be astonished to see these things!" They were, he blustered, worthless gadgets.

Within minutes the conversation about television sets and washing machines escalated into an ideological clash between communism and capitalism. A defensive Khrushchev charged that the American military wanted to destroy the Soviet Union. Jamming his thumb into Nixon's chest to underscore his point, Khrushchev warned, "If you want to threaten, we will answer threat with threat." Not to appear intimidated, Nixon brazenly waived his finger in Khrushchev's face, retorting that it was the Soviets, not the Americans, who threatened the world's peace. Later that evening at a state dinner Nixon, still gloating over the display of American affluence, told his Soviet hosts that the United States had achieved "the ideal of prosperity for all in a classless society."

This "Kitchen debate," appropriately set in the simulated kitchen of a suburban house, captured the conflicting currents of the decade. During the 1950s the United States experienced a "consumer revolution" as millions of Americans scrambled to buy a new home in the suburbs and fill it with the latest consumer gadgets. Television, the most popular of the new products, reinforced the celebration of traditional values under way by offering Americans a steady diet of shared images. America's love affair with the material benefits of prosperity bred contentment, especially among the expanding white middle classes, and reinforced traditional American optimism about the future.

What many Americans failed to realize at the time was that all these celebrations of prosperity and national unity raised expectations among groups that had been excluded from mainstream society. These years sharpened the paradox between expectations and social realities and laid the background for the social turmoil to come in the 1960s.

Boomer Nation

The nation experienced an unprecedented "baby boom" in the years following World War II. There is no agreement about the dates that make up the baby boom, although most observers define it as those born between 1946, when births started their dramatic climb, and 1964, when widespread use of the birth control pill contributed to a decline in birthrates. During that period, roughly 76 million babies were born, making the postwar baby boom the largest generation in history. The baby boom generation was unique in many ways and its influence would have a profound impact on American culture and politics for the rest of the century and beyond.

The rise in births following World War II caught everyone by surprise. In January 1953 General Electric announced that it would award five shares of stock to any employee who had a baby on October 15, which was the Company's 75th anniversary. After studying birth patterns for the past decade, the company said it expected about thirteen winners. Instead, there were 189 children born on that day! By 1959 there were over 50 million children under the age of fourteen living in the United States. Together they made up over 30 percent of the population. There were as many children in the United States in 1959 as there were people living in the United States in 1881.

Why the rush to have babies? Initially, young couples who had delayed getting married during World War II decided to make up for lost time. As the decade progressed, young couples started families earlier and continued to have children over a longer period of time. A general spirit of confidence about the future, and a growing economy, convinced young couples they could afford the demands of parenthood. Government policies played a key role in promoting the new optimism. The Serviceman's Readjustment Act, popularly known as the GI Bill, which Congress passed in 1944, pumped millions of dollars into the economy by providing veterans with unemployment compensation, medical benefits, loans to start new businesses, and tuition benefits for continuing education.

Gross National Product A number of factors, including pent-up consumer demands and profuse military spending, spurred the GNP upward after World War II. The climbing GNP figures reflect the prosperity of the 1950s and 1960s, with the numbers almost doubling from 1945 to 1960 and doubling again in the next decade. *(Source: Adapted from U.S. Bureau of the Census,* Historical Statistics of the United States, Colonial Times to 1970, *Bicentennial Edition, Washington, D.C.: U.S. Government Printing Office, 1975, 224.)*

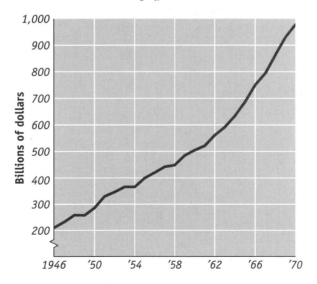

American Birthrates   The bulge in the birthrate from the end of World War II to the mid-1960s marks the height of the baby boom. By their sheer numbers, the members of this generation could not help but shape every aspect of American culture for the rest of the twentieth century. This generation did not choose to have as many children as their parents, as evidenced by the precipitous decline in the birthrate in the early 1970s. *(Source: National Center for Health Statistics, U.S. Dept. of Health and Human Services, as reported in* Statistical Abstract of the U.S., 1997, and World Almanac, 1998.*)*

Cold War fears also shaped the boom. Many Americans believed that stable and growing families would serve as the foundation of a thriving democracy. The family was the centerpiece of a domestic version of containment, providing the nurturance and support needed to limit the influence of communist propaganda. During the 1950s, television shows and magazine stories celebrated the joys of family life. Popular culture reinforced the message that fatherhood was a badge of masculinity and motherhood the ultimate expression of female sexuality.

At the same time, advances in medicine convinced parents it was safer to have children than ever before. Antibiotics and other new drugs subdued diseases such as tuberculosis, diphtheria, whooping cough, and measles. The most significant achievement was the victory over poliomyelitis (polio), most of whose victims were children. Between 1947 and 1951 this crippling disease struck an annual average of 39,000 Americans. In 1955, Dr. Jonas Salk of the Pittsburgh Medical School developed the first effective vaccine against polio, and by 1960 vaccines had practically eliminated the disease in the United States.

The End of Polio   By the 1950s, polio had killed or disabled thousands of children and young adults, and two epidemics in 1950 and 1952 afflicted ninety thousand more. A massive effort by medical researchers and ordinary Americans who contributed to the March of Dimes finally yielded success when on April 12, 1955 (the anniversary of polio-patient FDR's death), Dr. Jonas Salk, himself a victim of the disease, announced his vaccine was effective. By the end of the decade, most children had been inoculated, and the disease was virtually eradicated. Here six-year-old Michael Urnczis of San Diego reluctantly receives his vaccine while his twelve-year-old sister and polio survivor, Joanne, joyfully looks on.   *(© Bettmann/CORBIS)*

The Baby Boom and Generational Identity

The baby boom's special status is derived first and foremost from its enormous size, especially in comparison to the smaller generations that came immediately before and after. Some people have compared the baby boom to the image of a large python snake trying to digest a pig. The "Swing" generation that preceded the boomers produced only 30 million. The widespread use of the pill that began in 1964 reduced births for "Generation X" (1965–1977) to less than 45 million.

It was not just the generation's size that made boomers unique. More than any generations before or since, they have grown up thinking of themselves as members of a unique generation. A number of influences helped shape that sense of identity.

The first was prosperity. Boomers were raised in a period of unprecedented prosperity and unparalleled expectations about the future. Between 1940 and 1960, the gross national product (GNP) more than doubled and family income soared. Unlike in earlier boom times, runaway prices did not eat up rising income. "Never had so many people, anywhere, been so well off," the editors of *U.S. News and World Report* concluded in 1957.

Education played a central role in the development of a distinct baby boom culture. Many states passed mandatory school attendance laws after World War II in an effort to expose America's youth to middle-class values of respectability and hard work. In 1930, only 50 percent of children aged fourteen to seventeen were students. By 1950, the ratio increased to 73 percent. In response to the enormous demand for space, school districts rushed to open new schools and build new classrooms. During the 1950s, California opened one school every week. The hope was that these schools would introduce young people to middle-class standards of taste and behavior. Just the opposite happened. Large new schools swelling with thousands of teen-agers encouraged young people to look to their peers, and not their parents, for direction and approval.

New childrearing methods developed by Dr. Benjamin Spock meant that boomer babies were raised by more permissive rules than previous generations. Spock rejected his own upbringing, which emphasized strict feeding schedules and unchanging routines, and insisted that parents respond to the needs and schedules of their children. His bestselling book, *Baby and Child Care* (1946) offered practical advice on toilet training and temper tantrums, as well as sugar-coated doses of Freudian psychology. Whether they purchased his book (as one of five mothers did), borrowed it from their local library, read the excerpts in magazines and newspapers, or listened to him on television, boomer mothers found it impossible to escape Spock's influence. In a December 1955 episode of *I Love Lucy*, the husband-wife team of Lucille Ball and Desi Arnaz flipped through a dog-eared copy of Spock's book to decide whether to send "little Ricky" to nursery school. (The answer was yes.)

The growing influence of marketers and television also helped forge a sense of generational identity. Almost from the time they were conceived, boomers were dissected, analyzed, and pitched to by modern marketers. In the past, advertisers sold products to parents. Beginning in the 1950s, they bypassed parents and appealed directly to children as consumers. "By pitching so many things to us all the time that were only and specifically for us, the mass media insisted that *we* mattered," Susan Douglas wrote about the experience of young girls growing up in the 1950s. "Once you're a market—especially a really big market—you can change history."

Eugene Gilbert, who referred to himself as the "Pied Piper of the Youth Market," did more than anyone else to target the growing youth market. Gilbert estimated that the average teenager had $10 a week to spend in 1958 compared with $2.50 in 1944, and that teens spent more than $10 billion a year on products. He discovered that teenage girls spent $20 million on lipstick, $25 million on deodorant, and $9 million on permanents. Male teen-agers owned 2 million electric razors. Perhaps Gilbert's greatest insight was that teen-agers could convince their parents to purchase a new car or stylish clothing. Gilbert found that half of the four million kids who watched the popular children's show, *Captain Kangaroo,* went shopping with their mothers three times a week, and 80 percent of them pleaded with their mothers to buy products they had seen plugged on the show.

Toy companies led the way in selling products directly to children. By some estimates, children raised on shows like *The Mickey Mouse Club* and *Howdy Doody* saw more than 500 hours of ads by the age of six. By the time they were twenty-one, most boomers had seen more than 300,000 commercials.

The Consumer Republic

Although the consumer revolution traced its roots back to the 1920s, postwar affluence and the baby boom allowed it to blossom in the years following World War II. Parents purchased an endless number of products to support their growing families. In 1957 Americans spent $50 million on diapers. Toy sales skyrocketed. By the end of the decade Americans were buying over 2 million bicycles a year.

Advertising whetted America's appetite for these new products. The amount of money spent to advertise products doubled during the decade from $6 billion to over $12 billion. Advertising helped promote the rise of a credit society: if people did not have the money to purchase products, they borrowed it. The credit card business began in 1950 with the introduction of the Diner's Club card. By the end of the decade Sears Roebuck, a large department store, had more than 10 million accounts. As a result, total private debt in the United States increased from $104.8 billion to $263.3 billion during the 1950s.

The emergence of the credit card symbolized the evolving societal change from independence and frugality to consumption and debt. For generations many Americans had followed the advice of Benjamin Franklin: "A penny saved is a penny earned." But in the 1950s advertisers and their clients, like General Motors (GM), encouraged Americans to "Buy Now, Pay Later." The challenge for advertisers, noted a social scientist, was resolving "the conflict between pleasure and guilt"; not just to sell the product, but to give consumers "moral permission to have fun without guilt." Much of the advertising of the decade focused on consumer goods as rewards for years of hard work and sacrifice. "Here is the man who has earned the right to sit at this wheel," a Cadillac ad declared. McDonald's slogans ended by stating, "You deserve a break today."

Consumer demand for new products was just one force contributing to the postwar prosperity. Government spending played an important role as well. Overall government spending, which amounted to only 1 percent of

[handwritten margin note: encouraged to spend/buy rather than save]

the GNP in 1929, ballooned to more than 25 percent in 1960. Governments directly employed more than 8 million people by 1957, double the number in 1940. The military alone spent almost $40 billion a year, accounting for approximately 60 percent of the federal budget and 10 percent of the GNP. In addition, government programs, such as the Marshall Plan, opened new markets to American goods or, like the GI Bill, added millions of dollars directly to the economy.

The Rise of the Suburbs

The return of American servicemen following World War II produced a severe housing shortage. In 1945, 98 percent of American cities reported housing shortages. People were living in trolley cars, abandoned missile silos, and army barracks left over from World War II.

Many urban Americans looked to the suburbs to provide the additional space needed for their growing families, while rural residents and farmers moved to these same suburbs in search of better jobs and more opportunity. By 1960 almost 60 million people, making up about one-third of the total population, resided in suburban areas.

Builder William Levitt made the suburban dream a reality for millions of Americans. In 1949 Levitt bought 4,000 acres of potato fields in Hempstead, Long Island. Using mass-production methods meant every house was identical: one story high, with a 12-by-16-foot living room, a kitchen, two bedrooms, and a tiled bathroom. The price: $7,990, or $60 a month with no money down. Buyers snapped up 1,400 houses in the first three hours after sales began in March 1949. Levitt built a new home every sixteen minutes, as many as 150 homes a week. Builders throughout the country quickly followed his example.

Levitt built the houses, but government made the homes affordable for millions of young families. The Federal Housing Administration (FHA) and the Veterans Administration (VA) revolutionized home ownership in the United States by subsidizing home mortgages. By 1955 these two agencies insured 41 percent of all new nonfarm mortgages. Now, white veterans could buy homes in Levittown with a thirty-year mortgage and no money down for $56 a month at a time when the average apartment rental in many cities was $93.

The suburban home became more than just a place to live. Many Americans believed that home ownership would lessen class divisions, reinforce gender roles, and decrease the prospect of social unrest. The home became the center of America's new consumer-oriented family life. It also served as a powerful symbol of the superiority of American values—as Vice President Richard Nixon reminded Soviet leader Nikita Khrushchev.

For all of the opportunities opened by the development of suburbia, it was not the dream come true for all Americans. Blacks were systematically excluded from many of the new suburban communities and denied the opportunity of home ownership provided to white Americans. The suburbs may have lessened class divisions, but they hardened racial lines in America. Levitt banned African Americans from Levittown. "I have come to know," he said, "that if we sell one house to a Negro family, then 90 or 95 percent of our white customers will not buy into the community." Suburban communities used a variety of formal and informal methods to exclude blacks. In many cases, local real estate agents refused to sell houses to blacks and bankers rejected their mortgage applications. Some communities adopted zoning regulations designed to exclude lower income groups. The methods proved effective: by the end of the decade African Americans made up less than 5 percent of suburban residents. At the time that the white middle class was moving to the prosperous suburbs, African Americans were confined to decaying inner cities.

The Changing World of Work

Meeting the demands of the new consumer society produced enormous changes in the economy and in the nature of work. The 1950s witnessed an acceleration of the trend toward concentration of power in the hands of fewer corporations. By the end of the decade some 600 corporations, which made up only 0.5 percent of all U.S. companies, accounted for 53 percent of total corporate income. In the Cold War defense buildup the government contributed to the growth of big business by awarding military contracts to a handful of large corporations. Industrial giants used their vast resources to gobble up smaller competitors.

Expanding computer use represented the decade's most significant technological development. First developed to aid the defense effort during World War II, the original machines were massive: the Mark I, completed in 1944, stretched 50 feet in length and stood 8 feet high. In 1946, engineers at the University of Pennsylvania marketed the first commercial computer. International Business Machines, already a leader in the office-equipment industry, produced its first computer in 1953. The new technology was at the forefront of a wave of automation that promised to boost productivity and cut labor costs. By 1957 more than 1,250 computers were in use making airline reservations, forecasting elections, and helping banks process checks.

At the same time, important economic changes were disrupting the lives of millions of Americans. From 1947 to 1957, the number of factory workers dropped 4 percent. Automation alone eliminated an estimated 1.5 million blue-collar workers between 1953 and 1959. Those jobs were replaced by new service-sector positions. In 1956, for the first time in U.S. history, white-collar workers outnumbered their blue-collar counterparts.

The consumer economy presented organized labor with new challenges. At first glance, unions appeared to make tremendous gains during the decade. The number of union members in the United States climbed from 14.7 million in 1945 to 18 million in the mid-1950s. In 1955 the two most powerful labor organizations, the American Federation of Labor, headed by George Meany, and the Congress of Industrial Organizations, led by Walter Reuther, merged into one great federation. But unions faced serious problems making inroads into the fastest growing segment of the work force: white-collar employees. By 1960 unions had organized less than 184,000 of 5 million public employees and only 200,000 of 8.5 million office workers.

Labor-management relations became far less antagonistic than they had been in the 1930s, with few strikes or work stoppages. In 1950, General Motors and the United Automobile Workers signed a contract containing two provisions that would become standard in postwar contracts: (1) an automatic cost-of-living wage increase for workers and (2) a guarantee that wages would rise with productivity. Critics charged that the new accord between labor and management bred contentment and stagnation as union leaders who joined the middle class lost touch with the problems plaguing the working class.

Shaping National Culture: The Shared Images of Television

Television emerged as the most visible symbol of the new consumer society. It transformed the cultural landscape in America by bringing people from diverse backgrounds together in a shared experience. Along with the automobile, which broke down the geographical distance separating rural and urban, television helped promote a national culture.

Although television had been invented in the 1920s, it did not gain widespread acceptance until the 1950s. Mass production and technological advances in the 1950s allowed most American families to own a set. In 1946 about one of every eighteen thousand people owned a TV set. By 1960 nine out of every ten American homes had a TV.

Most shows avoided controversy and celebrated traditional American values. Families were intact, men worked during the day, women stayed at home. No one was ever sick. No one was poor. No one was African American. Shows such as *Ozzie and Harriet, Father Knows Best,* and *Leave It to Beaver* presented a glossy image of middle-class suburban life. Supportive wives spent their days minding the household and the clean-cut kids while their husbands provided for the family and solved the family crisis of the day. Millions of families gathered around the television set each week to watch as Superman, a comic-book hero turned television star, fought for "truth, justice, and the American way." Only a few shows, such as Jackie Gleason's *The Honeymooners,* which described life in a bleak urban apartment, hinted at the world beyond suburbia.

Television viewers also tuned into quiz shows that offered excitement and instant success. The format, which frequently saw taxi drivers and bricklayers outwit doctors and lawyers for huge cash prizes, reaffirmed the rags-to-riches notion that anybody could strike it rich in America. Charles Van Doren, a young Columbia University professor, dazzled millions of television viewers with his knowledge of everything from opera to chemistry on the popular show *Twenty-one*. In 1959, however, congressional investigators exposed Van Doren as a fraud: he had been given all the answers in advance. Quiz shows disappeared from prime time for over a decade, but the scandal did little to dampen public enthusiasm for television.

TV transformed American social habits. Studies showed that the average household watched five hours of television a day. Most viewers confessed to reading fewer books and magazines after purchasing a TV set. When a popular show was on, all the toilets in the nation flushed at the same time: during commercial breaks and when the program ended. By 1956, companies were spending over $488 million a year on network advertising. Advertising executives discovered that television could do what radio never could: "Show the product," one adman exclaimed, "and show it in use." Many advertisers did just that: a Remington razor shaved the fuzz off a peach, and a Band-Aid, as a demonstration of its strength,

A Family of Television Viewers   By the mid-1950s, most homes in America had a television in their living room, which quickly replaced the dining room as the center of family activity. While the screen was much smaller than on later televisions, families circled the "boob tube" to watch their favorite westerns, comedies, dramas, and variety and children's shows. Stations also provided news as it happened—live in the family's living room, as in this case of a mother watching the Army–McCarthy hearings.   *(© Bettmann/CORBIS)*

lifted an egg. Advertisers frequently used subtle psychological appeals to create consumer demand for their products. The Phillip Morris tobacco company, for example, created the Marlboro Man to create a link in the public mind between cigarette smoking and masculinity.

The combination of advertising, prosperity, and television produced overnight national fads. In 1954 the popular Disneyland show *Davy Crockett* produced the first fad of the decade. The "king of the wild frontier" became an instant hero among millions of children. Enterprising manufacturers flooded the market with Davy Crockett coonskin caps, knives, bow and arrow sets, and records of the show's theme song, "The Ballad of Davy Crockett." Before the fad was over, more than $100 million worth of Crockett paraphernalia had been sold.

As television absorbed millions of dollars of advertising money, it squeezed out other entertainment sources. Radio suffered most, losing nearly one-half of its audience between 1948 and 1956. Thousands of motion picture houses were forced to close their doors. "Why go to the movies," asked film executive Samuel Goldwyn in 1955, "when you can stay home and see nothing worse?" Many large-circulation magazines suffered a similar fate. General-interest magazines such as *Life,* the *Saturday Evening Post, Look,* and *Women's Home Companion* lost circulation and eventually ceased publication.

The irony of television was that an essentially conservative medium would, in time, produce such revolutionary changes in American society. By celebrating American prosperity, television contributed to America's grand expectations for the postwar world. The contrast between the idealized image of America as seen on the screen and the often harsh reality of everyday life for the nation's poor, women, and minorities contributed to the broad social movement in the 1960s to extend opportunity to all groups in society. Television avoided challenging racial stereotypes, but news coverage of white violence against blacks in the South would touch the nation's conscience and propel forward the civil rights movement.

Religious Revival

Television transformed religious preachers into overnight celebrities. The first clergyman to become a television star was the Most Reverend Fulton J. Sheen, who warned viewers that godless communism was infiltrating American institutions, especially government, and advised against making peace with the Soviets. At the height of his popularity, Sheen's *Life Is Worth Living* show played to an audience of 10 million people.

The most popular evangelist of the 1950s was undoubtedly Billy Graham. In 1954 *Time* magazine described Graham as "the best known, most talked about Christian leader in the world today, barring the Pope." Like other popular preachers of the day, he downplayed doctrinal differences, emphasized the common link between Christian teachings and American values, and warned of the evils of communism, which he called "a great sinister anti-Christian movement masterminded by Satan." When critics complained that Graham sold religion like Madison Avenue sold consumer products, the preacher responded, "I am selling the greatest product in the world; why shouldn't it be promoted as well as soap?"

PRIMARY SOURCE

4.1 | *America's Greatest Sin*
Billy Graham

Billy Graham began five weeks of evangelistic meetings in his hometown of Charlotte, North Carolina, on September 21, 1958. More than 4 million listened on the radio to Graham at the Charlotte Coliseum over the next month as he examined the problems of postwar society. Graham's fourth sermon, "America's Greatest Sin," explored the sins of a consumer society that needed to repent.

Americans are considered all over the world as materialistic, worldly, secular, greedy, and covetous. We are guilty of that sin as a nation, as a people, and as individuals. Americans have the highest standard of living the world has ever known. Never in history—in Rome, in Babylon, in the great nations of the

5   past—has there ever been a standard of living like we enjoy in America.

You say, "But, Billy, I'm not a rich person." You have shoes, don't you? You have a suit of clothes; you have a dress. Then you are rich by the world's standards. You had something to eat, didn't you? In India tonight, over a hundred million people will go to bed hungry tonight—if they have a bed to go to. And

10   when they drive the trucks down the streets of Calcutta tomorrow morning, they will pick up people that died of starvation, as I have seen them in India. The poorest person in this audience tonight is rich by the world's standards.

And in spite of our riches, in spite of our high standard of living, our whole economy is geared to getting more. The capitalist wants more profit. The laboring man

15   wants more wages for less hours. And all of us are engaged in a mad race—trampling over each other, cheating each other, lying, stealing, any way we can get it—to get another dollar. The Bible says it's the sin of covetousness. "Thou shall not covet." . . .

You are a rich man, and you are a rich person now. I'm not talking about the millionaire now. I'm talking about the man that makes twenty-five dollars a

20   week. I am talking about a rich American. . . .

God said that any man that will give himself to the making of money over and against the development and nature of his own soul is a fool, and doesn't deserve to live. Jesus said, "Out of the heart proceeds covetousness. These evil things come from within, in defilement of man" [see Mark 7:21–23]. . . .

25   God says that covetousness is actually idolatry, and He says a covetous person has no place in the kingdom of God. No place in the kingdom of God—the Bible says that in Ephesians 5:3 and 5. I just read it to you. If words mean anything, it means that a covetous person shall not go to heaven, shall not be saved. You say,

"Well, Billy, isn't a man supposed to take care of his family?" Yes. The Bible says
30   "Give me not poverty lest I steal" [see Proverbs 30:8, 9].

We are to have enough, but we're not to give our full attention to the things of
the world. Our first attention is to be on Christ. We are to seek first the kingdom
of God and his righteousness, then all of these things shall be added unto us [see
Matthew 6:33].

35   Is that what you're doing? Are you seeking God's kingdom first? Are you
seeking the things of Christ first? Or is your business, your pleasure, your amuse-
ment—the things of this world—first in your life? . . .

You can't work your way to heaven if you join every church in town. You
could work from now on, and you could never save yourself. Salvation is by the
40   grace and mercy of God. Ladies and gentlemen, we are all sinners. We all deserve
hell, and we are going to get hell, unless we are willing to repent and come to the
cross; hell in this life, and in the life to come.

Source: Text of Graham's "Wednesday Night Sermon" from the *Charlotte Observer,* September
25, 1958, 6A. Reprinted with permission from *The Charlotte Observer.* Copyright owned by *The
Charlotte Observer.* ■ ■ ■

Billy Graham's Revival at Madison Square Garden   The 1950s brought a major upswing
in church attendance in the United States and a growing awareness of the importance of religion in the lives of Americans facing the anxieties of the Cold War. Billy Graham, a young
Baptist minister, spent the decade organizing and preaching at evangelical rallies in every
major city in the nation and also in Africa, Europe, Asia, and South America. One of his most
successful revivals was his New York Crusade of 1957, which began as an eight-week series of
revival meetings, but which was quickly extended to sixteen weeks because of the overwhelming demand.   *(© Gjon Mili/Time Life Pictures/Getty Images)*

Graham's ecumenical message helped transform Christianity into a national religion. Church membership and professions of faith became popular methods of affirming "the American way of life" during the Cold War.

"Today in the U.S.," *Time* magazine claimed in 1954, "the Christian faith is back in the center of things." Considerable evidence existed to support the claim. Church membership skyrocketed from 64 million in 1940 to 114 million in 1960. Sales of Bibles reached an all-time high. In 1954 Congress added the phrase "under God" to the Pledge of Allegiance and the next year mandated "In God We Trust" on all U.S. currency.

However, in an influential 1955 study the theologian Will Herberg complained that modern religion was "without serious commitment, without real inner conviction, without genuine existential decision." Polls showed that a majority of Americans could not distinguish the New Testament from the Old or even name one of the Gospels. Religion offered Americans what they needed most in the 1950s: a sense of belonging in a rapidly changing society and divine support for traditional American values in the battle with communism. As the *Christian Century* noted in 1954, it had become "un-American to be unreligious."

The Car Culture

Television nationalized culture by projecting a common set of images, a shared language that Americans experienced in the comfort of their homes. At the same time, a dramatic increase in the number of automobiles and new highways narrowed the physical gap between rural and urban communities.

Manufacturers had halted the production of automobiles during World War II, but once the war was over, car sales boomed. Car registrations soared from 26 million in 1945 to 60 million in 1960. The number of two-car families doubled between 1951 and 1958. During these years General Motors developed a strategy of breaking down the consumer market into niches defined by economic and social status. The car was no longer just a means of transportation; it was now a reflection of status. GM designed the Chevy to appeal to blue-collar workers or young couples buying their first car; the Pontiac, to attract young professional types who wanted a sportier car; the luxurious Cadillac, to fit the ambitions of top executives. To keep people buying cars, GM instituted the annual model change, designed to make car owners eager for the latest equipment.

With millions of new cars on the road, Americans demanded better roads and highways. The Eisenhower administration backed the building of a nationwide network of four-lane highways to allow for the massive evacuation of urban areas in case of a nuclear war. Congress responded in 1956 by passing the Interstate Highway Act. The largest public works project in American history, this act appropriated $32 billion to build 41,000 miles of highway. The new highway system

The Transformation of the Chevrolet Tail Fin   To boost sales, automobile companies in the 1950s implemented a strategy of "planned obsolescence," redesigning car models yearly to encourage consumers to trade in the old for the new. GM's Chevy line, for example, saw longer and more detailed tail fins each year to entice buyers. For consumers concerned with keeping up the appearance of personal wealth and prosperity, it was necessary to purchase a new car every couple of years so as not to be labeled "behind the times." *(© Richard Cummins/CORBIS)*

made travel easier, faster, and more convenient. By the end of the decade the nation had over 3 million miles of roads, almost 75 percent of which were paved.

The car had a profound impact on American life during the 1950s. By the end of the decade the automobile was directly or indirectly responsible for one-sixth of the GNP and millions of jobs. In turn, the auto industry spurred production in related industries: petroleum, steel, tourism and travel, service stations, and highway construction and maintenance. The automobile also promoted the decline of metropolitan areas by accelerating the move to the suburbs, added to the decay of public transportation, and produced higher levels of air pollution.

Cars and new roads contributed to a massive population shift from the Northeast to the South and West. Florida's population boomed, fed by the tourist industry, an influx of retirees, and a rapid expansion of the fruit industry. The fastest growth occurred in California, which added 3.1 million residents and accounted for an astounding 20 percent of the nation's population growth in the 1950s.

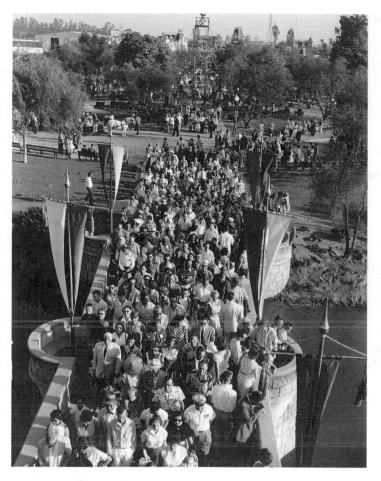

Crossing the Moat at Disneyland   Disneyland, which cost $17 million to build, opened its doors in Anaheim, California, in 1955. Its accessibility to the ordinary American made it a contemptible emblem of the "mass society," whose packaged commercialism and mindless entertainment intellectuals despised. But for American families, who had more kids and more money than ever before, Disneyland was a modern marvel. (*© AP/Wide World Photos*)

By 1963 California had moved past New York as the nation's most populous state. By 1960 half of the people living in the West were living in a state different from the one in which they had been born.

The automobile also made the United States a more homogeneous nation. In metropolitan areas across the country small mom-and-pop stores gave way to mammoth shopping malls housing national retail chains on the edges of the city. Interchangeable motels and fast-food chains materialized nearby. In August 1952, Kemmons Wilson opened the first Holiday Inn in Memphis, Tennessee. The hotel offered all the amenities needed by tired travelers and businessmen: a restaurant, a gift shop, a swimming pool, and a room with an air conditioner and television set. The cost was four dollars a night for a single, six dollars for a double.

In 1955 an ambitious salesman, Ray Kroc, established a chain of burger joints called McDonald's, which would become the symbol of the fast-food industry. "Our whole concept was based on speed, lower prices, and volume," noted Dick McDonald, who sold his name to Kroc. By the end of the decade Kroc had franchised 228 restaurants across the nation. Whether eating in California or Connecticut, customers would be served the same-sized hamburger, with one-fourth ounce of onion, 1 teaspoon of mustard, 1 tablespoon of ketchup, and a pickle 1 inch in diameter. "I put the hamburger on the assembly line," Kroc boasted.

The automobile boosted the travel industry and made possible new forms of entertainment. In July 1955, the vast Disneyland theme park opened in Southern California. The park attracted more than 1 million visitors in its first six months. Over 40 percent of the guests came from outside California, most of them by car. Inside the park, Main Street USA recalled America's small-town past, Frontierland brought back the thrill of the pioneers, and Tomorrowland suggested the future frontier of space. While enjoying the thrill of Disneyland's amusements, visitors shared in the celebration of common cultural images that reaffirmed the nation's mythic past and its promised future.

The Problem with Teens

During the 1950s, there were more young people in America than at any previous time in history. The word "teenager" entered the American language for the first time. American teens now had the purchasing power to taste the fruits of abundance, and to do so without having to seek parental approval.

Writers, directors, and advertisers appealed directly to the teenager's sense of alienation from the adult world. The publication of J.D. Salinger's *The Catcher in the Rye* (1951) marked the beginning of the youth culture. The novel traced the thoughts and actions of sixteen-year-old Holden Caulfield who roams around New York City recording his rejection of the phoniness and corruption of the adult world. In movies like *Rebel without a Cause*, teen idol James Dean abandons the middle-class values of his parents for the excitement of a lower-class car culture. Television made its contribution to the youth culture in 1957 with the debut of *American Bandstand*. The daily show hosted by Dick Clark showed clean-cut teen-agers dancing with each other while others watched from the bleachers.

For many adults a more troubling sign of the emergence of a separate youth culture was the dramatic rise in juvenile delinquency. As early as 1953, the federal government's Children's Bureau predicted that the exploding teenage population would soon produce an increase of 24 percent in car thefts, 19 percent in burglaries, and 7 percent in rapes. The *New York Daily News* reported in 1954 that "rowdyism, riot, and revolt" were the new three Rs in New York public schools.

Elvis Presley and the Power of Rock

Perhaps the most obvious symbol of the new youth culture was the emergence of rock and roll. A mix of black rhythm and blues, country, and white gospel music, rock and roll had gained enormous popularity among African Americans in the late forties. Because of its association with blacks and its strong sexual overtones, most whites dismissed the new sound as "race music."

At the beginning of the decade, it was being recorded only by small record companies and played only on African American radio stations. In 1951 a white disc jockey named Alan Freed began playing "race music" on his popular Cleveland radio station, renaming it "rock and roll," an urban euphemism for dancing and sex. "How y'all, everybody. This is Alan Freed, king of the Moondoggers, . . . Y'all ready to rock 'n' roll?" His white teen audiences loved it and, for the first time, started demanding the original black versions of the songs. By bringing "race music" to a white teenage audience, Freed's "Moondog's Rock and Roll Party" shattered musical barriers and instigated a national music craze.

Initially, most white radio stations refused to play rock and roll music that was performed by black singers. Pressed by growing teenage demand, major record companies produced white versions of songs originally recorded by black singers. In 1955 twelve of the year's top fifty songs were rock and roll, including "Rock Around the Clock," written by two white songwriters and recorded by an all-white group, Bill Haley and the Comets.

The Comets' success opened the door for the most popular rock and roll star of the decade: Elvis Aaron Presley (1935–1977). A nineteen-year-old truck driver from Tupelo, Mississippi, Presley emerged in 1956 with his hit single "Heartbreak Hotel." The young entertainer adapted the powerful rhythms and raw sexual energy of "race music" to create his own unique style and sound. The new white star enthralled screaming audiences of white teens. Between 1956 and 1958, Presley had ten number one hit records, including "Heartbreak Hotel," "Hound Dog," "All Shook Up," and "Jailhouse Rock."

In addition to challenging racial stereotypes at a critical time in the nation's history, Elvis tapped in to the spirit of rebellion among the army of American teens. "Without my left leg, Ah'd be dead," he drawled in 1956. Elvis acted out onstage the hostilities and confusion felt by most teen-agers. With his sensual pout, tight pants, and swinging hips, Elvis challenged the sexual and social conventions of the time. He was everything parents feared their children would become—cocky, brash, tough, and, most of all, sexual.

By the end of the decade, white audiences were rushing to record stores to buy the original black versions of songs. Radio stations and record companies now featured black artists. Little Richard (born Richard Wayne Penniman) sang, shouted, danced, gyrated, and sweated profusely through "Tutti Frutti."

Antoine "Fats" Domino, less threatening to whites than Little Richard, belted out songs such as "Blueberry Hill" (1956) and "Whole Lotta Loving" (1958). Guitar whiz Chuck Berry, who developed a famous "duck walk" across the stage, hit the charts with "Roll Over Beethoven" (1956) and "Johnny B. Goode" (1957).

At the beginning of the decade, there was a limited range of cultural options for young people. They were encouraged to wear the same style of clothing, watch the same television shows, listen to the same music, and admire the same people their parents did. Elvis Presley helped forge a wider range of cultural options by creating a musical style that appealed directly to the taste and sensibility of young people. Now, while their older brothers and sisters were still swooning over Doris Day and Perry Como, rebellious teens were twisting their hips to the beat of "Jailhouse Rock."

PRIMARY SOURCE

4.2 | *The New Teen Market*
LIFE MAGAZINE

A writer for the August 31, 1959, edition of *Life* magazine examined the new demands of America's teen-agers and their growing influence on the economy as consumers.

The time is past when a boy's chief possession was his bike and a girl's party wardrobe consisted of a fancy dress worn with a string of dime-store pearls. What Depression-bred parents may still think of as luxuries are looked on as necessities by their offspring. Today teen-agers surround themselves with a fantastic array of garish and often expensive baubles and amusements. They own
5 10 million phonographs, over a million TV sets, 13 million cameras. Nobody knows how much parents spend on them for actual necessities nor to what extent teen-agers act as hidden persuaders on their parents' other buying habits. Counting only what is spent to satisfy their special teen-age demands, the youngsters
10 and their parents will shell out about $10 billion this year, a billion more than the total sales of GM.

Until recently businessmen have largely ignored the teen-age market. But now they are spending millions on advertising and razzle-dazzle promotional stunts. Their efforts so far seem only to have scratched the surface of a rich lode.
15 In 1970, when the teen-age population expands from its present 18 million to 28 million, the market may be worth $20 billion. If parents have any idea of organized revolt, it is already too late. Teen-age spending is so important that such action would send quivers through the entire national economy. . . .

Some Fascinating Facts about a Booming Market

FOOD: Teen-agers eat 20% more than adults. They down 3½ billion quarts of
20   milk every year, almost four times as much as is drunk by the infant population
under 1. Teen-agers are a main prop of the ice cream industry, gobble 145 million
gallons a year.

BEAUTY CARE: Teen-agers spent $20 million on lipstick last year,
$25 million on deodorants (a fifth of total sold), $9 million on home permanents.
25   Male teen-agers own 2 million electric razors.

ENTERTAINMENT: Teen-agers lay out more than $1.5 billion a year for en-
tertainment. They spend about $75 million on single pop records. Although they
create new musical idols, they are staunchly faithful to the old. Elvis Presley, still
their favorite, has sold 25 million copies of single records in four years, an all-
30   time high.

HOMEMAKERS: Major items like furniture and silver are moving into the
teenage market because of [the] growing number of teen-age marriages. One
third of all 18- and 19-year-old girls are already married. More than 600,000 teen-
agers will be married this year. Teen-agers are now starting hope chests at 15.
35   CREDIT RISKS: Some 800,000 teen-agers work at full-time jobs and can buy
major items on credit.

Source: "A Young $10 Billion Power: The US Teen-age Consumer Has Become a Major Factor in
the Nation's Economy," *Life,* August 31, 1959, 78–84. Copyright © 1959 Life Inc. Reprinted by
permission. All rights reserved. ■ ■ ■

Mass Culture and the Crisis of American Identity

During the Great Depression of the 1930s, many writers worried about the prospect of class conflict in America. By the 1950s, however, pop psychologists and
social critics fretted that consumerism, suburbia, and materialism were corrupting American identity. Mass culture, they charged, was undermining individual
expression and initiative, which was at the core of American identity, replac-
ing it with a bland desire for conformity. The paradox of prosperity was that as
Americans became more secure and comfortable, they sacrificed their individual
identity.

In the popular book *The Lonely Crowd* (1950), the sociologist David Ries-
man suggested that consumerism had moved America from an "inner-directed"
culture in which people developed individualized goals to an "other-directed"
society molded by peer-group pressures. Other critics took aim at the new service economy, which emphasized teamwork and frowned on mavericks. "When
white-collar people get jobs, they sell not only their time and energy but their per-
sonalities as well," wrote the sociologist C. Wright Mills in *White Collar* (1951).

These critics pointed to the suburbs as evidence of the harmful impact of mass culture on contemporary society. Suburban communities, with their row after row of identical homes and well-manicured lawns, suggested a community that valued uniformity over individualism. Critic Lewis Mumford denounced Levittown as an "instant slum." Levittown, he suggested, represented the worst vision of America's future: bland people living in bland houses and leading bland lives.

"Beat" poets and artists joined the chorus of critics who decried American materialism and complacency. Writer Jack Kerouac, author of the best-selling novel *On the Road* (1957), coined the term *Beat* to express the "weariness with all the forms of the modern industrial state." In 1955 poet Allen Ginsberg, a Jew and homosexual who was deeply versed in Zen Buddhism, emerged as one of the leaders of the movement when he recited his poem "Howl" to a small audience in San Francisco. "Howl" railed against "robot apartments! invincible suburbs! skeleton treasuries! blind capitals! demonic industries!" The Beats embraced open sexuality and free drug use as keys to spiritual liberation. The Beat sensibility resonated with many disillusioned young people and helped inspire the counterculture movement of the 1960s.

PRIMARY SOURCE

4.3 | *Perils of Mass Culture*
U.S. News and World Report

In an article entitled "What TV Is Doing to America," a journalist with *U.S. News and World Report* sought to assess the impact of the medium on the mental and physical health of the nation's viewers.

Everywhere, children sit with eyes glued to screens—for three to four hours a day on the average. Their parents use up even more time mesmerized by this new marvel—or monster. They have spent 15 billion dollars to look since 1946.

5   Now, after nearly 10 years of TV, people are asking: "What hath TV wrought? What is this thing doing to us?"

Solid answers to this question are very hard to get. Pollsters, sociologists, doctors, teachers, the TV people themselves come up with more contradictions than conclusions whenever they start asking.

10   But almost everybody has an opinion and wants to air it.

What do these opinions add up to? People have strong views. Here are some widely held convictions, both against and for television:

That TV has kept people from going places and doing things, from reading, from thinking for themselves. Yet it is said also that TV has taken viewers

15 vicariously into strange and fascinating spots and situations, brought distinguished and enchanting people into their living rooms, given them a new perspective.

That TV has interfered with schooling, kept children from learning to read and write, weakened their eyesight and softened their muscles. But there are
20 those who hold that TV has made America's youngsters more "knowing" about life, more curious, given them a bigger vocabulary. Teaching by TV, educators say, is going to be a big thing in the future.

That TV arouses morbid emotions in children, glorifies violence, causes juvenile crime—that it starts domestic quarrels, tends to loosen morals and make
25 people lazy and sodden. However, it keeps families together at home, provides a realm of cheap entertainment never before available, stimulates new lines of conversation.

That TV is giving the U.S. an almost primitive language, made up of grunts, whistles, standardized wisecracks and clichés—that it is turning the average
30 American into a stereotype. Yet it is breaking down regional barriers and prejudices, ironing out accents, giving people in one part of the country a better understanding of people in other parts. That TV is making politics "a rich man's game," turning statesmanship into a circus, handing demagogues a new weapon. But it is giving Americans their first good look at the inside of their Government,
35 letting them judge the people they elect by sight as well as by sound and fury.

That TV has distorted and debased Salesmanship, haunting people with singing "commercials" and slogans. However, because or in spite of TV, people are buying more and more things they never before thought they needed or wanted.

These are just some of the comments that people keep on making about TV.
40 The experts say that it probably will be another generation before there is a firm basis of knowledge about television's impact on America.

Today's TV child, the boy or girl who was born with a TV set in his home, is too young to analyze his feelings. Older people, despite their frequent vehemence about TV, are still far from sure whether they have all Aladdin's lamp or hold a
45 bear by the tail. . . .

What Is It?

Why do people want TV? A $67.50-per-week shoe repairman in San Francisco, puts it about as plainly as anyone can. "TV," he says, "is the only amusement I can afford." That was the reason he gave for paying four weeks' wages for his set.
50 The cobbler's comment explains TV's basic lure. It is free entertainment except for the cost of [the] set, and repairs and electricity. It becomes so absorbing that a broken set is a family catastrophe. People will pay to have the set fixed before they will pay the milk bill, if necessary.

Source: "What TV Is Doing to America," *U.S. News & World Report,* September 2, 1955, 36–50. Copyright © 1955 U.S. News & World Report, L.P. Reprinted with permission. ■ ■ ■

While these critics were correct in highlighting the importance of mass culture, they frequently overplayed their hand. The public was not as passive, nor the dominant culture as monolithic, as they suggested. Despite dire warnings that television would overshadow other forms of information, Americans enjoyed a greater variety of cultural sources than at any time before. Book sales doubled during the decade. A dramatic increase in the number of specialized magazines, such as *Sports Illustrated* and *The New Yorker,* compensated for the decline of general-readership publications. Innovative newspapers increased their circulation by playing to the changing taste of suburban readers.

It is also difficult to measure how viewers interpreted the images they saw on their TV screens. Americans tended to filter the "messages" of mass media through the prism of their own experience. Italians in Boston's North End may have watched the same television show as African Americans in rural Alabama, but they responded to the images in different ways. By depicting America as a satiated and affluent society, television may actually have served as an unwitting vehicle of social change. TV's nightly diet of product advertising whetted the appetite of groups excluded from the consumer cornucopia, namely, the poor and minorities, and added momentum to their drive for inclusion.

Finally, suburbs, which appeared to some as manifestations of the growing conformity of modern life, were more diverse than critics recognized. Suburban communities included managers and workers, Democrats and Republicans, as well as a variety of ethnic and religious groups. Besides, most people viewed the move to the suburbs as a step up in life, the opportunity to own a piece of the American dream. One suburban resident reflected on the thrill of moving from an apartment in Brooklyn to Levittown. "We were proud," he recalled. "It was a wonderful community—and still is."

The rise of the consumer society reinforced America's optimism about the future and seemed to offer proof of the vital-center faith that economic growth could solve all social problems. During the 1950s many Americans believed that prosperity had muted ideological differences at the same time that the automobile and television were forging a common identity as consumers. By the end of the decade, however, clear signs emerged that the celebrations of consensus and prosperity were premature. The rise of teen culture and the emergence of rock and roll offered clear evidence of the social conflict that would consume the nation in the 1960s. Perhaps television offered the best insight into the impact of the consumer culture on the American paradox: while it trumpeted traditional values and the wonders of prosperity, it sowed the seeds of conflict by raising the expectations of groups excluded from the consumer culture.

SELECTED READINGS

▌ James T. Patterson focuses on the role of prosperity and the baby boom in transforming postwar ambition in *Grand Expectations* (1996). Steve Gillon looks at the impact of the baby boom on American politics and culture in *Boomer Nation* (2004). David Halberstam's *The Fifties* (1993) traces the major events and anxieties of the decade. Elaine Tyler May shows the relationship between the emphasis on families and the Cold War culture in *Homeward Bound* (1999). The transformation of America's self-image is the focus of Tom Englehardt's *The End of Victory Culture* (2nd ed., 1998). K.A. Cuordileone examines the impact of mass culture on American identity in *Manhood and American Political Culture in the Cold War* (2005).

▎ David P. Calleo's *The Imperious Economy* (1982) surveys the economic changes of the 1950s. John Kenneth Galbraith explores the postwar consumer culture in *The Affluent Society* (40th anniv. ed., 1998) and *The New Industrial State* (3rd ed., 1978). Lizabeth Cohen's *A Consumers' Republic* (2003) examines the importance of consumption in defining American citizenship and shaping politics. Martin Campbell-Kelly and William Aspray study the rise of computers and automation in *Computer* (1996). Alfred D. Chandler chronicles the rise of the modern corporation in *The Visible Hand* (1977).

▎ David M. Oshinsky provides an insightful account of the evolution of the polio vaccine in *Polio: An American Story* (2005). Kenneth T. Jackson's *Crabgrass Frontier* (1985) is a valuable survey of American suburbia. Herbert Gans's *The Levittowners* (1967) is a nuanced study that focuses on the diversity of suburban communities. Tom Lewis's *Divided Highways* (1997) examines the political support for highway projects and how the United States became an auto-oriented nation. Earl Swift examines the challenges engineers faced in constructing the highway system in *The Big Roads* (2011). The rise of the motel industry along the nation's new highways is told in Michael Witzel's *The American Motel* (2000), and Eric Schlosser traces the growth of fast-food chains and their impact on American diets in *Fast-Food Nation* (2001).

▎ Erik Barnouw's *Tube of Plenty* (2nd rev. ed., 1990) tracks the rise of television, with emphasis on its impact on American culture and politics. Lynn Spigel's *Make Room for TV* (1992) considers the transformation wrought by television on family life, as does Karal A. Marling's *As Seen on TV* (1994). Biographies of influential religious leaders include Carol George's *God's Salesman* (1994) about Norman Vincent Peale and William Martin's *A Prophet with Honor* (1991), which examines the work of Billy Graham. The history of rock and roll is examined in James Miller's *Flowers in the Dustbin* (1999), and the role of teens in the Cold War era is discussed by Grace Palladino in *Teen-agers* (1996).

5 The Politics of Moderation, 1951–1960

*I*n 1952, advertising pioneer Rosser Reeves asked a simple question: If television spots could be used to sell consumer products, why not use them to win votes for politicians? After all, Reeves would develop some of the most memorable commercials of the decade. To demonstrate how pain reliever Anacin performed, he showed how the pill quieted hammers pounding against the brain. Reeves once bragged about his Anacin spot that it "made more money [for Anacin] in seven years than *Gone with the Wind* did for . . . MGM in a quarter of a century." To convince viewers to buy Bic Pens, he shot the ball-points from rifles and crossbows, and to attract candy lovers, he announced that "M&M's melt in your mouth, not in your hands." Reeves proposed using the same method to sell Republican presidential candidate Dwight Eisenhower to the American people.

The centerpiece of the strategy was a series of fifty twenty-second commercials, called "spots," showing Eisenhower responding to questions from ordinary Americans. In early September Eisenhower met Reeves at a film studio in New York. For the next few hours Ike sat patiently, reading answers to hypothetical questions from giant cue cards. Uncomfortable with the whole process, Ike at one point remarked, "To think that an old soldier should come to this!"

Armed with Eisenhower's answers, Reeves needed to find a diverse group of people to ask the questions. He went to New York's Radio City Music Hall, chose a group of "everyday Americans," brought them to the studio, and filmed them asking questions of Eisenhower. When edited together, the spot showed Ike responding directly to the concerns of average Americans. An elderly woman remarked: "You know what things cost today. High prices are just driving me crazy." "My wife, Mamie," Ike answered, "worries about the same thing. I tell her it's our job to change that on November fourth." Though simplistic and devoid of any substance, such spots would become a standard feature of American politics.

Eisenhower's opponent, Illinois governor Adlai Stevenson, was uncomfortable with the new medium of television. Although he came across well on camera—a critic said he was "a television personality the like of which has not been seen before"—he did not like talking to an invisible audience of millions. "This is the worst thing I've ever heard of," he complained when he learned about the Eisenhower spots, "selling the president like cereal. Merchandising the presidency. How can you talk seriously about issues with one-minute spots!"

In the short run the ads carried Eisenhower's reassuring smile into millions of living rooms. In style and manner President Dwight D. Eisenhower served as a political symbol of the age. As one historian commented, "If he sought not to arouse the people to new political challenges, he was suited to reassure them that their elemental convictions were safe from doubt and confusion." At home Eisenhower's philosophy of dynamic conservatism reassured conservatives at the same time that it consolidated New Deal programs. Abroad Eisenhower's tough anti-Soviet rhetoric belied a policy that reflected caution and prudence in dealing with the Cold War adversary. The Republicans controlled the White House, but the basic ideas of the vital center still dominated thinking in Washington.

The Election of 1952

Eisenhower had not taken the typical route into politics. Born in Denison, Texas, on October 4, 1890, Eisenhower grew up in Abilene, Kansas. He was a diligent student, an eager reader, and a talented writer. After graduating from

West Point in 1915, he rose within the ranks of the army, serving with distinction on the War Department staff in Washington. He began World War II as a brigadier general and ended it as supreme commander in Europe. After leading the Anglo-American military forces that defeated Germany in 1945, Eisenhower remained in the army as chief of staff until 1948, when he accepted the presidency of Columbia University. Three years later he was called back to serve as the first supreme commander of North Atlantic Treaty Organization (NATO) forces in Europe.

Eisenhower's status as a war hero made him a popular choice to run for president in 1952. At first Eisenhower, who had never registered a party affiliation or voted in an election, expressed little interest, but he feared that if he did not run, the Republican Party would nominate Ohio senator Robert Taft. Though Taft enjoyed a large following among the party's Old Guard, his isolationist views and uninspiring manner limited his appeal to mainstream voters. When in February 1952 Taft advocated bringing American troops home from Europe, Eisenhower decided to run. He resigned from NATO and entered his name for the Republican nomination.

After a bitter convention struggle, Eisenhower won the nomination. To appease the party's right wing, he selected thirty-nine-year-old Senator Richard Nixon of California as his running mate. Because of his high-profile role in the Alger Hiss affair, Nixon had developed close ties to party conservatives. He was also a ferocious, frequently unscrupulous campaigner who could keep the Democrats on the defensive while Eisenhower took the high road. Hailing from California, Nixon added regional balance and was expected to deliver the state's electoral votes.

The Democrats faced a more difficult choice. In March a beleaguered President Harry Truman announced that he would not seek a second term. Recent investigations had linked appointees in Truman's administration to influence peddling and other corrupt practices. The scandals, added to the stalemate in Korea and Senator Joseph McCarthy's persistent accusations that the administration was "soft on communism," drove Truman's popularity to an all-time low of 26 percent. With Truman out of the picture, many Democrats looked to the popular Illinois governor Adlai Stevenson. Along with his ties to a large and powerful state, Stevenson had endeared himself to party loyalists by taking strong positions on civil rights and civil liberties. Like Eisenhower, Stevenson expressed little interest in the nomination, but he bowed to party leaders' insistence. To balance the ticket, Stevenson selected a segregationist senator, John Sparkman of Alabama, as his running mate.

Few substantive issues separated the two candidates. Ike and Stevenson subscribed to the basic precepts of the vital center. Both men were ardent Cold Warriors who feared the expansion of federal power at home. Stevenson abandoned many of the controversial programs of the Fair Deal, including public housing and national health insurance. On civil rights the Democratic nominee felt that it was the states' responsibility to address the problem and that the federal government should not "put the South completely over a barrel."

The GOP campaign correctly identified Korea, communism, and corruption as key issues. The Republicans complained of "plunder at home, blunder abroad" and promised to "clean up the mess in Washington." Nixon referred to "Adlai the Appeaser," who was a "Ph.D. graduate of Dean Acheson's cowardly College of Communist Containment." Eisenhower, just ten days before the election, declared, "I shall go to Korea." Though he did not say what he would do when he got there, his pledge was a masterful stroke. In a break with most presidential elections, which are decided primarily on domestic issues, more than one-half of the electorate regarded the war as the country's single most important problem, and most people believed Eisenhower's military background made him the best candidate to end the conflict.

The Republicans, however, had to endure an embarrassing scandal when the *New York Post* revealed that a group of wealthy California businessmen

Nixon's Televised "Checkers"Speech   Just days after Eisenhower selected Richard Nixon as his running mate in the fall of 1952, the *New York Post* reported that Nixon had received substantial gifts from wealthy businessmen. To save his political career, Nixon decided to plead his case to the American people with a televised speech. At the end of the speech, Nixon turned the tables on his opponents, questioning their ethics and challenging them to be as open with their finances as he had been. The American people rallied behind Nixon and Eisenhower kept him on the ticket. *(© Bettmann/CORBIS)*

had provided Nixon with an $18,000 private "slush fund" to pay for personal campaign expenses. On September 23 Nixon went on national television to defend himself, citing the emotional and material needs of his family, not personal ambition, as his reason for accepting the money. Near the end of the talk Nixon told the story of one special gift he had received—a "little cocker spaniel dog," which his daughter Tricia had named Checkers. He vowed his family would keep the dog "regardless of what they say about it." The address revealed the growing importance of television in politics. Over 9 million sets were tuned to Nixon's speech, and popular reaction was overwhelmingly favorable. Eisenhower, recognizing the positive response, assured Nixon, "You're my boy."

PRIMARY SOURCE

5.1 | *The Checkers Speech*

RICHARD NIXON

Utilizing the power of the new medium of television, Richard Nixon (with his wife, Pat, close by) made a passionate appeal for understanding from viewers as he explained his family's economic situation and confessed to accepting a dog for his daughters.

My Fellow Americans,
      I come before you tonight as a candidate for the Vice Presidency and as a man whose honesty and integrity has been questioned.

5   Now, the usual political thing to do when charges are made against you is to either ignore them or to deny them without giving details. I believe we have had enough of that in the United States, particularly with the present Administration in Washington, D.C.

To me the office of the Vice Presidency of the United States is a great office, and I feel that the people have got to have confidence in the integrity of the men 10 who run for that office and who might attain them.

I have a theory, too, that the best and only answer to a smear or an honest misunderstanding of the facts is to tell the truth. And that is why I am here tonight. I want to tell you my side of the case.

I am sure that you have read the charge, and you have heard it, that I, Senator 15 Nixon, took $18,000 from a group of my supporters.

Now, was that wrong? And let me say that it was wrong. I am saying it, incidentally, that it was wrong, just not illegal, because it isn't a question of whether it was legal or illegal, that isn't enough. The question is, was it morally wrong. I say that it was morally wrong—if any of that $18,000 went to Senator Nixon, for my personal use. I say that it was morally wrong if it was secretly given and secretly handled. And I say that it was morally wrong if any of the contributors got special favors for the contributions that they made.

And now to answer those questions let me say this: Not a cent of the $18,000 or any other money of that type ever went to me for my personal use. Every penny of it was used to pay for political expenses that I did not think should be charged to the taxpayers of the United States. . . .

. . . And so now, what I am going to do—and incidentally this is unprecedented in the history of American politics—I am going at this time to give to this television and radio audience, a complete financial history, everything I have earned, everything I have spent and everything I own, and I want you to know the facts. . . .

I own a 1950 Oldsmobile car. We have our furniture, we have no stocks and bonds of any type. We have no interest, direct or indirect, in any business. Now that is what we have. What do we owe?

I owe $3,500 to my parents, and the interest on that loan, which I pay regularly, because it is a part of the savings they made through the years they were working so hard—I pay regularly 4 percent interest. And then I have a $500 loan, which I have on my life insurance.

Well, that's about it. That's what we have. And that's what we owe. It isn't very much. But Pat and I have the satisfaction that every dime that we have got is honestly ours.

I should say this, that Pat doesn't have a mink coat.

But she does have a respectable Republican cloth coat, and I always tell her she would look good in anything.

One other thing I should probably tell you, because if I don't they will probably be saying this about me, too. We did get something, a gift, after the election.

A man down in Texas heard Pat on the radio mention the fact that our two youngsters would like to have a dog, and, believe it or not, the day we left before this campaign trip we got a message from Union Station in Baltimore, saying they had a package for us. We went down to get it. You know what it was?

It was a little cocker spaniel dog, in a crate that he had sent all the way from Texas, black and white, spotted, and our little girl Tricia, the six year old, named it Checkers. And you know, the kids, like all kids, loved the dog, and I just want to say this, right now, that regardless of what they say about it, we are going to keep it. . . .

And now, finally, I know that you wonder whether or not I am going to stay on the Republican ticket or resign. Let me say this: I don't believe that I ought to quit, because I am not a quitter. And, incidentally, Pat is not a quitter. After all, her name is Patricia Ryan and she was born on St. Patrick's Day, and you know the Irish never quit.

But the decision, my friends, is not mine. I would do nothing that would harm the possibilities of Dwight Eisenhower to become President of the United States.

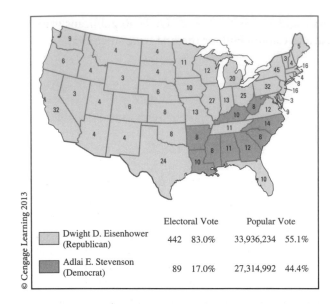

© Cengage Learning 2013

	Electoral Vote		Popular Vote	
Dwight D. Eisenhower (Republican)	442	83.0%	33,936,234	55.1%
Adlai E. Stevenson (Democrat)	89	17.0%	27,314,992	44.4%

The Election of 1952 Though a political novice, Dwight D. Eisenhower's persona as a war hero and man of the people gave him the edge over his more experienced, yet less-well-known opponent, Adlai Stevenson. Eisenhower's popularity and his promise to end the Korean War even swayed many southern Democrats to vote Republican for the first time.

And for that reason I am submitting to the Republican National Committee tonight, through this television broadcast, the decision which it is theirs to make.
65 Let them decide whether my position on the ticket will help or hurt. And I am going to ask you to help them decide. Wire and write the Republican National Committee whether you think I should stay on or whether I should get off. And whatever their decision is, I will abide by it.

Source: Excerpts from "The Fund Broadcast" speech, September 23, 1952. ■ ■ ■

Nixon had saved his spot on the ticket, but at a high price. Eisenhower remained suspicious of him, and although the public responded warmly to Nixon's speech, opinion makers found the whole episode unsavory. They were turned off by his self-pity and his willingness to use his wife, children, and even his dog to save his political life. For many people the episode underscored their perception of Nixon as a ruthless opportunist who would do almost anything to get what he wanted. That image would linger long after election night.

Few people were surprised on election day when Eisenhower scored a landslide victory. Ike won 55.1 percent of the popular vote and carried thirty-nine states. His vote total, 33.9 million, was nearly 12 million more than Dewey had received in 1948. Sweeping the electoral college 442 to 89, Eisenhower made inroads into the once solidly Democratic South by winning Florida, Tennessee, Texas, and Virginia. Stevenson, with 27.3 million votes, won 44.4 percent of the popular vote and carried nine states, all southern or border states. Most significantly, Eisenhower offset Democratic strength in major urban areas by scoring well in the growing suburbs. The Republicans gained majorities in both houses of

Congress, 48 to 47 in the Senate and 221 to 211 in the House. Republicans were in control of the White House and Capitol Hill for the first time since 1930.

Dynamic Conservatism at Home

Eisenhower came to office with a general idea of what he wanted to accomplish and where he wished to move the nation. The new president called his political philosophy "dynamic conservatism," which he interpreted as "conservative when it comes to money and liberal when it comes to human beings." The approach represented Ike's way of dealing with the paradox of rising expectations and traditional values. Like many conservatives, Eisenhower believed that the executive branch had grown too strong under Franklin Roosevelt and Harry Truman. Government regulation had strangled business, while the growth of executive power had disrupted the delicate constitutional balance among the branches of government. The solution, Ike argued, was to take a more restrained approach to the presidency. "I am not one of those desk-pounding types that likes to stick out his jaw and look like he is bossing the show," he said.

The new president was determined to reverse the direction taken by the New Deal and Fair Deal or, in his words, to remove "the Left-Wingish, pinkish influence in our life." The key was to control government spending—even on defense—and balance the budget. He believed that expanded federal power threatened individual liberty. The role of government was to tame special interests, restraining their excess demands and forcing them to work together for common purposes. The president should not use the federal budget to reward friends and punish enemies—as Eisenhower believed FDR and Truman had done—but instead to promote domestic harmony and economic stability. His strongest supporters referred to Eisenhower's approach to government as "modern Republicanism."

Acting on his conservative impulses, the president removed Truman's moderate wage and price controls, lowered price supports for farm products, cut the government payroll by two hundred thousand workers, and trimmed federal spending by 10 percent, or $6 billion, in his first year. Eisenhower's position on natural resource development clearly revealed his desire to limit federal involvement in the private sector. He reversed Truman's decision to proceed with federal construction of a hydroelectric plant in Hell's Canyon, Idaho, and licensed a private firm to complete the work. He opposed the Tennessee Valley Authority's request to build a new plant to furnish power for the Atomic Energy Commission. In May 1953, Eisenhower signed the Submerged Lands Act, which transferred control of about $40 billion worth of oil lands from the federal government to the states. The *New York Times* called it "one of the greatest and surely the most unjustified give-away programs in all the history of the United States."

Despite the hopes of many conservatives, and the fears of liberals, Eisenhower did not undermine the foundation of the modern welfare state. Political and economic realities prevented such a drastic step. "Should any political party attempt to abolish Social Security, unemployment insurance, and eliminate labor and farm programs," Ike warned, "you would not hear of that party again in our political history." In addition, congressional Democrats, who recaptured control of both houses in 1954 and retained it throughout the remainder of Eisenhower's presidency, would have blocked any attempt to repeal established programs. Meanwhile, sharp recessions in 1954 and 1958 led the president to abandon his budget-balancing efforts and to accelerate government spending.

Indeed, in the end Eisenhower's policies consolidated and strengthened the New Deal's economic and social programs. During his presidency spending on social welfare programs rose steadily, from 7.6 percent of the gross national product (GNP) in 1952 to 11.5 percent in 1961. The president and Congress agreed in 1954, and again in 1956, to increase social security benefits and to broaden the federal system to include an estimated 10 million new workers. In 1955 Congress and Eisenhower compromised on a new law that increased the minimum wage from seventy-five cents to one dollar an hour. In health and medical welfare Eisenhower carried forward the programs begun by Roosevelt and Truman. On April 1, 1953, Eisenhower signed a bill that raised the Federal Security Agency to cabinet rank as the Department of Health, Education, and Welfare. Barry Goldwater, a rising conservative star from Arizona, complained that Ike ran a "Dime Store New Deal."

Taking on McCarthy

While consolidating the New Deal, Eisenhower outflanked his party's right wing by intensifying the campaign against internal subversion. Soon after taking office, he issued Executive Order 10450, which toughened the government loyalty program. The new guidelines included not only loyalty and security but also an open-ended category called "suitability." Under his new guidelines almost ten thousand federal employees resigned or were dismissed. The president gave Federal Bureau of Investigation (FBI) director J. Edgar Hoover a free hand to wiretap suspected communists. The administration also supported the Communist Control Act. Passed by Congress in 1954, the law prohibited communists from running for public office.

Eisenhower hoped that his aggressive loyalty program would steal the limelight from Joseph McCarthy. But McCarthy had other ideas. In October 1953, McCarthy blasted the administration for conducting a foreign policy of "whiny, whimpering appeasement." At the same time, his investigations subcommittee

Roy Cohn and Senator McCarthy at the Army–McCarthy Hearings From April to June 1954, Senator Joseph McCarthy made his last great attempt to root out communism in the nation's government, this time targeting the U.S. Army. At the height of the Army–McCarthy hearings, which were televised live, the army's attorney, Joseph Welch, tenaciously cross-examined McCarthy's associate, Roy Cohn (seated to Senator McCarthy's left in this picture). In retaliation, McCarthy attacked one of the young lawyers in Welch's law firm who had been a member of a communist organization for a brief time in college. Watching McCarthy's vicious attack on a young man who had long ago rejected communism led many Americans to question McCarthy's motives for the hearings and to doubt McCarthy's ability to find any real communist infiltration into the American government. *(© Washington Post; reprinted by permission of the D.C. Public Library)*

conducted seventeen hearings, including ten that focused on current subversion in government.

Eisenhower had had enough. In March 1954, the president leaked to the press an army report that documented attempts by McCarthy and his staff to win preferential treatment for David Schine, a former staff member drafted into the army. The Senate, embarrassed by the army's accusations, decided to hold investigative public hearings carried live on national television. Beginning on April 27, as many as 20 million Americans watched the proceedings for thirty-five days. Toward the end McCarthy savagely attacked a lawyer for having once belonged to a left-wing organization. Outraged, Attorney Joseph Welch berated McCarthy, concluding: "Have you no sense of decency, sir, at long last? Have you left no sense of decency?" After watching McCarthy on television, a majority of Americans were asking the same question. As his appeal ebbed, the Senate roused itself against McCarthy, voting in December 1954, 67–22, to "condemn" him for bringing Congress into disrepute. Three years later, at the age of forty-eight, Joseph McCarthy, once the most feared man in America, died of hepatitis and other health problems caused by alcoholism.

The 1956 Presidential Campaign

McCarthy's fall removed a major source of embarrassment and virtually guaranteed Eisenhower's reelection in 1956. Polls showed Ike leading all Democratic challengers by wide margins. The president's enormous popularity had as much to do with his style and personality as it did with his policies. Most people viewed Eisenhower as a strong leader and a likable man who embodied traditional American values. He often spoke of old-fashioned virtues such as honor, duty, patriotism, and hard work. The White House seemed home to a traditional family, with First Lady Mamie Eisenhower playing the proper role of dutiful wife. "Ike took care of the office," she declared. "I ran the house."

Eisenhower used television not only when campaigning but also when building public support for his administration. Realizing that television allowed politicians to project themselves into the homes of millions of potential voters, Eisenhower hired movie star Robert Montgomery to help craft his media image. By 1955 Ike was so confident in his ability to perform for the cameras that he became the first president to allow television coverage of his press conferences. Eisenhower's appeal transcended the politics of personality: his modern Republicanism effectively straddled the contradiction between postwar expectations that government would do more to address social problems and the fear of expanding federal power.

After a spirited primary campaign, Democrats turned again to Adlai Stevenson to lead their party. Stevenson ran an energetic campaign for a "New America" where "poverty is abolished" and "freedom is made real for everybody."

Most commentators had trouble even pretending the race would be close. The confidence was well founded. The Eisenhower-Nixon ticket won with the largest popular vote in U.S. history up to that time. Eisenhower's support of 57.6 percent of the voters had been exceeded only by FDR's in 1936. The popular president carried such Democratic strongholds as Chicago and Jersey City, along with Baltimore, Milwaukee, Los Angeles, and San Francisco. He carried a majority of the Catholic vote and did well among African Americans.

The victory was, however, an endorsement of Eisenhower, not of his party. The Democrats actually increased their majorities in Congress and their governorships.

Ike and the "Bomb"

Eisenhower also managed to briefly ease American anxiety about the Cold War. Many Americans were reassured knowing that Eisenhower was in charge. Ike came to the White House better prepared to handle foreign policy than any other twentieth-century president. He had toured the globe and served as supreme wartime commander of Allied forces and NATO. He came to office with a clear vision of America's role in world affairs.

Eisenhower's foreign policy strategy depended heavily on "the bomb." America, he believed, should take advantage of its overwhelming superiority in nuclear weapons, attacking enemy forces with small nuclear weapons or even striking at the source of the aggression—Moscow or Beijing. Being cheaper than conventional forces, nuclear weapons offered "more bang for the buck." The administration called its defense strategy the "New Look."

To make credible the threat to use atomic arms, the administration dramatically increased the nation's nuclear arsenal. Between 1952 and 1959, the number of nuclear weapons in the American arsenal grew from around 1,500 to over 6,000.

In addition, the administration negotiated a number of regional defense treaties designed to deter Soviet aggression. By the end of the 1950s, the United States had signed agreements to defend forty-three different nations against "communist aggression." Eisenhower also unleashed the CIA to overthrow foreign governments—even popularly elected ones—that did not support American interests.

Despite his "New Look" strategy, Eisenhower discovered that the realities of international power and domestic politics prevented a radical departure from past practices. The first indication of the continuity in his approach to the world came in Korea, where Eisenhower was determined to end American involvement. But on what terms? As promised, he flew to Korea after the 1952 election to nudge the cease-fire talks. He also dropped hints to China that he was ready to use nuclear weapons in Korea. In July 1953, he agreed to terms that called for a division of Korea at approximately the same line that had marked the border in June 1950—the thirty-eighth parallel—with a demilitarized zone separating the two Koreas.

The president showed similar restraint in dealing with a potentially dangerous situation in China. During the fall of 1954, the Communist Chinese began to shell the offshore islands of Quemoy and Matsu, which were occupied by the

Nationalist Chinese. Conservatives urged Eisenhower to respond forcefully, perhaps by bombing the mainland. Instead, Eisenhower signed a security agreement with the Nationalists that committed the United States to protect the strategically important island of Formosa (Taiwan), but left ambiguous America's commitment to Quemoy and Matsu. Again, he and Secretary of State John Foster Dulles issued public statements hinting at the possibility of using nuclear weapons to stem communist attacks. Chinese leaders, uncertain whether Eisenhower was bluffing, stopped the bombardment.

Eisenhower also pursued a moderate course in his dealings with the Soviet Union. In March 1953, shortly after Eisenhower's election, Soviet leader Joseph Stalin died, raising hopes of a thaw in relations between the two countries. In July 1955, Eisenhower and Khrushchev, with their British and French counterparts, met in Geneva for the first top-level conference of the wartime Allies since the 1945 meeting at Potsdam. The cordial atmosphere produced a brief thaw in superpower tensions, which the press labeled "the spirit of Geneva."

The friendly words and smiling faces of Geneva could not mask the serious differences between the two countries. The thaw ended on October 29, 1956, when 200,000 Soviet soldiers and hundreds of tanks swept into Hungary to repress a popular uprising demanding democratic reforms. Once again, however, Eisenhower resisted calls for direct American intervention. He understood the military risks of attempting to intervene in a country so close to the Soviet border.

The Limits of the "New Look": The Middle East

Although President Eisenhower eased Cold War tensions in Europe, the administration had few answers to address growing nationalist movements in the Third World. Hungarians were not alone in their struggle for independence. Between 1945 and 1960 almost forty nations with 800 million people fought nationalist struggles against colonial rulers. The leaders of these countries tried to exploit superpower tensions to win concessions from both Washington and Moscow. These newly independent nations in Asia, the Middle East, Latin America, and Africa became the new battlegrounds of the Cold War. Henry Cabot Lodge, U.S. ambassador to the United Nations, first asked the question that plagued American policymakers in the years following World War II: "The U.S. can win wars," but "can we win revolutions?"

The Middle East confronted the administration with its first serious nationalist challenge. In 1954, Egyptian leader Colonel Gamal Abdel Nasser increased trade with the Soviet bloc and officially recognized China. Two years later,

Secretary of State Dulles, in an attempt to punish Egypt for its growing ties with communists, abruptly canceled American financing to build the Aswan Dam across the Nile. In response, Nasser seized control of the Suez Canal, the vital waterway between the Mediterranean and the Gulf of Suez, and used the revenue to complete the Aswan project. Arabs hailed Nasser as a hero for his strong stand against Western imperialism. Eisenhower worked behind the scenes to work out a compromise, but the British, who had controlled the canal, and the French, angered by Nasser's aid to rebels against French rule in Algeria, conspired to regain control of the canal and teach Nasser a lesson.

They got their chance on October 29, 1956, when, provoked by eight years of border attacks and fear of the Egyptian arms buildup, Israel invaded Egypt's Sinai Peninsula. Israeli forces advanced within ten miles of the Suez Canal. In an attack carefully coordinated with the Israelis, the British and French bombed Egyptian military targets and seized the northern third of the canal.

The Anglo-French military action angered Eisenhower. He feared it would alienate nationalist elements in the Middle East and drive the entire Arab world closer to the Russians. The president publicly condemned the attacks on Egypt and worked with the Soviets to oversee the withdrawal of all outside forces from Egypt. By December 1956, the crisis was over, but the Suez affair had shaken the Western alliance to its foundations and increased anti-Western sentiment in the region. Believing that Khrushchev's threat to intervene had stopped the invasion, Nasser accepted Soviet assistance in completing the Aswan project, providing the Russians with a foothold in the Middle East. In 1957 Eisenhower asked for, and both houses of Congress passed, a resolution that came to be called the "Eisenhower Doctrine." The new plan provided the president with broad authority to provide economic and military assistance to defend any Middle East ally from "international communism."

The Limits of Power: The CIA

In other regions of the world, the administration relied on the CIA to quell nationalist uprisings that appeared to threaten American interests. In Iran, when the government of Mohammed Mossadegh nationalized the Anglo-Iranian Oil Company in 1953, the CIA planned, financed, and orchestrated a coup to overthrow him. To replace him, the CIA worked with Iranian army officers to consolidate power behind the pro-Western Shah Reza Pahlavi. "I owe my throne to God, my people, my army—and to you!" exclaimed a grateful shah. The easy success of the operation in Iran encouraged the administration to use the CIA in other Third World hotspots.

5.2 | *Eisenhower's Diary*

DWIGHT EISENHOWER

On October 8, 1953, President Eisenhower, who kept a detailed diary of all his actions, wrote about the coup in Iran. He was clearly fascinated by the CIA and credited them for the overthrow of the government.

Another recent development that we helped bring about was the restoration of the Shah to power in Iran and the elimination of Mossadegh. The things we did were "covert." If knowledge of them became public, we would not only be embarrassed in that region, but our chances to do anything of like
5   nature in the future would almost totally disappear. Nevertheless our agent there, a member of the CIA, worked intelligently, courageously and tirelessly. I listened to his detailed report and it seemed more like a dime novel than an historical fact. When we realize that in the first hours of the attempted coup, all elements of surprise disappeared through betrayal, the Shah fled to
10   Baghdad, and Mossadegh seemed to be more firmly entrenched in power than ever before, then we can understand exactly how courageous our agent was in staying right on the job and continuing to work until he reversed the entire situation.

    Now if the British will be conciliatory and display some wisdom; if the
15   Shah and his new premier, General Zahedi, will be only a little but flexible, and the United States will stand by to help both financially and with wise counsel, we may really give a serious defeat to Russian intentions and plans in that area.

    Of course, it will not be so easy for the Iranian economy to be restored, even
20   if her refineries again begin to operate. This is due to the fact that during the long period of shut down of her oil fields, world buyers have gone to other sources of supply. These have been expanded to meet the need and now, literally, Iran really has no ready market for her vast oil production. However, this is a problem that we should be able to solve.

Source: Dwight D. Eisenhower's Papers as President, Diaries, Box 4, DDE Diary, Oct.–Dec. 1953.   ■ ■ ■

In 1954 the administration used the CIA to topple the leftist government of Jacobo Árbenz Guzmán in Guatemala. In 1953 the Arbenz government launched an ambitious land-reform program, which included seizing more than 200,000 acres controlled by the American-owned United Fruit Company. With an annual profit of $65 million, double the total revenue of the government, United Fruit became an obvious target of nationalist sentiment. Warning that the country could become an outpost for communism in the Western Hemisphere, the CIA trained a ragtag liberation army in Honduras. On June 18 the army crossed the border into Guatemala while the CIA provided the planes and pilots to support the assault. At the same time, the agency jammed the government's radio station and broadcast its own version of the fighting, one that emphasized how government troops were laying down their arms and refusing to fight (they were not). A few days later Dulles told the media that the coup represented "a new and glorious chapter for all the people of the Americas." A new government, approved by the CIA, took power and restored the appropriated lands to United Fruit.

Eisenhower's experiments in intervention revealed the flaws in the vital center's approach to nationalist revolutions. Viewing local struggles as part of the superpower competition and threats to U.S. security, Americans confused indigenous nationalist movements with Soviet-inspired aggression. America's attitude revealed an arrogance of power, a belief that U.S. power could and should shape the internal affairs of distant nations. In time America would pay a heavy price for its mistakes.

SELECTED READINGS

- Gary W. Reichard's *Politics as Usual* (1988) surveys politics at midcentury. Stephen E. Ambrose's *Eisenhower* (2 vols., 1983, 1984) is a comprehensive scholarly biography of the president, as is Geoffrey Perret's *Eisenhower* (1999). A number of scholars have challenged the notion that Eisenhower was a hands-off president. Among the best are Fred I. Greenstein's *The Hidden-Hand Presidency* (1982), and Jim Newton's *Eisenhower: The White House Years* (2011) Journalist Tom Wicker portrays Ike as a mediocre leader in his short biography, *Dwight D. Eisenhower* (2002).

- Eisenhower's efforts to protect national security by promoting a healthy economy is the basis of Gerard Clarfield's *Security with Solvency* (1999). Jeff Broadwater, in *Eisenhower and the Anti-Communist Crusade* (1992), argues that Eisenhower, while opposed to McCarthy's tactics, frequently failed to protect civil liberties in the name of national security.

- Robert Divine's *Eisenhower and the Cold War* (1981) provides an excellent survey of U.S.-Soviet relations in the 1950s, as does Victor Rosenberg's *Soviet-American Relations, 1953–1960* (2005). The essays collected by editors Richard Melanson and David Mayers in *Reevaluating Eisenhower* (1986) examine America's foreign policy around the globe. *Eisenhower's Atoms for Peace* (2002) by Ira Chernus analyzes Eisenhower's support for nuclear preparedness. Ray Takeyh's *The Origins of the Eisenhower Doctrine* (2000) traces the emergence of Eisenhower's foreign policy as he attempted to balance Cold War theory with the forces of nationalism in the Middle East. David A. Nichols provides an insightful account of Eisenhower's role in the Suez crisis in *Eisenhower 1956* (2011).

▌ The impact of a daring few in the CIA's early years is examined in Evan Thomas's *The Very Best Men* (1995). Richard Immerman provides a valuable case study of the CIA's actions in *The CIA in Guatemala* (1982). Philip Taubman's *Secret Empire* (2004) and Dino A. Brugioni's *Eyes in the Sky* (2010) highlight the role the CIA played in Eisenhower's foreign policy.

6 American Ideals and Social Realities, 1952–1960

In August 1955, Emmett Till, a fourteen-year-old African American youth from Chicago, visited relatives near Money, Mississippi. After buying some candy at a rural store, Till allegedly said "Bye, baby" to the white female clerk. A few days later, after midnight, her husband and brother dragged Till from the home of his uncle, Mose Wright. They shot Till in the head, cut off his testicles, and dumped him in the Tallahatchie River. His disfigured body was found three days later.

Mamie Bradley, Till's mother, decided to use his funeral to expose the evils of southern racism. She had the body sent back to Chicago and insisted on an open casket at the funeral so that, in her words, "All the world can see what they did to my boy." Over four days, thousands of people streamed by his casket. A popular magazine also published pictures of Till and his funeral. The image of Till's mutilated body seared itself into the consciousness of a generation of black leaders.

The murder trial attracted national attention. The NAACP sent lawyers to Mississippi to assist in the prosecution. Local whites resented the black assertiveness and rallied around the two defendants. The trial took place in a segregated courtroom before an all-white jury. For five long, hot summer days, the trial dragged on. In a dramatic moment, when asked to identify the two men who dragged his nephew from his house, Mose Wright stood and pointed at one of the defendants: "There he is."

His testimony, and that of a handful of other black witnesses, did no good. In his closing statement, the defense attorney exhorted the twelve white male jurors, "I am sure that every last Anglo-Saxon one of you has the courage to free these men. . . ." The jury deliberated for less than two hours, and despite overwhelming evidence of guilt, found the defendants innocent.

The brutal murder of Emmett Till focused a spotlight on racial injustice in the South at a time when the nation was engaged in a global struggle with the Soviet Union to convince people living in undeveloped countries of the superiority of American values. Prosperity allowed many Americans to join the middle class and buy new consumer goods to fill their new, more spacious suburban homes. But there was another side to the 1950s. Not only was the decade full of anxiety about the Cold War, but the celebration of family values limited opportunities for women, and signs of a booming economy obscured the growing gap between rich and poor. At a time when intellectuals and politicians proclaimed that prosperity had muted class and racial differences, the contradiction between American ideals and American reality provided the central paradox of the 1950s.

Intellectuals and the Celebration of Consensus

The tension went unnoticed by most intellectuals during the 1950s. Prosperity, the lure of suburbia, the stifling effects of McCarthyism, and the oppressive atmosphere of the Cold War discouraged critical social analysis, muted vigorous political debate, and reinforced the vital-center consensus. Intellectuals gave their scholarly blessing to the self-satisfied images that pervaded mass culture. In 1956 *Time* magazine observed that the intellectual "found himself feeling at home" in America.

Most intellectuals, ensconced in comfortable positions at major universities, foundations, and mass communication, benefited from the postwar prosperity and believed that capitalism was transforming America into a land of plenty. "American capitalism works," declared Harvard economist John Kenneth

Galbraith early in the decade. Meanwhile, McCarthy's attacks against leftist intellectuals intimidated many of them, who sought refuge in moderate liberalism. Many opinion makers, determined not to leave themselves vulnerable to right-wing attacks on their patriotism, expressed enthusiastic support for the Cold War, viewing it as a struggle between the free world and totalitarian communism.

Historians, sociologists, and political scientists heralded an "age of consensus," a time when prosperity, social programs, and fear of communism rendered social protest obsolete. At the end of the decade the sociologist Daniel Bell declared all radical alternatives dead in *The End of Ideology* (1960). Such historians as Daniel Boorstin and Henry Steele Commager minimized the role of conflict and change in American history and stressed the importance of continuity and consensus. Surveys showing that 75 percent of Americans considered themselves part of the middle class contributed to a growing sense that the nation was evolving toward a classless society.

Liberals joined in the celebration of consensus, abandoning or moderating the arguments born during the Great Depression for sweeping changes in the nation's economic institutions. Like earlier reformers, liberals in the 1950s believed that government needed to play a role in regulating the economy and guaranteeing social justice. But they also shared with many conservatives a reverence for the enormous potential of the free enterprise system and a fear of expansive federal power. Reflecting the broader consensus, liberals believed that sustained economic growth, with a minimum of government regulation, would eliminate class divisions, create opportunity for all citizens, and ensure a stable society.

A sizable number of intellectuals went even further, abandoning the pretense of moderation and embracing conservatism. While critical of the growth of government power in the years after World War II, these intellectuals celebrated the success of American capitalism and accepted the U.S. mission to redefine the world in its own image. Many conservative thinkers, fearful that the expanded state power would lead the nation down "the road to serfdom," and confident in the power of capitalism, offered a powerful defense of free market capitalism. Others, most notably Russell Kirk, worried about the decline of moral standards and called for a revival of traditional religious values. Finally, ex-communists who converted to conservatism, including Whittaker Chambers and James Burnham, carried into the postwar period a profound conviction that the West was involved in a titanic struggle with a ruthless adversary that sought nothing less than the conquest of the world.

The New Poverty

These intellectuals underestimated the persistence of profound poverty in America. Their celebration of a classless society proved unfounded. In spite of the widening prosperity, the distribution of income remained uneven. In 1960, the top 1 percent of the population held 33 percent of the national wealth, while the bottom 20 percent held only 5 percent. In 1959, a quarter of the population had no liquid assets; over half the population had no savings accounts. "If we made an income pyramid out of child's blocks, with each portraying $1,000 of income," the economist Paul Samuelson observed, "the peak would be far higher than the Eiffel Tower, but almost all of us would be within a foot of the ground."

Although poverty had declined significantly since the Great Depression, about 40 million Americans, representing 25 percent of the population, were poor in 1960. During the 1950s poverty moved from the rural farm to the inner city. By 1960 some 55 percent of the poor lived in cities. African Americans made up a majority of the new urban residents. Before World War II, 80 percent of African Americans lived in the South. During the war, defense-related jobs lured almost 3 million southern workers to the nation's cities. At one point in the 1950s, the black population of Chicago swelled by more than 2,200 new arrivals each week. By 1960, half of all African Americans lived in central cities.

African Americans, and other minorities, flooded the nation's cities just as the white middle class, and many jobs, were fleeing to the suburbs. Suburban communities used a variety of formal and informal methods to exclude blacks. In many cases, local real estate agents refused to sell houses to blacks and bankers rejected their mortgage applications. Some communities adopted zoning regulations designed to exclude lower-income groups. The methods proved effective: by the end of the decade African Americans made up less than 5 percent of suburban residents.

At the same time, many cities adopted ambitious "urban renewal" projects, which demolished neighborhoods and displaced poor people in the name of progress. By 1963, urban renewal uprooted 609,000 Americans, two-thirds of whom were minority group members. When planning the route of new superhighways to speed the commute between the suburbs and the central city, Los Angeles officials bypassed wealthy neighborhoods such as Beverly Hills, and plowed through densely populated Chicano communities in East Los Angeles and Hollenbeck. In October 1957, the city displaced the Chicano community in Chavez Ravine to make room for the building of Dodger Stadium.

Changing Gender Roles

A gap between popular perceptions and social realities also impacted gender roles during the decade. The problem was especially acute for women. In a special 1956 issue on American women, *Life* magazine concluded that the ideal modern woman married, cooked and cared for her family, and kept herself busy by joining the local Parent–Teacher Association and leading a troop of the Campfire Girls. The magazine praised the "increasing emphasis on the nurturing and homemaking values among women who might have at one time pursued a career."

As the *Life* magazine article revealed, women faced enormous social pressure to conform to traditional gender roles. Many people viewed marriage and child bearing as keys to a stable society and a bulwark against communism. Federal Bureau of Investigation (FBI) director J. Edgar Hoover lectured that marriage and motherhood would help in the fight against "the twin enemies of freedom—crime and Communism." Popular culture often reinforced the message as Hollywood screenwriters, still smarting from their confrontation with Red-hunters, required career women to acknowledge marriage as their top priority. "Marriage is the most important thing in the world," Debbie Reynolds said in *The Tender Trap* (1955). "A woman isn't really a woman until she's been married and had children."

The publication of Dr. Benjamin Spock's best-selling *The Common Sense Book of Baby Care* (1946) placed all the burden of child care on the mother. Children, he argued, needed constant motherly affection; otherwise they languished or would grow up to be juvenile delinquents. For Spock, a woman's place was in the home raising children. "If a mother realizes clearly how vital this kind of care is to a small child," he explained, "it may make it easier for her to decide that the

Life in Suburbia The domestic wife was an important component of the new suburban culture. She kept a tidy home and garden, cooked delicious meals, raised numerous children, all while looking beautiful, fit, and trim. In keeping with these trends, the fitness craze had its beginnings in postwar America. Here, suburban housewives exercise in front of another sign of the times, the television. *(Eve Arnold/Magnum Photos, Inc.)*

extra money she might earn, or the satisfaction she might receive from an outside job, is not so important after all."

Many leading educators discouraged women from seeking a college education. In 1950 the president of Mills College announced that education "frustrated" women. Instead of studying science and math, college women should learn the "theory and preparation of a basque paella, of a well-marinated shish-kebab, lamb kidney sauteed in sherry, an authoritative curry." In keeping with this philosophy, the college instituted a "marriage" major and introduced a course on "volunteerism." The president of Radcliffe College suggested changing the curriculum so that it would not "encourage women to compete with men." This oppressive atmosphere shaped the expectations of female students. "We don't want careers," explained one student. "Our parents expect us to go to college. Everybody goes. But a girl who got serious about anything she studied— like, wanting to go on and do research—would be peculiar, unfeminine. I guess everybody wants to graduate with a diamond ring on the finger. That's the important thing."

However, the decade's celebration of the American housewife failed to account for important changes in women's lives. Between 1940 and 1960 the number of women in the workforce doubled, rising from 15 percent to 30 percent. Even more striking, the proportion of married working mothers jumped 400 percent. By 1952, 2 million more women were at work than during World War II. Many of the women who joined the workforce were middle-aged wives looking for a second income to help their suburban families pay for their new consumer goods. By the early 1960s one worker in three was a woman and three of five women workers were married.

The expanding economy provided jobs for women, especially in the growing service sector. While millions of women went to work every day, they found themselves segregated in low-paying positions. The job ads that appeared in newspapers were divided by sex. On one side of the page were jobs for men; on the opposite page were ads that funneled women into "pink-collar work." In 1959 a white man with a high-school education earned an average of $4,429, while a white woman earned only $3,458. A greater portion of women's jobs than men's jobs were not covered by minimum wage or social security. In 1960 women represented only 3.5 percent of lawyers and 6.1 percent of physicians. But they made up 97 percent of nurses and 85 percent of librarians. Of high-school principals, 90 percent were male, while of elementary-school teachers, 85 percent were female.

Evidence of changing sexual behavior challenged the celebration of traditional family life. In 1947 Alfred Kinsey, an Indiana University zoologist best known as the world's foremost authority on the North American gall wasp, decided to abandon his work on insects and turn his attention to human sexuality. He became so obsessed by the topic that his wife remarked, "I hardly see him at night since he took up sex." His studies on *Sexual Behavior in the Human Male* (1948) and *Sexual Behavior in the Human Female* (1953) rocketed to the top of the best-seller list, where they stayed for twenty-seven weeks. The statistics shocked the nation: 86 percent of men said they had engaged in premarital sex, 50 percent said they had committed adultery before turning forty, 37 percent reported at least one episode of homosexual sex, and 17 percent who had grown up on farms claimed to have had sex with animals.

The Kinsey report exposed the contradiction between private behavior and public morality. Perhaps the most surprising revelation was about the promiscuity of women. Each generation of women, he reported, was more sexually active than the last. In addition, many women were engaging in sexual acts that previous generations of Americans had deemed immoral and illegal. Sexual activity previously labeled "deviant" or "immoral" seemed rampant among the very people who outwardly condemned it. All this was too much for many traditionalists. *Life* magazine condemned Kinsey's results as an "assault on the family as a basic unit of society, a negation of moral law, and a celebration of licentiousness."

The gap between the image and reality was the central focus of Betty Freidan's groundbreaking book, *The Feminine Mystique* (1963). Friedan dissected the pervasive myth of suburban women's domestic fulfillment that she called "the feminine mystique." She traced the evolution of the American woman from the independent, career-minded New Woman of the 1920s and 30s into the vacuous, overburdened housewife of the 1950s. As she pointed out, for a typical woman of the 1950s, life centered exclusively on chores and children. Experts and popular culture claimed that the new suburban life represented the fulfillment of every woman's dream, but Friedan found most of the women she talked to were unhappy and unfulfilled. As a Nebraska housewife with a Ph.D. in anthropology told her, "I wash the dishes, rush the older children off to school, dash out in the yard to cultivate the chrysanthemums, run back in to make a phone call about a committee meeting, help the youngest child build a blockhouse, spend fifteen minutes skimming the newspapers so I can be well-informed, then scamper down to the washing machines where my thrice-weekly laundry includes enough clothes to keep a primitive village going for an entire year. By noon I'm ready for a padded cell."

PRIMARY SOURCE

6.1 | *The Problem That Has No Name*
BETTY FRIEDAN

A political activist and supporter of working-class rights in the 1940s and early 1950s, Betty Friedan faced the pressure to live up to the middle-class image of the suburban wife and mother. Though she continued to write articles for women's magazines in the 1950s, Friedan increasingly felt trapped by the lack of alternatives for women. In 1957, she began interviewing other women who graduated with her from Smith College in preparation for their fifteenth reunion. Most of these women seemed to possess all the material needs that society deemed important—nice suburban homes, the latest home appliances, healthy children. But they were also unhappy. Friedan later wrote about this unhappiness, which she called "the problem that has no name," in her groundbreaking book, *The Feminine Mystique* (1963). Friedan challenged women to confront the problem and change their lives. "We can no longer ignore the voice within women that says: 'I want something more than my husband and my children and my home.'" The book, which sold more than 3 million copies, had finally broken the silence and forced Americans to deal with the reality of women's lives. The following is an excerpt from Chapter 1, "The Problem That Has No Name."

The problem lay buried, unspoken, for many years in the minds of American women. It was a strange stirring, a sense of dissatisfaction, a yearning that women suffered in the middle of the twentieth century in the United States. Each suburban wife struggled with it alone. As she made the beds, shopped
5   for groceries, matched slipcover material, ate peanut butter sandwiches with her children, chauffeured Cub Scouts and Brownies, lay beside her husband at night, she was afraid to ask even of herself the silent question—" Is this all?"

For over fifteen years there was no word of this yearning in the millions of
10 words written about women, for women, in all the columns, books and articles by experts telling women their role was to seek fulfillment as wives and mothers. . . . They learned that truly feminine women do not want careers, higher education, political rights—the independence and the opportunities that the old-fashioned feminists fought for. . . .

15 If a woman had a problem in the 1950s and 1960s she knew that something must be wrong with her marriage, or with herself. Other women were satisfied with their lives, she thought. What kind of a woman was she if she did not feel this mysterious fulfillment waxing the kitchen floor? She was so ashamed to admit her dissatisfaction that she never knew how many other women shared
20 it. . . .

When a woman went to a psychiatrist for help, as many women did, she would say, "I'm so ashamed," or "I must be hopelessly neurotic." . . . Most women with this problem did not go to see a psychoanalyst, however. "There's nothing wrong really," they kept telling themselves. "There isn't any problem."

25 Gradually I came to realize that the problem that has no name was shared by countless women in America. As a magazine writer I often interviewed women about problems with their children, or their marriages, or their houses, or their communities. But after a while I began to recognize the telltale signs of this other problem. . . . Sometimes I sensed the problem, not as a reporter, but as a subur-
30 ban housewife, for during this time I was also bringing up my own three children in Rockland County, New York. . . . The groping words I heard from other

women, on quiet afternoons when children were at school or on quiet evenings when husbands worked late, I think I understood first as a woman long before I understood their larger social and psychological implications.

Source: Betty Friedan, *The Feminine Mystique.* Copyright © 1983, 1974, 1973, 1963 by Betty Friedan. Used by permission of W. W. Norton & Company, Inc. ■ ■ ■

Men were also challenging traditional gender roles. During the 1950s, popular culture and pop psychologists idealized the "family man" who married early and focused his energy on providing for his stay-at-home wife and their growing family. Hugh Hefner challenged this notion of manhood with the founding of *Playboy* magazine in 1953. While the pictures of nude women on the cover attracted the most attention, the real subversion took place inside the magazine where the life-style articles presented an image of masculine identity based on high living and sexual pleasure unburdened by family obligations. The new "man" who read *Playboy* rejected the suburban house for a bachelor apartment and developed an identity separate from the obligations of marriage and family life.

The Struggle for Black Equality

Nowhere was the contradiction between ideals and reality more striking than in the lives of African Americans. The South's racially segregated schools formed only one piece in a vast mosaic of institutionalized racism. Wherever one looked in early postwar America, blacks were treated as second-class citizens.

Yet following World War II a combination of forces began undermining the structures of racial segregation in the South. The war had dramatically changed the lives of many blacks, luring millions into armaments plants and labor unions in the North and West. Cold War concerns further eroded ingrained patterns of racism. The reality of racism proved embarrassing to a nation that denounced the Soviets for ignoring human rights and courted newly independent nations in Asia and Africa.

For the previous half-century the NAACP had focused on fulfilling the constitutional promise of civil and political rights for African Americans by doggedly pursuing test cases in the courts. Gradually, the Supreme Court began to chip away at the legal bases of segregation. In 1951 the Reverend Oliver Brown tried to enroll his eight-year-old daughter, Linda, in an all-white elementary school in Topeka. School officials refused to admit her, citing a law in force in Kansas and in sixteen other states requiring black children to attend segregated educational facilities. Instead of walking the four blocks to her neighborhood school, Linda had to board a bus every morning for the 5-mile journey to an all-black school across town. With the help of a small team of skilled black lawyers from Howard University and the NAACP, led by Thurgood Marshall, Reverend Brown took the case to court.

The suit claimed that refusal to admit Linda Brown violated the equal protection clause of the Fourteenth Amendment, which states that "no State . . . shall deprive any person of life, liberty, or property, without due process of law; nor deny to any person within its jurisdiction the equal protection of the laws." The case quietly worked its way up the appeal system and reached the Supreme Court in 1954. The Court overturned the legal justification for one of the principal pillars of white supremacy in a unanimous decision popularly known as *Brown* v. *Board of Education*. The *Brown* decision declared segregation in public schools to be illegal, claiming that "in the field of public education the doctrine of 'separate but equal' has no place." Two days after *Brown* the *Washington Post* declared, "It is not too much to speak of the court's decision as a new birth of freedom." A year later the Supreme Court instructed federal district courts to require local authorities to show "good faith" and to move with "all deliberate speed" toward desegregation of all public schools.

The historic decision triggered massive resistance to ending Jim Crow—the legal segregation of the races that dated back to the 1890s—among state and local politicians in the South. In March 1956 nineteen southern senators and seventy-seven representatives signed a manifesto, composed by Virginia Senator Harry Byrd, which expressed their dissatisfaction with the Court's ruling. This Southern Manifesto bound the signatories to "use all lawful means to bring about a reversal of this decision which is contrary to the Court and to prevent the use of force in its implementation."

PRIMARY SOURCE

6.2 | *The Southern Manifesto, 1956*

A year after the *Brown* decision, the Supreme Court ordered public schools desegregated with "all deliberate speed," thereby angering many southern whites, who vowed to fight back. Unable to obtain enough votes for a congressional resolution denouncing *Brown,* Virginia Senator Harry Byrd composed the Southern Manifesto in March 1956 to express his dissatisfaction with the Court's ruling. Nineteen southern senators and seventy-seven representatives signed the manifesto, encouraging white defiance of desegregation.

W̄e regard the decision of the Supreme Court in the school cases as clear abuse of judicial power. It climaxes a trend in the Federal judiciary undertaking to legislate, in derogation of the authority of Congress, and to encroach upon the reserved rights of the states and the people.

5   The original Constitution does not mention education. Neither does the Fourteenth Amendment nor any other amendment. The debates preceding the

submission of the Fourteenth Amendment clearly show that there was no intent that it should affect the systems of education maintained by the states. . . .

10 When the amendment was adopted in 1868, there were thirty-seven states of the Union. Every one of the twenty-six states that had any substantial racial differences among its people either approved the operation of segregated schools already in existence or subsequently established such schools by action of the same law-making body which considered the Fourteenth Amendment. . . .

15 This unwarranted exercise of power by the court, contrary to the Constitution, is creating chaos and confusion in the states principally affected. It is destroying the amicable relations between the white and negro races that have been created through ninety years of patient effort by the good people of both races. It has planted hatred and suspicion where there has been heretofore friendship and understanding. . . .

20 With the gravest concern for the explosive and dangerous condition created by this decision and inflamed outside meddlers:

We reaffirm our reliance on the Constitution as the fundamental law of the land.

We decry the Supreme Court's encroachments on rights reserved to the states 25 and to the people, contrary to established law and to the Constitution.

We commend the motives of those states which have declared the intention to resist forced integration by any lawful means.

We appeal to the states and people who are not directly affected by these decisions to consider the constitutional principles involved against the time when 30 they too, on issues vital to them, may be the victims of judicial encroachments.

Source: Brown v. Board of Education, 347 U.S. 483 (1954).　■ ■ ■

The first outright defiance of the federal courts occurred in Little Rock, Arkansas. Desegregation of Central High School was scheduled to begin in September 1957, but many whites wished to obstruct the plan. The state's ambitious governor, Orville Faubus, believed that supporting desegregation would mean political suicide. Faubus called out the National Guard to prevent black students from entering Central High. The guardsmen, with bayonets drawn, turned back the nine young African American students who planned to attend Central and thereby sidelined segregation for nearly three weeks until a federal judge ordered the Guard removed.

The students managed to enter the school, but a mob of unruly whites outside pelted and pushed the police who tried to protect the students, forcing the administration to send the nine students home for fear the mob might get into the school. National television cameras recorded the ugly events. President Dwight Eisenhower, who privately deplored the *Brown* decision, responded by sending federal troops to uphold the court order. The president told a southern senator that "failure to act in such a case would be tantamount to acquiescence in anarchy and the dissolution of the union." For the first time since post-Civil War Radical Reconstruction, the federal government demonstrated that it would use military force to protect rights guaranteed to blacks by the Constitution. Troops patrolled the high school for months, but the controversy over desegregation convulsed the city for two more years.

The *Brown* decision and Eisenhower's forceful response in Little Rock offered hope that Washington had finally decided to join the black struggle for civil rights. African Americans, however, were not going to wait for the federal government in their effort to end the daily humiliation of legal segregation. Even before *Brown,* African Americans living in the South had laid the foundation of a powerful social movement that would challenge white supremacy.

The Montgomery Bus Boycott

The image of Emmett Till was fresh on people's minds when on December 1, 1955, a forty-two-year-old civil-rights advocate named Rosa Parks boarded a city bus in Montgomery, Alabama. When asked to give up her seat to a white person as required by Alabama law, Parks refused. "I felt it was just something I had to do," Parks said. Her simple act of courage became a challenge to the edifice of racial injustice in the South. After police arrested Parks for her defiance, black leaders decided to boycott the city bus system. They sought the support of black ministers, the traditional leaders of African American communities, whose churches had for decades served as the community's social, political, and organization center. One of the key organizations supporting the boycott was the Women's Political Council (WPC). Made up of middle-class African American women, the WPC organized a "telephone tree" to inform members of developments and to coordinate activities. The night that Parks was arrested, Jo Ann Robinson, the chair of the WPC, composed and printed more than thirty thousand mimeographed copies of a leaflet pleading with Montgomery's citizens to "please stay off all buses on Monday."

Twenty-six-year-old Martin Luther King Jr., pastor of the Dexter Baptist Church, agreed to head the Montgomery Improvement Association (MIA), created to promote and support the boycott. King had grown up in Atlanta, the son of a prosperous minister of one of the largest Baptist congregations in the country. After graduating from Atlanta's Morehouse College, he attended Crozer Seminary in Pennsylvania and earned his doctorate at Boston University. A brilliant speaker, he could inspire blacks and whites alike with his words. King preached a philosophy of nonviolent resistance that represented a synthesis of the teachings of Jesus and Mahatma Gandhi. His goal was to use the power of love and the tactic of nonviolence—boycotts, strikes, marches, and mass civil disobedience— to combat social evil. "We must meet the forces of hate with the power of love; we must meet physical force with soul force." King planned to use nonviolent confrontations to expose to the nation the viciousness of southern society, and to highlight the compelling moral contrast between peaceful blacks demanding basic American rights and a violent white political leadership determined to deny them those rights.

6.3 | *Montgomery Bus Boycott Inauguration Speech*
MARTIN LUTHER KING JR.

On December 5, 1955, the day Rosa Parks's trial began for her refusal to give her seat to a white man, African Americans in Montgomery boycotted buses to show their support for her efforts. That evening, the Montgomery Improvement Association held their first meeting at Holt Street Baptist Church. President of the Association, Martin Luther King Jr., addressed the crowd of around 7,000 citizens, emphasizing the importance of religion and the power of democracy to end segregation. The crowd then overwhelmingly voted for a continuation of the boycott until the bus companies desegregated their vehicles.

M y friends, we are certainly very happy to see each of you out this evening. We are here this evening for serious business. We are here in a general sense because first and foremost we are American citizens and we are determined to apply our citizenship to the fullness of its meaning. We are here also because of our
5   love for democracy, because of our deep-seated belief that democracy transformed from thin paper to thick action is the greatest form of government on earth. . . .

Just the other day, just last Thursday to be exact, one of the finest citizens in Montgomery—not one of the finest Negro citizens but one of the finest citizens in Montgomery—was taken from a bus and carried to jail and arrested because
10   she refused to get up to give her seat to a white person. . . .

Mrs. Rosa Parks is a fine person. And since it had to happen I'm happy that it happened to a person like Mrs. Parks, for nobody can doubt the boundless outreach of her integrity. Nobody can doubt the height of her character, nobody can doubt the depth of her Christian commitment and devotion to the teachings
15   of Jesus. . . .

And you know, my friends, there comes a time when people get tired of being trampled over by the iron feet of oppression. There comes a time, my friends, when people get tired of being plunged across the abyss of humiliation where they experience the bleakness of nagging despair. There comes a time when peo-
20   ple get tired of being pushed out of the glittering sunlight of life's July, and left standing amid the piercing chill of an alpine November. There comes a time.

We are here, we are here this evening because we're tired now. And I want to say, that we are not here advocating violence. We have never done that. I want it to be known throughout Montgomery and throughout this nation that we are

25 Christian people. We believe in the Christian religion. We believe in the teachings of Jesus. The only weapon that we have in our hands this evening is the
weapon of protest. That's all.

And certainly, certainly, this is the glory of America, with all of its faults. This
is the glory of our democracy. If we were incarcerated behind the iron curtains of
30 a Communistic nation we couldn't do this. If we were dropped in the dungeon of
a totalitarian regime we couldn't do this. But the great glory of American democracy is the right to protest for right. . . .

As we stand and sit here this evening and as we prepare ourselves for what lies
ahead, let us go out with a grim and bold determination that we are going to stick
35 together. We are going to work together. Right here in Montgomery, when the
history books are written in the future, somebody will have to say, "There lived a
race of people, a *black* people, 'fleecy locks and black complexion,' a people who
had the moral courage to stand up for their rights. And thereby they injected a
new meaning into the veins of history and of civilization." And we're gonna do
40 that. God grant that we will do it before it is too late. As we proceed with our
program let us think of these things.

Source: Reprinted by arrangement with the Estate of Martin Luther King Jr., c/o Writers House
as agent for the proprietor, New York, NY Copyright 1969 Martin Luther King Jr., copyright
renewed 1997 Coretta Scott King. ■ ■ ■

To deal with the loss of public transportation, the bus boycotters organized a
massive and complicated system of carpools that involved twenty thousand people every day. Some preferred to walk, as far as 12 miles a day, to underline their
determination and hope. "I'm not walking for myself," said an elderly woman
turning down a ride. "I'm walking for my children and my grandchildren." Another elderly woman, known as Mother Pollard, vowed to King that she would
walk until it was over. "But aren't your feet tired?" he asked. "Yes," she said, "my
feets is tired, but my soul is rested."

In June 1956 a panel of federal judges struck down Montgomery's segregation
ordinances. The state appealed to the Supreme Court, which upheld the lower
court decision a few months later. On December 21 a bus pulled up to a street
corner where King was standing. The white driver greeted him with a smile.
"I believe you are Reverend King." "Yes, I am," King responded. "We are glad to
have you with us this morning," the driver said.

The Montgomery boycott demonstrated that intimidation, which had served
for so long to repress black aspirations, would no longer work. In doing so, the
boycott laid the foundation for the civil-rights struggle of the 1960s. It also established Martin Luther King as a persuasive and articulate spokesman for the
movement. In the past white leaders in the South had served as both judge and
jury, but the news media nationalized the struggle, exposing the South to the
critical eye of public opinion. The boycott forced changes in one institution that
mistreated blacks, but it could not attack the most important problem facing
blacks in the South—segregation.

Montgomery Bus Boycotters   For a year, African Americans in Montgomery refused to ride public buses, instead forming carpools and even walking miles to work each day. These black workers are walking to work instead of riding the bus during the third month of the bus boycott. Their sacrifices reduced the profits on city buses by 65 percent and produced a Supreme Court decision that declared segregation on city buses unconstitutional. *(Time & Life Pictures/Getty Images)*

American Identities

African Americans were not the only minority group challenging the fragile Cold War consensus. During the 1940s and 1950s, the combination of technological innovation and a population explosion in Mexico produced massive new waves of immigrants across America's southern border. When Puerto Rico mechanized its sugarcane production, many workers who lost their jobs migrated to the mainland.

At the same time, the United States recruited millions of Mexican laborers through the Bracero Program. Created to address the agriculture labor shortage during World War II, the program continued for more than two decades. By 1960, Spanish speakers, almost all of them of Mexican origin, made up 12 percent of the population in the Southwest.

Hispanic veterans, inspired by their service in World War II and by the evolving African American freedom struggle, spearheaded their own civil-rights movement. In 1948, when a funeral home in Three Rivers, Texas, refused to conduct a burial service for a Mexican American veteran, local leaders formed the

American GI Forum (AGIF) to protest discrimination. Over the next decade, AGIF led voter-registration drives, filed lawsuits to end discrimination, and helped educate Mexican American veterans about their rights under the GI Bill.

Like AGIF, many of the new Hispanic organizations established after World War II were made up of middle-class leaders who worked to remove the barriers preventing integration into American life. In a series of lawsuits, the League of United Latin American Citizens (LULAC), which had chapters in cities with large Hispanic populations between Texas and California, filed lawsuits to end segregation of Hispanic students in public schools. The courts agreed, banning intentional segregation, but local school officials developed clever ways to avoid the court decisions.

While many government agencies promoted policies that intentionally separated races, Native Americans faced renewed pressure after World War II to abandon their tribal associations and integrate into mainstream society. Leading politicians from both parties stressed the need to terminate Indian tribes' semi-sovereign political status and the practice of self-rule on the reservation. Policymakers believed the move would rid the nation of its enduring "Indian problem" while also allowing Washington to cut funding for Indian tribes. As Utah Senator Arthur Watkins declared, it was time for the federal government to "get out of the Indian business." Some Indians welcomed the initiative, and the possible opportunities it afforded. But they also wanted to maintain their sense of tribal identity.

In 1952, the Bureau of Indian Affairs (BIA) introduced a "voluntary relocation program" to encourage Indians to move from the reservations to cities. The BIA recruited Indians, paid their moving expenses, and promised them housing and jobs in an urban destination of their choice. By 1960, more than 30,000 Indians migrated through the program to begin new lives in places like Chicago, Los Angeles, and Denver. Estimates suggest that over twice that number left of their own accord, without financial support from the Indian Bureau. By the end of the decade, roughly 140,000 Indians, about one-third of the native population, were living in major cities. By 1980, half of all American Indians resided in urban areas.

For many Native people, the harsh realities of urban life, and the failure of the BIA to live up to its end of the bargain, often crushed their hopes of gaining better opportunities in distant cities. As a survival technique, many Native Americans established small, often poor, enclaves that provided resources for job networking and community organizing. Still, most of the job opportunities were low-paying, entry-level positions that were the first cut when business slowed down. "You get placed on the job, and your first job don't work out, where are you?" asked a frustrated Indian. "Several thousand miles from your home and broke." Despite the challenges of the city, many urban Indian migrants learned valuable lessons about how the mainstream American political and legal system worked. Over time they would use that knowledge to protect tribal interests back on the reservation.

Sputnik and the Quest for National Purpose, 1957–1960

As the 1950s drew to a close, many Americans began to question their view of themselves as a prosperous, satisfied, and secure society. The Soviets' successful launch of a satellite to orbit the earth shocked the American public's confidence in Eisenhower's New Look. A combination of other events, at home and abroad, contributed to the sense that America had lost its way. Echoing this conviction, the young senator from Massachusetts, John F. Kennedy, made the issue of national purpose the centerpiece of his 1960 campaign for president.

On October 4, 1957, the Soviet Union launched a 184-pound space satellite called *Sputnik,* or "Little Traveler." On October 13, Sputnik and its rocket were visible over New York. NBC filmed it and aired it that night on television. It was the first time that the air space over the continental United States had been violated. Every three seconds radio operators on the ground picked up the distinctive beeps from the satellite. They were the first sounds ever recorded from space.

One month later, it launched a second satellite carrying a small dog, the first living creature to leave Earth's atmosphere. The Soviets gloated, claiming the achievement demonstrated the superiority of their "socialist society." The Soviet success eroded America's status abroad and raised questions about the competitive capability of American capitalism. A Gallup poll revealed that U.S. prestige dropped in six of seven foreign countries included in the survey.

The Soviet success in space, and its earlier launch of an Intercontinental Ballistic Missile (ICBM), dealt a serious blow to American national pride and created a widespread and unfounded fear of a "missile gap" between the United States and the Soviet Union. Asked by reporters what Americans would find should they ever reach the moon, Edward Teller, father of the hydrogen bomb, replied: "Russians."

Sputnik brought to the surface America's underlying anxiety about atomic power. If the USSR had rockets powerful enough to launch satellites, it could also bombard the United States with nuclear weapons. Newspaper articles, books, and government studies reminded people they were vulnerable to Soviet nuclear bombs. A generation of schoolchildren learned to "duck and cover" in classroom drills for a nuclear attack. A 1959 congressional study concluded that 28 percent of the population likely would be killed by such an attack. Many wealthy Americans responded by building private bomb shelters.

It was not just nuclear-armed missiles that worried Americans. Secret government documents declassified in 2010 showed that government officials worried about the possibility of Soviet spies smuggling small "suitcase" bombs into American cities. An FBI memo from 1953 warned that "a saboteur could easily pose as a Mexican 'wetback' and get into the country without detection, presumably carrying an atomic weapon in his luggage." The government spent millions of dollars to install radiation detectors at airports and seaports to stop nuclear devices being carried into the country.

Many people blamed the educational system for allowing the Soviets to pass America in the development of space-age rockets. To remedy the situation, Congress passed the National Defense Education Act (NDEA) of 1958. The legislation provided loan funds for college students and fellowships for advanced study, and it promised more resources to strengthen the instruction in mathematics, the sciences, and foreign languages at the elementary and secondary school levels.

Concern about Soviet missiles also pushed Congress to accept the statehood applications of Alaska and Hawaii, areas positioned to provide an early warning system for potential Soviet rocket attacks.

Americans also feared the by-products of the nuclear age—in particular, the health consequences of radioactive fallout from bomb tests. The United States exploded 217 nuclear weapons over the Pacific and in Nevada between 1946 and 1962. The Soviet Union conducted 122 tests in the 1950s, Great Britain at least 50. By the mid-1950s Americans were growing increasingly alarmed by radioactive substances turning up in the soil and in food.

The fears of atomic energy found creative outlet in popular culture. *Mad,* a favorite humor magazine among teens, fantasized that after a nuclear war the "Hit Parade" would include songs that lovers would sing as they "walk down moonlit lanes arm in arm in arm." Science fiction writers such as Ray Bradbury, Isaac Asimov, and Arthur C. Clarke penned imaginative novels about space travel, time travel, and the dangers of atomic weapons.

Hollywood produced a series of monster and mutant movies suggesting that nuclear tests had either dislodged prehistoric monsters or created new genetically altered creatures. Though universally panned for their cinematic quality, movies such as *The Beast from 20,000 Fathoms* (1953) played to public concern about life in the nuclear age. In the movie an atomic blast in the Arctic melts an iceberg, releasing a "rhedosaurus" that decides to visit Brooklyn's Coney Island. In *The Day the Earth Stood Still* (1951) a superior race of aliens invades Earth to warn humans of the dangers of nuclear weapons, threatening to destroy the planet if all nations do not abolish atomic weapons. *On the Beach* (1959), perhaps the best science fiction film of the decade, presented a chilling picture of the final days of the human race after a nuclear war. The film ended showing a tattered Salvation Army poster declaring, "THERE IS STILL TIME, BROTHER."

6.4 | *How to Respond to a Nuclear Attack, 1950*

During the height of America's anxiety concerning atomic strikes by the Soviet Union, the federal Civil Defense Agency sought to relieve fears by publishing tips on how to survive a nuclear attack, like this one printed in 1950.

(Continued)

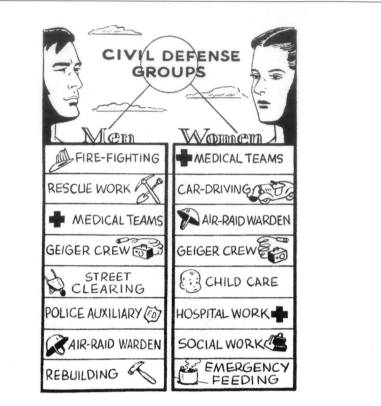

Here are some of the civil defense jobs open to men and women.

SECLUDED 15 ACRE ESTATE

on fair sized lake beyond Luzerne. 25 minutes from Saratoga. Large well furnished and equipped main house. 4-room guest house, large garage, accessory buildings, woods, gardens, boats, fishing, swimming. Good bomb immunity. Attractive summer home or could be converted for resort or institutional purposes. $30,000.

Box H 70, The Wall Street Journal.

Sources: Paul Boyer, *By the Bomb's Early Light: American Thought and Culture at the Dawn of the Atomic Age* (New York: Pantheon Books, 1985), 310–311. Reprinted by permission; Richard Gerstell, *How to Survive an Atomic Bomb* (New York: Bantam, 1950); *Life,* February 27, 1950. Copyright 1950 Life Inc. Reprinted with permission. ■ ■ ■

Blows to American Pride

Sputnik was only the first of a series of blows to Americans' pride and stature at the end of the decade. In May 1960, the Soviets shot down an American U-2 spy plane and its pilot, Gary Powers. Washington initially called the flight a weather-data–gathering mission that had strayed off course, but when the Soviets produced Powers and his espionage equipment, Eisenhower confessed responsibility for the U-2 flight. The incident took place two weeks before a scheduled summit meeting in Paris between Eisenhower and Khrushchev. An angry Khrushchev, who paraded the captured American pilot before the world media, canceled the summit and withdrew an invitation for Eisenhower to visit Moscow.

At home, a persistent recession contributed to the sense of unease. Unemployment, which had held steady at 4 percent from 1955 to 1957, jumped to 8 percent in 1959. Since fewer people were working and paying taxes, the floundering economy produced huge budget deficits.

Potentially the greatest threat to American pride occurred 90 miles off the coast of Florida on the small island of Cuba. On January 1, 1959, a young lawyer turned revolutionary, Fidel Castro, led a successful insurrection against the American-supported dictatorship of Fulgencio Batista. American economic interests expressed concern when Castro began breaking up large cattle ranches and sugar plantations. When the United States threatened to cut off economic aid, Castro responded by declaring his support for communism, signing a trade agreement with the Soviets, and confiscating about $1 billion in U.S. property.

John F. Kennedy and the 1960 Presidential Election

Politically, Democrats planned to capitalize on the growing unease about national purpose. The Republicans, forced by the Twenty-second Amendment—which limited a president to two terms—to seek a new leader, turned to Vice President Richard Nixon to counter the Democratic offensive.

After a tough primary campaign, the Democrats turned to the youthful and attractive John F. Kennedy. The forty-two-year-old senator was the first Catholic to contend for the presidency since Al Smith in 1928. "Jack" Kennedy grew up in a conservative Boston Irish family. After graduating from Harvard he enlisted in the navy during World War II. When a Japanese destroyer rammed his patrol boat, *PT-109*, Kennedy spent hours swimming in shark-infested waters trying to save his crew. He returned from the war a hero, ready to fulfill the ambitions of his father, Joseph P. Kennedy, a wealthy businessman who had served under Roosevelt as ambassador to Great Britain. "It was like being drafted," Kennedy reflected. "My father wanted his eldest son in politics. 'Wanted' isn't the right word. He demanded it."

The political journey began in 1946 when Kennedy won a congressional seat. He served three terms in the House before winning election to the Senate in 1954. Six years later voters reelected him to the Senate by the widest popular margin in Massachusetts history.

Kennedy attracted considerable media attention. With the help of his talented group of advisers, he carefully cultivated the image of a youthful, robust leader, hero of *PT-109* and the brilliant author of the Pulitzer Prize–winning book *Profiles in Courage* (1956). In later years, historians would discover that Kennedy had manufactured much of the image. In reality, he suffered from various illnesses, including Addison's disease, which required regular injections of cortisone. Many liberals also complained that Kennedy's failure to vote with other Democrats to censure Joseph McCarthy revealed that he was long on profile and short on courage.

Whatever his shortcomings, Kennedy possessed considerable political skill and broad popular appeal. He revealed his shrewd political instincts at the 1960 Democratic convention. Realizing he needed a running mate who could provide regional balance and help diminish criticism of his religion, Kennedy asked Texas senator Lyndon Johnson to join the ticket.

Few substantive differences separated Kennedy and Nixon. Kennedy, however, understood better than Nixon the public's desire for dynamic leadership. Throughout the campaign he struck the right tone with his calls for positive leadership, public sacrifice, and a bold effort to "get America moving again."

Despite Kennedy's appeal, the election remained close. Nixon skillfully played to public concern about Kennedy's inexperience, especially in foreign affairs. Most of all, many Americans were reluctant to vote for a Catholic for president.

The turning point in the campaign came in a series of four televised debates between September 26 and October 24. Kennedy used the debates—the first ever televised face-off between presidential contenders—to demolish the Republican charge that he was inexperienced and badly informed. And he succeeded far better than his opponent in communicating the qualities of boldness, imagination, and poise. The performance energized Kennedy's campaign, and the debates institutionalized television's role as a major force in American politics.

The momentum from the debate carried Kennedy to victory—though just barely. Of the nearly 68,500,000 popular votes cast, Kennedy won 34,226,731 and Nixon 34,108,157. Kennedy's popular majority of two-tenths of 1 percent was the smallest since 1880. His vote in the electoral college was only slightly more convincing, 303 to 219.

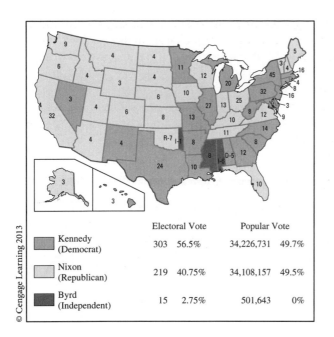

	Electoral Vote		Popular Vote	
Kennedy (Democrat)	303	56.5%	34,226,731	49.7%
Nixon (Republican)	219	40.75%	34,108,157	49.5%
Byrd (Independent)	15	2.75%	501,643	0%

© Cengage Learning 2013

The Election of 1960

The 1960 election was not only the closest presidential race in the twentieth century, it also had the highest voter turnout (63 percent). Yet the discontent of white southerners over the issue of civil rights was evident as all of Mississippi's delegates and some of Alabama's rejected both parties and voted for prosegregationist Senator Harry Byrd of Virginia.

Kennedy's victory signaled a desire for change, but the narrowness of his triumph reflected the caution with which Americans approached the challenges of the new decade. During the campaign, Kennedy managed to convey a message of change and continuity. The tension between American ideals and social realities, which sharpened during the decade, foreshadowed the difficult balancing act that would confront the new president in the next decade.

SELECTED READINGS

■ Michael Harrington's *The Other America* (1962) is still a classic exposé of the 1950s have-nots. Thomas Sugrue's *The Origins of the Urban Crisis* (1996) focuses on how blacks were denied houses in the suburbs and confined to inner-city Detroit. Nicholas Lemann covers the postwar black migration in *The Promised Land* (1991). James T. Patterson's *America's Struggle Against Poverty* (1981) provides a sweeping survey of the American underclass. Rodolfo Acuna's *Occupied America* (4th ed., 2000) has useful material on Hispanic poverty in the 1950s. Donald Fixico's *The Urban Indian Experience in America* (2000) provides a general overview of Indian urbanization. For two case studies see: James LaGrand's *Indian Metropolis* (2002), which examines Indian migration to Chicago, and Coll Thrush's *Native Seattle* (2007).

■ Glenna Matthews's *Just a Housewife* (1987) explores the world of 1950s homemakers, while Wini Brienes, in *Young, White, and Miserable* (1992), analyzes the conflicting sentiments of their daughters. Susan Strasser's *Never Done* (1982) paints a bleak picture of the demands placed on housewives.

The essays in Joanne Meyerwitz's *Not June Cleaver* (1994) examine women who did not fit the domestic stereotype. The unrealistic image of the ideal family is the theme of Stephanie Coontz's *The Way We Never Were* (1992). The complexities and nontraditional images of the Cold War family structure are revealed in *To Have and to Hold* (2000) by Jessica Weiss. K.A. Cuordileone examines changing male identities in *Manhood and American Political Culture.* (2005). Elizabeth Fratterrigo examines the impact of Hugh Heffner in *Playboy and the Making of the Good Life in Modern America* (2009).

▌ Harvard Sitkoff's *The Struggle for Black Equality* (2008) stands as the best one-volume survey of the movement. Also valuable is Robert Weisbrot's readable *Freedom Bound* (1989). Editor Stewart Burns provides a well-documented account of the bus boycott in Montgomery in *Daybreak of Freedom* (1997). The death of Emmitt Till and the subsequent trial and protest are the focus of Stephen Whitfield's *A Death in the Delta* (1991). Martin Luther King Jr.'s role in the making of the movement is the focus of the first volume of Taylor Branch's brilliant trilogy, *Parting the Waters* (1989). Robert F. Burk evaluates Eisenhower's performance on race issues in *The Eisenhower Administration and Black Civil Rights* (1984).

▌ W.J. Rorbaugh provides the most up-to-date analysis of the 1960 election in *The Real Making of the President* (2009). Paul Dickson highlights the impact of the Soviet successful satellite launch in *Sputnik* (2011). David Snead analyzes the impact of the Gaither Report on the acceleration of the arms race in *The Gaither Committee, Eisenhower, and the Cold War* (1999). Thomas Paterson's *Contesting Castro* (1994) examines U.S.-Cuban relations during Castro's uprising and successful revolution. The U-2 spy plane incident is related in Michael Beschloss's *Mayday* (1986). The heightened awareness of the destructive force of nuclear weapons and its impact on popular culture is analyzed in Margot Henriksen's *Dr. Strangelove's America* (1997). Fred Kaplan outlines the challenges the nation confronted at the end of the decade in *1959: The Year That Everything Changed* (2009).

7 The Kennedy Presidency, 1961–1963

*I*n November 1963, President John F. Kennedy began laying the foundation for his 1964 reelection campaign by visiting the key state of Texas. Shortly after noon on the twenty-second his entourage arrived at Dallas's Love Field airport. Kennedy, handsomely attired in a gray suit and pin-striped shirt, exited the plane with his wife, Jacqueline, who was wearing a strawberry-pink wool outfit and matching pillbox hat and cradling a bouquet of red roses. After shaking a few hands, the president, the first lady, and Texas Governor John Connally and his wife, Nellie, hopped into the back of their open-top Lincoln limousine. Since it was a bright autumn day, Kennedy chose not to use the bulletproof bubble top.

Friendly crowds greeted the president's motorcade—eighteen cars and three buses—as it traveled along a 10-mile route through downtown Dallas. The crowds became denser when the cars turned onto Main Street and moved westward toward Dealey Plaza. People were everywhere, waving from office buildings, filling the streets, cheering. At the corner of Main and Houston the motorcade turned right and headed north. As it approached Elm Street, Nellie Connally said, "Mr. President, you can't say Dallas doesn't love you." Kennedy answered, "That's obvious." The time was 12:30 PM.

Suddenly, the sound of gunfire ripped through the air. "Oh no!" Jacqueline Kennedy cried. The president clutched his neck with both hands and slumped down in his seat. One bullet had passed through his throat; another had shattered his skull. Governor Connally had also been hit, seriously but not mortally. The driver pulled the limousine out of the motorcade line and sped to Parkland Hospital.

The president's limousine arrived at the hospital's emergency entrance at 12:36 PM. A Secret Service agent lifted Kennedy from his wife's arms, placed him on a stretcher, and rushed him into Trauma Room 1. Doctors were shocked by the extent of his wounds. "I looked at the President's head," recalled one physician. "A considerable portion of the skull, of the brain, was gone. It looked like a wound we just could not salvage." As a grieving Jacqueline Kennedy looked on, doctors worked feverishly to revive her husband. Their efforts were in vain. The president was pronounced dead at 1:00 PM.

Secret Service agents placed the slain president's body in a casket and loaded it onto the presidential plane for the trip back to Washington. In the central compartment of the plane Judge Sarah T. Hughes of the Northern District of Texas administered the oath of office to Lyndon Johnson. A stunned and blood-soaked Jackie Kennedy stood to the left of the new president. Within hours of the assassination Dallas police arrested Lee Harvey Oswald and charged him with assassinating the president of the United States. Two days later Jack Ruby, a Dallas nightclub owner, shot and killed Oswald as police were transferring him to another prison.

For a generation of Americans Kennedy's assassination served as a symbolic marker separating a confident age of consensus from the period of social conflict that followed. The president's death may have been the most traumatic, but it was only one of a series of shocks that challenged the pervasive optimism of the consumer society. By the summer of 1963 Kennedy was questioning some of the assumptions of vital-center liberalism. The possibility of nuclear war, brought home in dramatic fashion by the Cuban missile crisis, led to a softening of Cold War attitudes and a new emphasis on cooperation. More important, the confrontation between the black freedom struggle and the intransigence of southern whites threatened to expose the gap between expectations and social realities and to undermine the fragile vital-center consensus. The president's tragic death in November 1963 cut short his evolution and left future generations asking, What if Kennedy had lived?

JFK and the New Frontier

At the age of forty-three John F. Kennedy was the youngest man ever elected president and the first American president born in the twentieth century. Kennedy's inaugural address, delivered on a cloudless and cold January day in 1961, captivated the nation's imagination and captured the hope and expectations of the decade. His vigor and youth stood in sharp contrast with the staid and stodgy Eisenhower style. Calling for "a struggle against the common enemies of man: tyranny, poverty, disease, and war," he promised a "New Frontier" of opportunity and challenge.

Kennedy surrounded himself with bright young men who shared his faith in activist government. Among "the best and the brightest" were McGeorge Bundy, a forty-one-year-old former Harvard dean who became Kennedy's chief foreign-relations counselor. As secretary of defense Kennedy chose Robert McNamara, a

The King and Queen of Camelot   The Kennedys captivated the American people with their style and elegance, as evidenced in this picture of the couple leaving a performance at Ford's Theater. A week after her husband's death, Jackie spoke to *Life* journalist Theodore H. White about one of Kennedy's favorite songs from the musical about the mythical King Arthur called *Camelot*. The song included the line "Don't let it be forgot that for one brief shining moment there was Camelot." The term *Camelot* became synonymous with the glamour of the Kennedy administration. *(National Archives)*

past president of Ford Motor Company with a passion for systems analysis and organizational management. To head the State Department, Kennedy chose Dean Rusk, a Rhodes scholar and former diplomat. The most controversial choice was Robert Kennedy, the president's brother, as attorney general. Critics complained about his lack of legal experience, but the president trusted his brother's shrewd political instincts, clear judgment, and firm support.

The liberals who surrounded Kennedy shared the vital center belief that America had entered an age of consensus. Building on the ideas developed by liberal intellectuals during the 1940s and 1950s, they argued that economic growth, when combined with prudent government social programs, would provide every American with a minimum standard of living and boundless opportunity for success. Prosperity offered the added benefit of rendering obsolete ideological conflict and social struggle. "Politics," Kennedy said in 1962, was to avoid "basic clashes of philosophy and ideology" and be directed to "ways and means of achieving goals." Proponents of consensus believed that international communism presented the greatest threat to American institutions and values. "The enemy," Kennedy declared with typical flourish, "is the Communist system itself—implacable, insatiable, increasing in its drive for world domination." Convinced that Dwight Eisenhower had failed to fight the Cold War with sufficient vigor, Kennedy moved to increase military pressure on the Soviet Union.

Acting on the assumptions of the consensus, the new president focused much of his energy at home on revitalizing a stagnant economy. During the last two years of the Eisenhower administration, economic growth had slowed to about 2 percent and unemployment had started creeping upward. At Kennedy's request, Congress extended unemployment benefits, raised the minimum wage, broadened social security benefits, increased the defense budget by almost 20 percent, and approved over $4 billion in long-term spending on federally financed housing. In 1962, Congress passed the Revenue Act of 1962, which granted $1 billion in tax breaks to businesses.

By 1963 a brief economic downturn convinced Kennedy that he needed to take bolder action. In January the president proposed a tax reduction of $13.5 billion that he hoped would stimulate consumer spending, create new jobs, and generate economic growth. His support of a tax cut revealed Kennedy's willingness to experiment with unconventional ideas. Many liberals, who wanted higher government spending, not more tax cuts, opposed the plan. Conservatives blustered at the idea of intentionally running a budget deficit. Ignoring criticisms from the Left and the Right, Kennedy submitted his proposal to Congress, claiming that "the unrealistically heavy drag of federal income taxes on private purchasing power was the largest single barrier to full employment."

Kennedy gave tepid support to efforts to address gender inequities in the workplace. The president appointed Esther Peterson to head the Women's Bureau, a division of the U.S. Labor Bureau. Peterson used her position to mobilize a coalition of women and labor organizations to pressure the president to create a special commission to explore the rights of women. In 1961 Kennedy responded by issuing an executive order establishing the President's Commission on the Status of Women, which was chaired by former First Lady Eleanor Roosevelt. Kennedy had little personal interest in the issue of women's rights, and he viewed the commission as a way of rewarding Roosevelt for her support during the 1960 presidential campaign. The commission, however, took its responsibilities seriously. Its final report, presented in October 1963, documented the discrimination that women faced in the workplace and helped legitimize public debate about the role of women in American society. Within a year of its publication the national commission spawned dozens of state commissions. By 1967 all fifty states boasted one.

On many other issues, however, Kennedy ran into resistance from Congress. His narrow victory had denied him a clear mandate. He also presided over a divided party. Democrats controlled Congress, but conservative southern Democrats who were unsympathetic to Kennedy's liberal proposals controlled key congressional committees.

The result was often legislative stalemate. Congress enacted only seven of twenty-three bills that the president submitted in his early months in office. Among the bills defeated were an ambitious health care plan for the elderly and a proposal for federal aid to education. But Kennedy shares part of the blame. He showed little interest either in domestic issues or in the political brokering necessary to court Congress. "Foreign affairs is the only important issue for a President to handle, isn't it?" he once remarked. "I mean, who gives a shit if the minimum wage is $1.15 or $1.25, compared to something like Cuba."

Despite his limited legislative success, Kennedy remained personally very popular. JFK's youth and charm suited him to the new medium of television. Kennedy was the first president to allow live broadcast of his press conferences. By May 1961, nearly 75 percent of the public had seen one, and the vast majority—over 91 percent—gave him high marks for his performance. With the help of a media-conscious staff, the administration produced a constant flow of captivating Kennedy images. His sophisticated and glamorous wife, Jacqueline, and two handsome children, Caroline and John, added to the Kennedy mystique.

JFK and Civil Rights

Civil rights confronted Kennedy with the most important test of his domestic policy. Late in the afternoon on Monday, February 1, 1960, four well-dressed black students sat down at a segregated lunch counter at a Woolworth's department store in Greensboro, North Carolina, and ordered a cup of coffee. "I'm sorry," the waitress said, "we don't serve you here."

The next day twenty-seven black students occupied the Woolworth's lunch counter; on Wednesday, sixty-three. By Friday more than three hundred protesters jammed the store and the nearby Kress's five-and-dime. As news of the sit-ins reached other cities, the protest spread "like a fever." By the end of 1960 more than seventy thousand people in over 150 southern cities and towns had participated in the protests. "I guess everybody was pretty well fed up at the same time," observed a Greensboro activist. Lunch counters were the most popular focus of action, but protesters also organized "wade-ins" at segregated pools and beaches, "kneel-ins" at churches, "read-ins" at public libraries, and "bowl-ins" at recreational areas.

The sit-in movement represented an important change in the strategy of civil-rights protesters. It revealed the growing frustration of many younger blacks who were impatient with the slow pace of change and convinced that more aggressive tactics could force the government to take bolder action to redress existing wrongs. In April 1960 these younger, more militant protestors formed the Student Nonviolent Coordinating Committee (SNCC). The sit-ins also underscored the decentralized, grass-roots approach of the civil-rights movement. The success of national figures such as Martin Luther King Jr. rested on a foundation forged by the courage and commitment of ordinary "local people" such as Fannie Lou Hamer, Robert Moses, Amelia Boynton, and Fred Shuttlesworth.

In 1961 members of the Congress of Racial Equality (CORE) decided to challenge another aspect of racial segregation. By 1960 the Supreme Court had barred racial segregation in bus and train stations, airport terminals, and other facilities related to interstate transit. But southerners widely ignored these decisions. In May 1961, seven black and six white "freedom riders" left Washington on two buses headed for Alabama and Mississippi. "Our intention," declared CORE national director James Farmer, "was to provoke the southern authorities into arresting us and thereby prod the Justice Department into enforcing the law of the land."

As the vehicles moved into the Deep South, white racists mobilized. At stops along the way the Freedom Riders were assaulted by gangs of thugs brandishing baseball bats, lead pipes, and bicycle chains. A white mob in Birmingham, Alabama, beat the riders so badly that an informant for the Federal Bureau of Investigation (FBI) reported that he "couldn't see their faces through the blood." President Kennedy, fearful that the violence would undermine American prestige abroad, negotiated a compromise with southern authorities: if local officials would guarantee the safety of the riders, the federal government would not protest their arrest. During the next few months over three hundred Freedom Riders were arrested. In September 1961, after hundreds of Freedom Riders had risked their lives, the Interstate Commerce Commission enforced the ban against segregation in interstate terminals.

Ole Miss

The president also tried to negotiate a settlement when James Meredith, a twenty-eight-year-old black Air Force veteran, attempted to register at the all-white University of Mississippi. Kennedy believed that he had worked out a deal with the state's segregationist governor Ross Barnett that would guarantee Meredith's safety. But Barnett double-crossed Kennedy. The presence of 500 federal marshals who accompanied Meredith to campus failed to intimidate Barnett and his supporters. On September 30 a white mob attacked the federal marshals, killing 2 and injuring 375. Outraged by the violence, the president ordered 30,000 regular army troops and federalized national guardsmen to Oxford to restore order. The massive show of force worked: Barnett backed down, and Meredith enrolled.

President Kennedy nevertheless moved cautiously on the issue of civil rights. Despite the rising tide of protest, the public outside the South remained largely indifferent to the black struggle, and powerful southern Democratic congressmen fiercely opposed the demands to end segregation. Kennedy feared that pushing too hard would alienate the South, risk his domestic agenda, and siphon off votes he needed for reelection in 1964. The president also worried that social unrest at home would diminish U.S. prestige in the world and undermine his negotiating position with the Soviets. During the Freedom Riders campaign Robert Kennedy pleaded for a cooling-off period, claiming the need for national unity at a critical stage in the Cold War. One civil-rights leader responded that blacks "have been cooling off for 150 years. If we cool off any more, we'll be in a deep freeze."

Letter from a Birmingham Jail

In March 1963 the civil-rights struggle focused on Birmingham, Alabama, perhaps the most segregated city in the South. White terrorists had blown up so many buildings there that some called the town "Bombingham." King's immediate focus was on ending discrimination at the city's department stores and lunch counters, but his larger goal was to send a strong signal across the South that racial intolerance was no longer acceptable. "As Birmingham goes, so goes the South," King declared.

When King and fifty other protest marchers violated a state court injunction against protest marches, they were promptly arrested and thrown into jail. He spent his week behind bars responding to criticism from white Alabama clergy that his tactics were too militant, asking him to cancel his "unwise and untimely" demonstrations. King used a smuggled yellow, legal-sized pad to produce his powerful argument for civil disobedience, "Letter from Birmingham Jail." "I submit," he wrote, "that an individual who breaks a law that conscience tells him is unjust, and who willingly accepts the penalty of imprisonment in order to arouse the conscience of the community over its injustice, is in reality expressing the highest respect for law."

King's passionate defense of nonviolence energized the Birmingham movement. In May, after his release from jail, King organized a peaceful march to City Hall. In response, the police commissioner, Eugene ("just call

Children's Crusade in Birmingham, Alabama   Following in their parents' footsteps, the black children of Birmingham staged marches through the city in early May, carrying signs denouncing segregation. Birmingham Police Chief Eugene "Bull" Connor responded by calling out the Fire Department, which turned fire hoses on the children to disperse them, and by ordering his officers to use police dogs to attack the peaceful protestors. Police arrested close to nine hundred children during the demonstrations. Photographs and video of the events shocked the nation, increasingly aware of the violence white southerners were willing to use, even on children, to prevent integration. (© *Charles Moore/StockPhoto.com*)

me 'Bull' ") Connor, and his officers set upon the marchers with dogs, clubs, and fire hoses. "Let those people come to the corner, Sergeant," shouted Connor to a group of whites gathered to watch the spectacle. "I want 'em to see the dogs work. Look at those niggers run." Television coverage of the clubbings aroused the indignation of the nation and turned Connor's victims into martyrs. Eventually, the business community, stung by the national publicity and a black boycott, broke with the city government and agreed to most of King's demands.

A Moral Issue

In June 1963, the stage shifted to Montgomery, where Governor George Wallace planned to fulfill his campaign promise to "stand in the schoolhouse door" if the courts ordered the integration of his alma mater, the University of Alabama.

For weeks the Kennedy brothers tried negotiating with Wallace, and a federal judge warned him against defying a court order demanding that the students be accepted. On the morning of June 11, under such a court order, two black students arrived to register at the Huntsville branch of the state university. With television cameras recording the drama, Wallace stood in the doorway, where a deputy attorney general confronted him. Having made his point, Wallace made a brief speech for the television cameras and then allowed the students to register.

Wallace's theatrical defiance convinced Kennedy that it was no longer possible to negotiate the issue of civil rights. That evening Kennedy delivered one of the most eloquent, moving, and important speeches of his presidency. For the first time he referred to civil rights as a moral issue, one that was, he said, "as old as the scriptures and as clear as the American constitution." The confrontations between blacks demanding civil rights and local white leaders insisting on preserving the status quo underscored the postwar paradox. Kennedy now realized that the liberal promise to provide equal opportunity to all citizens could not be accomplished within the framework of consensus. Economic growth and promises of gradual reform failed to satisfy African American expectations of a better life. The growing militancy of the movement exposed the gap between liberal promises and social realities and forced Kennedy to make a difficult choice. Eight days after his speech Kennedy asked Congress for laws to support voting rights, to provide assistance to school districts that were desegregating, to ban segregation of public facilities, and to empower the attorney general to initiate proceedings against the segregation of schools.

To build support for the legislation and to appeal to the conscience of the nation, black leaders organized a march on Washington in August 1963. Polls showed that the vast majority of Americans opposed the proposed march. Some feared the possibility of racial violence, but most white Americans were simply uncomfortable with African American demands. Responding to the public concerns, President Kennedy tried unsuccessfully to convince the organizers to call off the demonstration. City residents fled for the day. Anticipating violence, the Pentagon readied more than 4,000 troops in the event of trouble.

On August 28 more than a quarter million people gathered under a cloudless sky at the Lincoln Memorial for the largest civil-rights demonstration in the nation's history. The high point of the sweltering afternoon came when Martin Luther King took the speakers' podium. "Even though we face the difficulties of today and tomorrow," King intoned in his powerful cadence, "I still have a dream. It is a dream chiefly rooted in the American dream. . . . that my four little children will one day live in a nation where they will not be judged by the color of their skin but by the content of their character." For a brief moment the nation embraced King's vision of interracial brotherhood, but no speech, no matter how moving, was going to tame the pent-up demands of the freedom struggle.

Martin and Malcolm

King's "I Have a Dream" speech captivated the nation, but his was not the only powerful voice speaking on behalf of the African American freedom struggle. At the same time, Malcolm X, a spellbinding preacher and a charismatic leader, was delivering a very different message.

Born in 1925, Malcolm Little had a tragic childhood. After being orphaned at age fourteen, he assumed many different identities—pimp, drug dealer, thief. In 1946, while serving a six-year prison sentence for robbery, Malcolm converted to the Nation of Islam, or Black Muslims. Upon joining, Little abandoned his "slave name" in favor of Malcolm X; the X stood for his lost African name. Dismissing the aspirations of white civil-rights leaders, he said that black nationalists did not want "to integrate into this corrupt society, but to separate from it, to a land of our own, where we can reform ourselves, lift up our moral standards, and try to be godly." While civil-rights leaders called for nonviolent change, Malcolm insisted on a "black revolution." Moderates like King wanted to desegregate; the black revolutionary demanded land, power, and freedom. King preached the Christian philosophy of "love thy enemy," but black nationalists had no love or respect for their oppressor.

King and Malcolm X represented two very different resistance traditions in African American history. As W.E. B. Du Bois noted at the turn of the century, the institutions of slavery and segregation forced African Americans to struggle with a "double-consciousness." "What, after all, am I?" he wrote. "Am I an American or am I a Negro? Can I be both?" Integrationists like King believed that blacks could be both African and American. Nationalists like Malcolm X rejected the American dimension of their identity and emphasized racial solidarity. King's message resonated with northern white liberals and served as an effective weapon in exposing the injustice of legal, or de jure, segregation in the South. Malcolm X tapped into the anger and frustration of African Americans living in the poverty of northern ghettos, where de facto discrimination was based on custom but not always codified into law.

For all of their philosophical differences, the two leaders shared much in common. Both were religious men whose faith shaped their activism. They were both fighting the same enemy, but employing different strategies. "Despite their many differences," observed James Baldwin, "they *needed* each other, *learned* from each other, and *helped* make each other." They understood the value of offering more than one approach to dealing with deeply ingrained racism, and King appreciated that Malcolm's angry rhetoric provided whites with greater motivation to respond to his more modest demands.

They also were moving closer together. In 1963, Malcolm X broke with the Nation of Islam, and after a 1964 African pilgrimage to Mecca, the holy City of Islam, in Saudi Arabia, his ethical position shifted. He embraced multiracial Islam, rejected racism, spoke of the common bond linking humanity, and suggested that blacks build alliances with like-minded whites. But he emphasized the need for blacks to unify themselves before they reached out for help from whites and liberals. His evolution remained incomplete, however. In February 1965, he was gunned down at a Harlem rally, apparently by Black Muslim loyalists. The historian Manning Marable speculates that the police had advance warning of the assassination but did nothing to stop it and then intentionally bungled the investigation, convicting two innocent men and allowing the real gunman to go free.

PRIMARY SOURCE

7.1 | *The Black Revolution*
Malcolm X

On April 8, 1964, Malcolm X spoke to a mostly white audience at Palm Gardens in New York. Focusing on increasingly violent protests by young African Americans, Malcolm X encouraged an international struggle against racism and warned of a potential bloody revolution brewing against white America.

Friends and enemies: Tonight I hope that we can have a little fireside chat with as few sparks as possible being tossed around. Especially because of the very explosive condition that the world is in today. Sometimes, when a person's house is on fire and someone comes in yelling fire, instead of the person who is awak-
5 ened by the yell being thankful, he makes the mistake of charging the one who awakened him with having set the fire. I hope that this little conversation tonight about the black revolution won't cause many of you to accuse us of igniting it when you find it at your doorstep. . . .
  And by the hundreds of thousands today we find our own people have be-
10 come impatient, turning away from your white nationalism, which you call democracy, toward the militant, uncompromising policy of black nationalism. I point out right here that as soon as we announced we were going to start a black nationalist party in this country, we received mail from coast to coast, especially from young people at the college level, the university level, who expressed com-
15 plete sympathy and support and a desire to take an active part in any kind of political action based on black nationalism, designed to correct or eliminate immediately evils that our people have suffered here for 400 years. . . .
  1964 will be America's hottest year; her hottest year yet; a year of much racial violence and much racial bloodshed. But it won't be blood that's going to
20 flow only on one side. The new generation of black people that have grown up in this country during recent years are already forming the opinion, and it's a just opinion, that if there is to be bleeding, it should be reciprocal—bleeding on both sides. . . .

So today, when the black man starts reaching out for what America says are
25 his rights, the black man feels that he is within his rights—when he becomes the
victim of brutality by those who are depriving him of his rights—to do whatever
is necessary to protect himself. An example of this was taking place last night at
this same time in Cleveland, where the police were putting water hoses on our
people there and also throwing tear gas at them—and they met a hail of stones,
30 a hail of rocks, a hail of bricks. A couple of weeks ago in Jacksonville, Florida, a
young teen-age Negro was throwing Molotov cocktails.

Well, Negroes didn't do this ten years ago. But what you should learn from
this is that they are waking up. It was stones yesterday, Molotov cocktails today; it
will be hand grenades tomorrow and whatever else is available the next day. The
35 seriousness of this situation must be faced up to. You should not feel that I am
inciting someone to violence. I'm only warning of a powder-keg situation. You
can take it or leave it. If you take the warning, perhaps you can still save yourself.
But if you ignore it or ridicule it, well, death is already at your doorstep. There
are 22 million African-Americans who are ready to fight for independence right
40 here. When I say fight for independence right here, I don't mean any nonviolent
fight, or turn-the-other-cheek fight. Those days are gone. Those days are over.

If George Washington didn't get independence for this country nonviolently,
and if Patrick Henry didn't come up with a nonviolent statement, and you taught
me to look upon them as patriots and heroes, then it's time for you to realize that
45 I have studied your books well. . . .

So in this country you find two different types of Afro-Americans—the type
who looks upon himself as a minority and you as the majority, because his scope
is limited to the American scene; and then you have the type who looks upon
himself as part of the majority and you as part of a microscopic minority. And
50 this one uses a different approach in trying to struggle for his rights. He doesn't
beg. He doesn't thank you for what you give him, because you are only giving
him what he should have had a hundred years ago. He doesn't think you are doing him any favors. . . .

So this kind of black man is thinking. He can see where every maneuver that
55 America has made, supposedly to solve this problem, has been nothing but political trickery and treachery of the worst order. Today he doesn't have any confidence in these so-called liberals. (I know that all that have come in here tonight
don't call yourselves liberals. Because that's a nasty name today. It represents hypocrisy.) So these two different types of black people exist in the so-called Negro
60 community and they are beginning to wake up and their awakening is producing
a very dangerous situation.

You have whites in the community who express sincerity when they say
they want to help. Well, how can they help? How can a white person help the
black man solve his problem? Number one, you can't solve it for him. You can
65 help him solve it, but you can't solve it for him today. One of the best ways that
you can help him solve it is to let the so-called Negro, who has been involved
in the civil-rights struggle, see that the civil-rights struggle must be expanded
beyond the level of civil rights to human rights. Once it is expanded beyond the
level of civil rights to the level of human rights, it opens the door for all of our

70 brothers and sisters in Africa and Asia, who have their independence, to come
to our rescue. . . .

Source: Malcolm X Speaks. Copyright © 1965, 1989. ■ ■ ■

New Frontiers Abroad

Frustrated by a stubborn Congress and deep divisions over civil rights at home,
Kennedy was freer to express his activist instincts in foreign affairs. Kennedy
and his military advisors believed that Eisenhower had relied too heavily on the
threat of the bomb to deter Soviet aggression. The Soviets, taking advantage of
American vulnerability, moved to expand their influence in the Third World. The
administration believed that by expanding America's conventional capability,
and by developing more tactical nuclear weapons, they could expand the options
available for confronting Soviet aggression. The goal was to come up with new,
more creative and dynamic ways of waging the Cold War. They called their new
strategy "flexible response."

Kennedy's instinctive activism led him into the first foreign policy blunder
of his presidency. As president-elect, Kennedy learned of a secret plan, approved
by Eisenhower in the spring of 1960, for the invasion of Cuba by anti-Castro
refugees.

The goal was to make the invasion appear like a domestic revolt, hoping that
news of the rebellion would lead the Cuban people to join the uprising and overthrow the communist leader. Almost from the beginning, everything that could
possibly go wrong went wrong.

Shortly before midnight on April 17, 1961, over 1,400 CIA-trained Cuban
exiles landed on Cuba's southern coast at Bahia de Cochinos (Bay of Pigs). The
invasion was supposed to be a surprise, but Castro's army was waiting in ambush.
His planes sunk ships carrying essential communications equipment and ammunition while his well-trained army prevented the invaders from establishing a
beachhead. At the last minute, Kennedy called off a planned air strike, fearing it
would expose U.S. involvement in the attack. After three days of intense fighting,
the rebels surrendered.

Instead of inspiring an insurrection, the invasion aroused Cuban nationalist
sentiment, strengthened Castro's control over the nation, and pushed him closer
to the Soviet Union. The United States suffered widespread international condemnation and humiliating loss of prestige in Latin America.

The affair represented a humiliating disaster for the Kennedy administration, but the president, and his brother, remained determined to get rid of
Castro. Within six months, they launched "Operation Mongoose," a secret CIA-
coordinated program to destabilize the Cuban government. Operatives hatched
various plans to humiliate Castro, including placing a special powder in his shoes

that would make his "magical" beard fall out, and pumping LSD into his radio booth to make him sound crazy on the air. There were also more sinister plots to assassinate him. Among the plans: providing Castro with poisoned cigars and harpooning him while he went snorkeling at a resort.

PRIMARY SOURCE

7.2 | *Kennedy Deals with the Bay of Pigs Fiasco*

On April 20, 1961, the day after the failed Bay of Pigs mission, Undersecretary of State Chester Bowles attended a somber cabinet meeting and recorded how members of the administration, including the president, dealt with the defeat. His notes provide a unique window into how the Kennedy White House handled the news.

I attended the Cabinet meeting in Rusk's absence and it was about as grim as any meeting I can remember in all my experience in government, which is saying a good deal.

The President was really quite shattered, and understandably so. Almost
5 without exception, his public career had been a long series of successes, without any noteworthy setbacks. Those disappointments which had come his way, such as his failure to get the nomination for Vice President in 1956 were clearly attributable to religion.

Here for the first time he faced a situation where his judgment had been mis-
10 taken, in spite of the fact that week after week of conferences had taken place before he gave the green light.

It was not a pleasant experience. Reactions around the table were almost savage, as everyone appeared to be jumping on everyone else. The only really coherent statement was by Arthur Goldberg, who said that while it was doubtful that the ex-
15 pedition was wise in the first place, the Administration should not have undertaken it unless it was prepared to see it through with United States troops if necessary.

At least his remarks had an inherent logic to them, although I could not agree under any circumstances to sending troops into Cuba—violating every treaty obligation we have.
20 The most angry response of all came from Bob Kennedy and also, strangely enough, from Dave Bell, who I had always assumed was a very reasonable individual.

The discussion simply rambled in circles with no real coherent thought. Finally after three-quarters of an hour the President got up and walked toward his
25 office. I was so distressed at what I felt was a dangerous mood that I walked after him, stopped him, and told him I would like an opportunity to come into his office and talk the whole thing out.

Lyndon Johnson, Bob McNamara, and Bob Kennedy joined us. Bobby
30 continued his tough, savage comments, most of them directed against the Department of State for reasons which are difficult for me to understand.

When I took exception to some of the more extreme things he said by suggesting that the way to get out of our present jam was not to simply double up on
everything we had done, he turned on me savagely.

35 What worries me is that two of the most powerful people in this
Administration—Lyndon Johnson and Bob Kennedy—have no experience in
foreign affairs, and they both realize that this is the central question of this period and are determined to be experts at it.

The problems of foreign affairs are complex, involving politics, econom-
40 ics and social questions that require both understanding of history and various
world cultures.

When a newcomer enters the field and finds himself confronted by the
nuances of international questions, he becomes an easy target for the military-
CIA-paramilitary type answers which are often in specific logistical terms which
45 can be added, subtracted, multiplied, or divided.

This kind of thinking was almost dominant in the conference and I found it
most alarming. The President appeared the most calm, yet it was clear to see that
he had been suffering an acute shock and it was an open question in my mind as
to what his reaction would be.

50 All through the meeting which took place in the President's office and which
lasted almost a half hour, there was an almost frantic reaction for an action program which people would grab onto.

Source: U.S. Department of State, *Foreign Relations of the United States,* 1961–63, Volume X,
Cuba, 1961–62. ■ ■ ■

The Berlin Wall

West Berlin, buried deep in the Soviet-controlled part of East Germany, remained a flash point between the two nations. In June 1961, Kennedy traveled to Vienna to meet with Khrushchev. The Soviet leader blustered about his
willingness to go to war over Berlin. The immediate problem was that many
East Germans were defecting to the West. Between 1949 and 1961, almost
2.7 million East Germans used West Berlin to escape Soviet-controlled East
Germany. The rate of defections accelerated through the summer of 1961,
threatening the viability of the East German state. Khrushchev felt he needed
to act—and fast.

Before dawn on August 13, 1961, the Soviets responded by starting construction of a wall separating East and West Berlin. The wall not only stopped the
flow of people, it separated families and made West Berlin a prison inside Soviet-
controlled East Germany.

Kennedy opposed the construction of the wall, but he was unwilling to go to war to stop it from being constructed. "It's not a very nice solution," Kennedy said, "but a wall is a hell of a lot better than a war." Rejecting the advice of some hawks who wanted him to take a dramatic step, perhaps using American forces to knock down the wall, JFK settled for a restrained and reasoned approach. He sent a token force of 1,500 troops to Berlin, making clear that the United States would defend the beleaguered city. Tensions between the superpowers eased—but only temporarily.

The Cuban Missile Crisis

On October 14, 1962, an American U-2 spy plane discovered offensive nuclear missile sites in Cuba. The photographic images were shocking: The Soviet Union had installed between 16 and 32 missiles with a maximum range of over 1,000 miles. Once they were loaded with nuclear warheads the missiles could hit American cities up and down the East Coast. The CIA estimated as many as 80 million Americans would die in an attack.

Kennedy initially supported an air strike to destroy the missile sites, but an air strike alone would not destroy all the missile sites. On October 22, Kennedy decided to impose a naval quarantine of the island. A blockade would provide more time for each side to contemplate the costs of its actions and possibly provide the Russians with a graceful way to back out of the crisis.

The nation, and the world, teetered on the edge of nuclear war. The crisis intensified as a dozen Soviet ships headed toward a possible confrontation with the American Navy off the coast of Cuba. Raising the stakes, Kennedy ordered B-52 aircraft carrying nuclear weapons to stand ready and moved troops south to prepare for a possible invasion. Then he and his advisors waited for the Soviets' response.

The danger was far greater than Kennedy realized at the time. We now know that the U.S. military estimates were grossly wrong. The Soviets had 42,000 troops on the island, not the 8,000–10,000 that JFK had been told. More importantly, the Soviets had deployed tactical nuclear weapons to repel any land invasion of Cuba. Had Kennedy pursued the military option of air strikes followed by a land invasion the situation could easily have escalated into a nuclear war between the two nations.

On October 28, Khrushchev retreated, ordering the Soviet ships to turn around. Over the next few days the two superpowers hammered out an agreement to end the confrontation. The United States promised not to invade Cuba if the missiles were quickly withdrawn. Privately, Kennedy also agreed that American missiles in Turkey would be removed.

In the short run, the missile crisis set the stage for a gradual improvement in United States–Soviet relations. Both nations, traumatized by their close brush

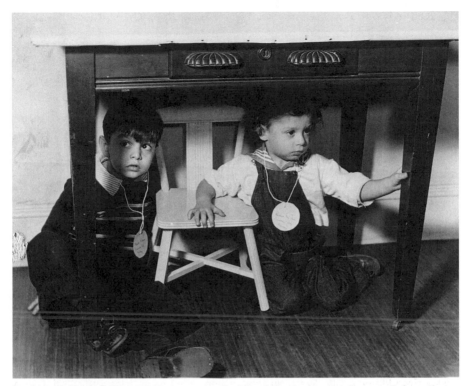

Duck-and-Cover Drill While Americans had faced the threat of nuclear attack from the Soviet Union since 1949, the fear of such an attack never seemed as real or possible as it did in October 1962 during the Cuban missile crisis. The number of bomb shelters built skyrocketed during the fall, as did the diligence with which the nation's schools practiced their air-raid drills. Known as duck-and-cover drills, teachers trained children to scramble under their desks and cover their faces as quickly as possible when an alarm sounded *(AP/Wide World Photos)*

with nuclear war, appeared ready to lessen tensions. Taking the initiative in a speech at American University in June 1963, Kennedy called for a reexamination of American attitudes toward the Soviet Union and the Cold War. "In the final analysis," he said, "our most common link is that we all inhabit this small planet. We all breathe the same air. We all cherish our children's future. And we are all mortal." The White House and the Kremlin agreed to install a "hot line" to establish direct communications between the leaders of the world's two superpowers. Perhaps the most tangible evidence of the new thaw in relations was the nuclear test ban treaty. The treaty, initialed on July 25, banned atmospheric and underwater nuclear testing.

The Missile Crisis also impacted America's relationship with its European allies. While Europe supported the U.S. actions in Cuba, many leaders were concerned that the United States was willing to push the world toward nuclear war

Location of Missiles in Cuba, 1962   In the summer of 1962, Soviet premier Nikita Khrushchev began secretly sending troops and weapons into Cuba. By sending medium-range ballistic missiles and intercontinental-range ballistic missiles, Khrushchev ensured the Soviet Union's first-strike capability. Cuban and Soviet technicians assembled the missiles on the western end of Cuba, as close to the U.S. Florida Keys as possible and as far from the prying eyes of the American military at Guantanamo Bay in southeastern Cuba as possible. (*Source: James T. Patterson,* Grand Expectations: The United States, 1945–1974 [OHUS Volume 10]. *By permission of Oxford University Press.*)

without consulting them. French President Charles De Gaulle worried that his nation might one day face "annihilation without representation." De Gaulle distanced himself from the United States, and pushed for the creation of a separate independent French nuclear force.

JFK and the Third World

While the most intense conflicts between the superpowers took place in familiar places, Kennedy devoted a great deal of energy to winning hearts and minds in the Third World. The Kennedy years witnessed the continuation of the process of decolonization—the withdrawal of occupying forces and the end of economic exploitation of Third World countries by European powers—that began after World War II. Between 1960 and 1963, twenty-four new nations emerged, and Kennedy worked hard to win their allegiance with a mix of idealism and realism.

JFK provided rhetorical support to independence movements in Africa, invited their leaders to the White House, and appointed ambassadors who understood their culture. He created new programs designed to provide economic and humanitarian aid to struggling Third World countries. "Food for Peace" provided nourishment for 92 million people a day, including 35 million children. The Peace Corps sent American volunteers to foreign countries, fostering closer cultural ties. As president, he visited Latin America three times, drawing large, enthusiastic crowds along the way. In 1961, he announced the Alliance for Progress and pledged $1 billion to support economic development for Latin America.

Kennedy was also willing to use military support to sustain repressive governments and to overthrow leftist governments. On the African continent, the administration failed to support a nationalist leader in the Congo and acquiesced to Portugal's brutal repression in Angola. In Latin America, the administration supported Haiti's repressive dictator Jean Claude "Papa Doc." When Brazil's government tried to establish a neutral position in the Cold War, the CIA spent $5 million to overthrow the government and establish a military dictatorship.

The Space Program

The competition between the United States and Soviet Union extended into space. After the successful launch of Sputnik, the Soviets beat the Americans to another first on April 12, 1961, when Yuri Gagarin completed one orbit of the Earth. "Let the capitalist countries try to catch up," Premier Nikita Khrushchev boasted. The following month, Alan Shepard became the first American in space when he took Freedom 7, a Project Mercury capsule, on a 15-minute suborbital flight. Shepard did not fly as high, as far or as fast as Gagarin, but his successful mission—"Everything's A-OK," he radioed from space—was a psychological boost for a nation unsettled by another Soviet success.

On May 25, 1961, just three weeks after Shepard had taken America's first step into space, Kennedy stood before Congress and declared "I believe this nation should commit itself to achieving the goal, before the decade is out, of landing a man on the moon and returning him safely to Earth." The decision set in motion the greatest peacetime mobilization of men and resources for science and exploration in history. Congress responded by doubling the budget of the National Aeronautics and Space Administration (NASA). While the president galvanized the nation with his call for action, his plan also attracted criticism. Liberals worried that the program would drain resources from thirsty domestic programs. Conservatives, on the other hand, complained that the money could be better spent developing the military potential of space.

The space program transformed astronauts into national heroes. All of them had been under 40 when they were recruited in 1959, all possessed IQs above 130 and all were under 5 feet 11 inches in height. Many became household names, as well-known as sports stars and Hollywood celebrities. The journalist James Reston wrote that Shepard was elevated to hero status "because he symbolized what Washington was created to celebrate but had begun to doubt: the free and natural man: simple, direct, thoughtful, and modestly confident."

The Life of Kennedy's Death

Within months of Kennedy's assassination, polls showed a majority of Americans questioning whether Lee Harvey Oswald had acted alone. To quell the doubts, President Johnson appointed a blue-ribbon commission of seven prominent public figures chaired by Chief Justice Earl Warren. On September 24, 1964, only ten months after the events in Dallas, the President's Commission on the Assassination of President Kennedy, popularly known as the Warren Commission, presented its 888-page report. There was no conspiracy, foreign or domestic; it declared that Lee Harvey Oswald had acted alone.

The Warren Commission's findings failed to convince skeptics. A *Newsweek* poll taken in 1983 on the twentieth anniversary of the assassination showed that 74 percent of Americans believed that "others were involved." Critics charged that Oswald could not have fired three shots in 5.6 seconds from a mail-order, bolt-action rifle. More improbable was the contention that one bullet, dubbed the "magic bullet," could have traveled through the president's body, inflicted extensive injury to Governor Connally, and remained in nearly pristine condition. Skeptics charged that in a "rush to judgment" the Warren Commission ignored witnesses who claimed to hear more than three shots and repressed evidence of other groups with a motive to shoot the president. Such suspicions would gain a new lease on life in 1992 with the release of the Hollywood film *JFK*, directed by Oliver Stone. The film portrayed an elaborate web of conspiracy involving Vice President Johnson, the FBI, the CIA, the Pentagon, defense contractors, and assorted other officials and agencies.

While critics have poked holes in the Warren Commission's findings, they have failed either to undermine its final conclusion that Oswald acted alone or to develop a convincing alternative interpretation of events on November 22, 1963. Numerous reenactments, along with new computer-enhanced models, have confirmed the core of the ballistic evidence: Oswald could have fired all three shots, and a single bullet could have cut its deadly path through both the president and Governor Connally. The opening of nearly all records related to the assassination undercuts suggestions of a government cover-up.

If the evidence supports the Warren Commission, why do the conspiracy theories persist? Sloppiness on the part of the Warren Commission, intense media interest, and Cold War paranoia all played a part in keeping Kennedy's death alive. Perhaps most of all, people find the theories of conspiracy attractive because they imbue Kennedy's death with meaning. Believing that great tragedies require great causes, Americans reject the notion that a single lunatic can change history. By making Kennedy a victim of some sinister, powerful force, conspiracy theories transform Kennedy's death into something more than a senseless act of violence.

Kennedy's death, and the debate that it generated, would fascinate Americans for decades. Television played a role in cementing Kennedy's image with the public. Kennedy was the first president to use television to bypass the Washington opinion makers and communicate directly with the American public. The trauma of his death, played over seventy-five straight hours on television, was burned into the national consciousness. Four of five Americans felt "the loss of someone very close and dear," and more than one-half cried.

More than anything else, however, Kennedy's inspiring rhetoric and youthful style projected an image of America moving forward to a better future. The consensus was unraveling all around him, but for many Americans Kennedy represented a time when the United States stood strong in the world, the nation felt united, and life seemed simpler. Events in the years following his death—the defeat in Vietnam, campus unrest, urban rioting, Watergate, and stagflation—would shatter that faith. As the nation's faith in government and hope for the future diminished, Americans clung more tenaciously than ever to a mythic view of Kennedy.

Ultimately, America's fascination with Kennedy revealed more about the nation's tenacious belief in progress and its need for heroes than it did about the man. Kennedy was mortal, very much a product of his times, and he offered few solutions to the day's pressing issues. Like his postwar predecessors, JFK relied upon the vital-center consensus to deal with the American paradox. By 1963 the seams of the consensus were already beginning to split under the strain of the civil-rights movement, which exposed the tension between expectations and reality.

SELECTED READINGS

▮ Robert Dallek's *An Unfinished Life* (2003) provides the most balanced assessment of Kennedy's life and legacy. Also valuable is James Giglio's *The Presidency of John F. Kennedy* (1991). Former prosecutor Vincent Bugliosi makes a strong case against Lee Harvey Oswald in *Four Days in November* (2008).

▮ Garry Wills's *The Kennedy Imprisonment* (1982) offers a critical meditation on the troubling aspects of Kennedy's charismatic leadership. Thomas Brown casts a skeptical eye on the use of the media to create an aura surrounding the Kennedy image in his *JFK: The History of an Image* (1988). Irvin Bernstein's *Promises Kept* (1990) focuses on the domestic programs, such as civil rights, that provided Kennedy with opportunities to act.

▮ A detailed account of the sit-ins at the Woolworth in Greensboro, North Carolina, can be found in Miles Wolff's *Lunch at the 5 and 10* (1990), while Clayborne Carson traces the evolution of black consciousness through the process of grass-roots mobilization and protest in his definitive history of SNCC, *In Struggle* (1981). In *An American Insurrection* (2001), William Doyle examines the tumultuous events surrounding James Meredith's admission to the University of Mississippi and its impact on southern resistance. Diane McWhorter's *Carry Me Home* (2001) tells the story of her own white, middle-class family, but in the context of the wider civil-rights struggle occurring in her hometown of Birmingham. In *Ella Baker and the Black Freedom Movement* (2003) Barbara Ransby chronicles the life and political activities of one of the movement's most influential women. James Cone offers an insightful account of the similarities and differences in the two leaders of the civil-rights movement in *Martin & Malcolm & America* (2009). Manning Marable's *Malcolm X: A Life of Reinvention* (2011) stands as the definitive account of the slain civil-rights leader's life.

▌ Gerard Rice's *The Bold Experiment* (1985) traces the early history of the Peace Corps. Lawrence Freedman's *Kennedy's Wars* (2000), examines JFK's foreign policy. Michael Dobbs provides new insight into the Cuban Missile Crisis in *One Minute to Midnight* (2008). Robert Weisbrot analyzes the role of public perception and Kennedy's leadership qualities during the crisis in *Maximum Danger* (2001).

8

Lyndon Johnson, the Great Society, and the Unraveling of America, 1963–1967

On May 22, 1964, President Lyndon Johnson outlined his utopian vision for America's future in a twenty-minute commencement address at the University of Michigan. Having come to the presidency by the whim of an assassin's bullet and having spent the past few months completing his predecessor's legislative agenda, Johnson was ready to place his own mark on the office. Americans, he told the appreciative audience of eighty thousand who interrupted him for applause twenty-nine times, had conquered a continent and mastered the levers of prosperity. Now it was time for the nation to address the problems of poverty and racial injustice. The challenge for the future, he charged, was "to move not only toward the rich society and the powerful society, but upward to the Great Society." In this "Great Society" people would be "more concerned with the quality of their goals than with the quantity of their goods."

Johnson's speech that day captured the essence of vital-center liberalism: the faith in economic growth, the belief that social and economic conflict had faded, and the optimism that the federal government could improve the quality of life for all its citizens without imposing sacrifice or hardship. At the heart of the Great Society was a belief that economic growth provided all Americans—rich and poor, urban blacks and rural whites, young and old—with the historic opportunity to forge a new national consensus. Growth would eliminate the need for higher taxes at the same time that it produced a social surplus that would replenish new social programs. Social progress would be painless. *Time* magazine declared that Johnson added two new phrases to the American vocabulary—"let us reason together" and "I want to be President of all the People."

Following his 1964 landslide victory Johnson moved aggressively to enact his Great Society legislation. "Hurry, boys, hurry," he told his aides. "Get that legislation up to the Hill and out. Eighteen months from now ol' Landslide Lyndon will be Lame-Duck Lyndon." In a whirlwind of legislative activity, the administration asked Congress for 200 major pieces of legislation. By October 1966, Congress had approved 181 of them. Yet Johnson's larger goal of achieving a "Great Society" remained unfulfilled. Like many reformers, he raised expectations about the possibilities of change but offered only modest proposals for reform. The gap between promise and performance intensified ideological and cultural divisions and exposed the limits of Johnson's cherished "consensus." The growing polarization between black and white, and between young and old, highlighted the tension between American ideals and social realities and exposed the painful paradox of postwar American politics.

Lyndon Johnson Takes Charge

John Kennedy's death brought to the White House a man with a strikingly different background and temperament. Born in 1908, Lyndon Johnson grew up in the depressed rural area of the Texas Hill country outside of Austin. His hardscrabble roots instilled in him a passionate desire to help the less fortunate and an idealistic faith in the power of government to provide opportunity, but it had also left him with a nagging inferiority complex—a fear that those of better background and more refined upbringing would never accept him.

From an early age Johnson was determined to make his mark in politics. In 1937, he won election to Congress. In 1948 he won a disputed election to the Senate by 87 votes, earning him the nickname "Landslide Lyndon."

Once in the Senate, Johnson impressed everyone with his energy and ambition. As minority leader and then as majority leader, he became a master of parliamentary maneuver and a skillful behind-the-scenes negotiator. Johnson was not afraid to twist arms to bend recalcitrant Senators to his will. Standing six feet four inches tall he towered over many of his peers, and he was not afraid to use his size to intimidate his opponents. Two journalists described this process as the "Johnson treatment." "He moved in close, his face a scant millimeter from his target, his eyes widening and narrowing, his eyebrows rising and falling." Minnesota senator Hubert Humphrey once described an encounter with Johnson as "an almost hypnotic experience. I came out of that session covered with blood, sweat, tears, spit—and sperm."

During the 1950s, many observers considered him the second most powerful man in Washington behind President Dwight Eisenhower. Johnson was not only one of the most powerful men in Washington, he was one of the most colorful, controversial, and complicated. While often deferential to superiors, Johnson could be vicious to his subordinates, and overbearing with anyone who got in his way. He worked long, 18-hour days and pushed his staff to exhaustion. He demanded unquestioned loyalty from everyone who worked for him. "I want real loyalty," he once said. "I want someone who will kiss my ass in Macy's window, and say it smells like roses." He was reckless about his health. He drank heavily—Cutty Sark whiskey was his favorite—and was a chain smoker. His bad habits almost killed him in 1955 when he suffered a serious heart attack. Doctors gave him a fifty-fifty chance of surviving. "Will I ever be able to smoke again?" he asked in the ambulance. On being told that he would not, LBJ muttered: "I'd rather have my pecker cut off." After a short break, Johnson resumed his rigorous schedule, but without the cigarettes.

Johnson had hoped to win the presidency in 1960, but he was outmaneuvered by JFK. He reluctantly accepted the vice presidency believing that he could infuse the office with new powers. His hopes were quickly disappointed. Worried that LBJ's enormous ego could hurt more than help on Capitol Hill, Kennedy failed to include him in deliberations on key legislative initiatives. Johnson sat helplessly on the sidelines as the great promise of the New Frontier stalled in Congress.

Launching a "War on Poverty"

Always the political tactician, Johnson realized that Kennedy's death provided him with a powerful symbol to build political support for an expansive liberal agenda. Johnson used his political talent to push Congress into enacting a number of Kennedy's initiatives. In February 1964, Congress passed the Kennedy tax package, reducing personal income taxes by more than $10 billion. Many economists believe the tax cut contributed to an economic boom that saw the nation's gross national product (GNP) rise from $591 billion in 1963 to $977 billion in 1970. Johnson also pushed through Congress Kennedy's stalled housing and food-stamp programs.

Johnson was not content merely to pass Kennedy's agenda, however. He sought to create a program that would bear his personal brand. In January 1964, in his first State of the Union message, Johnson declared "unconditional war on poverty. . . . We shall not rest until that war is won. The richest Nation on earth can afford to win it. We cannot afford to lose it." Reflecting the grand expectations that animated liberals in the 1960s, Johnson believed that a constantly expanding economy could fund needed social problems and solve nearly all of the nation's domestic problems.

The resulting war on poverty actually had its roots in the Kennedy administration. Like many Americans, Kennedy took office believing that economic growth alone would solve the problems of poverty. In 1962 the social activist Michael Harrington passionately challenged that notion in a popular book entitled *The Other America*. Estimating the ranks of the poor at 40 to 50 million, or as much as 25 percent of the U.S. population, Harrington argued that poverty resulted from long-term structural problems, such as unemployment and low wages, which only the federal government could address. On November 19, 1963, just three days before his death, Kennedy asked Walter Heller, the chairman of the Council of Economic Advisors, to design a legislative proposal for fighting poverty. The day after the assassination Johnson enthusiastically endorsed the plan. "That's my kind of program," the president said. "Move full speed ahead."

Congress passed the poverty bill, called the Economic Opportunity Act, in the summer of 1964. It authorized almost $1 billion for a wide range of antipoverty programs, including Head Start for preschoolers and the Job Corps for inner-city youth. Volunteers in Service to America, a domestic version of the Peace Corps, provided volunteers with the opportunity to work in poor urban areas and depressed rural communities. The law also authorized creation of the Office of Economic Opportunity (OEO) to coordinate the antipoverty battle. Johnson chose Peace Corps director R. Sargent Shriver, a Kennedy brother-in-law, to administer the OEO.

The centerpiece of the new legislation was the community action program (CAP). The initiative, intended to stimulate sustained involvement among the poor, called for the "maximum feasible participation" of local community members in shaping antipoverty programs. In many cases, OEO ended up funding projects that bypassed local Democratic machines and supported controversial groups. In Chicago, OEO money allowed a street gang to set up a Head Start Program. In San Francisco, black power advocates tried to use antipoverty money to establish an independent political party. Within a year, powerful Democratic leaders were denouncing the program and Johnson quickly retreated.

By some measures the various programs that made up the war on poverty succeeded. The proportion of Americans below the federal poverty line fell from 20 percent in 1963 to 13 percent in 1968. For African Americans, who faced the most desperate conditions, the statistics were even more impressive. The percentage of blacks living below the poverty line dropped from 40 percent to 20 percent between 1960 and 1968. However, a booming economy contributed to these statistics as much as did the antipoverty program.

Like many of the social programs of the 1960s, the war on poverty was characterized by grand ambition and limited gains. In submitting his bill to Congress, Johnson called for "total victory." "Conquest of poverty is well within our power," he declared. But ingrained conservative attitudes toward the poor, and toward government's role in promoting social welfare, limited the choice of weapons used to fight the war. With polls showing that large numbers of Americans believed that poverty resulted from "lack of effort" and that the poor were partly to blame for their plight, the administration developed a program that emphasized opportunity and promised to help the poor to help themselves. From 1965 to 1970 OEO spent an average of $1.7 billion per year—less than 1.5 percent of the federal budget, or one-third of 1 percent of the GNP. If all OEO money had gone directly to the poor, it would have amounted to between $50 and $70 per person.

The ultimate irony of the war on poverty was that a program launched as the result of renewed faith in the power of government was to undermine public faith in Washington's ability to solve social problems. "Perhaps no government program in modern American history promised so much more than it delivered," noted the historian James T. Patterson. The contrast between promise and performance infuriated some of the poor. In 1967 when rioting hit Detroit, Mayor Jerome Cavanagh blamed the OEO and other federal programs. "What we've been doing, at the level we've been doing it, is almost worse than nothing at all. . . . We've raised expectations, but we haven't been able to deliver all we should have." The experience also soured a generation of intellectuals who viewed the war on poverty as a metaphor for government ineptitude. "There are limits to the desirable reach of social engineering," observed the sociologist Nathan Glazer. Increasingly, the public shared many of these doubts. By 1967 more than 67 percent of the public thought the administration had gone "too far." In 1969 a total of 84 percent agreed with the statement: "There are too many people receiving welfare who ought to be working."

The 1964 Election

To oppose Johnson in November, the Republicans nominated Arizona Senator Barry Goldwater. Tall, trim, and handsome, Goldwater was an outspoken critic of liberal reform who hoped to rally millions of conservative voters in the South and West with his calls for smaller government and aggressive anticommunism. During the 1950s Goldwater had developed a loyal group of conservative followers, but he burst on the national scene in 1960 with publication of *The Conscience of a Conservative*. The book challenged the prevailing faith in consensus, arguing that government intervention had restricted individual freedom and that coexistence with Russia had rewarded unchecked Soviet aggression. "A tolerable peace . . . must *follow* victory over Communism."

In 1962 Goldwater loyalists developed elaborate plans to seize control of the Republican Party at the grass roots. Instead of winning the support of governors and senators, conservatives would organize precinct by precinct to control the delegates at the 1964 convention. Rather than cultivating traditional Republican votes in the Northeast, they would focus their efforts in the white South. "We're not going to get the Negro vote as a bloc in 1964 and 1968," Goldwater declared, "so we ought to go hunting where the ducks are." As civil-rights tensions mounted in the South, and Kennedy's approval rating among whites dropped, pundits began speculating that Goldwater could ride the discontent into the White House. Goldwater energized the party's vocal right wing, but he alienated Republican moderates and liberals. He suggested that nuclear weapons be used against Cuba, China, and North Vietnam if they failed to accede to American demands. "Our job, first and foremost," he wrote, "is to persuade the enemy that we would rather follow the world to Kingdom Come than consign it to Hell under communism." GOP campaign posters asserted, "In Your Heart You Know He's Right." (Democrats retorted, "In Your Guts You Know He's Nuts.")

By waging a campaign to win over the right, Goldwater conceded the broad middle ground to Johnson, who brilliantly exploited the opportunity. At the party's Atlantic City convention, Johnson won the nomination by acclamation. As his running mate, he chose Minnesota senator Hubert Humphrey, a passionate proponent of civil rights and a leading liberal. Throughout the campaign Johnson played the role of the fatherly figure committed to continuing the policies of the nation's fallen leader. Campaigning eighteen hours a day, he reminded voters of his party's past accomplishments and promised to carry the nation to new heights.

The election was never close. Johnson's portion of the popular vote, 61 percent, matched Roosevelt's in 1936. Voters gave Johnson 43.1 million votes to Goldwater's 27.2 million. Carrying all but six states, Johnson gathered 486 electoral votes to Goldwater's 52. Congressional Democrats coasted to victory on the president's coattails, providing the administration with large majorities in both houses: 68 to 32 in the Senate and 295 to 140 in the House. The *New York Times* opined that Goldwater had "wrecked his party for a long time to come," while *The New Yorker* predicted that Johnson's landslide victory had "finished the Goldwater school of political reaction."

The Democrats may have triumphed on election day, but Goldwater won the debate in the long run. He was a prophet of the new conservatism. While mainstream Republicans were still debating balanced budgets, Goldwater tapped into a growing discontent with the unfulfilled expectations of postwar liberalism. In the final months of the campaign Goldwater taught Republicans how to appeal to the cultural frustrations and anxieties of white voters by addressing such issues as racial quotas, law and order, and fear of moral decline. The message helped the Republicans make dramatic inroads into the once solidly Democratic South. Goldwater

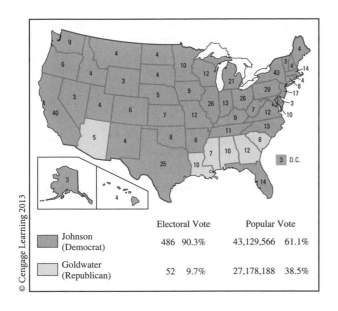

	Electoral Vote		Popular Vote	
Johnson (Democrat)	486	90.3%	43,129,566	61.1%
Goldwater (Republican)	52	9.7%	27,178,188	38.5%

© Cengage Learning 2013

The Election of 1964
Republicans tried a new political strategy with their candidate Barry Goldwater, attacking the liberal domestic policies of Democratic presidents, including the New Deal and the war on poverty. Lyndon Johnson retaliated by campaigning to as wide an audience as possible and urged people at every point of the political spectrum to join him. Ultimately this broad appeal worked, except in the Deep South states where whites dominated the polls and voted for Goldwater.

received 70 percent of the vote in Alabama and 87 percent in Mississippi. Even in southern states that he lost, Republicans won a majority of white voters.

The Goldwater campaign revealed the fragile nature of the postwar consensus and foreshadowed the growing political power of conservatism. The new liberalism had raised expectations of a secular utopia: prosperity would solve the problems of poverty and racism without challenging traditional values of limited government or individual rights. By 1964 the contradiction between expectations and social realities was becoming apparent to those on both the left and the right. It was becoming apparent that Lyndon Johnson planned to build the foundation of his reform agenda on the quicksand of the American paradox.

The Great Society

Following his victory over Goldwater in November, Johnson launched his Great Society. The administration's top priorities were to rescue two staples of the Democratic agenda since the Fair Deal that had been held hostage by congressional conservatives: medical insurance for the elderly and education funding for the young. Johnson and his new allies in Congress overwhelmed the opposition. Along with providing medical assistance to people on social security (Medicare), the legislation included a Medicaid program that would pay the medical expenses of the poor regardless of age. "No longer will older Americans be denied the healing miracle of modern medicine," a triumphant Johnson declared. The president also managed to quiet opponents of federal aid to education and convince Congress to pass his Elementary and Secondary Education Act of 1965.

Its heart was Title I, which provided more than $1 billion for textbooks, library materials, and special-educational programs for poor children.

Mounting momentum enabled Johnson to push through a wide range of legislation. In the first six months of 1965 the administration submitted eighty-seven bills to Congress and saw eighty-four of them become law. Congress passed consumer protection acts and provided aid for mass transit, urban development, and slum clearance.

Johnson made concern for the environment a central tenet of his Great Society. Prodded by the White House, Congress passed legislation mandating tougher regulation of water and air pollution. The Wilderness Act of 1964 set aside over 9 million acres of national forest to be preserved in their unspoiled state. A companion measure, the Wild and Scenic Rivers Act of 1968, similarly protected a number of rivers from the threat of development. The first lady, Lady Bird Johnson, supported environmental awareness as an eloquent and effective leader of a campaign for national beautification.

Signing a Piece of the Great Society into Law   Lyndon Johnson went further than any previous president to employ the federal government to meet people's needs and solve social problems. Key to his program was ensuring that every American child had an adequate education, from preschool through high school. Johnson, raised in poor, rural Texas, justified his generous education package by claiming that "education is the only valid passport from poverty." Here he signs the bill, accompanied by his first-grade teacher at the site of the one-room schoolhouse he attended as a boy. *(AP/Wide World Photos)*

Whether the Great Society programs were successful is a subject of heated scholarly debate. Supporters point out that programs such as Medicare and Medicaid provided essential medical benefits to the elderly and the poor. Critics, however, point out that the middle class, not the poor, was the chief beneficiary of many Great Society programs. By refusing to impose restrictions on what doctors could charge patients, Medicare and Medicaid contributed to spiraling medical costs that benefited doctors. A similar problem plagued Johnson's compensatory education program. To avoid raising fears of encroaching government power, Johnson gave local school districts authority for developing and implementing education programs. In a classic case of the "curse of localism," school officials skirted federal guidelines and redirected money toward middle-class students.

The Unintended Consequences of Immigration Reform

In July, standing in the shadow of the Statue of Liberty, Johnson signed the Immigration Act of 1965. "The bill that we sign today is not a revolutionary bill," he said, but it did "repair a very deep and powerful flaw in the fabric of American justice." Since 1924 the United States had allocated visas in ratios determined by the number of persons of each nationality in the United States in 1890. Not surprisingly, the "national origins" clause favored people from northern Europe, who consumed 98 percent of the quota, leaving only 2 percent for the rest of the world. The new legislation replaced national origins with a family preference system. Congress believed the new law would eliminate discriminatory quotas without producing an increase in the overall number of immigrants or significantly altering the sources of immigration.

In a classic case of unintended consequences, the Immigration Act of 1965 opened the door to an increased flow of immigrants from Asia and Latin America that would profoundly affect American life in the decades ahead. Legislators never considered how family unification could produce a chain of migration that would confound efforts to control immigration. Under the new preference system an engineering student from India could come to the United States to study, find a job after graduating, get labor certification, and become a legal resident alien. His new status would then entitle him to bring over his wife, and six years later, after being naturalized, his brothers and sisters. They in turn could begin the process all over again by sponsoring their wives, husbands, children, and siblings. Within a dozen years one immigrant entering as a skilled worker could generate dozens of visas for distant relatives.

Despite large numbers in the United States, many northern European immigrants lacked the close family ties needed to benefit from the new system. Many came over as single men, applied for jobs, married Americans, and raised families. However, immigrants from southern Europe and especially from Asia emigrated as families and were therefore better positioned to take advantage of the family unification provisions. In the twenty years following the 1965 Immigration Act, the Asian population in the United States soared from 1 million to 5 million; nearly four times as many Asians entered the country during that period as had emigrated in the previous hundred years. Most of these came from a handful of countries: the Philippines, China, Korea, and India.

The Conservative Revival

Growing concern about the expansion of federal power during the 1960s helped to heal divisions that had plagued modern conservatives, allowing them to emerge as an energetic and unified political force during the decade. The New Right attacked the moral relativism of the vital center, which they claimed blurred the distinction between right and wrong. The new conservatives called for an aggressive foreign policy, dramatic increases in military spending, and an end to most social welfare programs. The *National Review,* founded in 1955 by William F. Buckley, played a key role in promoting the new conservatism. "We are in opposition," the magazine declared, "and we have to fight conformity." The message struck a responsive chord. Between 1960 and 1964 the circulation of the conservative monthly magazine tripled to ninety thousand.

Also growing in size was the ultraconservative John Birch Society (JBS), founded in 1958 by Robert Welch. The United States, Welch declared, was at war with "a gigantic conspiracy to enslave mankind." The list of conspirators included Dwight Eisenhower, the justices of the Supreme Court, and just about anyone else who supported nuclear disarmament or civil rights. President John Kennedy's softening position toward the Soviets following the Cuban missile crisis caused alarm among anticommunists and helped swell the JBS membership. By 1964 the JBS claimed about fifty thousand members and received more than $7 million a year in contributions.

During the 1950s and 1960s conservatives developed a base of support in thriving suburban communities, especially in the South and West. In Orange County, California, for example, middle-class whites, worried about the decline of morality and the growth of federal power, organized at the grass-roots level to support right-wing causes. As small property owners, they fought to maintain the racial homogeneity of their communities and to resist Washington's efforts to force integration. Heavily dependent on military contracts for their survival, local residents supported an aggressive anticommunism and opposed efforts to negotiate with the Soviets. Although the federal government supplied the loans used to pay the mortgage and helped build the roads that tied the communities together, many suburban residents developed a virulent hatred of Washington.

The Right also established an energetic presence on college campuses. In 1960 more than one hundred conservative students gathered at William Buckley's family estate in Sharon, Connecticut, to develop an agenda for conservative youth. "Now is the time for Conservative youth to take action to make their full force and influence felt," declared the invitation. The conference marked the birth of the Young Americans for Freedom (YAF). The group issued a statement of principles calling for restrictions on government power to allow "the individual's use of his God-given free will," and urged "victory over, rather than co-existence with," the Soviet Union. By 1961 YAF claimed twenty-four thousand members at 115 schools. Noting the proliferation of conservative clubs on college campuses, one conservative proclaimed a "new wave" of campus revolt. These new campus conservatives, he predicted, would be the "opinion-makers—the people who in ten, fifteen, and twenty-five years will begin to assume positions of power in America."

PRIMARY SOURCE

8.1 | *"A Time for Choosing"*
Ronald Reagan

In the fall of 1964 actor Ronald Reagan gave a nationally televised address in support of Barry Goldwater's campaign for the presidency. In the brief speech, Reagan articulated many of the themes that would dominate the conservative movement for the next few decades and help launch his own successful career in politics.

I am going to talk of controversial things. I make no apology for this.

It's time we asked ourselves if we still know the freedoms intended for us by the Founding Fathers. James Madison said, "We base all our experiments on the capacity of mankind for self-government."

5   This idea that government was beholden to the people, that it had no other source of power is still the newest, most unique idea in all the long history of man's relation to man. This is the issue of this election: Whether we believe in our capacity for self-government or whether we abandon the American Revolution and confess that a little intellectual elite in a far-distant capital can plan our lives

10   for us better than we can plan them ourselves.

You and I are told we must choose between a left or right, but I suggest there is no such thing as a left or right. There is only an up or down. Up to man's age-old dream—the maximum of individual freedom consistent with order—or down to the ant heap of totalitarianism. Regardless of their sincerity, their humanitar-

15   ian motives, those who would sacrifice freedom for security have embarked on

this downward path. Plutarch warned, "The real destroyer of the liberties of the people is he who spreads among them bounties, donations and benefits."

The Founding Fathers knew a government can't control the economy without controlling people. And they knew when a government sets out to do that, it
20 must use force and coercion to achieve its purpose. So we have come to a time for choosing.

Public servants say, always with the best of intentions, "What greater service we could render if only we had a little more money and a little more power." But the truth is that outside of its legitimate function, government does nothing as
25 well or as economically as the private sector.

Yet any time you and I question the schemes of the do-gooders, we're denounced as being opposed to their humanitarian goals. It seems impossible to legitimately debate their solutions with the assumption that all of us share the desire to help the less fortunate. They tell us we're always "against," never "for"
30 anything.

We are for a provision that destitution should not follow unemployment by reason of old age, and to that end we have accepted Social Security as a step toward meeting the problem. However, we are against those entrusted with this program when they practice deception regarding its fiscal shortcomings, when
35 they charge that any criticism of the program means that we want to end payments. . . .

We are for aiding our allies by sharing our material blessings with nations which share our fundamental beliefs, but we are against doling out money government to government, creating bureaucracy, if not socialism, all over the
40 world.

We need true tax reform that will at least make a start toward restoring for our children the American Dream that wealth is denied to no one, that each individual has the right to fly as high as his strength and ability will take him. . . . But we cannot have such reform while our tax policy is engineered by people who
45 view the tax as a means of achieving changes in our social structure. . . .

Have we the courage and the will to face up to the immorality and discrimination of the progressive tax, and demand a return to traditional proportionate taxation? . . . Today in our country the tax collector's share is 37 cents of every dollar earned. Freedom has never been so fragile, so close to slipping from our grasp.

50 Are you willing to spend time studying the issues, making yourself aware, and then conveying that information to family and friends? Will you resist the temptation to get a government handout for your community? Realize that the doctor's fight against socialized medicine is your fight. We can't socialize the doctors without socializing the patients. Recognize that government invasion of public
55 power is eventually an assault upon your own business. If some among you fear taking a stand because you are afraid of reprisals from customers, clients, or even government, recognize that you are just feeding the crocodile hoping he'll eat you last.

If all of this seems like a great deal of trouble, think what's at stake. We are
60 faced with the most evil enemy mankind has known in his long climb from the swamp to the stars. There can be no security anywhere in the free world if there

is no fiscal and economic stability within the United States. Those who ask us to trade our freedom for the soup kitchen of the welfare state are architects of a policy of accommodation.

65 They say the world has become too complex for simple answers. They are wrong. There are no easy answers, but there are simple answers. We must have the courage to do what we know is morally right. Winston Churchill said that "the destiny of man is not measured by material computation. When great forces are on the move in the world, we learn we are spirits—not animals." And he said,

70 "There is something going on in time and space, and beyond time and space, which, whether we like it or not, spells duty."

You and I have a rendezvous with destiny. We will preserve for our children this, the last best hope of man on earth, or we will sentence them to take the first step into a thousand years of darkness. If we fail, at least let our children and our children's

75 children say of us we justified our brief moment here. We did all that could be done.

Source: Ronald Reagan Presidential Campaign Papers, 1964–1980, Series I, Box 20, Ronald Reagan Library. ■ ■ ■

The Reforms of the Warren Court

The same activist spirit that guided the president and Congress infused the third branch of government—the courts. Under the leadership of Chief Justice Earl Warren, the Supreme Court asserted its right to review and declare unconstitutional legislation that it believed infringed on individual rights.

On civil rights, justices built on the foundation of *Brown v. Board of Education* (1954) by upholding the right of demonstrators to participate in public protests. The Court disallowed the use of the poll tax in state and local elections. And in 1967 the Court struck at the core of white supremacy doctrine in *Loving v. Virginia* by unanimously declaring laws prohibiting interracial marriages to be unconstitutional.

The Court extended the definition of individual rights to other explosive social issues. In the early 1960s twelve states required Bible reading in public schools. Children in New York State recited a nonsectarian Christian prayer: "Almighty God, we acknowledge our dependence upon Thee, and we beg Thy blessings upon us, our parents, our teachers and our country." The Supreme Court, in *Engel* v. *Vitale* (1962), ruled the New York prayer unconstitutional on the grounds that it was a religious activity that placed an "indirect coercive pressure upon religious minorities."

Nowhere did the Court break more decisively with the past than in the area of sexual freedom. In 1965, in *Griswold* v. *Connecticut,* the Court struck down a Connecticut statute banning the sale of contraceptives. In a ruling that would influence future debates about a woman's right to an abortion, Justice William O. Douglas wrote that the Constitution guaranteed "a right to privacy." In *Jacobellis* v. *Ohio* (1964), the Court ruled that states could not ban sexually explicit material unless "it is found to be utterly without redeeming social value." Under that standard nearly all restrictions on the right of an adult to obtain sexually explicit material vanished.

A number of decisions overruled local electoral practices that had prevented full participation in the political process. In 1962 the Court ruled in *Baker* v. *Carr* that the state of Tennessee had to reapportion its legislature to reflect changes in the population. The Court expanded on the ruling two years later when, in *Reynolds* v. *Sims,* it established the principle of "one man, one vote." Legislative districts, the Court ruled, had to be apportioned so that they represented equal numbers of people. "Legislators represent people, not acres or trees," Warren said.

Perhaps the Court's most controversial decisions concerned criminal justice. In *Gideon* v. *Wainwright* (1963), the Court ruled that a pauper accused in state courts of a felony had to be provided an attorney at public expense. The following year, in *Escobedo* v. *Illinois,* it voided the murder confession of a man who had been denied permission to see his lawyer. In the most controversial criminal-rights case, *Miranda* v. *Arizona* (1966), a divided Court required police to inform suspected criminals of their right to remain silent and to have an attorney present during interrogation.

This expansion of judicial activism touched a raw nerve among Americans fearful of encroaching federal power. One congressman said that the justices were "a greater threat to this Union than the entire confines of Soviet Russia." Rulings on pornography, school prayer, and contraception outraged Catholics, fundamentalists, and other religious groups. Reverend Billy Graham called the decision banning school prayer part of a "diabolical scheme" that was "taking God and moral teaching from the schools" and ushering in a "deluge of juvenile delinquency." The Court's involvement in apportionment offended traditionalists, who charged that questions of representation were best handled by elected leaders. The Court's rulings on criminal rights irked white, middle-class Americans worried about rising crime. A 1966 poll showed that 65 percent of Americans opposed recent rulings on criminal rights.

We Shall Overcome

After Kennedy's death in November, civil-rights supporters looked to Lyndon Johnson for leadership. Using the skills he had learned from years on Capitol Hill, the president assumed personal control of the fight to pass the civil-rights package. In the House opponents of the legislation attempted to divide liberal forces by adding a provision that would bar employment discrimination against women as well as blacks. But the measure backfired when Congress adopted the amendment without controversy. Still, for seventy-five days opponents filibustered against the bill, until, on June 10, Senate minority leader Everett Dirksen (R-Ill.) announced his support for allowing a vote. The next day, the Civil Rights

Act of 1964 passed the Senate. Three weeks later the House followed suit. On July 2 President Johnson signed the measure into law.

The Civil Rights Act of 1964 was the most far-reaching law of its kind since Reconstruction. At its heart was a section guaranteeing equal access to public accommodations. The legislation created the Equal Employment Opportunity Commission and charged it with investigating discrimination in employment and included sex, along with race, color, religion, and national origin, as a protected class. Though slow to act, the commission later became a major bulwark in the effort to abolish practices that discriminated against women workers. The law also empowered the government to file school desegregation suits and cut off funds wherever racial discrimination was practiced in the application of federal programs.

Many black leaders believed that racism would never be overcome until blacks exercised political power. In 1964 only 2 million of the South's 5 million voting-age blacks were registered to vote. The Fifteenth Amendment, passed almost a century earlier, had guaranteed the right to vote, but the U.S. system of federalism had allowed states to deny voting privileges through such measures as the poll tax, literacy tests, and grandfather clauses (until 1939). When laws failed to keep blacks off the rolls, segregationists resorted to physical violence and economic intimidation.

In 1964 the Student Nonviolent Coordinating Committee (SNCC) organized a voting rights campaign in Mississippi, where only 5 percent of blacks were registered to vote. The volunteers working to help blacks register included many white college students, and they encountered fierce and sometimes fatal resistance. In June federal agents pulled the decaying bodies of three such workers, Michael Schwerner, James Chaney, and Andrew Goodman, from an earthen dam near Philadelphia, Mississippi. Before the summer ended, opponents of this Freedom Summer had burned or bombed thirty-five houses, churches, and other buildings. "It was the longest nightmare I have ever had," recalled one organizer.

Despite daily beatings and arrests, the volunteers expanded their program to challenge the state's lily-white Democratic organization. They formed their own Mississippi Freedom Democratic Party (MFDP) and elected a separate slate of delegates to the 1964 Democratic National Convention. On August 22 the credentials committee listened to the MFDP's emotional appeal: "Is this America, the land of the free and the home of the brave, where we are threatened daily because we want to live as decent human beings?" asked Fannie Lou Hamer, the daughter of sharecroppers who had lost her job and been evicted from her home because of her organizing efforts. When the regular all-white delegation threatened to walk out if the convention seated the protestors, Johnson feared the controversy would hurt his election in the South. "If you seat those black buggers," Texas governor John Connally warned, "the whole South will walk out." In response, the president offered the dissidents two at-large seats and agreed to bar from future conventions any state delegation that practiced discrimination. The Freedom Democrats rejected the compromise. "We didn't come all this way for no two seats," protested Hamer. In the end, however, Johnson and his liberal allies prevailed and the convention voted to accept the compromise.

The "compromise" at Atlantic City angered many blacks, who no longer felt they could achieve justice through the system. "Things could never be the same," SNCC's Cleveland Sellers wrote. "Never again were we lulled into believing that our task was exposing injustice so that the 'good' people of America could eliminate them. We left Atlantic City with the knowledge that the movement had turned into something else. After Atlantic City, our struggle was not for civil rights, but for liberation."

Selma and the Voting Rights Act of 1965

The growing militancy of the movement further complicated Martin Luther King's efforts, making it essential that he score a quick victory in order to restore confidence in his moderate approach. In 1965 King chose Selma, Alabama, as the site of a renewed voting rights campaign. "We are not asking, we are demanding the ballot," he declared, just weeks after accepting the Nobel Peace Prize. Selma was home to 14,400 whites and 15,100 blacks, but its voting rolls were 99 percent white. SNCC workers had spent several frustrating months organizing local residents to vote. But their efforts had reaped few rewards. The chief obstacle was Sheriff Jim Clark, a bulldog-visaged segregationist who led a group of deputy volunteers, many of them members of the Ku Klux Klan. In response to blacks singing "We Shall Overcome," Clark penned a button reading, "Never."

Clark, however, fell into King's trap, the purpose of which was to provoke confrontation. The sheriff steadfastly turned away the waves of blacks who tried to register. During one week more than three thousand protesters were arrested. As police patience wore thin, police actions became more violent. In February a mob of state troopers assaulted a group of blacks, fatally shooting twenty-six-year-old Jimmie Lee Jackson as he tried to protect his mother and grandmother.

Jackson's death inspired black leaders to organize a 54-mile march from Selma to Montgomery to petition Governor George Wallace for protection of blacks registering to vote. On March 7, ignoring an order from Wallace forbidding the march, 650 blacks and a few whites began walking through Selma. Conspicuously absent from the march was Martin Luther King, who, after private pressure from the White House, had returned to Atlanta.

On the other side of the Alabama River a phalanx of 60 state policemen, wearing helmets and gas masks, stood at the foot of the Edmund Pettus Bridge waiting to greet the marchers. After a few tense minutes the patrolmen moved on the protesters, swinging bullwhips and rubber tubing wrapped in barbed wire. White spectators cheered the police on, while Sheriff Clark bellowed, "Get those

God-damned niggers!" The marchers stumbled over each other in retreat. The images, shown that evening on all the networks, horrified the nation and pushed the administration into action.

The strategy of massive demonstrations had paid off. Supporters staged marches in Detroit, New York, Chicago, and Los Angeles. Sympathizers in Washington conducted sit-ins at the White House, at the Capitol, and along Pennsylvania Avenue. On March 15 Johnson went before Congress to make his case for a powerful new voting rights bill. Selma, he told the hushed chambers, marked a turning point in American history equal to Lexington and Concord. "Because it is not just Negroes, but really all of us who must overcome the crippling legacy of bigotry and injustice. And," he concluded, "we shall . . . overcome." Martin Luther King called Johnson's speech one of "the most eloquent, unequivocal and passionate pleas for human rights ever made by a President of the United States."

Five months later, on August 6, in the President's Room of the Capitol, where 104 years earlier Abraham Lincoln had signed a bill freeing slaves impressed into the service of the Confederacy, Johnson signed into law the Voting Rights Act of 1965. The legislation authorized federal examiners to register voters, and it banned the use of literacy tests.

A Former Slave Finally Gets the Vote   The Voting Rights Act of 1965 authorized the attorney general to suspend local and state regulations that interfered with voter registration. The act transformed southern politics in particular, admitting hundreds of thousands of citizens into the political process for the first time. One hundred years after he was freed from slavery, this 106-year-old Mississippi man registers to vote in Batesville. He is escorted by members of the Mississippi Freedom Democratic Party. *(© Bettmann/CORBIS)*

The Voting Rights Act permanently changed race relations in the South. The most dramatic result was in Mississippi. In 1965 just 28,500 blacks, a mere 7 percent of the voting-age population, had been registered; three years later 250,770 blacks were registered. Between 1964 and 1969 the number of black adults registered to vote increased from 19.3 percent to 61.3 percent in Alabama and from 27.4 percent to 60.4 percent in Georgia. One of the many white office-holders removed from office by the surge in black voting was Sheriff Jim Clark, who was defeated in the 1966 Democratic primary.

The legislation also had the unintended consequences of increasing mobilization of white voters and undermining support for the Democratic Party in the South. On the night that Congress passed the act, a somber Johnson told an aide, "I think we've just handed the South over to the Republican Party for the rest of our lives." The prediction proved painfully accurate for Democrats. Despite the massive mobilization of black voters between 1960 and 1980, the increase of white registration surpassed black by almost five to one. Before 1964 nearly 55 percent of all southern counties voted consistently Democratic in presidential elections. By 1980 that number had dropped to only 14 percent. While many forces conspired to erode Democratic support in the once-solid South, race ranked at the top of the list.

Burn, Baby, Burn!

Ironically, just when Johnson was legislating into law the most progressive domestic legislation in history, African American discontent reached a new high. Between 1964 and 1968 the United States experienced the most intense period of civil unrest since the Civil War. In 1964 blacks rioted in Harlem and in the Bedford-Stuyvesant section of Brooklyn. In August 1965, five days after Johnson signed the Voting Rights Act into law, the Watts section of Los Angeles exploded in violence. Two-thirds of the 250,000 blacks living in Watts were on welfare, and unemployment stood at 34 percent. Complaints about the police were common. The population was 98 percent black, but only 5 of the 205 police officers were black.

On August 11, 1965, a white police officer stopped a car driven by a twenty-one-year-old, unemployed black man. When the man resisted arrest, a crowd gathered, forcing police to summon reinforcements. Within an hour a thousand blacks were on the street hurling rocks and bottles at the cops and shouting, "Burn, baby, burn!" For four nights marauding mobs in the black suburb burned and killed, while 500 policeman and 5,000 national guardsmen struggled to contain the fury. Before the rioting ended, thirty-four were dead, nearly four thousand were arrested, and property damage had reached $45 million. Fourteen thousand national guardsmen and several thousand local police needed six days to stop the arson, looting, and sniping.

The Watts explosion marked the first of four successive "long hot summers." In the summer of 1966 thirty-eight disorders destroyed ghetto neighborhoods in cities from San Francisco to Providence, Rhode Island. The result was seven deaths, four hundred injuries, and $5 million in property damage. The following year Newark erupted, leaving twenty-five dead and some twelve hundred wounded. In Detroit forty-three were killed, and more than four thousand fires burned large portions of the city. *Newsweek* called the riots "a symbol of a domestic crisis grown graver than any since the Civil War."

The paradox of American prosperity, and the revolution of rising expectations that it produced, contributed to the success of the civil-rights movement, but it also sowed the seeds of discontent and rebellion. Between 1963 and 1969 blacks were experiencing the most significant gains since the Civil War. The Civil Rights Act of 1964 and Voting Rights Act of 1965 had removed the last vestiges of legal discrimination. In 1967 African Americans were elected mayors in Gary, Indiana, and Cleveland, Ohio—the first blacks to govern major cities. That same year Thurgood Marshall became the first black to serve on the Supreme Court. Economically, blacks were faring better, thanks to Great Society programs and an overheated economy. Median black family income rose from $5,921 to

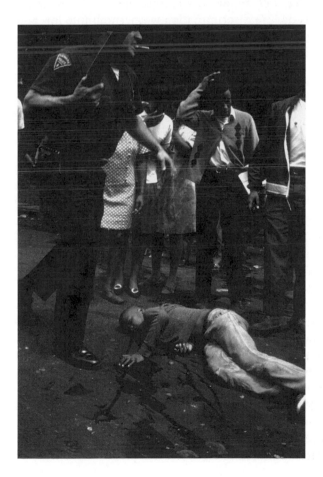

Newark Riot, July 28, 1967 Despite passage of the Civil Rights Act of 1964 and the Voting Rights Act of 1965, northern black communities suffered poverty in the ghettos of the nation's larger cities and discrimination at the hands of white police officers. The summer of 1967 saw the greatest number of riots, beginning with a riot in Newark, New Jersey, in late July. The four-day riot left twenty-five people dead and approximately twelve hundred wounded, including twelve-year-old Joe Bass Jr., who was accidentally hit by fragments from a police officer's shotgun blast. The riot cost over $10 million in property damage. (© Bud Lee/The Serge Group)

$8,074; the percentage of black families below the poverty line declined from 48.1 percent in 1959 to 27.9 percent in 1969. Polls showed that the majority of blacks were optimistic about their personal futures.

With expectations of the "good society" stimulated by the acquisition of legal and political rights, many younger northern African Americans demanded social and economic rights as well. While the struggle in the South raised the hopes of blacks living in northern ghettos, it did little to improve their condition. Violence became a means of expressing their rage at the limited pace and scope of racial change and their bitterness over increased white opposition to their minimal advances. "The Negro masses are angry and restless," observed the author Louis Lomax, "tired of prolonged legal battles that end in paper decrees."

The riots highlighted the differences between the struggle for political rights in the South and the new campaign for economic rights in the North. They also highlighted how Martin Luther King's strategy of nonviolence seemed inappropriate for addressing the new problems. In the South, King confronted a political system that systematically prevented blacks from exercising rights that most Americans considered essential—the right to vote, the right of access to public facilities. This de jure discrimination was written into law and enforced by the state. An intransigent white power structure allowed King to convey to the nation the sharp moral contrast between the black struggle for rights and the reality of an oppressive society still struggling with the legacy of slavery.

In the North blacks suffered from economic inequality and more informal, but no less pernicious, forms of discrimination. This de facto discrimination developed over years and found expression in profoundly segregated housing, limited job opportunities, poor schools, and minimal health care. Sometimes the discrimination was written into law through various covenants that prevented blacks from moving into white neighborhoods. Sometimes it was practiced by government officials even without the clear sanction of law. For decades school boards consciously redirected resources away from predominately black schools, for example. For the most part, however, the discrimination developed through voluntary habits and custom and served as a reminder of the deep racial divide in America. Blacks in the North could vote, board public buses, and occasionally join unions, but they had little choice in where they worked or lived.

The result was deeply imbedded poverty and unemployment in many black communities. In 1966, 41.7 percent of nonwhites in urban America lived below the federal poverty line. The infant mortality rate for African Americans was 90 percent higher than it was for whites. President Johnson's National Advisory Commission on Civil Disorders, created to investigate the causes of the riots, speculated that despair, black militancy, and white racism combined to create a combustible situation. Ominously, the commission warned, "Our nation is moving toward two societies, one black, one white—separate and unequal."

By the mid-1960s many black leaders had repudiated King's message of integration and nonviolence in favor of separatism and self-defense. The change could be seen in the evolution of SNCC, the organization that helped organize sit-ins and freedom rides. By 1965 bruised and angry SNCC members were unwilling to turn the other cheek when confronted by violence. SNCC members felt betrayed when Lyndon Johnson refused to support the Mississippi Freedom Democratic Party's challenge to the all-white delegation at the Democratic National Convention in 1964. Believing that liberal white college students only helped to reinforce the feelings of inferiority in southern blacks, SNCC kicked whites out of the organization, ending the biracial coalition that had been so successful in the South.

Black Power!

SNCC leader Stokely Carmichael captured the anger of many urban blacks when he coined the phrase *Black Power*. Picking up on the theme of black nationalism of the slain Malcolm X, Carmichael called integration "a subterfuge for the maintenance of white supremacy." Instead, he urged blacks to develop their own cultural heritage and become self-dependent. "We don't need white liberals," Carmichael told supporters. "We have to make integration irrelevant." Rejecting nonviolence, Carmichael said, "Black people should and must fight back."

Martin Luther King urged Carmichael to tone down his rhetoric, arguing that the cry of Black Power would "confuse our allies, isolate the Negro community and give many prejudiced whites . . . a ready excuse for self-justification." Roy Wilkins of the National Association for the Advancement of Colored People (NAACP) branded Black Power "the father of hatred and the mother of violence." Others pointed out that a racial minority could not achieve anything of substance without allies. But Carmichael refused to back down. He was frustrated and angry with the slow pace of progress, disillusioned with King, and eager to build a mass movement that would include young radicals and the urban poor.

PRIMARY SOURCE

8.2 | "Black Power": A Statement by the National Committee of Negro Churchmen

BLACK POWER

In 1966, The National Committee of Negro Churchmen (NCNC), an organization made up of 300 members from twelve Protestant denominations, issued a statement designed to clarify the meaning of Black Power. While rejecting violence, they acknowledged that the need for blacks to demand and exercise power—political and economic—was at the heart of the civil-rights struggle.

We, an informal group of Negro churchmen in America, are deeply disturbed about the crisis brought upon our country by historic distortions of important human realities in the controversy about "black power." What we see shining through the variety of rhetoric is not anything new but the same old problem of power and race which has faced our beloved country since 1619.

We realize that neither the term "power" nor the term "Christian Conscience" is an easy matter to talk about, especially in the context of race relations in America. The fundamental distortion facing us in the controversy about "black power" is rooted in a gross imbalance of power and conscience between Negroes and white Americans. It is this distortion, mainly, which is responsible for the widespread, though often inarticulate, assumption that white people are justified in getting what they want through the use of power, but that Negro Americans must, either by nature or by circumstances, make their appeal only through conscience. As a result, the power of white men and the conscience of black men have both been corrupted. The power of white men is corrupted because it meets little meaningful resistance from Negroes to temper it and keep white men from aping God. The conscience of black men is corrupted because, having no power to implement the demands of conscience, the concern for justice is transmuted into a distorted form of love, which, in the absence of justice, becomes chaotic self-surrender. Powerlessness breeds a race of beggars. We are faced now with a situation where conscienceless power meets powerless conscience, threatening the very foundations of our nation. . . .

It is of critical importance that the leaders of this nation listen also to a voice which says that the principal source of the threat to our nation comes neither from the riots erupting in our big cities, nor from the disagreements among the leaders of the civil rights movement, nor even from mere raising of the cry for "black power." These events, we believe, are but the expression of the judgment of God upon our nation for its failure to use its abundant resources to serve the real well-being of people, at home and abroad.

We give our full support to all civil rights leaders as they seek for basically American goals, for we are not convinced that their mutual reinforcement of one another in the past is bound to end in the future. We would hope that the public power of our nation will be used to strengthen the civil rights movement and not to manipulate or further fracture it.

We deplore the overt violence of riots, but we believe it is more important to focus on the real sources of these eruptions. These sources may be abetted inside the ghetto, but their basic causes lie in the silent and covert violence which white middle-class America inflicts upon the victims of the inner city. The hidden, smooth and often smiling decisions of American leaders which tie a white noose of suburbia around the necks and which pin the backs of the masses of Negroes against the steaming ghetto walls—without jobs in a booming economy; with dilapidated and segregated educational systems in the full view of unenforced laws against it; in short: the failure of American leaders to use American power to create equal opportunity in life as well as in law—this is the real problem and not the anguished cry for black power.

From the point of view of the Christian faith, there is nothing necessarily wrong with concern for power. . . . At issue in the relations between whites and

Negroes in America is the problem of inequality of power. Out of this imbalance grows the disrespect of white men for the Negro personality and community, and the disrespect of Negroes for themselves. This is a fundamental root of human
50 injustice in America. In one sense, the concept of "black power" reminds us of the need for and the possibility of authentic democracy in America.

We do not agree with those who say that we must cease expressing concern for the acquisition of power lest we endanger the "gains" already made by the civil rights movement. The fact of the matter is, there have been few substantive
55 gains since about 1950 in this area. The gap has constantly widened between the incomes of non-whites relative to the whites. Since the Supreme Court decision of 1954, de facto segregation in every major city in our land has increased rather than decreased. Since the middle of the 1950s unemployment among Negroes has gone up rather than down, while unemployment has decreased in the white
60 community.

While there has been some progress in some areas for equality for Negroes, this progress has been limited mainly to middle-class Negroes who represent only a small minority of the larger Negro community.

These are the hard facts that we must all face together. Therefore, we must not
65 take the position that we can continue in the same old paths.

When American leaders decide to serve the real welfare of people instead of war and destruction; when American leaders are forced to make the rebuilding of our cities the first priority on the nation's agenda; when American leaders are forced by the American people to quit misusing and abusing American
70 power; then will the cry for "black power" become inaudible, for the framework in which all power in America operates would include the power and experience of black men as well as those of white men. In that way, the fear of the power of each group would be removed. America is our beloved homeland. But, America is not God. Only God can do everything. America and the other nations of the
75 world must decide which among a number of alternatives they will choose.

Source: National Committee of Negro Churchmen Collection, Special Collections Research Center, Syracuse University Library. ■ ■ ■

The reorientation of the civil-rights movement away from integration and assimilation and toward separatism and racial pride spread like wildfire across black America. But this reorientation meant different things to different people. It was more a cry of rage than a systematic doctrine. For some, the emphasis on black solidarity would allow African Americans to gain political power. To overcome racism, this argument went, blacks had to work together. "Before a group can enter the open society," read one manifesto, "it must first close ranks." In theory, this was similar to the model of liberal pluralism used by European ethnic groups in America and celebrated by political scientists.

Another theme stressed cultural nationalism as a way for black people to uncover their roots and recognize the uniqueness of their culture and traditions. African American parents pushed school boards to approve the teaching of black history and culture. College students pressured administrators to recruit black teachers and students, create Afro-American cultural centers, and institute Black Studies classes and departments. Young people let their hair grow in what became known as the "Afro" and began wearing African-styled clothing. Singer James Brown declared, "Say it loud, I'm black and I'm proud." In this sense the Black Power movement represented a new spirit of pride and assertiveness.

Another, more militant theme crystallized with the Black Panther Party, formed in Oakland in October 1966, following the killing of an unarmed black youth by a San Francisco police officer. Huey Newton and Bobby Seale created the Panthers to embody Malcolm X's doctrine of community self-defense. Above all, the Panthers believed that the black community needed to arm to defend itself from the brutality of the white police: "Only with the power of the gun can the black masses halt the terror and brutality perpetuated against them by the armed racist power structure." Black people constituted a colony in the mother country of the American empire, Newton said, and, like all victims of oppression, could legitimately resort to revolution—meaning guns. "The heirs of Malcolm X," Newton rejoiced, "have picked up the gun."

Uninterested in legislative or political reform, the Panthers called themselves "armed revolutionaries." In May 1967, Newton, Seale, and thirty followers armed with shotguns and M-16 rifles marched into the California state legislature in Sacramento to protest a bill that would have made it illegal for people to carry unconcealed weapons. In October 1967, Panther Huey Newton went to jail for killing a police officer. In April 1968, thirteen Panthers ambushed an Oakland police car, hitting it with 157 shots and badly wounding one officer. By 1970 the Panthers had killed eleven police officers. Beyond their rhetoric and their shootouts with the police, a few committed Panthers, many of them women, set up free breakfast programs, medical clinics, and other community-based programs in several cities.

Backlash

Urban riots were part of what appeared to be a crime epidemic that swept the nation in the 1960s. Property crime (burglary, larceny, and auto theft) soared 73 percent between 1960 and 1967. The rate of violent crime (murder, robbery, rape, and aggravated assault) doubled. Between 1965 and 1969 the crime rate in America increased by double digits every year, and it grew fastest in rural areas and small towns. "Crime Runs Wild," cried a 1965 headline in *U.S. News & World Report*. "Will It Be Halted?"

The rising crime rate was directly tied to the aging of the baby boomer generation—there were simply greater numbers of people in the young adult age group that was most likely to commit crime. A genuine fear that society was unraveling fueled the backlash. But most white Americans viewed the breakdown of law and order through the lens of race and politics. Concern over the rising crime rate, combined with racial unease and worry that traditional values were under assault, produced a potent new political issue.

Even before the riots and the rise of black nationalism, white America revealed its general discomfort with African American appeals for racial justice. During the 1940s and 1950s, urban whites in cities such as Detroit had split their ballots. They voted for pro-civil-rights candidates for president, but in local elections that directly impacted their communities, they consistently voted against any effort to end residential segregation. In 1963 a *Newsweek* magazine survey found that 55 percent of whites objected to having a black family living next to them; 90 percent would object to having their daughters date a black man. "I don't like to touch them. It just makes me squeamish," said one northerner. In 1964 voters in California, who elected Lyndon Johnson in a landslide, also passed by a 2–1 margin a referendum, Proposition 14, repealing the state's new fair housing act. "The essence of freedom is the right to discriminate," observed a leader of the repeal movement.

Most whites responded to the riots and the new militancy with increased fear and anger. While liberals failed to appreciate the growing public anxiety, conservatives realized that the white backlash offered a powerful political weapon to undermine support for the Democratic Party. In 1966, California movie actor Ronald Reagan won the governorship by blaming the Watts riot on liberal policymakers. Even his defeated opponent, liberal Pat Brown, declared in his concession speech that "whether we like it or not the people want separation of the races." Republican candidates across the country pounced on the law and order issue. That same year, Republicans campaigning on a tough "law-and-order" platform gained forty-seven seats in the House and three in the Senate. The Democrats lost more seats in 1966 than they had won in 1964. After November 1966, there were 156 northern Democrats in the House, 62 short of a majority. Johnson, a meteorologist of the public mood, tailored his program to suit the times. Only once in his 1967 State of the Union message, a thirteen-page, single-spaced text, did he refer to the Great Society.

The Youth Culture

Racial conflict exposed one of the fault lines in the vital center's faith in consensus. At the same time, many young people challenged the cultural and political assumptions of their parents, exposing another tear in the fabric of consensus. Young Americans in the 1960s were not the first to speak against the injustice and hypocrisy of their elders, but social and demographic forces provided this generation with new clout. The postwar baby boom had dramatically increased the number of college-age students in America. In 1965, 41 percent of all Americans were under the age of twenty. College enrollments soared from 3.6 million in 1960 to almost 8 million in 1970. Because colleges contained the largest concentration of young people in the country, they became the seedbed of youth protest.

By the early 1960s the Beat message, popularized in inexpensive paperback novels, television, and movies, had gained wide acceptance among young people and formed the backbone of the "counterculture" movement. The movement lacked a coherent ideology but shared a core of attitudes and beliefs. In search of a "higher consciousness," the counterculture rejected the tenets of modern industrial society: materialism, self-denial, sexual repression, and the work ethic. To the alarm of many older Americans, counterculture fashion promoted long hair for men, eastern symbols, and clothes purchased from the Salvation Army.

Drug use was part of the message. The prophet of the new drug culture was Timothy Leary, a Harvard psychologist who preached to his students (and anyone else who would listen) about the wonders of magic mushrooms and LSD. "Tune in, turn on, drop out," he advised the young. LSD was widely available on college campuses, and many of the world's most popular rock groups used it and wrote songs about it. According to *Life* magazine, by 1966 over 1 million people had experimented with LSD. But marijuana remained the drug of choice for young people. By 1969 more than 30 percent of all college students in the United States had smoked pot.

Sexual expression and freedom were central to the counterculture's rejection of mainstream morality. The media offered extensive coverage of "Summer of Love" festivals. Music, which once celebrated the wonders of dating, soon made explicit reference to sex acts. In 1964 the Beatles topped the charts with "I Want to Hold Your Hand." By 1967 they were singing, "Why don't we do it in the road?" During the decade sexual images became a part of the nation's public culture. By 1970 there were 830 adults-only bookstores and 200 theaters showing hardcore sex films. An estimated 45 million pieces of sexually oriented material were sent through the mail each year. Studies showed that roughly 80 percent of boys and 70 percent of girls had seen visual depictions or read descriptions of sexual intercourse by the age of eighteen.

The ability to enjoy sex without the burden of procreation was enhanced by new methods of birth control. Developed in 1957 and licensed by the Food and Drug Administration in 1960, the birth control pill—which quickly became known as "the pill"—gave women a greater sense of sexual freedom than any previous contraceptive device. By 1962 an estimated 1,187,000 women were using the pill. Ten years later 10 million women were doing so. *Time* magazine called it "a miraculous tablet." The pill divorced sex from the danger of unwanted pregnancy. It gave women the freedom to have sex when and where they wished and made contraception acceptable to the mainstream. The pill put birth control on the front pages of newspapers and on the cover of magazines, forcing people to confront the gap between public morality and private behavior.

The counterculture also defined itself through music. Bob Dylan's rapid rise to fame was emblematic of the newly emerging cultural sensibility. Dylan, born Robert Zimmerman in Hibbing, Minnesota, joined the New York Greenwich Village folk music scene in 1961. Blending poetic economy with poetic diction, Dylan accompanied himself on an acoustic guitar and a harmonica harnessed around his neck. His hugely successful second album, *The Freewheelin' Bob Dylan* (1963), which included political songs such as "A Hard Rain's Gonna Fall," and "Blowin' in the Wind," sold two hundred thousand copies in two months. The last song, with its call to political action and challenge to consensus—"How many times can a man turn his head pretending he just doesn't see?"—sold more than 1 million copies. The following month the folk group Peter, Paul, and Mary released their own single of "Blowin' in the Wind" that sold over three hundred thousand copies in less than two weeks.

After 1964 Dylan had to compete with a host of new rock bands from England. The most popular, the Beatles, captured the hearts of teenage America following a TV appearance on the popular *Ed Sullivan Show* in 1964. Initially, the Beatles, with ties, jackets, and well-kempt, if long, hair, hoped to reach a mass consumer market by avoiding a clear association with the counterculture. But their music, which seemed to mock the adult world, contained a message of freedom and excitement that belied their sometimes subdued lyrics. By 1967, however, with the release of *Sergeant Pepper's Lonely Hearts Club Band,* the Beatles were celebrating their new role as cultural antagonists. "When the Beatles told us to turn off our minds and float downstream," recalled one fan, "uncounted youngsters assumed that the key to this kind of mind-expansion could be found in a plant or a pill."

The Beatles changed their tune, in part, to keep ahead of other groups that were gaining widespread popularity by preaching a more potent message. In 1967 Mick Jagger, lead singer of the Rolling Stones, also a British import, was arousing young audiences with a mixture of anger and sexual prowess. During concerts Jagger would thrust the microphone between his legs and whip the floor with a leather belt in a blatantly erotic demonstration. "The Beatles want to hold your hand," said one critic, but "the Stones want to burn your house."

The New Left

At the heart of the youth rebellion of the 1960s was a desire to challenge the established political and cultural order. In 1962 Students for a Democratic Society (SDS), the leading New Left organization on college campuses, composed the Port Huron Statement. The founding document of the New Left, it called for tackling the nation's problems through "self cultivation, self direction, self understanding, and creativity." While recognizing the need to address issues of poverty and racism, the statement suggested the crisis of modern life was primarily moral. "A new left," SDS proclaimed, "must give form to the feelings of helplessness and indifference, so that people may see the political, social, and economic source of their personal troubles and organize to change society." Despite many differences, both the New Left and the counterculture rejected their parents' definition of reality and searched for ways to express their individuality and find self-fulfillment in an age of mass conformity.

In 1963, 125 SDS members, mostly middle-class white men and women, set up chapters to organize poor whites and blacks in nine American cities. Other members traveled to Mississippi in 1964 as part of the Freedom Summer organized by the Student Nonviolent Coordinating Committee (SNCC). Direct exposure to the brutality of southern justice radicalized many of the students, who returned to campus the following fall searching for an outlet for their fear and anger.

In October 1964 the administration of the University of California at Berkeley provided one outlet. Chancellor Clark Kerr decided to enforce campus regulations prohibiting political demonstrations at the entrance of campus—a traditional site for student political expression. When police tried to arrest protester Jack Weinberg, a crowd of students surrounded the car and organized a sit-in. The next day the university backed down and dropped charges, but the Free Speech Movement (FSM) had been born. At a December 2 rally FSM leader Mario Savio told a spirited crowd that "there is a time when the operation of the machine becomes so odious . . . [that] you can't even passively take part." When he finished, the crowd of eight hundred stormed Sproul Hall, Berkeley's administration building, for a sit-in. The movement soon broadened its focus to protest

The Free Speech Movement at the University of California, Berkeley Though their grievances against the administration varied, undergraduate and graduate students at UC Berkeley worked together to organize a sit-in of Sproul Hall on December 2. Early the next morning, police began emptying the building, arresting eight hundred students who refused to leave voluntarily. Their action prompted change at the university. In early January, the new acting chancellor loosened the rules for political activity on campus and opened up the steps of Sproul Hall to political speeches.

the "multiversity machine." Many students began wearing computer punch cards marked: "I AM A STUDENT. DO NOT FOLD, SPINDLE, OR MUTILATE." The revolt quickly spread to other campuses and championed many causes, from opposing dress codes to fighting tenure decisions.

The New Left never articulated a coherent alternative vision for America. They shared a sense of anger with the existing system, but they often fought over tactics. The New Left also fractured along gender lines. Women joined the ranks of the new left organizations for the same reasons as men—they wanted to challenge the consensus by participating in social activism. However, many women felt marginalized by their male colleagues and alienated from the inner circle of the movement. The assumption of male superiority, they charged, left many "competent, qualified, and experienced" women relegated to "female kinds of jobs," such as "typing, desk work, and telephone work." Women activists also faced physical and sexual abuse from the police and from men within their own movement. "What is the position of women in SNCC?" Stokely Carmichael joked in response to a feminist complaint. "The position of women in SNCC is prone!"

Many idealistic women who joined organizations like SNCC and SDS to promote equality became disillusioned with the rampant sexism. They charged that men who would risk their lives to fight for racial equality failed to appreciate the reality of gender inequality. While a few men were sympathetic to these efforts to address gender discrimination in the New Left, most were either indifferent or openly hostile. When a coalition of leftist organizations banded together in August 1967 to form the National Conference for New Politics, women participants wanted to debate a resolution regarding women's issues. Many of the male leaders dismissed the notion. One man responded by patting a female representative on the head, saying "Move on little girl; we have more important issues to talk about here than women's liberation." Feeling rejected by existing New Left organizations, which considered women's rights as secondary to the bigger problems of imperialism and capitalism, many women activists formed their own independent caucuses and workshops, seeking personal identities that rejected traditional expectations.

PRIMARY SOURCE

8.3 | *To the Women of the Left*

After the National Conference for New Politics meeting in August 1967, a group of women delegates, frustrated with their treatment inside the male-dominated New Left movement, decided to meet independently. The Westside Group, one of a handful of women's groups that formed in Chicago, created a Preliminary Statement of Principles to lay out the most important issues of women who had become activists in the civil-rights and students movements and who now believed that true liberation would only come with gender equality. *New Left Notes,* an SDS publication in Chicago, printed the statement in its November 13, 1967, edition.

We have been meeting weekly for the last two months to discuss our colonial status in this society and to propound strategy and methods of attacking it. Our political awareness of our oppression has developed thru the last couple years as we sought to apply the principles of justice, equality, mutual respect and
5 dignity which we learned from the Movement to the lives we lived as part of the Movement; only to come up against the solid wall of male chauvinism.

Realizing that this is a social problem of national significance not at all confined to our struggle for personal liberation within the Movement we must approach it in a political manner. Therefore it is incumbent on us, as women, to
10 organize a movement for woman's liberation. . . .

Specifically, it is imperative that we unite behind the following points as a beginning step towards full and equal participation of women in our society.

1. As women are 51% of the population of this country, they must be proportionally represented on all levels of society rather than relegated to trivial func-
15 tions that have been predetermined for them. . . .

2. We condemn the mass media for perpetuating the stereotype of women as always in an auxiliary position to men, being no more than mothers, wives or sexual objects. . . .

3. There should be total equality of opportunity for education, at all levels and
20 in all fields. . . .

4. Equal employment opportunities must be enforced. . . .

5. The labor movement and all labor organizations, unions and groups must admit women on an equal basis to all executive and policy levels while encouraging women to assume leadership roles in their organizations. . . .
25 6. Women must have complete control of their own bodies. This means (a) the dissemination of birth control information and devices, free of charge by the state, to all women regardless of age and marital status; (b) the availability of a competent, inexpensive medical abortion for all women who so desire.

7. The structure of the family unit in our society must be reconsidered and
30 the following institutional changes must be incorporated: (a) a fundamental revamping of marriage, divorce and property laws and customs which cause an injustice to or a subjection of either sex; (b) the equal sharing by husbands and wives of the responsibility for maintaining the home and raising the children; (c) the creation of communal child care centers which would be staffed by women
35 and men assuming equal responsibility. . . .

Towards this end, we identify with those groups now in revolutionary struggle within our country and abroad. Until the movement recognizes the necessity that women be free and women recognize the necessity for all struggles of liberation, there can be no revolution.

Source: Excerpts from "To the Women of the Left," *New Left Notes* (Chicago), November 13, 1967, 2. ■ ■ ■

Lyndon Johnson came to office promising to create a "Great Society." Using his considerable legislative skill, he pushed Congress to enact legislation to aid the poor and elderly and to guarantee equal rights for African Americans. The legislative success, however, did not produce the social harmony that Johnson promised. By 1967 the contradiction between expectations and social realities was becoming apparent to those on both the left and the right. African Americans, realizing that southern racism could not be uprooted without the use of coercive federal power, grew disillusioned by Washington's halfhearted response to their plight. At the same time, conservatives were becoming resentful of federal activism, complaining that it had usurped rights reserved to individuals and the states. Adding to the explosive mix were young people who were questioning the cultural pillars supporting the faith in consensus. Confused thinking and poor planning plagued the Great Society, but it was a distant war in Southeast Asia that would mark its demise.

SUGGESTED READINGS

▌ John A. Andrew III offers a brief overview of LBJ's reform initiatives in *Lyndon Johnson and the Great Society* (1998). Michael W. Flamm and David Steigerwald offer competing views of the politics of the decade in *Debating the 1960s* (2008). Robert Caro's multivolume biography, *The Years of Lyndon Johnson: Path to Power* (1982); *Means of Ascent* (1990); and *Master of the Senate* (2002), needs to be balanced with Robert Dallek's masterful volumes, *Lone Star Rising* (1991) and *Flawed Giant* (1998). James T. Patterson's *America's Struggle Against Poverty, 1900–1994* (1995) analyzes the fateful consequences of the Great Society's "welfare explosion." Michael Beschloss uses White House tape recordings to provide a rare glimpse inside the Johnson administration in *Taking Charge* (1997). Lucas Powe, in *The Warren Court and American Politics* (2000), argues that the Court worked to impose national liberal-elite values on the country. In *Earl Warren* (1982), G. Edward White discusses the formative influences on Warren's progressive worldview. Anthony Lewis brings to life the personal stakes of judicial activism in his classic account of one man's extraordinary involvement in a landmark criminal-rights decision, *Gideon's Trumpet* (1964).

▌ John Dittmer's study of the civil-rights movement in Mississippi, *Local People* (1994), reveals the commitment and grit of ordinary people that sustained an extraordinary social movement. Doug McAdam's *Freedom Summer* (1988) studies the impact of SNCC's watershed moment on a generation of activists. David Garrow's *Bearing the Cross* (1986) digs deep into the complex life of Martin Luther King. Nick Kotz uses newly released taped conversations between Johnson and King to reveal the efforts of both men after Kennedy's death in *Judgment Days* (2005). The Kerner Commission's *Report of the National Advisory Commission on Civil Disorders* (1968) and Stokely Carmichael and Charles Hamilton's *Black Power* (1967) are both important primary sources on the later civil-rights movement. Michael Flamm offers insight into the white backlash in *Law and Order* (2005).

▌ Godfrey Hodgson traces liberalism's cathartic passage through the 1960s in his masterful synthesis, *America in Our Time* (1976). The tendency to see the student protest movements as harbingers of a profound society-wide awakening of political activism and consciousness was influenced early on by two widely read essays, Theodore Roszak's *The Making of a Counter-Culture* (1969) and Charles Reich's *The Greening of America* (1971). Terry Anderson's *The Movement and the Sixties* (1995) looks closely at underground sources to draw connections among the many protests. For a gripping, dizzying journey into the lives of some pioneers of the counterculture, see Tom Wolfe's *The Electric Kool-Aid Acid Test* (1968). Kevin Mattson's *Intellectuals in Action* (2002) traces the origins of the New Left and reasons for its demise. On the decade's political legacy, see Maurice Isserman and Michael Kazin's *America Divided* (1999).

▌ There is a growing body of work on the rise of conservatism in the 1960s. The most insightful is Rick Perlstein's *Before the Storm* (2002). Also valuable are Jonathan Schoenwald, *A Time for Choosing* (2002); John Micklethwatt, *The Right Nation* (2004); and Mary C. Brennan, *Turning Right in the Sixties* (1995).

9

"Into the Big Muddy": America in Vietnam, 1945–1968

At about 2:00 PM on February 7, 1965, the sentry at Camp Holloway, an American air base outside the Vietnamese city of Pleiku, spotted the shadows of men moving along the perimeter of the base. Seconds later a series of explosions shattered the concrete wall surrounding the installation, dozens of mortar shells rained from the sky, and thousands of rounds of small-arms fire pelted the area. By the time the attack ended, 7 men were dead, 109 wounded. Three days later the Vietcong hit a U.S. Army barracks at Qui Nhon, killing 8 Americans and wounding 21.

Over the next several days President Lyndon Johnson met with the National Security Council (NSC) to discuss the American response. NSC adviser McGeorge Bundy, sent to Vietnam after the attacks, returned with a startling report. "The prospect in Vietnam is grim," he informed the president. "The stakes in Vietnam are extremely high." The president's leading civilian and military advisers had been eager to expand U.S. military involvement in Vietnam by initiating a campaign of sustained bombing of selected targets. The attack on Pleiku provided the administration with the justification for escalation. "Pleikus are like streetcars," Bundy told a reporter, meaning that you jump onto one when you need it.

Following the attack on Pleiku, the administration committed the nation to its fateful course in Vietnam. Not only did the United States decide to begin a program of sustained bombing but it also agreed to commit American ground troops to protect air bases from attacks similar to Pleiku. In order to launch a bombing campaign, Johnson said the only way to stop the attacks was by "sending a very large number of U.S. troops to Vietnam." Secretary of Defense Robert McNamara told the president that guarding American bases would require "at least 100,000 men, 44 battalions." The president also made another key decision: he would keep the change in policy a secret. When William Bundy, an assistant secretary of state and brother of McGeorge, suggested that "at an appropriate time we could publicly announce that we have turned a corner and changed our policy," Johnson said that since the United States was already committed to helping the South Vietnamese, he did not have to announce any change in strategy.

Since the days of Harry Truman, American policymakers had walked a fine line in Vietnam: taking incremental steps to prevent a communist victory while avoiding a major commitment of resources to the region. With the military situation deteriorating, Johnson could no longer maintain that delicate balancing act. Johnson found his Vietnam policy impaled on the horns of the same paradox that confounded his domestic programs. At home, the president wanted to eradicate poverty without a dramatic expansion of federal power; abroad, he wanted to defeat communist aggression in Vietnam without the sacrifices of war—full mobilization, increased taxes, and a shift away from domestic priorities.

By 1968, the contradictions in America's approach to Vietnam and the limits of vital-center liberalism were painfully obvious and found full expression in that year's presidential campaign.

The First Fateful Steps

America's postwar policy of containment shaped the nation's approach to Vietnam. In 1949, the "fall" of China had transformed a local nationalist struggle against French rule in Indochina into a globally strategic battleground. During

World War II Franklin Roosevelt had expressed support for Vietnamese nationalist forces led by Ho Chi Minh, a communist educated in Paris and Moscow, and called for an end to French colonial rule. After Jiang's collapse American policy shifted. Fearing that a communist "victory" in Indochina would become a sweep of Southeast Asia and tilt the global balance of power, the United States abandoned its pretense of neutrality and openly endorsed French policy in Asia. In 1950, when the Soviet Union and China extended diplomatic recognition to Ho's government, which controlled a part of Northern Vietnam, Truman supplied military aid to the French. America had taken its first step into the Vietnam quagmire.

Eisenhower, like Truman, viewed Ho as a communist puppet and believed that if southern Vietnam fell to the communists, all Southeast Asia would be at risk. The administration's approach to Vietnam was also influenced by its priorities in Europe. Ike supported the French effort, providing up to 75 percent of the cost of the war by 1954, because he wanted France to join NATO.

The poorly led French army, however, was no match for the resourceful Vo Nguyen Giap, the commander-in-chief of the Vietminh troops in the South. In 1954 Vietnamese and Communist Chinese forces surrounded 12,000 French troops at Dien Bien Phu, a remote jungle fortress. The French pleaded for direct American intervention to rescue their troops. For weeks the administration debated a course of action. Secretary of State John Foster Dulles wanted to take the nation to the brink of war by launching air strikes against the North Vietnamese. Vice President Nixon went further, suggesting the introduction of ground troops or even the use of tactical nuclear weapons. He was supported by the air force chief of staff, who favored dropping "small tactical A-bombs," to "clean those Commies out of there" so that "the band could play the Marseillaise and the French would come marching out of Dien Bien Phu in fine shape."

Eisenhower preferred caution. The president had little faith in the military capability of the French, whom he called "a hopeless, helpless mass of protoplasm." He also doubted the abilities of France's Vietnamese allies whom he felt lacked the "high morale based upon a war purpose or cause in which it believes" needed to win a war. European allies, especially the British, opposed American intervention. At home leading Democrats, including Senators Lyndon Johnson of Texas and John F. Kennedy of Massachusetts, warned against using American soldiers in Indochina. Eisenhower also worried about the moral implications of using tactical nuclear weapons in Asia. "You boys must be crazy," Eisenhower replied. "We can't use those awful things against Asians for the second time in ten years. My God." Without American support the French garrison surrendered in May 1954.

Eisenhower was not opposed to some form of intervention, however. When asked a question about Indochina at a press conference, Ike spelled out for the first time what would become known as the "domino theory," establishing a policy for the region that guided succeeding administrations.

9.1 | *The Domino Theory*

DWIGHT EISENHOWER

President Eisenhower laid out the need for stronger American resolve to prevent communism from spreading throughout Southeast Asia. During his April 7 news conference Eisenhower explained why support of the French in Indochina was vital to American interests in the entire region, promoting what became known as the domino theory.

*R*obert Richards, Copley Press: Mr. President, would you mind commenting on the strategic importance of Indochina to the free world? I think there has been, across the country, some lack of understanding on just what it means to us.

5　*The President:* You have, of course, both the specific and the general when you talk about such things.

First of all, you have the specific value of a locality in its production of materials that the world needs.

Then you have the possibility that many human beings pass under a dictator-
10　ship that is inimical to the free world.

Finally, you have broader considerations that might follow what you would call the "falling domino" principle. You have a row of dominoes set up, you knock over the first one, and what will happen to the last one is the certainty that it will go over very quickly. So you could have a beginning of a disintegration that
15　would have the most profound influences.

Now, with respect to the first one, two of the items from this particular area that the world uses are tin and tungsten. They are very important. There are others, of course, the rubber plantations and so on.

Then with respect to more people passing under this domination, Asia, after
20　all, has already lost some 450 million of its people to the Communist dictatorship, and we simply can't afford greater losses.

But when we come to the possible sequence of events, the loss of Indochina, of Burma, of Thailand, of the Peninsula, and Indonesia following, now you begin to talk about areas that not only multiply the disadvantages that you would suf-
25　fer through loss of materials, sources of materials, but now you are talking really about millions and millions and millions of people.

Finally, the geographical position achieved thereby does many things. It turns the so-called island defensive chain of Japan, Formosa, of the Philippines and to the southward; it moves in to threaten Australia and New Zealand.

30　It takes away, in its economic aspects, that region that Japan must have as a trading area or Japan, in turn, will have only one place in the world to go—that is, toward the Communist areas in order to live.

So, the possible consequences of the loss are just incalculable to the free world.

Source: Public Papers of the Presidents of the United States: Dwight D. Eisenhower, 1954 (Washington, D.C.: Government Printing Office, 1958), 381–390. ■ ■ ■

In July the French government signed the Geneva Accords, which temporarily divided Indochina at the seventeenth parallel until the holding of free democratic elections in 1956. To prevent future losses in the region Dulles set up yet another anticommunist military alliance, the Southeast Asia Treaty Organization, in September. The treaty pledged the United States to defend Australia, New Zealand, Thailand, Pakistan, and the Philippines against communist aggression.

The Geneva Accords gave the administration two years to develop a viable government in South Vietnam. Realizing that the popular Ho Chi Minh would win in a free election, the administration installed as head of state in South Vietnam Ngo Dinh Diem, an ardent Vietnamese nationalist who hated the French. Diem was also a staunch anticommunist and devout Catholic. The United States poured economic and military aid into the South in hopes of making Diem a viable leader. Between 1954 and 1956 the CIA launched plans to harass the North, destroying printing presses, contaminating the fuel supply, and distributing leaflets designed to undermine support for Ho Chi Minh. Critics pointed out that Diem was a weak leader, "a messiah without a message" whose goal was "to ask immediate American assistance in every form." But Diem was the only option, and the administration feared the consequences of abandoning his government.

With American support, Diem announced that the South would not participate in free elections as mandated by the Geneva Accords. Publicly he claimed that his government had never signed the accords and that free elections would be impossible given the repressive nature of the North Vietnamese government. It would turn out to be one of the most fateful decisions of the Cold War.

JFK and Vietnam

Between 1955 and 1961 the United States had provided over $1 billion in aid to South Vietnam and sent more than 1,500 advisers to provide economic and military assistance. The American effort, however, focused on transforming Ngo Dinh Diem's government into an effective anticommunist fighting force, not on helping him to establish a firm base of public support.

Diem had inherited from the French a crippled economy, a poorly trained army, and a corrupt and incompetent government bureaucracy. Ho Chi Minh, the nationalist leader of the communist forces in North Vietnam, added to Diem's problems by creating the communist National Liberation Front, called Vietcong, in the South to fight a guerrilla war against the Diem government. Diem's aloof personality and authoritarian style contributed to his failure to win popular support. Indifferent to the concerns of peasants living in the countryside, he ruthlessly suppressed dissenters, including powerful Buddhist groups.

Like others of his generation, Kennedy accepted the domino theory of communist conquest. If the United States abandoned Vietnam to the communists, he said in September 1963, "pretty soon Thailand, Cambodia, Laos, Malaya would go and all of Southeast Asia would be under control of the Communists and under the domination of the Chinese."

The president believed that American credibility was at stake in Vietnam. The United States needed to demonstrate its strength in order to reassure its allies and discourage potential adversaries. Yet Kennedy also harbored doubts about whether Diem could unite the country, and he questioned the wisdom of using American ground forces in the jungles of Southeast Asia. In fact, with the exception of an occasional crisis, Vietnam was never a high priority for Kennedy. During these early years the cost of losing Vietnam far outweighed the price the nation had to pay to maintain stability. Kennedy had little doubt that the United States would prevail, that its vast military might would intimidate the North Vietnamese at the same time that counterinsurgency measures would help stabilize the South. Kennedy never seriously considered that the conflict would escalate into a wider war. In 1961, when Undersecretary of State George Ball warned Kennedy that Vietnam could lead to the deployment of hundreds of thousands of American troops, Kennedy laughed: "George, you're supposed to be one of the smartest guys in town, but you're crazier than hell. That will never happen."

During his nearly three years in office, Kennedy increased both economic aid and the number of American military advisers. The infusion of American support did little to stabilize the Diem regime, however. The North Vietnamese–supplied Vietcong established control over large portions of the countryside. At the same time, American officials watched helplessly as Diem gradually lost control. He squandered millions of dollars in American aid, refused to call free elections, and used the army to crush even peaceful noncommunist demonstrations.

Kennedy's advisers offered conflicting advice on Vietnam. With the exception of the U.S. ambassador to Vietnam, who advocated a policy of "sink or swim with Ngo Dinh Diem," both the State Department and the Pentagon believed that the United States needed to take a tougher line with Diem and introduce combat troops to stabilize the government. The chairman of the Joint Chiefs of Staff urged Kennedy to "grind up the Vietcong with 40,000 American ground troops. . . . Grab 'em by the balls and their hearts and minds will follow." Robert McNamara supported the introduction of combat troops but stressed that the military had to avoid fighting a conventional war and instead develop a counterinsurgency strategy to battle the communists. Ball counseled caution, claiming that Vietnam was not a vital American interest.

Caught in the middle, Kennedy initially tried taking a hard line with Diem, insisting that American aid was contingent on his willingness to reform his corrupt government and seek accommodation with dissident groups in South Vietnam. When Diem ignored the pressure, the administration backed down. Kennedy, however, was deeply skeptical about the proposal to send combat troops to Vietnam. He worried about the difficulty of fighting in the jungles of Southeast Asia, the lack of support from major U.S. allies, and the possibility of Chinese intervention in the conflict. While he accepted the domino theory, Kennedy doubted whether Vietnam was the place to draw a line in the sand.

In the summer and fall of 1963 the situation in South Vietnam seriously deteriorated when Diem ordered his troops to fire on Buddhist leaders holding banned religious celebrations. Anti-Diem forces immediately rallied to the Buddhists, and civil war threatened within the principal cities. Several Buddhists responded by publicly burning themselves to death, an act that Diem's government ridiculed as a "barbecue show." The deaths, flashed on the evening news in the United States, dramatized the growing opposition and grabbed the administration's attention.

Confronted by the possibility of a massive revolt against the Diem government, Kennedy reconsidered his support of the beleaguered ally. When South Vietnamese generals approached Washington with plans for a coup, Kennedy reluctantly agreed. On November 1, 1963, the generals seized key military

Buddhist Monks Protest the Diem Government President Ngo Dinh Diem ruled autocratically, abolishing local elections, curbing the press, and harassing his enemies. By 1963, his actions literally drew fire from devout Buddhist priests, who set themselves ablaze to protest his administration. Photographs such as this one horrified the American public, who questioned why the United States supported a government that provoked this kind of defiance. President Kennedy, also disturbed, gave his tacit approval to a military coup that overthrew the hated government. *(AP/Wide World Photos)*

and communications installations and demanded Diem's resignation. Later that day Diem was captured and, despite American assurances of safe passage, murdered.

Although Kennedy resisted pressure to commit American troops, he spent nearly $1 billion in South Vietnam and increased the number of American military "advisers" to more than 16,000. But the Vietcong was stronger than ever. Two weeks after the coup Kennedy ordered a "complete and very profound review of how we got into this country, what we thought we were doing, and what we now think we can do." Kennedy would never see the report.

Vietnam: The Decision to Escalate

Like Kennedy, Johnson was torn between his commitment to preventing a communist victory in Vietnam and his reluctance to get pulled into a major confrontation in Southeast Asia. Johnson, in a press conference in 1965, explained that America's defeat in South Vietnam "would encourage and spur on those who seek to conquer all free nations within their reach. This is the clearest lesson of our time."

The president's key advisers, all leftovers from the Kennedy administration, urged a strong U.S. military response to the deteriorating situation in Saigon. In March 1964, North Vietnam sent 23,000 fresh recruits south, swelling the ranks of the Vietcong. North Vietnam improved and extended the Ho Chi Minh Trail, a network of trails and roads on which supplies flowed south. The increased military pressure added to the political instability in the South. Desertions in South Vietnam's military, the Army of the Republic of Vietnam, reached epidemic levels. The Central Intelligence Agency estimated that the Vietcong controlled up to 40 percent of the territory of South Vietnam and more than 50 percent of the people.

The president's senior advisers believed the war could not be won without severing the flow of supplies from North Vietnam. They recommended a campaign of strategic bombing both to shore up the government in the South and to send a clear signal of U.S. resolve to the North. In March the Joint Chiefs of Staff advocated a "progressive and selective attack" against targets in North Vietnam.

Like Kennedy, Johnson dreaded getting mired in a protracted ground war in Southeast Asia. A wider war, he feared, would distract attention from his Great Society programs and provide critics with ammunition to scale back domestic spending. He told biographer Doris Kearns "that bitch of a war" would destroy "the woman I really loved—the Great Society." At the same time he remembered the chastising Harry Truman had received when China "fell" to the communists. Johnson told the U.S. ambassador to Vietnam, "I am not going to be the president who saw Vietnam go the way China went."

Privately, Johnson anguished over the war, often questioning whether the United States could win a military struggle in Southeast Asia. In private conversations he recorded on the White House taping system, the president described himself as "depressed" and "scared to death" about the conflict. On the one hand he was convinced that the United States needed to expand the war to maintain its credibility, but on the other hand he doubted whether the nation could win a war in Vietnam without using nuclear weapons and "kicking off World War III." At one point early in the conflict he cried to Lady Bird, "I can't get out [of Vietnam], and I can't finish it with what I have got. And I don't know what the hell to do!" Trying to decide what to do about Vietnam, he told her, was "like being in an airplane—and I have to choose between crashing the plane or jumping out. I do not have a parachute."

Despite his private doubts, the president approved the recommendation of his military advisers calling for an incremental escalation in Vietnam. Before implementing the new tactics, Johnson wanted to neutralize potential critics by securing congressional support for a wider war. He needed a dramatic incident to convince the nation to support his plans. He did not have to wait long. On August 4, 1964, while operating in heavy seas about 60 miles off the North Vietnamese coast in the Tonkin Gulf, the U.S. destroyers *C. Turner Joy* and *Maddox* reported they were under attack by North Vietnamese torpedo boats. Neither saw any enemy boats, however, and afterward crew members speculated that poor weather conditions may have contributed to the confusion. Johnson expressed doubts. "For all I know our navy might have been shooting at whales out there," he said.

The reported attack nonetheless gave Johnson the opportunity he needed to establish congressional support for his actions in Vietnam. With little debate and strong public support, Congress overwhelmingly ratified the Gulf of Tonkin Resolution, which authorized the president to take "all necessary measures." The resolution provided the legislative foundation for the Vietnam War. As Lyndon Johnson observed, it was "like Grandma's nightshirt, it covers everything."

PRIMARY SOURCE

9.2 | *The Gulf of Tonkin Resolution, 1964*

On August 4, Johnson reported to the American people the attack on the *Maddox* and his decision to launch retaliatory strikes. Three days later the House unanimously approved the Gulf of Tonkin Resolution (H.J. RES 1145) and only Wayne Morse of Oregon and Ernest Gruening of Alaska opposed it in the Senate.

Whereas naval units of the Communist regime in [North] Vietnam, in violation of the principles of the Charter of the United Nations and of

international law, have deliberately and repeatedly attacked United States naval vessels lawfully present in international waters, and have thereby created a serious
5 threat to international peace; and

Whereas these attacks are part of a deliberate and systematic campaign of aggression that the Communist regime in North Vietnam has been waging against its neighbors and the nations joined with them in the collective defense of their freedom; and
10 Whereas the United States is assisting the peoples of southeast Asia to protect their freedom and has no territorial, military, or political ambitions in that area, but desires only that these peoples should be left in peace to work out their own destinies in their own way: Now, therefore, be it

Resolved by the Senate and House of Representatives of the United States of
15 *America in Congress assembled,* That the Congress approves and supports the determination of the President, as Commander in Chief, to take all necessary measures to repel any armed attack against the forces of the United States and to prevent further aggression.

Sec. 2. The United States regards as vital to its national interest and to world
20 peace the maintenance of international peace and security in Southeast Asia. Consonant with the Constitution of the United States and the Charter of the United Nations and in accordance with its obligations under the Southeast Asia Collective Defense Treaty, the United States is, therefore, prepared, as the President determines, to take all necessary steps, including the use of armed force,
25 to assist any member or protocol state of the Southeast Asia Collective Defense Treaty requesting assistance in defense of its freedom.

Sec. 3. This resolution shall expire when the President shall determine that the peace and security of the area is reasonably assured by international conditions created by action of the United Nations or otherwise, except that it may be
30 terminated earlier by concurrent resolution of the Congress.

Source: Department of State Bulletin, Vol. 51, No. 1313 (August 24, 1964), 268. ■ ■ ■

Armed with congressional support for a wider war, Johnson considered further action. The military recommended intense air strikes and the commitment of a large American ground force. Senior civilian advisers viewed the conflict as a political issue resulting from the weakness of the South Vietnamese government. As a result, they stressed pacification programs combined with an effective counterinsurgency program in the South. But Undersecretary of State George Ball rejected the premise of intervention, arguing that Vietnam was not a vital American interest. In a brilliant sixty-page, single-spaced memorandum he systematically challenged every argument used to support the U.S. commitment to South Vietnam. He took special aim at the logic for bombing. "Once on the tiger's back," he observed, "we cannot be sure of picking the place to dismount."

By the end of 1964 Johnson had agreed to a phased escalation of the Vietnam War. He waited for the right opportunity to implement his new strategy. When the Vietcong launched the mortar attack against Pleiku, Johnson initiated "a carefully orchestrated bombing attack" against the North. The bombing accomplished none of its objectives. The enemy intensified its efforts, and the political situation in the South continued to deteriorate. In March 1965, the administration responded by launching Operation Rolling Thunder, the sustained bombing of North Vietnam that would last until 1968. Once again Johnson privately expressed doubts that an expanded military effort in Vietnam would produce an American victory. "Now we're off to bombing these people," he was recorded telling Secretary of Defense McNamara as he gave the bombing order on February 26. "We're over that hurdle. I don't think anything is going to be as bad as losing, and I don't see any way of winning."

Instead of intimidating the North Vietnamese, the bombing raids only stiffened their resolve; the flow of arms into the South actually increased. America believed that its commitment to South Vietnam would deter Chinese aggression. Just the opposite occurred: Chinese leader Mao Zedong promised assistance to the North, beginning a flow of arms that would continue throughout the war. The South Vietnamese government, weakened by corruption and constant political intrigue, seemed incapable of stemming the communist advance. "The situation is very disturbing," McNamara informed the president at the end of 1964. "Current trends, unless reversed in the next 2–3 months, will lead to neutralization at best and more likely to a Communist-controlled state."

PRIMARY SOURCE

9.3 | *Memorandum for the President*
GEORGE BALL

In a July 1, 1965, memorandum to President Johnson (later published in the *Pentagon Papers*), George Ball warned of the futility of American military intervention and recommended an alternative plan: a compromise solution that would allow the United States to extract itself from Vietnam.

A Compromise Solution in South Vietnam

(1) A Losing War: The South Vietnamese are losing the war to the Viet Cong. No one can assure you that we can beat the Viet Cong or even force them to the conference table on our terms, no matter how many hundred thousand *white, foreign* (U.S.) troops we deploy.

5   No one has demonstrated that a white ground force of whatever size can win a guerrilla war—which is at the same time a civil war between Asians—in jungle terrain in the midst of a population that refuses cooperation to the white forces

(and the South Vietnamese) and thus provides a great intelligence advantage to
the other side. Three recent incidents vividly illustrate this point: (a) the sneak
10   attack on the Da Nang Air Base which involved penetration of a defense perimeter
guarded by 9,000 Marines. This raid was possible only because of the cooperation
of the local inhabitants; (b) the B-52 raid that failed to hit the Viet Cong who
had obviously been tipped off; (c) the search and destroy mission of the 173rd
Air Borne Brigade which spent three days looking for the Viet Cong, suffered
15   23 casualties, and never made contact with the enemy who had obviously gotten
advance word of their assignment.

(2) The Question to Decide: Should we limit our liabilities in South Vietnam
and try to find a way out with minimal long-term costs?

The alternative—no matter what we may wish it to be—is almost certainly a
20   protracted war involving an open-ended commitment of U.S. forces, mounting
U.S. casualties, no assurance of a satisfactory solution, and a serious danger of
escalation at the end of the road.

(3) Need for a Decision Now: So long as our forces are restricted to advising
and assisting the South Vietnamese, the struggle will remain a civil war between
25   Asian peoples. Once we deploy substantial numbers of troops in combat it will
become a war between the U.S. and a large part of the population of South Vietnam, organized and directed from North Vietnam and backed by the resources
of both Moscow and Peiping.

The decision you face now, therefore, is crucial. Once large numbers of U.S.
30   troops are committed to direct combat, they will begin to take heavy casualties in
a war they are ill-equipped to fight in a non-cooperative if not downright hostile
countryside.

Once we suffer large casualties, we will have started a well-nigh irrevers-
ible process. Our involvement will be so great that we cannot—without national
35   humiliation—stop short of achieving our complete objectives. *Of the two possibilities I think humiliation would be more likely than the achievement of our
objectives—even after we have paid terrible costs.*

(4) Compromise Solution: Should we commit U.S. manpower and prestige to a
terrain so unfavorable as to give a very large advantage to the enemy—or should
40   we seek a compromise settlement which achieves less than our stated objectives
and thus cut our losses while we still have the freedom of maneuver to do so.

(5) Costs of a Compromise Solution: The answer involves a judgment as to
the cost to the U.S. of such a compromise settlement in terms of our relations
with the countries in the area of South Vietnam, the credibility of our commit-
45   ments, and our prestige around the world. In my judgment, if we act before
we commit a substantial U.S. force to combat in South Vietnam we can, by
accepting some short-term costs, avoid what may well be a long-term catastrophe. I believe we tended grossly to exaggerate the costs involved in a compromise settlement. An appreciation of probable costs is contained in the attached
50   memorandum.

Source: The Pentagon Papers, Senator Gravel Edition, Volume IV (Boston: Beacon Press),
615–619.   ■ ■ ■

In July 1965, Johnson, enacting a decision made months earlier, announced that he was committing American ground forces to offensive operations in Vietnam. He scaled back McNamara's request for 100,000 troops to 50,000, though privately he assured the military that he would commit another 50,000 before the end of the year. While planning for war, Johnson talked about peace, deliberately misleading Congress and the American people about his intended escalation of the conflict. While confidently predicting victory in public, he privately feared defeat. Unwilling to distract attention from his Great Society programs, he refused to admit that he had dramatically increased America's involvement in Vietnam.

America's War

To lead the combat troops in Vietnam, Johnson chose General William Westmoreland, a veteran of World War II and former superintendent of West Point. Westmoreland planned to limit ground action to "search-and-destroy" missions launched from fortified bases in the countryside. Rather than confronting the enemy in large-scale ground assaults, he would depend on firepower from

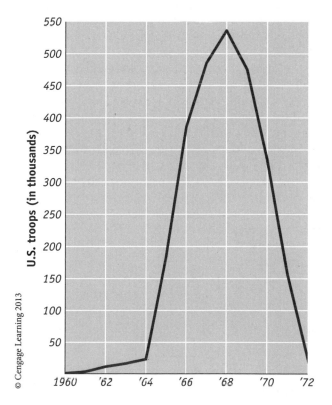

American Troop Levels in Vietnam After Johnson's decision to send marines to Danang in 1965, the American presence in Vietnam skyrocketed. Not until the Tet Offensive in 1968, though, did Americans begin loudly to demand an end to the war. The outcry led to the election of a new president in 1968 and the deescalation of American ground forces in Vietnam.

© Cengage Learning 2013

ground artillery, helicopter gunships, fighter aircraft, and B-52 bombers. "We'll just go on bleeding them," he said, "until Hanoi wakes up to the fact that they have bled their country to the point of national disaster for generations."

Westmoreland's optimism proved premature. The air war failed to sever the flow of supplies between North and South. Thousands of peasants worked daily to rebuild parts of the Ho Chi Minh Trail damaged by American bombs. By the time the war ended, the Ho Chi Minh Trail had 12,500 miles of roads, complete with portable bridges, underground fuel storage tanks, hospitals, and supply

Vietnam, to 1968 Despite the number of soldiers (see graph, page 199) and military bases in South Vietnam and Thailand, American troops could not confine and fight an enemy as mobile as the North Vietnamese. With a constant supply line, known as the Ho Chi Minh trail, the North Vietnamese circumvented the border between the North and South, smuggling men and supplies through Laos and Cambodia to supporters in the South.

warehouses. Since the North had an agricultural economy with few industries vital to the war effort, aerial sorties against cities in North Vietnam had little impact on supplies. The civilian toll, however, was heavy. All told, U.S. bombs killed an estimated 100,000 North Vietnamese civilians.

Unable to win the war from the air, the administration gradually increased the number of ground troops, from 184,000 in late 1965 to more than 500,000 in 1968. The Vietcong continued its guerrilla tactics, avoiding fixed positions and striking from ambush. Hanoi's strategy was to fight a war of attrition, confident that American public opinion would sour on an inconclusive war. As the U.S. death count mounted, North Vietnamese General Vo Nguyen Giap predicted, "their mothers will want to know why. The war will not long survive their questions."

Along with trying to crush the enemy with massive bombing and a ground war, the United States launched a pacification and nation-building program in South Vietnam to build support for the noncommunist regime in Saigon. But the military effort directly undermined the political goals. By the end of 1968 almost 4 million South Vietnamese had lost their homes in aerial bombardments. Between 1965 and 1972 more than 1.4 million civilians died or were wounded by American forces. One American official observed, "It was as if we were trying to build a house with a bulldozer and wrecking crane."

The military's failure in Vietnam, despite its enormous advantages in firepower, underscored the fundamental problem with America's Vietnam policy. Blinded by a rigid anticommunism, American policymakers rejected the nationalist impulse behind the Vietnamese revolution. Insisting on viewing Ho as a puppet of Soviet and Chinese aggression, the United States aided in the transformation of a local struggle into a superpower conflict. "We both overestimated the effect of South Vietnam's loss on the security of the West and failed to adhere to the fundamental principle that, in the final analysis, if the South Vietnamese were to be saved, they had to win the war themselves," the contrite former Secretary of Defense Robert McNamara reflected in 1995.

The Soldier's War

Early in the war most men went to Vietnam confident they were doing the right thing. "There was nothing we could not do because we were Americans," wrote Philip Caputo, who joined the Marines in 1960 looking forward to a "splendid little war." At one end of the spectrum service in Vietnam could be easy for those working in the rear handling paperwork, moving supplies, helping the wounded. For soldiers in the field it could be hell. Climate and country imposed horrible conditions. Malaria, blackwater fever, and dysentery took their toll. "Our days were spent hacking through mountainous jungles," Caputo remembered. "At night we squatted in muddy holes, picked off the leeches that sucked on our

On the Ground in Vietnam For the "grunts" who faced the day-to-day reality of the Vietnam War, harrowing scenes such as this were all too common. These two GIs wait for a helicopter to carry them and their fallen comrade out of the jungle in Long Khanh province. *(National Archives)*

veins, and waited for an attack to come rushing at us from the blackness beyond the perimeter wire."

Combat involved constant patrolling, days and days of suspense waiting for an ambush or a booby trap, and then a short, intense firefight followed by more suspense. The war was fought not on set battlefields but in villages and rice paddies. The strategy for victory eluded most ground soldiers. No clear objectives were set; no territory was captured. Units swept across the same area repeatedly, taking casualties each time, never seeming to achieve any lasting effect. One day they were trying to win the "hearts and minds" of local villagers; the next day they had orders to destroy the village. Repeated over and over, such actions bred a sense of hopelessness.

In a war of attrition, as Vietnam had become, the "body count" was the primary measure of success. It inflicted a terrible emotional toll on the nineteen-year-olds ordered to fight. "What am I doing here?" asked a young soldier. "We don't take any land. We don't give it back. We just mutilate bodies." The tragic consequences of that policy played out in March 1968, when an American platoon led by Lieutenant William L. Calley descended on the tiny village of My Lai. Not a single shot was fired at them, and almost no men of military age were present in the village. Nonetheless, the American soldiers slaughtered more than 450 people. In an orgy of violence they gang-raped girls, blew apart children with hand grenades, slaughtered domestic animals, and burned the village to the ground.

In the final years of the war as American troop withdrawals increased, many soldiers refused to risk their lives in what they deemed a futile effort. Who wanted to be, asked Lieutenant John Kerry, "the last man to die in Vietnam?" Desertion and absent-without-leave rates skyrocketed. Incidents of *fragging*—the term soldiers used to describe the assassination of overzealous officers—multiplied. Drug abuse reached epidemic proportions. In 1969 the Pentagon estimated that nearly two-thirds of combat soldiers had used marijuana, while one-third had tried heroin. "What the hell is going on?" asked a bewildered general. "Is this a goddamned army or a mental hospital?"

The change in tone from the expansive optimism of JFK, who promised to "bear any burden" to defend freedom around the world, to a frustrated Johnson, burdened by a war that he could not understand or win, symbolized the perils of the American paradox. Johnson had the misfortune of presiding over a nation that was forced to confront the contradiction between its expansive expectations of change and its commitment to older notions of limited government. At home Johnson's war on poverty served as a fitting symbol of a reform approach that tried to solve major social problems without challenging existing notions of government power. Abroad Johnson struggled to uphold America's global commitment to resisting the spread of communism in Vietnam without sacrificing his domestic agenda or requiring full mobilization. Perhaps the greatest victim of the 1960s was the cherished notion of an American consensus.

The irony was that Johnson's desire to preserve a fragile consensus by obscuring the true nature of the war actually divided the nation. His yearning to maintain credibility by fighting in Vietnam eroded his authority and diminished America's stature in the world. And his faith that economic growth could sustain reform at home and a war abroad produced spiraling inflation that crippled the economy. The decade exposed not only Johnson's personal limitations but also the flawed assumptions of the vital center.

The Draft

During World War II and the Korean War an entire generation of young men were drafted. During Vietnam, LBJ wanted to avoid a full mobilization, so he depended on draft laws that were full of loopholes and exemptions. The reality is that only a small number of draft-age baby boomers actually fought in Vietnam. During the years 1964 to 1973, 27 million men came of draft age. Less than 10 percent went to Vietnam.

Most of those who fought and died in Vietnam were drawn from among the poor and working-class. U.S. forces in Vietnam were also among the youngest to fight an American war. The average age of the volunteers and draftees was nineteen. In WW II, by contrast, the average American soldier was twenty-six years old.

Many middle-class baby boomers were able to take advantage of the loop-holes in the draft law to avoid service. Colleges were the main sanctuary from the draft, and many teachers and administrators did what they could to help students. College grades were referred to as "A, B, C, D, and Nam."

A vast network of professionals helped middle-class men avoid the draft. For anyone who found a competent lawyer, avoiding the draft was virtually assured. One attorney claimed that "any kid with money can absolutely stay out of the Army—with one hundred percent certainty." A local prosecutor agreed. "If you got the dough, you don't have to go."

The draft, and how to avoid it, was a constant topic of conversation in the school cafeteria and around the family dinner table. Many men made key decisions about their future in an effort to avoid it. In 1968, for example, when the New York City draft boards announced that teachers qualified for deferments, the city received nearly 20,000 more applications for teacher's licenses than the year before. The following year, city universities experienced an 800 percent increase in draft-age men taking teacher education courses.

Protesting the War

The threat of the draft pushed a generation of young people to protest the war. The protests started with mild mannered "teach-ins" in 1965 where organizers planned lectures and discussions about the war in the hope of "educating" students to the dangers of American involvement in Vietnam. By late 1965, students were planning mass demonstrations, burning draft cards, and chanting "Hey, Hey, LBJ, how many kids did you kill today?" Student anger reached a new level when, in January 1966, Johnson ended automatic draft deferments for college students. The demonstrations swelled in size and intensity as protestors burned draft cards and an occasional American flag.

Antiwar spirits were bolstered by establishment figures who joined the cause. In 1966, Democratic Senator J.W. Fulbright, the powerful chairman of the Senate Foreign Relations Committee, held nationally televised hearings on the war. Fulbright charged that by displaying an "arrogance of power," the United States was "not living up" to its "capacity and promise as a civilized example for the world." The nation listened as George Kennan, the father of containment, complained that the administration's preoccupation with Vietnam was stretching America's power and prestige. In April 1967, Martin Luther King criticized the government for sending young black men "to guarantee liberties in Southeast Asia which they had not found in Southwest Georgia and East Harlem."

Students viewed the war as immoral, a reflection of fundamental problems in American society. "There is something sick," commented the University of Michigan daily paper, "about a nation that can deploy thousands of soldiers to go off shooting Vietcong . . . but can't spare a few hundred to avert the murder" of civil-rights workers in the South. Students hoped to use opposition against the war to lead a broader assault on Americans institutions and values.

To the great majority of Americans, however, the war was not immoral. It was a tragic mistake. They wanted to end the war because winning no longer seemed worth the price. Class resentment reinforced the ideological differences among war opponents. A large number of working-class Americans opposed the war, but they disliked privileged student protestors even more. Many working-class war critics opposed college protestors largely because they saw the antiwar movement as an elitist attack on American troops by people who could avoid the war.

Upheaval

During the summer of 1967, wrote *Time*, "a profound malaise overcame the American public." In August, Johnson sent 45,000 more troops to Vietnam and asked for higher taxes to finance the war. The horror of the war, flashed into the homes of most Americans on the evening newscasts, was matched by that of racial violence in the nation's cities. Flames tore through thirty cities. In one week alone in August, forty-five people were killed and thousands injured, and property damage ran into the billions of dollars.

In October the antiwar movement staged a march on the Pentagon, later celebrated by Norman Mailer's *Armies of the Night*. One thousand angry students converged on the Pentagon to shut down "the American military machine" in one act of civil disobedience.

The discontent and revolt was not limited to the United States. In 1967 and 1968 a wave of student protest movements broke out across Europe. Like their counterparts in the United States, young people took to the streets to challenge established governments, to force institutions to be more responsive to their needs, and to protest the war in Vietnam. In Paris, students joined workers to organize a general strike that paralyzed the government. Universities across Poland were forced to shut down. Riots broke out at 33 universities in Rome. The Soviets were forced to send tanks into the streets of Prague to repress a powerful freedom movement.

The Tet Offensive

A North Vietnamese military offensive on January 31, 1968, the lunar New Year, called Tet, added fuel to the fires of discontent, both at home and abroad. In a bold and risky move, the Vietcong invaded the U.S. embassy compound in Saigon and waged bloody battles in the capitals of most of South Vietnam's provinces.

From a military perspective, the Tet Offensive was a failure for the North Vietnamese. They suffered heavy casualties and failed to gain new ground or incite a popular rebellion against the United States. But if a military defeat for the North, the Tet Offensive represented a striking psychological victory. The ferocity of the offensive belied the optimistic reports of General Westmoreland that the U.S. strategy was working.

Television pictures of marines defending the grounds of the American embassy in Saigon shocked the nation. Television anchorman Walter Cronkite, echoing many Americans, declared the United States was "mired in stalemate." At that moment, Johnson turned to an aide and said, "It's all over." If he had lost Cronkite, he had lost "Mr. Average Citizen."

The Tet offensive dealt Johnson's credibility a crowning blow. The public registered its discontent with Johnson's policies in the first presidential primary of the year in New Hampshire. He was almost defeated by a little-known antiwar senator, Eugene McCarthy. Four days after Johnson's embarrassment, Robert F. Kennedy, who had been a senator from New York since 1964, entered the race for the Democratic nomination. Many Democrats believed that Kennedy was the only politician in America who could pull together the fractured liberal coalition. On Vietnam, Kennedy, who had supported his brother's military escalation of the conflict, now called for a negotiated settlement. He focused most of his attention, however, on domestic issues. Kennedy believed that convincing poor people of all colors to pursue their shared class interests offered the only solution to the deep racial hostility that was tearing the nation apart. "We have to convince the Negroes and poor whites that they have common interests," Kennedy told a journalist. "If we can reconcile those two hostile groups, and then add the kids, you can really turn this country around."

Seeing the writing on the wall, Johnson announced on March 31 that he would not be a candidate for reelection. Three weeks later, Vice President Hubert Humphrey announced that he would run in Johnson's place.

The Assassinations of MLK and RFK

While Kennedy and McCarthy tried rallying antiwar Democrats, another outspoken critic of the administration was raising his voice in protest. Like Kennedy, Martin Luther King argued that America's racial problems could not be solved without addressing the issue of class. King now considered himself a revolutionary, not a reformer. "We are engaged in [a] class struggle . . . dealing with the problem of the gulf between the haves and the have nots."

In March 1968, King supported striking garbage workers in Memphis, Tennessee, hoping a peaceful, successful strike would further his new, more militant message of redistribution of power and his enduring commitment to nonviolence. While in Memphis he reaffirmed his faith in the possibility of racial justice: "I may not get there with you. But we as a people will get to the promised land." The following day, April 4, King was killed, shot to death by assassin James Earl Ray, a white ex-convict.

King's death touched off an orgy of racial violence. Rioters burned twenty blocks in Chicago where Mayor Daley ordered police to "shoot to kill." The worst violence occurred in Washington, D.C., where seven hundred fires burned and nine people lost their lives. For the first time since the Civil War armed soldiers guarded the steps to the Capitol. Nationally the death toll was forty-six.

With King dead, Robert Kennedy became for many disaffected people, black and white, the only national leader who commanded respect and enthusiasm. Kennedy may have had the broadest base of support, but party leaders selected most convention delegates. A large majority of these delegates, remaining loyal to the administration, pledged their support to Humphrey. Kennedy's strategy was to sweep the remaining major primaries, showing such support at the polls that the convention delegates would have no choice but to nominate him.

Kennedy won a decisive victory over Humphrey and McCarthy in Indiana but lost in Oregon. The California primary on June 4 was critical, and Kennedy won. But that evening, after giving his victory speech, he was shot by Sirhan Sirhan, a Palestinian who opposed the Senator's pro-Israel position. Twenty-five hours later, Robert Kennedy died, dimming Democrats' hopes of uniting their disparate coalition of blacks and whites, hawks and doves, young and old.

The 1968 Democratic Convention

Robert Kennedy's death assured Humphrey of the nomination on the first ballot. His victory was overshadowed, however, by the violent clashes between protestors and police outside the Chicago convention hall.

While most protestors planned peaceful marches, many demonstrators had come to Chicago with the clear intent of taunting the police and provoking a violent response. In response, the city's powerful mayor, Richard Daley, turned the city into a fortress.

Television cameras focused the nation's attention on the violent clashes in the streets of Chicago. Demonstrators hurled bricks, bottles, and nail-studded golf balls at the police lines. Chicago police charged blindly into crowds, which included peaceful protestors, journalists, and innocent bystanders. "The cops had one thing on their minds," one journalist said, "club and then gas, club and then gas, club and then gas."

Chicago, 1968 At the Democratic National Convention, the tensions that had been building over the course of the decade came to a head. Twenty-eight thousand police, national guardsmen, federal troops, and secret service agents confronted a smaller contingent of protestors from over one hundred different antiwar organizations. The violence lasted throughout the convention as the city tried to remove protestors from parks where they had gathered, or to prevent them from marching on the convention hall. The public's reaction to the police riot gave an indication of the American mood in 1968. Most Americans sympathized with the police. In a poll taken shortly after the Democratic convention, most blue-collar workers approved of the way the Chicago police had handled the protestors; some of them thought the police were "not tough enough" on them. Bumper stickers, declaring "WE SUPPORT MAYOR DALEY AND HIS CHICAGO POLICE," blossomed across the country. *(© Bettmann-CORBIS)*

The Center Holds: The Election of 1968

The public's reaction to the police riot gave an indication of the American mood in 1968. Most Americans sympathized with the police. In a poll taken shortly after the Democratic Convention, most blue-collar workers approved of the way the Chicago police had handled the protestors; some even thought the police were "not tough enough" on them.

Two candidates were vying for the allegiance of these angry voters. The most direct appeal came from American Independence Party candidate George Wallace, whose symbolic stance in a university doorway had made him a hero to southern whites. In 1968, Wallace's antiestablishment populism also appealed to many northern Democrats angry over the party's association with protest and integration. A ranting orator who seemed to intentionally mangle his syntax and mispronounce his words, Wallace's appeal was blatantly racist and anti-intellectual. One survey showed that more than half of the nation shared Wallace's view that "liberals, intellectuals, and long-hairs have run the country for too long."

Joining Wallace in pursuit of the hearts and minds of America's angry white voters was the Republican nominee, Richard Nixon. The party's 1960 presidential nominee campaigned as the candidate of unity, reflecting his belief that most Americans wanted an end to the civil discord. To capitalize on the yearning for tranquility, Nixon promised the restoration of law and order. Nixon appealed to the "forgotten Americans," those whose values of patriotism and stability had been violated by student protestors, urban riots, and arrogant intellectuals.

Humphrey emerged from the debacle in Chicago a badly damaged candidate. Antiwar protestors blamed him for LBJ's Vietnam policies, while many working-class Democrats associated him with the violent protest and civil unrest of the convention. On September 30, Humphrey discovered his independent voice and announced that he would "stop the bombing of North Vietnam as an acceptable risk for peace." On October 31, less than a week before election day, Johnson helped Humphrey's cause by announcing a bombing pause in Vietnam.

It was not enough to win. On election day, Nixon won by a razor-thin majority in the popular vote, receiving 31,770,222 votes compared to Humphrey's

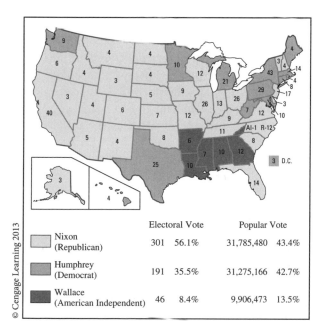

	Electoral Vote		Popular Vote	
Nixon (Republican)	301	56.1%	31,785,480	43.4%
Humphrey (Democrat)	191	35.5%	31,275,166	42.7%
Wallace (American Independent)	46	8.4%	9,906,473	13.5%

© Cengage Learning 2013

The Election of 1968
With Johnson out of the race, both Richard Nixon and Hubert Humphrey pursued voters with promises to end the war in Vietnam. A third-party candidate, Alabama governor George Wallace, won the Deep South with a segregationist platform, while Nixon carried all but four states west of the Mississippi. Vice President Humphrey, unable to shake his ties to Johnson, made inroads predominantly in the Northeast.

31,267,744. Less than seven-tenths of 1 percent separated the two candidates. Nixon scored a more decisive triumph in the electoral college, amassing 301 votes to Humphrey's 191. Wallace carried five states, receiving 9.9 electoral votes and 13.5 percent of the popular vote—the best showing for a third party candidate in forty-four years.

The 1968 election may have produced a conventional political result, but the social conflict that shaped it was anything but conventional. The decade sharpened, and in many ways, redefined the American paradox: consensus and prosperity had sown the seeds of social conflict by producing a generation that rejected the tenets of consensus and stressed the value of ideology. Many middle-class college students were angered by the perceived gap between the American ideals and social realities, especially the rhetoric of social justice and the brutality of southern racism, and the escalation of violence in Vietnam. For them, the "vital center" had lost its vitality: gradual change and compromise had done little to improve the lives of African Americans in the South, narrow the gap between rich and poor, or prevent Lyndon Johnson from escalating the war in Vietnam. Despite extraordinary progress—like the passage of the most important civil-rights legislation since Reconstruction—expectations far outpaced the possibility of change, producing disillusion and despair. For now, in a decade marked by bold challenges to established institutions, Americans looked to a familiar face and old values to help forge a new consensus in the troubled days ahead.

SUGGESTED READINGS

▌ The literature on the conduct of the Vietnam War is immense. George Herring's *America's Longest War* (3rd ed., 1996) and Stanley Karnow's *Vietnam* (1983) are good starting points. Randy Roberts and James Olson offer a highly readable account of the war in *Where the Domino Fell* (2nd ed., 1996). Christian Appy provides an international perspective in *Patriots: The Vietnam War Remembered from All Sides* (2003). For a useful collection of essays and primary sources, see Jeffrey P. Kimball, *To Reason Why* (1990). On JFK, see David Kaiser's *American Tragedy* (2000). David Halberstam, who made his name reporting from Vietnam, reveals in *The Best and the Brightest* (1972) the atmosphere of brash optimism and technocratic assurance that accompanied the U.S. commitment.

▌ On the fateful decision to send troops, see Larry Berman's *Planning a Tragedy* (1982). Neil Sheehan captures the tragic dimensions of Americans' commitment to winning the war in his elegantly written *A Bright Shining Lie* (1988). *In Retrospect* (1995) offers Robert McNamara's reflections on mistakes made and lessons learned, while H. R. McMaster picks apart the decisions McNamara made that contributed to the disaster in Vietnam in *Dereliction of Duty* (1997). Also useful in understanding LBJ are Lloyd C. Gardner, *Pay Any Price* (1995), and Herbert Y. Schandler, *Lyndon Johnson and Vietnam* (1977).

- The impact of the war on the American men who fought in it, especially those from poor families, is detailed in Christian Appy's *Working-Class War* (1993). David Maraniss offers a compelling account of the war at home and on the battlefield in *They Marched into Sunlight* (2003). The story of the war from a soldier's point of view can be found in Phillip Caputo's *A Rumor of War* (1977); Al Santoli's *Everything We Had* (1981); and *The Bad War* by Kim Willenson (1987). For the African American experience see Wallace Terry's *Bloods* (1984).
- David Caute's *The Year of the Barricades* (1988) identifies 1968 as a critical turning point in world history, a point also made effectively by Mark Kurlansky in *1968: The Year that Rocked the World* (2005). Also see David Farber's study of the Yippies, the antiwar protesters, and the Daley machine at the Democratic convention in *Chicago '68* (1988). On the decade's political legacy, see Maurice Isserman and Michael Kazin's *America Divided* (1999).

10 Richard Nixon and the New Republican Majority, 1969–1974

At noon on Monday, May 4, 1970, students at Kent State University in Ohio organized for an antiwar rally on the Commons, a grassy campus gathering spot. For the previous three days the lush lawns and green elms and maple trees of this 790-acre campus had been the site of violent confrontation between students and police. What had ignited the protest was President Richard Nixon's announcement on April 30 of his decision to widen the war in Vietnam by sending American ground troops into neighboring Cambodia. The surprise announcement had come as a shock to a nation lulled into complacency by troop withdrawals and declining body counts.

A National Guard jeep drove onto the Commons, and an officer ordered the crowd to disperse. A platoon of guardsmen, armed with M-1 rifles and tear-gas equipment, followed, moving methodically across the green and over the crest of a hill chasing the protesters. The crowd taunted the poorly trained guardsmen, chanting, "Pigs Off Campus" and hurling stones and bricks. The troops, most of them local townspeople—accountants, bankers, barbers—responded by firing volleys of tear gas into the crowd.

Suddenly, the crackle of gunfire cut through the tear-gas-laced air. A girl screamed, "My God, they're killing us!" Some students fled; others fell to the ground. It took only a few seconds, but by the time the shooting stopped, four students lay dead and another eleven were seriously wounded. None of those hit at Kent State had broken any law, and none was a campus radical. Among them were two women simply walking to class who had never been part of the protest. An investigation by the Federal Bureau of Investigation called the shootings "unnecessary, unwarranted, and inexcusable."

Death at Kent State University   Richard Nixon promised an end to the American involvement in Vietnam with his plan of "Vietnamization," but in April 1970 Nixon expanded America's role in the region by sending U.S. troops into Cambodia to protect that nation's new government from possible North Vietnamese aggression. Antiwar activists quickly prepared a number of rallies after Nixon's announcement of his Cambodian plan. At Kent State University, student demonstrators were met by National Guard forces that opened fire on the crowd, killing four and wounding eleven. This photograph, of a young woman grieving over the body of one of the victims, stirred opposition to Nixon's Southeast Asia policy and also led administrators to close many state universities before finals, fearing a repeat of Kent State on another college campus. (© *John Filo*)

After the Kent State killings over 400 colleges had to cancel some classes and 250 campuses were closed as young people expressed their outrage. But not everyone was sympathetic to the students. One poll indicated that 58 percent of the public blamed the students for the Kent State deaths. A local resident told the town newspaper that the guardsmen "should have fired sooner and longer."

During the late 1960s and early 1970s the American paradox produced unprecedented social strife. On one side of the divide were those Americans, like protesting students at Kent State, who were frustrated by the government's slow and half-hearted response to the civil-rights struggle, angered by the nation's continued involvement in the Vietnam War, and disillusioned by the gap between American ideals and social realities. Made up largely of middle-class baby boomers nurtured on postwar affluence and filled with grand expectations about the possibilities of reform, they took to the streets to challenge the establishment. On the other side of the debate were the millions of Americans whom Richard Nixon called the "silent majority." A broad cross section of Americans, they were united by fears of social disorder, by resentment of middle-class youth who questioned traditional values, and by anxiety about the consequences of dramatic social and political changes. Richard Nixon was elected on a promise to bring harmony to American politics, but his efforts to create a durable base of political support by mobilizing the backlash against protest clarified and hardened the divisions separating Americans.

Richard Nixon and the Two Americas

For most political observers, the surprising popularity of George Wallace's third-party candidacy and the election of Richard Nixon represented an important shift in the nation's political life. By 1969 it appeared that the radical 1960s were giving way to the mainstream 1970s. The signs were everywhere: car windows were plastered with American flag decals and bumper stickers reading, "Honor America" had replaced the 1960s mantra "Make Love Not War." In big cities, fearful voters worried about rising crime rates were turning to elected tough law-and-order mayors like former police officer Frank Rizzo in Philadelphia.

Middle Americans were driving the nation's rightward drift. The journalist Joseph Kraft first coined the phrase in 1967, and Richard Nixon made numerous references to these voters during his 1968 campaign. *Time* described them best when it referred to Middle America as "a state of mind, a morality, a construct of values and prejudices and a complex of fears."

The sources of Middle American discontent were easy to identify: an unresolved war in Vietnam, race riots in major cities, rebellious student protesters, and rising inflation. More than the specific grievances, many Americans were troubled by a general sense that middle-class values were under assault.

"The values that we held so dear are being shot to hell," noted a typical Middle American. "Everything is being attacked—what you believed in, what you learned in school, in church, from your parents."

This frustration with American society may have been palpable, but many Middle Americans were conflicted about possible solutions as well. Most wanted peace in Vietnam but refused to accept the possibility of defeat, preferring instead "an honorable withdrawal." They believed that African Americans deserved a quality education, but they were also appalled by "the idea of sacrificing their own children's education to a long-range improvement for blacks." Middle Americans were a diverse group, divided by sex (women tended to be less hawkish on the war), education (those with college degrees were more tolerant on race issues), and geography (racial attitudes in the South tended to be harsher). According to *Newsweek,* what they all shared was a desire for "stability—or at least the illusion of stability."

Nixon's political strategy was to pursue policies that would attract the support of frustrated Middle Americans, allowing him to forge a new majority that was made up of traditional Republicans and angry ex-Democrats. He believed that race riots, student protest, and an unpopular war in Vietnam could do for the Republicans what a depression and world war had once done for the Democrats. And he, Richard Nixon, the man scorned by the eastern establishment, would be the architect of the new coalition, the Roosevelt of the new majority. Though he courted big business and powerful conservative interests, Nixon identified with the fears and resentments of the struggling middle class. "My source of strength," he once observed, "was more Main Street than Wall Street."

Constructing his new majority required Nixon to appeal to the shifting ideological center of American politics. He hoped to reach out to the two-thirds of the country he called the "constituency of uneducated people." They were the angry voters who flirted with George Wallace's antiestablishment populism in 1968. "These are my people," Nixon said. "We speak the same language." Since the days of the New Deal, Democrats had used the language of economic populism to cement the loyalties of the working class, charging that an economic elite was out of touch with the concerns of average voters. Nixon's goal was to articulate a new lexicon of cultural populism, arguing that a cultural elite associated with the Democratic Party had lost touch with the mainstream values of average Americans.

In his early years in office Nixon adopted moderately progressive positions. As the first elected president since 1849 forced to work with a Congress controlled by the opposition party, he favored cooperation over confrontation. In addition to signing Democratic bills raising social security benefits, Nixon increased federal funds for low-income public housing and even expanded the Job Corps. His first term saw steady increases in spending on mandated social-welfare programs, especially social security, Medicare, and Medicaid. His most innovative and surprising proposal was the Family Assistance Plan, which provided a guaranteed minimum income of $1,600 to every U.S. family. Although the proposal died in the Senate, it revealed Nixon's capacity for domestic innovation. Michael Harrington, whose *The Other America* had helped inspire the war on poverty, called it "the most radical idea since the New Deal."

Vietnam: The War at Home and Abroad

Nixon understood that his administration's success hinged on diffusing the crisis in Vietnam. "It is essential that we end this war, and end it quickly," he declared during the presidential campaign. He believed, however, that the United States could not simply "cut and run"; instead he promised "peace with honor." Nixon wanted to intimidate the North Vietnamese, raising the stakes by threatening an expanded war. Nixon explained his approach as "the Madman Theory." "I want the North Vietnamese to believe I've reached the point where I might do *anything* to stop the war," he confided in 1968.

In developing his strategy for dealing with the conflict, Nixon relied heavily on his national security adviser, Henry Kissinger. Born in Germany in 1923, Kissinger immigrated to the United States in 1938. After serving in World War II, he attended Harvard, earned a Ph.D. in government, and joined the faculty. Both men shared a personal style and a similar view of America's role in the world. They possessed a desire for power and a penchant for secrecy and intrigue. Together they concentrated decision making in the White House and excluded even close aides from sensitive diplomatic initiatives. An observer suggested that Kissinger's aides were like mushrooms: "They're kept in the dark, get a lot of manure piled on them, and then get canned." Nixon, who took great pride in his knowledge of international relations, functioned as his own secretary of state until Kissinger assumed the post in 1973. Nixon and Kissinger also shared an essentially pessimistic view of the behavior of nations known as realpolitik. Power, they believed, not ideals or moral suasion, counted in international affairs. Nations could be expected to act on their own narrowly defined interest.

For Nixon, Vietnam was a two-front war, with battle lines in Asia and America. He saw himself engaged in a contest "with the antiwar movement for the public mind in the United States and the private mind in Hanoi." To make his threats credible to the North Vietnamese, Nixon needed to diffuse domestic opposition. Hostility to the war had forced his predecessor from office, but by the time Nixon entered the presidency, the peace movement was in disarray, demoralized by the Republican victory, splintered into rival factions, and reeling from the public backlash at protest. By the spring of 1969, a majority of Americans—52 percent—opposed peaceful demonstrations and 82 percent believed students who participated in demonstrations should be expelled from school.

The centerpiece of the president's strategy of deflating the peace movement was the policy of Vietnamization. Nixon believed that by reducing the number of combat troops, which stood at 530,000 on the day he took office in 1969, he could cut the casualties that fueled home-front protest. In June the White House announced the withdrawal of 25,000 troops in the first large-scale reduction of troop strength. Within weeks U.S. combat losses dropped to their lowest level of the war. In December Nixon announced a draft lottery system that eliminated many of the inequities of the older system. By 1973 troop withdrawals would allow him to end the draft and create an all-volunteer army.

While official announcements focused on troop withdrawals, the president dramatically enlarged the bombing campaign. In January 1969, in keeping with his madman theory, Nixon authorized Operation Menu—the secret bombing of North Vietnamese bases and supply routes in Cambodia. "Breakfast" was followed by "Lunch," "Snack," "Dinner," "Dessert," and "Supper." Over the next fifteen months American B-52 bombers served up a deadly diet of explosives. "We were dropping a hell of a lot of bombs," said a military official. "I refuse to believe that a little fourth-rate power like North Vietnam does not have a breaking point," Kissinger told his staff.

The bombings not only failed to intimidate the North Vietnamese; they also did little to stem the losses on the ground in South Vietnam. The South's government was failing miserably in its efforts to win popular legitimacy and to build an effective military force. Its army suffered from massive desertions and poor, often corrupt and brutal, leadership. In July, Nixon warned Ho Chi Minh that unless significant progress was made, he would be forced to turn to "measures of great consequence and force," later described by Kissinger as a "savage, punishing blow." Operation Duck Hook called for intensive bombing of North Vietnamese population centers and military targets, mining of harbors and rivers in the North, and bombing of the dike and rail system connecting North Vietnam and China.

Appealing to the "Silent Majority"

With his efforts to bomb the North Vietnamese into submission failing and discontent with the war rising, Nixon decided to go on the offensive. Dismissing the peace movement as a "brotherhood of the misguided, the mistaken, the well-meaning, and the malevolent," Nixon tried to buy time for his policy by redirecting public anger against antiwar protesters. The centerpiece of Nixon's counteroffensive was a November 3 address to the American people on national television. More than 80 million Americans listened to Nixon outline his Vietnamization policy and explain why the United States could not cut and run. After establishing his war strategy, the president attacked the antiwar movement, saying that he would be "untrue" to his "oath of office" if he allowed national policy to be "dictated" by a "vocal minority" that attempted to "impose" its views on others "by mounting demonstrations in the street." Nixon called for the support of "the great silent majority of my fellow Americans" in his struggle to win the peace. "Let us understand: North Vietnam cannot defeat or humiliate the United States," he said. "Only Americans can do that."

PRIMARY SOURCE

10.1 | *The Silent Majority*

RICHARD NIXON

Faced with mounting pressure to remove American troops from Vietnam, President Nixon defended his plan of Vietnamization in a televised speech on November 3, 1969. In his address Nixon explained why American troops remained in Vietnam, calling on those Americans not openly protesting the war, whom he called the "silent majority," to support his policy.

My fellow Americans, I am sure you can recognize from what I have said that we really only have two choices open to us if we want to end this war.

I can order an immediate, precipitate withdrawal of all Americans from Vietnam without regard to the effects of that action. Or we can persist in our
5 search for a just peace through a negotiated settlement if possible, or through continued implementation of our plan for Vietnamization if necessary, a plan in which we will withdraw all of our forces from Vietnam on a schedule in accordance with our program, as the South Vietnamese become strong enough to defend their own freedom.
10 I have chosen this second course. It is not the easy way. It is the right way.

It is a plan which will end the war and serve the cause of peace—not just in Vietnam but in the Pacific and in the world.

In speaking of the consequences of a precipitate withdrawal, I mentioned that our allies would lose confidence in America.
15 Far more dangerous, we would lose confidence in ourselves. Oh, the immediate reaction would be a sense of relief that our men were coming home. But as we saw the consequences of what we had done, inevitable remorse and divisive recrimination would scar our spirit as a people.

We have faced other crises in our history and have become stronger by reject-
20 ing the easy way out and taking the right way in meeting our challenges. Our greatness as a nation has been our capacity to do what had to be done when we knew our course was right.

I recognize that some of my fellow citizens disagree with the plan for peace I have chosen. Honest and patriotic Americans have reached different conclusions
25 as to how peace should be achieved. . . .

And now I would like to address a word, if I may, to the young people of this nation who are particularly concerned, and I understand why they are concerned, about this war.

30 I respect your idealism. I share your concern for peace. I want peace as much
as you do. There are powerful personal reasons I want to end this war. This week
I will have to sign 83 letters to mothers, fathers, wives and loved ones of men who
have given their lives for America in Vietnam. It is very little satisfaction to me
that this is only one-third as many letters as I signed the first week in office. There
is nothing I want more than to see the day come when I do not have to write any
35 of those letters.

I want to end the war to save the lives of those brave young men in
Vietnam.

But I want to end it in a way which will increase the chance that their younger
brothers and their sons will not have to fight in some future Vietnam someplace
40 in the world.

And I want to end the war for another reason. I want to end it so that the energy and dedication of you, our young people, now too often directed into bitter
hatred against those responsible for the war, can be turned to the great challenges
of peace, a better life for all Americans, a better life for all people on this Earth. . . .
45 Let historians not record that when America was the most powerful nation
in the world we passed on the other side of the road and allowed the last hopes
for peace and freedom of millions of people to be suffocated by the forces of
totalitarianism.

And so tonight—to you, the great silent majority of my fellow Americans—I
50 ask for your support.

I pledged in my campaign for the presidency to end the war in a way that
we could win the peace. I have initiated a plan of action which will enable me to
keep that pledge.

The more support I can have from the American people, the sooner that
55 pledge can be redeemed; for the more divided we are at home, the less likely the
enemy is to negotiate at Paris.

Let us be united for peace. Let us also be united against defeat. Because let us
understand: North Vietnam cannot defeat or humiliate the United States. Only
Americans can do that. . . .
60 As president I hold the responsibility for choosing the best path to that goal
and then leading the nation along it. I pledge to you tonight that I shall meet this
responsibility with all of the strength and wisdom I can command in accordance
with our hopes, mindful of your concerns, sustained by your prayers.

Thank you and good night.

Source: Address on Vietnam to American public, November 3, 1969. ■ ■ ■

The speech was a brilliant tactical move that undercut public support for the
organized antiwar movement. A poll showed that nearly 75 percent of the public
considered themselves part of the "silent majority." By a margin of 65 percent to
25 percent, the public agreed with Nixon's point that "protestors against the war
are giving aid and comfort to the Communists."

Nixon's appeal to the "silent majority" tapped into the deep class resentments
that shaped attitudes toward the war and toward antiwar protesters. By 1969
many white, middle-class Americans—even those who opposed the war—were

convinced that a willful minority of violent youth, militant blacks, and arrogant intellectuals had seized control of the public debate, showing contempt for mainstream values and threatening social stability. At the same time, 55 percent of Americans called themselves "doves" and nearly 80 percent said they were "fed up and tired of the war." Yet as frustrated as Americans were with the war, they disliked protesters even more. The "silent majority" speech intensified the cultural clash of the decade. Middle Americans viewed the antiwar movement as an elitist attack on American troops by privileged students who had avoided the war. More importantly, by using the antiwar movement as the foil, Nixon managed to transform himself into an antiestablishment figure, a cultural populist fighting for mainstream values against a liberal cultural elite.

The Cambodian Incursion

Having gained a tactical victory at home, Nixon was ready to send another message to the North Vietnamese. With the war going badly, Nixon talked about a "bold move" in Cambodia, which U.S. military officials believed the North Vietnamese were using as a staging ground for attacks on South Vietnam. At a meeting in April Nixon was warned that if he invaded Cambodia, "the campuses will go up in flames." The president was determined to prove to the North Vietnamese that he was in charge. In the days leading up to the invasion, Kissinger recalled, "Richard Nixon was virtually alone, sitting in a darkened room in the Executive Office Building, the stereo softly playing neoclassical music— reflecting, resenting, collecting his thoughts and his anger."

Nixon ordered American ground troops into the neutral country on April 29, 1970. The next day, in a national televised address, a visibly nervous president explained his decision to a war-weary public. Claiming that an American defeat in Vietnam would unleash the forces of totalitarianism around the globe, he insisted that the invasion of Cambodia was a guarantee of American "credibility." "The most powerful nation in the world," he said, could not afford to act "like a pitiful helpless giant."

The raids achieved some of the short-term goals set by military planners, but on the whole the invasion was a strategic failure. At home the invasion reinflamed antiwar sentiment and eroded support for Nixon's policy. Angry senators submitted legislation repealing the Gulf of Tonkin Resolution. South Dakota's Democratic senator George McGovern told his Senate colleagues, "This chamber reeks of blood." Campuses erupted in marches and protests. On May 4, at Kent State University in Ohio, panicked national guardsmen fired into a crowd of student protesters. A week later, at Jackson State College in Mississippi, two black students were killed and eleven wounded when police fired indiscriminately into a dormitory. Student protests reached a fever pitch in the weeks that followed. "The overflow of emotion seemed barely containable," observed the *Washington Post*.

"The nation was witnessing what amounted to a virtual general and uncoordinated strike by its college youth."

In public Nixon made a deliberate effort to appear nonchalant about the protest and about the growing signs of discontent with his policies. He made a point of telling reporters that he watched a Washington Redskins football game during one large demonstration outside the White House. Behind the confident façade, however, Nixon was growing increasingly isolated and embattled, paranoid that his enemies in Congress, the press, and the antiwar movement were conspiring to destroy him. "Within the iron gates of the White House, quite unknowingly, a siege mentality was setting in," a Nixon aide recalled. "It was now 'us' against 'them.' Gradually, as we drew the circle closer around us, the ranks of 'them' began to swell."

The circle tightened even further in June 1971 when the *New York Times* began publishing *The Pentagon Papers,* a secret Defense Department study of American decision making in Vietnam before 1967. Leaked to the press by former Pentagon official Daniel Ellsberg, the report showed that John Kennedy and Lyndon Johnson had consistently misled the public about their intentions in Vietnam. Nixon tried to block further publication, claiming it would damage national security. The Supreme Court, by a vote of 6 to 3, ruled against the administration, citing the First Amendment freedoms of speech and the press. The decision enraged Nixon.

As support for the war evaporated, and the public appeared more divided than ever, Nixon desperately tried to refocus public anger away from his policies and toward the antiwar movement. Shrewdly playing to the public's mood, Nixon wrapped himself in the flag and questioned the patriotism of those who challenged his policies.

The president's strategy reached a fever pitch in the final weeks of the 1970 midterm elections. In a desperate attempt to unseat Democrats and increase Republican power in Congress, Nixon engaged in a campaign that the historian James T. Patterson described as "among the most aggressive and divisive" in modern politics. Hitting twenty-three states during the final days of the campaign, Nixon orchestrated confrontations with protesters as a way of arousing the indignation of his cherished Middle Americans. But this time the public failed to respond to Nixon's shrill rhetoric. The Democrats gained nine House seats, lost two in the Senate, and gained eleven governorships. Overall, Democrats received 4.1 million more votes than their Republican challengers.

Peace with Honor?

The poor showing in the midterm election convinced Nixon that he had to neutralize Vietnam as a political issue before the 1972 presidential campaign. In March 1972 North Vietnam's forces launched a massive invasion of the South. In April the U.S. ambassador in Vietnam cabled Nixon, "ARVN [South Vietnamese] forces are on the verge of collapse." Nixon, refusing to allow South Vietnam to fall, initiated a risky plan to use American air power to give the North a "bloody nose." By approving the campaign, code-named "Linebacker," Nixon ran the risk of inflaming public opinion at home and jeopardizing a planned summit with the Russians. The gamble succeeded. The Soviets offered only tepid protest, and most Americans believed the North's invasion required a tough American response.

The North Vietnamese invasion and Nixon's forceful response created an opportunity for negotiations. Both sides had reason to seek accommodation. North Vietnam wanted to end the punishing American bombings; the United States needed to end the war quickly. Since early in 1971 Kissinger had been holding private meetings in a suburb of Paris with his North Vietnamese counterpart, Le Duc Tho. The key stumbling block had been Tho's insistence that South Vietnam's president Nguyen Van Thieu be removed from power and that North Vietnamese troops be allowed to remain in the South. For a year neither side budged. The only thing they had agreed on was the shape of the negotiating table.

Nixon decided that only a dramatic demonstration of American power could reassure the South Vietnamese and intimidate the North. On December 18, 1972, he ordered Operation Linebacker II, a massive, eleven-day bombing campaign over North Vietnam. The raids were directed at military targets, but inevitably bombs also fell on schools, hospitals, and prisoner-of-war camps. The American costs were heavy as well: the loss of fifteen B-52 planes and the capture of 98 American airmen. During the previous seven years only one of these high-flying bombers had been downed.

The resumption of bombing, along with pressure from China and the Soviet Union, pushed North Vietnam back to the negotiating table. They did not, however, change the terms for peace. The stumbling block remained the same: Thieu refused to accept a settlement that would allow the North Vietnamese to keep troops in the South. With polls showing overwhelming public support for ending the war and with Congress threatening to cut off funding for the effort, Nixon needed an agreement. This time he privately warned Thieu of grave consequences if he rejected the agreement. Nixon matched the threat with a promise to "respond with full force should the settlement be violated by North Vietnam."

The Paris Peace Accords, signed on January 27, 1973, officially ended U.S. involvement in the Vietnam War. The treaty required the United States to remove its remaining 23,700 troops and the North Vietnamese to return all American prisoners of war. As a face-saving measure for the United States, the accords also called for "free and democratic general elections" to create a government for a unified Vietnam. More importantly, however, was the American and South Vietnamese concession that North Vietnamese troops could remain in the South.

Nixon told a national television audience that the United States had achieved peace with honor. In fact, it had achieved neither peace nor honor. The North Vietnamese had no intention of abandoning their dream of unification. Kissinger hoped that the treaty would provide a "decent interval" between the U.S. military withdrawal and the North's complete military conquest of the South. As Kissinger predicted, the North violated the cease-fire within a few months and continued its relentless drive south. Thieu appealed to the United States for help, but a war-weary Congress refused to provide assistance. By April 1975, when the North's troops captured the South Vietnamese capital of Saigon, America had already turned its attention away from the nation's longest war. In April the House of Representatives voted down the administration's request for $474 million in additional military aid for South Vietnam. The *Washington Post* called it "a stunning defeat" for the administration.

Détente

For Nixon and Kissinger, achieving "peace with honor" in Vietnam represented only one piece in the larger puzzle of global politics. The key players, they argued, were the Soviet Union and China. Because they believed that the United States and the Soviet Union had reached a rough military parity, Nixon and Kissinger wanted to abandon the costly pursuit of weapons superiority and instead focus on peaceful economic competition. Nixon and Kissinger hoped that such a relationship, which they called *détente*, would lessen the threat of nuclear war, encourage the Soviets to pressure the North Vietnamese into a peace settlement, and diminish the possibility of another war like Vietnam beginning elsewhere in the Third World.

Shrewdly, Nixon and Kissinger began working to improve relations with Communist China, using the Sino–Soviet tension to America's strategic advantage. As an incentive Nixon offered the Chinese access to American technology, capital goods, and foodstuffs. With a solid groundwork established, Nixon made a historic trip to China in February 1972, becoming the first sitting American president to visit that nation and reversing more than twenty years of Sino–American hostility.

The Soviets watched nervously as anticommunist Richard Nixon embraced the world's largest communist country. Fearing closer ties between the United States and China, they pushed for their own deal with the Americans. Nixon reached an agreement with the Soviets on the terms of the Strategic Arms Limitation Talks (SALT), an unprecedented breakthrough in Soviet–American relations. Thereafter, the aim of American nuclear doctrine shifted from achieving "superiority" to maintaining "sufficiency."

Détente did not mean an end to the U.S.–Soviet competition in other parts of the world. Because he believed that a communist victory anywhere in the world tipped the global balance of power away from the United States, Nixon supplied arms to a number of repressive regimes willing to oppose the regional interests of the Soviet Union. Among others, Nixon sent aid and approved arms sales to the shah of Iran, President Ferdinand Marcos in the Philippines, and Balthazar Vorster's white-supremacist government of South Africa. He also intervened more actively to douse potential hotspots. When a Marxist, Salvador Allende, won election as president of Chile, Nixon directed the CIA to support Allende's opponents.

PRIMARY SOURCE

10.2 | *The Principles of Détente*

In May 1972, three months after his groundbreaking visit to China, Nixon traveled to the Soviet Union where he and Leonid Brezhnev signed a document titled: "Basic Principles of Relations Between the United States of America and the Union of Soviet Socialist Republics." The summit, which also included the signing of a strategic arms limitations treaty, represented the high point of Nixon diplomacy and the clearest statement of the goals of détente.

The United States of America and the Union of Soviet Socialist Republics, Guided by their obligations under the Charter of the United Nations and by a desire to strengthen peaceful relations with each other and to place these relations on the firmest possible basis,

5   Aware of the need to make every effort to remove the threat of war and to create conditions which promote the reduction of tensions in the world and the strengthening of universal security and international cooperation,

Believing that the improvement of US-Soviet relations and their mutually advantageous development in such areas as economics, science and culture,

10   will meet these objectives and contribute to better mutual understanding and business-like cooperation, without in any way prejudicing the interests of third countries, Conscious that these objectives reflect the interests of the peoples of both countries,

Have agreed as follows:

15   *First*. They will proceed from the common determination that in the nuclear age there is no alternative to conducting their mutual relations on the basis of peaceful coexistence. Differences in ideology and in the social systems of the USA and the USSR are not obstacles to the bilateral development of normal relations based on the principles of sovereignty, equality, non-interference in

20   internal affairs and mutual advantage.

Second. The USA and the USSR attach major importance to preventing the development of situations capable of causing a dangerous exacerbation of their relations. Therefore, they will do their utmost to avoid military confrontations and to prevent the outbreak of nuclear war. They will always exercise restraint

25   in their mutual relations, and will be prepared to negotiate and settle differences by peaceful means. Discussions and negotiations on outstanding issues will be

conducted in a spirit of reciprocity, mutual accommodation and mutual benefit. Both sides recognize that efforts to obtain unilateral advantage at the expense of the other, directly or indirectly, are inconsistent with these objectives. The pre-
30 requisites for maintaining and strengthening peaceful relations between the USA and the USSR are the recognition of the security interests of the Parties based on the principle of equality and the renunciation of the use or threat of force.

Third. The USA and the USSR have a special responsibility, as do other countries which are permanent members of the United Nations Security Council, to
35 do everything in their power so that conflicts or situations will not arise which would serve to increase international tensions. Accordingly, they will seek to promote conditions in which all countries will live in peace and security and will not be subject to outside interference in their internal affairs.

Fourth. The USA and the USSR intend to widen the juridical basis of their
40 mutual relations and to exert the necessary efforts so that bilateral agreements which they have concluded and multilateral treaties and agreements to which they are jointly parties are faithfully implemented.

Fifth. The USA and the USSR reaffirm their readiness to continue the practice of exchanging views on problems of mutual interest and, when necessary, to con-
45 duct such exchanges at the highest level, including meetings between leaders of the two countries. The two governments welcome and will facilitate an increase in productive contacts between representatives of the legislative bodies of the two countries.

Sixth. The Parties will continue their efforts to limit armaments on a bilateral
50 as well as on a multilateral basis. They will continue to make special efforts to limit strategic armaments. Whenever possible, they will conclude concrete agreements aimed at achieving these purposes. The USA and the USSR regard as the ultimate objective of their efforts the achievement of general and complete disarmament and the establishment of an effective system of international security in
55 accordance with the purposes and principles of the United Nations.

Seventh. The USA and the USSR regard commercial and economic ties as an important and necessary element in the strengthening of their bilateral relations and thus will actively promote the growth of such ties. They will facilitate cooperation between the relevant organizations and enterprises of the two countries and
60 the conclusion of appropriate agreements and contracts, including long-term ones.

Source: Public Papers of the Presidents, Richard Nixon, 1972 ■ ■ ■

The Middle East

The Nixon-Kissinger diplomacy faced a tough challenge in the Middle East. The region represented a tangle of competing interest: the United States supplied military and economic aid to ensure Israel's survival, but it was also heavily dependent on oil from the Arab states. Complicating the picture, the Mideast had become a Cold War battleground between Washington and Moscow. In 1967

Arab nations, which had never conceded Israel's right to exist, prepared to invade their neighbor. Forewarned, Israel attacked first, and in six days of fighting the Israeli army captured the Gaza Strip and Sinai Peninsula from Egypt, the West Bank and East Jerusalem from Jordan, and the Golan Heights from Syria.

On October 6, 1973—the most sacred Jewish holy day, Yom Kippur—Syria and Egypt attacked Israel. In the first three days of fighting, Egyptian troops advanced into the Sinai and crossed the Suez Canal while Syria's army in the North threatened to cut Israel in half by penetrating through the Golan Heights.

With Israel's survival at stake, the United States ordered a massive supply of arms to its ally. The American aid proved decisive. Israel recovered and took the offensive before the fighting ended in late October. Over the next two years Kissinger pursued "shuttle diplomacy," traveling between capitals in the Middle East to promote peace.

He met with limited success. He made progress with Egypt, but the other Arab states, bruised by America's pivotal intervention, imposed an oil embargo against the United States, Europe, and Japan. The embargo, which lasted from October 17, 1973, to March 18, 1974, produced dramatically higher energy costs. Thereafter, the OPEC nations continued to raise oil prices, which increased 400 percent in 1974 alone, with devastating consequences for the oil-dependent U.S. economy.

Kissinger also made little progress in addressing the thorny issue of a Palestinian homeland. In 1964, Palestinian Arabs created the Palestine Liberation Organization (PLO), which called for an end to the Jewish state and the creation of a Palestinian homeland. Under the aggressive leadership of Yasser Arafat, PLO factions launched a series of terrorist attacks against Israeli targets, including the murder of eleven Israeli athletes at the 1972 Olympic games in Munich. In 1975, after Arafat offered to settle the issue peacefully through the United Nations, the United States acknowledged that "the legitimate interests of the Palestinian Arabs must be taken into account in the negotiating of an Arab-Israeli peace." The issue of "land for peace" would prove a source of continuing friction in the region.

Playing the Race Card

At home, Nixon escalated his efforts to tap into the frustrations of the "silent majority" by exploiting the Democrats' vulnerability on race issues. Though he came to office on a tough law-and-order platform, Nixon had always been a racial moderate. During his first two years in office he reached out to black voters, dramatically expanding government enforcement of desegregation and institutionalizing racial quotas in all government contracts. In 1969 the president approved the Philadelphia Plan, which required construction unions in Philadelphia employed on government contracts to establish "goals and timetables" for hiring minorities.

Nixon proved to be a fair-weather friend of racial quotas, and as political winds shifted to the right, he repudiated one of his administration's major legacies. The pivotal event was the hard hat march in the spring of 1970, during which thousands of New York City construction workers marched in support of Nixon's Vietnam policies. According to journalist William Safire, "Most of the zip went out of [the Philadelphia Plan] after the hard hats marched in support of Nixon and the war." Nixon saw an opportunity to win over the working class to the Republican Party and now viewed his support of quotas as an obstacle.

In 1971 the Supreme Court, losing patience with southern resistance to desegregation, ordered the busing of students to promote racial mixing in the public schools. Polls showed that by a three-to-one majority, whites opposed busing. Nixon was quick to capitalize on white resistance and win their allegiance. In the months leading up to the 1972 election the president fired off memos to his

The Prowar Demonstration by New York's "Hard Hats"   On the morning of May 8, 1970, hundreds of antiwar activists gathered along Wall Street to protest Nixon's sending of U.S. troops into Cambodia. About five minutes to noon, construction workers, often called "hard hats" in New York, began arriving on the scene and started hitting students with their helmets, scattering the crowd. Then the hard hats marched to City Hall and demanded that the American flag, lowered to half-staff to commemorate the Kent State deaths, be fully raised. Nixon used the action of the hard hats as an example of how average working Americans supported their country and Nixon's actions in Southeast Asia. Nixon invited the leaders of the local union to a White House ceremony, where he donned a hard hat for photographers. *(© Paul Fusco/Magnum Photos)*

staff, insisting that they emphasize his opposition to "forcibly integrated housing or forcibly integrated education."

In an explicit appeal to the white South, Nixon nominated conservative southern judges to fill Court vacancies. In 1969 he successfully nominated conservative Warren Burger to replace departing Chief Justice Earl Warren. Later that year when another vacancy opened on the court, Nixon turned to South Carolina Judge Clement Haynsworth. Though no one questioned Haynsworth's legal credentials, his strong opposition to desegregation angered Senate liberals and worried many moderate Republicans. For the first time since the administration of Herbert Hoover, the Senate rejected a Supreme Court nominee. Nixon responded by nominating Judge G. Harrold Carswell, an undistinguished jurist who had once declared his belief in white supremacy. The Senate again refused to confirm the president's nominee. Nixon lost the battle, but he won the political war because he skillfully used the Senate rejection to score political points in the South by playing on Southerners' sense of victimization.

To highlight his position on social issues, Nixon unleashed Vice President Spiro Agnew, who traveled the country denouncing the media, radical professors, student protesters, and liberals. Realizing that the administration needed to break the hold of the Democratic Party on white voters, Agnew promised a "positive polarization" of the electorate. "Will America be led by a President elected by a majority of the American people," he demanded, "or will it be intimidated and blackmailed into following the path dictated by a disruptive radical and militant minority—the pampered prodigies of the radical liberals in the United States Senate?" Agnew called the Kent State killings "predictable and avoidable," and he attacked the "elitists" who regarded the Bill of Rights as a protection "for psychotic and criminal elements in our society."

While denouncing Democrats for being soft on social issues, Nixon tried to co-opt their economic message by intentionally overheating the economy. Nixon began his administration by embracing the monetarist theories of economist Milton Friedman. The conservative Friedman claimed that prices could be lowered by reducing the quantity of money in the economy. If there was less money and it was more expensive to borrow, reasoned Friedman, economic activity would ease and there would be less upward pressure on prices. In practice a reduced money supply did slow economic growth, but it did not stop prices from rising. By 1970 the unemployment rate had increased from 3.6 percent to 4.9 percent, while the consumer price index rose by 11 percent. This new and troubling phenomenon, dubbed stagflation, haunted the economy for the rest of the decade.

Deeming monetarism a failure, Nixon tried other policies. In August 1971, Nixon shocked conservatives and delighted liberals by declaring, "I am now a Keynesian." Acting on his new faith, the president advocated traditionally liberal solutions: imposing wage and price controls, devaluing the dollar, and abandoning the gold standard. Fearing the political consequences of high unemployment in an election year, Nixon pressured the Federal Reserve Bank, the nation's central institution for setting interest rates and regulating the money supply, to turn on the money spigot. Commenting on Nixon's dramatic switch, a journalist quipped, "It's a little like a Christian crusader saying 'All things considered, I think Mohammed was right!' " Later that year Nixon announced a "new economic policy," imposing a 10 percent surcharge on U.S. imports. "My basic approach," said Secretary of Treasury John Connally, "is that the foreigners are out to screw us. Our job is to screw them first."

The policies realized their short-term political and economic goals. During the 1972 election year the gross national product grew by 7.2 percent and the unemployment rate plunged from 6 percent to 5.1 percent. In the long run, however, Nixon's policies proved disastrous. By ignoring clear signs of inflation and intentionally expanding the economy, he contributed to a cycle of spiraling inflation that would soon cripple it.

The 1972 Presidential Campaign

In 1972 the Democratic Party nominated as its presidential candidate Senator George McGovern, an outspoken liberal critic of the Vietnam War. McGovern and the delegates at the Democratic Party convention adopted an aggressively liberal platform. Among its more controversial points were a call for the immediate withdrawal of U.S. troops from Vietnam, amnesty for those who had fled the draft, and the abolition of capital punishment.

When a would-be assassin shot and critically wounded George Wallace during the 1972 primaries, Nixon inherited many of his angry white supporters. Most were former Democrats who disapproved of their party's liberal position on domestic issues. They saw McGovern not as their champion but as the candidate of a liberal, intellectual, northeastern establishment.

On election day Nixon scored a resounding victory, winning 60.7 percent of the popular vote, while McGovern received only 37.5 percent. Nixon carried every state except Massachusetts and the District of Columbia, for a margin in the electoral college of 520 to 17. Nixon's shrewd appeals to the "silent majority" touched a responsive chord with many working-class Democrats who felt their party had abandoned them in pursuit of more liberal voters. Almost 10 million Democrats, nearly one-third of all registered Democrats, voted for Nixon. An overwhelming 70 percent of the white working class voted for him. But it was a lonely landslide. The Democrats gained two seats in the Senate, and the Republicans gained only a dozen House seats. Nixon carried 72 percent of the once-solid South. In a clear reflection of the success of his campaign, he won over 90 percent of white southerners who had voted for Wallace in the primaries. Nixon also won 65 percent of middle-income voters, and he scored well with ethnic voters, winning a majority of Italian and Irish voters.

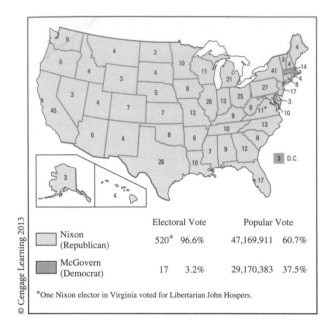

© Cengage Learning 2013

	Electoral Vote		Popular Vote	
Nixon (Republican)	520*	96.6%	47,169,911	60.7%
McGovern (Democrat)	17	3.2%	29,170,383	37.5%

*One Nixon elector in Virginia voted for Libertarian John Hospers.

The Election of 1972

The assassination attempt on George Wallace and Edward Kennedy's personal crisis over Chappaquiddick removed two of the leading Democratic candidates for president, leaving Senator George McGovern of South Dakota to take the nomination. Nixon won by the largest majority of any Republican in American history.

Watergate and the Downfall of Richard Nixon

The Nixon administration actually began unraveling before the 1972 election. On June 17, 1972, a security guard foiled a break-in at the Democratic Party's national headquarters in the Watergate Hotel. The story might have died had it not been for two industrious young reporters at the *Washington Post*, Bob Woodward and Carl Bernstein. Using leads from a confidential source they called "Deep Throat," who was later revealed to be Mark Felt, second in command at the FBI, the reporters connected the burglary to the president's reelection committee. In February 1973, Congress created a bipartisan select committee to probe further into the Watergate affair. The committee, headed by North Carolina Democrat Sam Ervin, uncovered a trail of corruption leading to higher and higher levels of the White House staff. Republican senator Howard Baker from Tennessee posed the central question: "What did the president know and when did he know it?"

On June 25 White House Counsel John Dean gave a disturbing answer to that question when in flat, unemotional tones he told the committee of the president's personal involvement in a scheme to cover up the Watergate burglary. Dean's proximity to the president and the concrete details he offered in his 245-page testimony made him a compelling witness. While much of official Washington seemed mesmerized by the growing White House scandal, the public was becoming increasingly angry about the economy. The president's wage and price controls had artificially dampened inflation pressures. When he lifted controls, prices climbed. At the same time, higher oil prices raised the inflation rate from 8.4 percent during 1973 to 12.1 percent in 1974. *Time* magazine reported in August that "each costly ring of the check-out cash register seemed to eat away at public patience with the Administration far more than the revelations of the Watergate scandal."

It was Watergate, however, that doomed the Nixon presidency and derailed his strategy of creating a new majority. Former aide Alexander Butterfield revealed to the Ervin committee that Nixon had installed a secret taping system to record, "for posterity," his private conversations in the White House and the Executive Office Building. A special prosecutor, Harvard law school professor Archibald Cox, asked the courts to order Nixon to release the tapes. Nixon refused.

When Cox persisted in his efforts to secure the tapes, Nixon ordered him fired. Members of Congress demanded that a new special prosecutor be appointed and that the tapes be released. Compelled by this unified opposition, Nixon yielded some of the tapes and named a new special prosecutor, Leon Jaworski of Texas. Once again Nixon declared his innocence, this time on television. "I am not a crook," he insisted.

Nixon professed his innocence, but Vice President Spiro Agnew was forced to plead no contest in federal court to charges of income-tax evasion and admitted that he had accepted hundreds of thousands of dollars in bribes while governor of Maryland. Agnew resigned from the vice presidency, and Congress quickly confirmed Nixon's choice, House minority leader Gerald R. Ford, a veteran Michigan Republican, to succeed Agnew under the terms of the Twenty-fifth Amendment.

More bad news followed: one of the tapes Nixon had turned over contained a suspicious eighteen-and-one-half-minute gap of a conversation between the president and White House adviser H. R. Haldeman on June 20, 1972, three days after the break-in. Nixon's secretary Rosemary Woods took responsibility, claiming that she had accidentally erased the tape while transcribing it. Experts testified, however, that the tapes had been deliberately tampered with by "manual" erasures. By December 1973, Nixon's own personal finances had come under increasingly critical scrutiny. The Internal Revenue Service disclosed that the president owed more than $400,000 in back taxes and penalties.

The air of scandal and uncertainty continued to hang over the capital until July 24, 1974, when a unanimous Supreme Court ordered President Nixon to turn over all relevant tapes. Just as Dean had contended, the tapes revealed that Nixon had personally intervened to stifle an investigation by the Federal Bureau of Investigation into the Watergate break-in and that he had authorized payments of more than $460,000 in hush money to keep the Watergate burglars from implicating higher-ups in the administration. It was not just the content of the tapes, but Nixon's demeanor and profane language that, in the words of noted columnist Joseph Alsop, engendered "sheer flesh-crawling repulsion."

PRIMARY   SOURCE

10.2 | *The Smoking Gun*

One tape turned over by the White House after the Supreme Court order was a recorded conversation between the president and domestic adviser H. R. Haldeman. Recorded six days after the break-in, the two men discussed covering up the Watergate break-in, thereby proving Nixon's culpability. Notice the reference to FBI assistant director Mark Felt, who was later identified as "Deep Throat."

June 23, 1972

[H. R.] HALDEMAN: Now, on the investigation, you know the Democratic break-in thing, we're back in the problem area because the FBI is not under control, because [Director Patrick] Gray doesn't exactly know how to control it and they have—their investigation is now leading into some productive area. . . .
5   They've been able to trace the money—not through the money itself—but through the bank sources—the banker. And it goes in some directions we don't want it to go. Ah, also there have been some [other] things—like an informant came in off the street to the FBI in Miami who was a photographer or has a friend who is a photographer who developed some films through
10   this guy [Bernard] Barker and the films had pictures of Democratic National Committee letterhead documents and things. So it's things like that that are filtering in. . . . [John] Mitchell came up with yesterday, and John Dean analyzed very carefully last night and concludes, concurs now with Mitchell's recommendation that the only way to solve this . . . is for us to have [CIA
15   Assistant Director Vernon] Walters call Pat Gray and just say, "Stay to hell out of this—this is ah, [our] business here. We don't want you to go any further on it." That's not an unusual development, and ah, that would take care of it.
PRESIDENT: What about Pat Gray—you mean Pat Gray doesn't want to?
20   HALDEMAN: Pat does want to. He doesn't know how to, and he doesn't have any basis for doing it. Given this, he will then have the basis. He'll call [FBI Assistant Director] Mark Felt in, and the two of them—and Mark Felt wants to cooperate because he's ambitious—
PRESIDENT: Yeah.
25   HALDEMAN: He'll call him in and say, "We've got the signal from across the river to put the hold on this." And that will fit rather well because the FBI agents who are working the case, at this point, feel that's what it is.
PRESIDENT: This is CIA? They've traced the money? Who'd they trace it to?
HALDEMAN: Well, they've traced it to a name, but they haven't gotten to the guy yet.
30   PRESIDENT: Would it be somebody here?
HALDEMAN: Ken Dahlberg.

PRESIDENT: Who the hell is Ken Dahlberg?

HALDEMAN: He gave $25,000 in Minnesota and, ah, the check went directly to this guy Barker.

PRESIDENT: It isn't from the Committee though, from [Maurice] Stans?

35 HALDEMAN: Yeah. It is. It's directly traceable and there's some more through some Texas people that went to the Mexican bank which can also be traced to the Mexican bank—they'll get their names today.

PRESIDENT: Well, I mean, there's no way—I'm just thinking if they don't cooperate, what do they say? That they were approached by the Cubans? That's what

40 Dahlberg has to say, the Texans too.

HALDEMAN: Well, if they will. But then we're relying on more and more people all the time. That's the problem and they'll [the FBI] . . . stop if we could take this other route.

PRESIDENT: All right.

45 HALDEMAN: [Mitchell and Dean] say the only way to do that is from White House instructions. And it's got to be to [CIA Director Richard] Helms and to—ah, what's his name? . . . Walters.

PRESIDENT: Walters.

HALDEMAN: And the proposal would be that . . . [John] Ehrlichman and I call

50 them in, and say, ah—

PRESIDENT: All right, fine. How do you call him in—I mean you just—well, we protected Helms from one hell of a lot of things.

HALDEMAN: That's what [John] Ehrlichman says.

PRESIDENT: Of course; this [Howard] Hunt [business.] That will uncover a lot of

55 things. You open that scab there's a hell of a lot of things and we just feel that it would be very detrimental to have this thing go any further. This involves these Cubans, Hunt, and a lot of hanky-panky that we have nothing to do with ourselves. Well, what the hell, did Mitchell know about this?

HALDEMAN: I think so. I don't think he knew the details, but I think he knew.

60 PRESIDENT: He didn't know how it was going to be handled though—with Dahlberg and the Texans and so forth? Well who was the asshole that did? Is it [G. Gordon] Liddy? Is that the fellow? He must be a little nuts!

HALDEMAN: He is.

PRESIDENT: I mean he just isn't well screwed on, is he? Is that the problem?

65 HALDEMAN: No, but he was under pressure, apparently, to get more information, and as he got more pressure, he pushed the people harder.

PRESIDENT: Pressure from Mitchell?

HALDEMAN: Apparently. . . .

PRESIDENT: All right, fine, I understand it all. We won't second-guess Mitchell

70 and the rest. Thank God it wasn't [Special White House Counsel Charles] Colson.

HALDEMAN: The FBI interviewed Colson yesterday. They determined that would be a good thing to do. To have him take an interrogation, which he did, and the FBI guys working the case concluded that there were one or two possibilities—

75 one, that this was a White House (they don't think that there is anything at

the Election Committee) they think it was either a White House operation and they have some obscure reasons for it—non-political, or it was a—Cuban [operation] and [involved] the CIA. And after their interrogation of Colson yesterday, they concluded it was not the White House, but are now convinced
80   it is a CIA thing, so the CIA turnoff would—

PRESIDENT: Well, not sure of their analysis, I'm not going to get that involved. I'm (unintelligible).

HALDEMAN: No, sir, we don't want you to.

PRESIDENT: You call them in.

85 HALDEMAN: Good deal.

PRESIDENT: Play it tough. That's the way they play it and that's the way we are going to play it. . . .

PRESIDENT: O.K. . . . Just say (unintelligible) very bad to have this fellow Hunt, ah, he knows too damned much. . . . If it gets out that this is all involved,
90   the Cuba thing, it would be a fiasco. It would make the CIA look bad, it's going to make Hunt look bad, and it is likely to blow the whole Bay of Pigs thing which we think would be very unfortunate—both for CIA, and for the country, at this time, and for American foreign policy. Just tell him to lay off. Don't you [think] so?

Source: Transcript of White House tapes, June 23, 1972, published by the Hearings Before the Committee on the Judiciary, House of Representatives, 93rd Congress, 2nd session (Washington, D.C.: Government Printing Office, 1974), 512–514.   ■ ■ ■

On August 8, 1974, facing certain impeachment, a disgraced Richard Nixon became the first American president to resign from office. Many forces conspired to create America's national nightmare. The extraordinary growth of presidential power during the Cold War, the social upheaval and intense partisan divisions of the 1960s and early 1970s, and the emergence of a skeptical and assertive media played important roles in Nixon's downfall. But it is impossible to understand Watergate without coming to terms with the ambitious, paranoid personality of Richard Nixon. Though he occupied the world's most powerful office, Nixon remained surprisingly insecure, fearful that his enemies in the establishment—liberals, media, and Congress—were out to destroy him. Since he equated his own political survival with the fate of the nation, Nixon felt justified in using whatever means necessary to destroy his opponents. "You were either for us or against us," recalled one aide, "and if you were against us we were against you." In a chilling disregard for civil liberties Nixon maintained that to curb domestic dissent, "everything is valid, everything is possible." Perhaps Nixon offered the most insight into his own downfall in his farewell speech to the White House staff. "Never be petty," he said, and "always remember, others may hate you, but those who hate you don't win unless you hate them, and then you destroy yourself."

In 1968 Richard Nixon won election preaching social harmony, but he governed by political polarization. Postwar contradictions provided much of

Nixon's Good-bye
After fellow Republicans made it clear that Nixon would be impeached and removed from office for his role in the Watergate cover-up, Nixon chose to resign. Gerald Ford, the House minority leader who had replaced Spiro Agnew as vice president the year before, was then sworn in as president. In this picture, Nixon and his family are boarding the helicopter on the White House lawn for the last time August 9, 1974. *(Nixon Presidential Materials Project, National Archives and Record Administration)*

the fuel Nixon needed. Affluence, and the rising expectations it produced, had nurtured a younger generation impatient for reform. Rejecting the vital-center faith in slow and gradual progress, the youth culture planned to narrow the gap between American ideals and social realities by forcing a quick end to the Vietnam War and refocusing attention on problems closer to home. Nixon frustrated these plans by playing to the social and cultural anxieties of the "silent majority." Although a majority of Americans opposed the war by 1969, Nixon tapped into the white working class's fear of social disorder, their intense patriotism, and their class resentment. Watergate derailed Nixon's effort to forge a new Republican majority, but it also produced more lasting damage. Nixon not only destroyed himself; he also disgraced the presidency and raised even more doubts about government's ability to produce a meaningful response to the American paradox.

SELECTED READINGS

▌ Historians are still trying to come to terms with Richard Nixon and his presidency. For the best accounts, see Melvin Small, *The Presidency of Richard Nixon* (2003) and Richard Reeves, *President Nixon* (2002). Robert Dallek presents the most incisive account of Nixon's foreign policy, and his complicated relationship with Henry Kissinger, in *Nixon and Kissinger* (2007). Allen Matusow offers a critical appraisal of the president's economic policy in *Nixon's Economy* (1998). David Greenberg uncovers the many competing images that Americans had of Richard Nixon in *Nixon's Shadow* (2003). Rick Perlstein provides the best account of Nixon's efforts to mobilize the "silent majority" in *Nixonland* (2009).

▌ Stanley Kutler's *Abuse of Power* (1997) and *The Wars of Watergate* (1992) are essential reading for understanding Nixon's downfall. Bob Woodward and Carl Bernstein's *All the President's Men* (1974) and *The Final Days* (1976) are both captivating journalistic accounts. For an insightful look at how Americans have remembered the events that led to Nixon's resignation, see Michael Schudson, *Watergate in American Memory* (1992).

▌ William Shawcross indignantly describes Nixon and Kissinger's Cambodia policy in *Sideshow* (1979). Melvin Small outlines the impact of the peace protesters on the administration's policies in *Johnson, Nixon, and the Doves* (1988). Jeffrey Kimball, Nixon's Vietnam War (2002) and Larry Berman's in *No Peace, No Honor* (2001) present devastating critiques of Nixon''s foreign policy. For Nixon's efforts toward disarmament, see Franz Schurmann's *The Foreign Policies of Richard Nixon* (1987). Jussi Hanhimaki analyzes Kissinger's role in American foreign policy in *The Flawed Architect* (2004). Edy Kaufman's *Crisis in Allende's Chile* (1988) details the events leading to the 1973 coup. Stephen Rabe covers the crises in the Middle East in *The Road to OPEC* (1982). Raymond Garthoff charts American–Soviet relations in the 1970s in *Detente and Confrontation* (rev. ed., 1994).

11 The Clash of Cultures, 1969–1980

On August 15, 1969, a half a million like-minded young people gathered on Max Yasgur's 600-acre farm near Bethel, New York, for a weekend festival of "peace and love and music." Woodstock included a stellar lineup of musical talent that included Jimi Hendrix, the Who, the Grateful Dead, Joe Cocker, Janis Joplin, and Sly and the Family Stone. "It was a very magical, once-in-a-lifetime thing to be part of," said guitarist Carlos Santana. Whether they attended the concert or not, the generation that came of age during the 1960s embraced Woodstock's freedom-espousing spirit: Hendrix's screaming guitar rendition of the national anthem, the rampant drug use, sexual freedom, long hair, and bell bottoms.

The concert was about more than just music. Disillusioned with the Vietnam War and with the state of American politics, young people who traveled to Woodstock hoped to create an alternative community. Instead of seeking to change society, they chose to withdraw from it, forging a separate identity of like-minded young people who rejected the values of contemporary society.

Not everyone experienced the magic of Woodstock. Organizers, who had expected about 150,000 people, were overwhelmed by the size of the crowds. Tickets were priced to sell

237

for $18, but the organizers had failed to have fences installed or ticket booths set up, so it turned into a free event. Heavy rains turned the grounds into a mud pit. There were traffic jams that led many people to abandon their cars miles from the site. There was such a severe shortage of water, food, and medical and sanitation facilities, that New York Governor Nelson Rockefeller declared a state of emergency.

The challenges of creating and sustaining the spirit of Woodstock became apparent the following December when organizers planned a follow-up west coast concert in Altamont, California. The scene was marred by violence. Hired to provide security, members of the Hell's Angels motorcycle gang assaulted concert goers, beating one man to death. Three other people died during the festival.

Many critics wrote that the 1970s were a cultural wasteland, a time when Americans retreated into personal pursuits and abandoned the higher idealism and public engagement of the 1960s. The journalist Tom Wolfe called it the "me decade." But

The Counterculture at the Woodstock Music Festival   For three days, August 15–17, 1969, the counterculture took center stage at the Woodstock music festival. Organizers booked some of the greatest music artists of the baby-boom generation, but failed to anticipate the number of rock music fans who would descend on Woodstock. As a result the crowd found that there were few facilities available. Despite the problems, those assembled enjoyed themselves in the true spirit of the counterculture—with three days of sex, drugs, and rock and roll. *(© John Filo)*

the critics may have rushed to an unfair judgment, overlooking the central paradox of the decade: while America experienced a political backlash against the 1960s, most Americans absorbed the cultural values of that decade, transforming radical ideas of personal liberation into mainstream values.

The decade also witnessed an intense cultural clash over the legacy of the 1960s. On one side stood reformers—homosexuals, Native Americans, Hispanics, and women—who tried to build on the foundation of the "rights consciousness" established during the 1960s. Opposing them were traditionalists—Christian fundamentalists and neoconservative intellectuals—who appealed to traditional values, charging that the emphasis on rights and self-fulfillment had eroded personal responsibility and encouraged a cancerous permissiveness. The tension between reform and traditional values produced a clash between the two sides over a series of contentious issues—busing to achieve racial integration, passage of the Equal Rights Amendment (ERA) to the Constitution, and gay rights—that shaped both the culture and the politics of the decade.

The Great Shift

The culture of the 1970s represented a flowering of the youth culture's rebellion, the desire to discover the inner self and find self-fulfillment. "In the '70s, hardly anybody was a hippie, because everybody was," declared one observer. Emblems of sixties protest, like long hair and casual dress, gained mainstream appeal during the 1970s. Even notable fashion failures—blue polyester leisure suits and wide, pointy collars—reflected a rebellion against the formality of an older generation. "Many of the changes the hippies spearheaded in the '60s became major cultural phenomena," noted a designer, "particularly the belief that nobody could tell them what to wear."

Not everyone rebelled in polyester, however. Many Americans turned to clothes made from natural fabrics, such as cotton caftans and gauze blouses and dresses. The Earth Shoe, designed by a yoga teacher in Denmark, became a big hit claiming that it provided the natural feel of walking on sand. Rock and roll, the anthem of the youth rebellion during the 1960s, joined the mainstream in the seventies. "Rock," noted an observer, "was becoming a common language, the reference point for a splintered culture." The new music expressed the pent-up frustration and utopian idealism of the young in a language that most adults could not understand. "Don't criticize what you can't understand/ Yours sons and your daughters are beyond your command," folk artist Bob Dylan warned mothers and fathers of the baby boom. Dylan's music often had an explicit political message, but most rockers were more interested in free expression than radical action. Many of the decade's most popular rock and roll artists—David Bowie, Rod Stewart, Elton John, Al Green, the Rolling Stones, and Pink Floyd, among others—wore outrageous costumes, made explicit references to sex and drugs, and often included biting social commentary. American culture embraced them: young people packed stadiums for concerts and spent millions buying their records. In 1976 presidential candidate Jimmy Carter told audiences that his favored performers were Bob Dylan, Led Zeppelin, and the Grateful Dead.

The real musical sensation of the decade was disco. This new musical craze, popularized by the hit movie *Saturday Night Fever* and by vocalists such as Donna Summer, mesmerized its audiences with glitzy dance halls and pulsating lights. The most famous disco was New York's fashionable Studio 54, where celebrities and powerbrokers lined up outside hoping to gain admission.

Most discos, however, were housed in abandoned factories, churches, and hotels. By 1975, there were over 10,000 discos in North America—over 200 in New York City alone. The patrons of these clubs were often the disenfranchised: gays, African-Americans, and Latinos who were excluded from mainstream society. They were attracted to disco because it preached a message of inclusion, a blurring of racial and gender identities. Disco was music made openly for and by gays as well as straights. It merged and recombined elements of soul, jazz, Latin, and R&B. More than anything else, it provided a needed escape from a nation traumatized by the Vietnam War and hard economic times.

On the dance floor, people from different backgrounds and races danced to the rhythmic beats of Donna Summer and Gloria Gaynor. Straight men and women swooned to the "Village People," who presented themselves as cartoon homosexual pinups—a cowboy, construction worker, leather man, Native American, policeman, and soldier—as they wiggled their way through hits such as "In the Navy," "YMCA," and "Macho Man."

Changes in clothing styles, the widespread appeal of rock music, and the rise of disco were just a few examples of the great shift in cultural values. The consciousness revolution, once confined to the youthful counterculture, mushroomed into a mass movement, particularly among the white middle-class. Many Americans looked to Eastern religions "to get in touch with their feelings," with others, and with the forces of nature. Most employed some form of meditation or breathing exercises to expand consciousness beyond the routine of everyday intellectual experience. The most popular fad, Transcendental Meditation (TM), required two 20-minute periods daily of repeating a word called a "mantra."

Drugs remained the method of choice for many Americans trying to escape the drudgery of everyday life. Marijuana use became a rite of passage for most college students in the 1970s. Use of mind altering drugs spread to older Americans, who managed to get their drugs legally. In 1975, doctors issued 229 million prescriptions. The most popular drug of the decade was the tranquilizer Valium.

The search for self-fulfillment found expression in a health and fitness craze during the 70s. Natural food stores sprouted from coast to coast. Between 1968 and 1972, the number of health-food stores in the United States more than doubled, from 1,200 to 2,600. By the end of the decade, Stow-Mills, the largest health-food distributor in New England, was selling 12 tons of granola each month. Supermarkets in major cities offered leeks, fresh herbs, and organically grown produce. Salad bars, which started as a hippie novelty, became commonplace at fancy restaurants and fast-food eateries.

Americans by the millions started jogging to stay fit and improve their overall health. "If the emblem of the '60s was the angry banner of a protest marcher, the spirit of '79 was the jogger, absorbed in the sound of his own breathing—and wearing a smile button," observed *Newsweek*.

In 1978, Gallup estimated that 15 million American men and women jogged regularly. In 1970, 126 runners participated in the first New York Marathon; by the end of the decade the number had soared to nearly 15,000.

The jogging craze was part of a larger public fascination with fitness. Jogging and tennis led in popularity, but racquetball, handball, squash, and sailing also found new recruits. Sales of roller skates exploded over 500 percent during the decade. Austrian-born Arnold Schwarzenegger raised bodybuilding to a new art form with the publication of his book, *Pumping Iron: The Art and Sport of Bodybuilding*.

The Sexual Revolution

Sexual feelings were high on the list of emotions that Americans explored during the decade. By the mid-1970s Americans were bombarded with sexual images. Off Broadway plays featured frontal nudity, magazines displayed centerfolds, sexual themes pervaded daytime television, and dinner table conversation revolved around previously taboo subjects such as birth control, abortion, and homosexuality. *The Joy of Sex* (1972), which billed itself as "the first explicitly sexual book for the coffee table," sold more than 3.8 million copies in its first two years.

Explicitly sexual messages permeated popular culture. Disco queen Donna Sumner moaned her way through "Love to Love You Baby," and followed up that hit with "More, More, More," sung to a backdrop of orgasmic yelps by porn star Andrea True. Among the most popular television shows were *Get Christie Love!*, *Love, American Style*, and *The Love Boat*.

The 1972 release of the pornographic movie *Deep Throat*, staring Linda Lovelace, gained critical acclaim and emerged as one of the year's most popular films, earning more than $25 million in sales. Many cities saw a proliferation in the number of bathhouses, both gay and straight. The most famous, Plato's Retreat in New York City, treated over six thousand men and women every month to an assortment of sexual experiences.

The pervasiveness of sexual images reflected a loosening of sexual values. A majority of Americans, both male and female, expressed more liberal views on premarital sex, living together outside of marriage, and abortion. Between 1960 and 1977, the number of unmarried couples living together more than doubled. A survey in 1967 found that 85 percent of parents condemned premarital sex as morally wrong. By 1980, 63 percent condoned it. According to the pollster Daniel Yankelovich, the new attitude had become: "If two people loved each other, there's nothing morally wrong with having sexual relations."

In an age that emphasized personal fulfillment, self-awareness, and sexual freedom, there was less incentive to remain in marriages. The divorce rate, which climbed almost 100 percent in the 1960s, increased another 82 percent in the 1970s. More than two out of five marriages during the decade ended in divorce. "In the 1950s as in the 1920s, diamonds were 'forever,' " observed the historian Sheila Rothman. "In the 1970s diamonds were for 'now.' "

Just as important, boomer couples that stayed together rewrote the rules of marriage. By the end of the 1970s, three-quarters of baby boomers said they preferred an "equal marriage" with the husband and wife sharing responsibility. Only 10 percent wanted a "traditional marriage" with clearly defined male and female roles.

Television and Movies

The anti-authority streak of the 1960s counterculture seeped into the popular culture of the 1970s. *Saturday Night Live* broke all conventions when it aired on NBC on October 11, 1975. Creator Lorne Michaels wanted to create a comedy show that would appeal to the sensibilities of the baby boom generation. It was edgy, topical, and pushed boundaries. The show's cast of young comics, including Chevy Chase, John Belushi, Dan Aykroyd, and Gilda Radner, infused their skits with pointed barbs at anyone in a position of authority. The most provocative television show of the decade was Norman Lear's eccentric soap opera *Mary Hartman, Mary Hartman*. Its heroine, a befuddled, angst-ridden housewife residing in the mythical blue-collar town of Fernwood, Ohio, dealt with daily travails that included an impotent husband, a promiscuous sister, and a senile grandfather known to police as "the Fernwood Flasher." "There is something sick, sick and twisted, twisted about *Mary Hartman, Mary Hartman*," observed a critic.

But popular culture also revealed the struggle of a culture attempting to reconcile new ideas with old realities. The popular ABC miniseries *Roots* (1976) provided audiences with a rich portrayal of the African American experience. Norman Lear's popular sitcom *All in the Family* pitted Archie Bunker, who preferred an older, simpler America expressed in the theme song "Those Were the Days," against the progressive views of his liberal son-in-law, Michael. "Why fight it?" Michael asked Archie in the first episode. "The world's changing." But Archie, refusing to accept defeat, continued his fight against the forces of change, especially minorities, liberals, and radicals. "I'm against all the right things," Archie shouted, "welfare, busing, women's lib, and sex education."

A number of blockbuster movies also touched on sensitive issues and revealed the decade's conflicting social currents. In the 1976 Academy Award-winning film *Rocky*, film writer Sylvester Stallone played a streetwise white roughneck named Rocky Balboa, "the Italian Stallion," who challenged the outspoken and black Apollo Creed, for the heavyweight championship of the world. Movie audiences cheered for the white ethnic underdog, whom one movie critic called "the most romanticized Great White Hope in screen history." *Breaking Away* (1979), the story of blue-collar youth competing in a bicycle race in Bloomington, Indiana, offered a more subtle and sensitive portrayal of working-class frustration. *Kramer vs. Kramer*, the biggest box office hit of 1979, used the story of a painful divorce and child custody battle to deal with changing gender roles and the breakup of the family.

Hollywood, and the nation, struggled during the decade to come to terms with Vietnam. The film *M*A*S*H* (1970), later made into a television sitcom, used the backdrop of an Army field hospital in Korea to present a black comedy about Vietnam. In 1978, two Vietnam films, *Coming Home* and *The Deer Hunter*, swept the Oscars with their vivid portrayal of how the war traumatized ordinary Americans. The message of *Coming Home*, which starred peace activist Jane Fonda, was solidly antiwar. *The Deer Hunter* was more ambiguous. In tracing the tragic journey of three friends from a steel-mill town in western Pennsylvania who volunteered for the war, director Michael Cimino showed the tremendous price, both physical and psychological, many Americans paid during the conflict. At the same time, critics charged that by depicting the Viet Cong as "brutes and dolts" and the Americans as "innocents in a corrupt land," the movie took a subtle prowar position.

American Identities

Dreams of social change, and the struggles over racial identity, did not end with the changing of the calendar. The 1970s witnessed a continuation of the struggles over American identity that were unleashed during the previous decade. The civil-rights struggle inspired an explosion in "rights consciousness," as other disadvantaged groups organized to fight for a broader, more inclusive vision of what it meant to be an American.

African Americans: Progress and Poverty

African Americans were once again at the center of that movement, building on the success of the civil-rights movement of the 1960s, moving beyond demands for political rights and calling for expanded economic opportunities. The Civil Rights Act of 1964 and the Voting Rights Act of 1965 had destroyed the last vestiges of legal discrimination. The courts gave legal sanction to the demands of civil-rights groups for affirmative action programs that sought to achieve equality by reserving opportunities for minorities. In 1978 a white man, Allan Bakke, sued the University of California Medical School at Davis, claiming that the university had rejected him in favor of less-qualified minority candidates. A divided Supreme Court, in *Bakke* v. *University of California* (1978), ruled that the university's absolute quota for minorities was illegal, but it also agreed that schools could consider race as a "plus factor" in admissions so as to foster "diversity" in the classes.

With vigorous government enforcement of the Voting Rights Act of 1965, African Americans began voting in unprecedented numbers and dramatically increased their representation in Congress, in statehouses, and in town halls across the nation. The most dramatic gains took place on the local level. In 1964 there were 70 elected black officials at all levels of government; by 1980, there were 4,600, including more than 170 mayors.

The end of legal segregation opened up new opportunities for African Americans. Many took white-collar jobs and held union memberships for the first time, earning higher incomes and enjoying advances in job security. In the 1970s the earnings of between 35 and 45 percent of African American families rose to middle-class levels. By 1977 more than 1 million blacks were attending college, a 500 percent increase since 1960.

Unfortunately, legal and economic gains took place against a backdrop of increasing misery for many African Americans. In the 1970s black America increasingly divided into a two-class society: while some black families rose to middle-class income levels during the decade, about 30 percent slid deeper into poverty. African Americans had long suffered disproportionately from poverty, but that of the 1960s and 1970s was in many ways new, marked by a deeper isolation and hopelessness. The economic gap between blacks and whites also widened during the decade. Those African Americans who held jobs earned less than their white counterparts. In 1978 only 8.7 percent of white families lived below the poverty line, compared to 30.6 percent of African American families.

Frustrated by the persistence of discrimination, many African Americans abandoned the integrationist ideal of the early civil-rights struggle. In the words of African American scholar Harold Cruse, discussions about race in America shifted from a "politics of civil rights" to a "politics of black ethnicity." "The Negro Integrationist runs afoul of reality in pursuit of an illusion," Cruse noted. While the vast majority of African Americans rejected militant expressions of black power, they embraced expressions of black cultural nationalism.

Native Americans

Throughout the 1960s, Native Americans led various political reform efforts of their own that in some respects mirrored the larger Civil Rights movement but were unique in their origins and ideologies. Similar to "Black Power" advocates of the African American civil-rights movement, numerous Native American activists cried "Red Power" while embracing militant reform tactics. Despite parallels with the Black Power movement, however, the Red Power movement was unique in its ability to place issues of land, political sovereignty, and treaty rights at the center of their reform efforts. Influenced by Dakota intellectual Vine Deloria Jr.'s bestselling *Custer Died for Your Sins: an Indian Manifesto* (1969), they protested the Bureau of Indian Affairs' program to "assimilate" them into mainstream society and the lack of economic and education opportunities not just on reservations, but also in urban neighborhoods—where by 1970 almost half of all Native people resided. Additionally, they advocated a policy of self-determination that would allow for Indians to manage their own political and economic affairs.

In 1969, a group of urban Indians from the San Francisco Bay Area calling themselves the "Indians of All Tribes" led a takeover of the abandoned federal prison on Alcatraz Island in hopes of establishing an Indian center and drawing symbolic parallels between the prison and the nature of life on various Indian reservations. For nineteen months the occupation drew attention from a national media that overwhelmingly sided with charismatic Indian leaders like Richard Oakes and John Trudell. In the process, the news media helped the Native activists in their efforts to bring attention to the problems that Indians faced in contemporary American society.

Meanwhile, a group of urban Indian activists based in Minneapolis-St. Paul, Minnesota, calling themselves the American Indian Movement (AIM), was steadily gaining adherents. Established in 1968 as a neighborhood patrol group modeled after the Black Panthers, AIM railed against police abuse, unemployment, and poor housing conditions, while advocating a return to traditional Indian ways that stressed the importance of treaty rights, spirituality, and tribal community. AIM gained the national media spotlight in December 1972, when they orchestrated a one-week seizure of the Bureau of Indian Affairs headquarters in Washington, D.C.

The movement's influence peaked in February 1973, when two hundred AIM members occupied the town of Wounded Knee, South Dakota, on the Pine Ridge Lakota reservation to protest the light sentences of four white men found guilty of torturing and murdering a Lakota man. They occupied a small church on a hill for 71 days, demanding that the government honor hundreds of broken treaties and calling for major changes in reservation government.

Other Native activist groups like the Native American Rights Fund employed more conservative tactics to win a series of legal actions that restored violated treaty rights and extended legal rights. Armed with copies of old treaties, numerous Native activists demonstrated legal savvy in using the Supreme Court to win the return of land wrongly taken from them. They also won legal battles to block strip-mining and to preserve rights to fishing and mineral resources on reservation land. Two new laws, the 1975 Indian Self-Determination and Education Assistance Act and the 1976 Indian Health Care Improvement Act, alongside future amendments, fortified tribal sovereignty while increasing tribal control of programs affecting their welfare.

Native American Seizure of the Wounded Knee Church, April 1973 The American Indian Movement, partly inspired by the African American civil-rights movement, seized the trading post and Catholic church at Wounded Knee, on the South Dakota Pine Ridge Reservation, on February 28, 1973. Site of the infamous massacre of over 200 Lakota Ghost Dancers in 1890, Wounded Knee was seen as the perfect place to air the grievances of twentieth-century Native Americans living on reservations and suffering from staggering poverty and poor health facilities. Members of AIM and local Oglala Lakota people fought attempts by the FBI to extricate them from the church, and the ensuing violence led to the deaths of two AIM activists and a serious injury to one U.S. Marshal. After seventy-one days, AIM surrendered, but their actions forced public discourse about the civil rights of Native Americans and furthered the debate over tribal self-governance. *(Photographer: Owen Luck)*

Despite impressive gains over the final decades of the twentieth century, however, Native Americans continued to face overwhelming obstacles. Shrunken by treaty violations and geographically distant from national employment networks, Indian reservations provided dismal economic and education opportunities at best. In 1971 unemployment among reservation Indians ranged from 40 to 75 percent and annual family incomes averaged about $1,500. Life expectancy was only forty-six years, compared to the national average of seventy. Infant mortality rates were the highest in the nation. Perhaps most tragically, reservations counted an alarmingly high suicide rate among Native young people. Such monumental challenges and grim prospects make Native people's late twentieth-century strides in the legal, professional, and educational spheres all the more impressive in hindsight.

Latinos

Many young Mexicans and Puerto Ricans were inspired by the militancy of the civil-rights struggle and by the early victories of labor organizers who appealed to the ethnic pride of Hispanics. In 1965 César Chávez and the United Farm Workers (UFW) organized a strike against powerful California grape growers. Despite the UFW gaining the support of Walter Reuther and the United Auto Workers, and of influential politicians such as Robert F. Kennedy, the growers continued to import workers to replace the strikers. In 1966 Chávez organized a 250-mile march from Delano to Sacramento to call attention to the strike, or *la huelga*. The cry *huelga* became symbolic of a broad, nonviolent crusade for civil rights—*la Causa*. Between 1968 and 1970 Chávez orchestrated a national boycott of California grapes, which eventually forced the growers to recognize the UFW.

PRIMARY SOURCE

11.1 | *The Grape Boycott*

CÉSAR CHÁVEZ

During a UFW boycott of grape growers, union founder César Chávez initiated a hunger strike in February 1964, as a show of solidarity with the UFW. On March 10, after three weeks of fasting, a weak Chávez met with eight thousand farm workers and political leaders, including Senator Robert Kennedy, to pray and end the fast. Because Chávez was unable to deliver his prepared speech, a minister who worked with the UFW read the address to the assembled crowd.

    I have asked the Reverend James Drake to read this statement to you because my heart is so full and my body too weak to be able to say what I feel. . . . I do not want any of you to be deceived about the fast. The strict fast of water only which I undertook on February 16 ended after the twenty-first day because of
5 the advice of our doctor, James McKnight, and other physicians. Since that time I have been taking liquids in order to prevent serious damage to my kidneys.

We are gathered here today not so much to observe the end of the fast but because we are a family bound together in a common struggle for justice. We are a union family celebrating our unity and the nonviolent nature of our movement.
10 Perhaps in the future we will come together at other times and places to break bread and to renew our courage and to celebrate important victories.

The fast has had different meanings for different people. Some of you may still wonder about its meaning and importance. It was not intended as a pressure against any growers. For that reason we have suspended negotiations and arbitra-
15 tion proceedings and relaxed the militant picketing and boycotting of the strike during this period. I undertook this fast because my heart was filled with grief and pain for the sufferings of farm workers. The fast was first for me and then for all of us in this union. It was a fast for nonviolence and a call to sacrifice.

Our struggle is not easy. Those who oppose our cause are rich and powerful
20 and they have many allies in high places. We are poor. Our allies are few. But we have something the rich do not own. We have our own bodies and spirits and the justice of our cause as our weapons.

When we are really honest with ourselves we must admit that our lives are all that really belong to us. So it is how we use our lives that determines what kind
25 of men we are. It is my deepest belief that only by giving our lives do we find life. I am convinced that the truest act of courage, the strongest act of manliness, is to sacrifice ourselves for others in a totally nonviolent struggle for justice. To be a man is to suffer for others. God help us to be men!

Source: TM/© 2006 the César E. Chávez Foundation by CMG Worldwide www.cmgww.com. Reprinted by permission. ■ ■ ■

New immigrants from Mexico helped make Hispanic Americans the fastest growing minority group in America during the 1960s and 1970s. By 1980 Mexicans and Mexican Americans made up about 60 percent of the nation's 14.6 million Hispanics. They were followed in numbers by Puerto Ricans and Cubans. While lumped together on census forms, Hispanics reflected a wide variety of cultures. The diversity is evident in the different names used to describe them: the most commonly used term was *Hispanic,* but many people of Spanish descent preferred to describe themselves as *Latino.* Others identified with their native country: Cuban, Puerto Rican, Dominican. Some Mexican Americans used the term *Chicano.* "A Chicano," observed the journalist Ruben Salazar, "is a Mexican-American with a non-Anglo image of himself."

Hispanics developed different strategies for adapting to American society. Mexican immigration was circular, made up of poor workers who traveled back and forth between the United States and Mexico in search of better jobs. Immigrants from South and Central America tended to be middle class or professionals who either fled their homeland because of political instability or were attracted to America by the dream of a better life. These immigrants were often downwardly mobile, abandoning high-status jobs at home for menial work in the United States. When Fidel Castro assumed power in Cuba and began nationalizing industry, the professional and middle class fled to the United States and created a thriving community in Miami, Florida. In 1979 Cuban Americans had the highest median family income of all Hispanic groups, although they still lagged behind white non-Hispanics. In 1979 more than one-third of Puerto Rican families had no workers in the household, earned less than any other ethnic group on the mainland, and had the highest school-dropout rate of all ethnic groups.

During the 1970s Hispanic intellectuals and labor leaders rejected traditional notions of the "melting pot" and espoused a militant message of cultural pluralism. In 1972 Rodolfo Acuña, who established a pioneering Chicano Studies Program at the California State University, Northridge, published *Occupied America: The Chicano's Struggle Toward Liberation.* Acuña claimed that America was a "European term of occupation and colonization," and he advised Chicanos to resist integration and "captivity." In Denver, Rodolfo "Corky" Gonzales, a former boxer and Democratic Party official, rejected conventional reform politics and established a separate organization, the Crusade for Justice. In addition to calling for better housing and greater economic opportunity, the crusade openly discussed declaring its independence from the United States. In New Mexico the Federal Alliance of Land Grants, a militant separatist group, attempted to reclaim land, water, and grazing rights that had been usurped by Anglos. The nationalist sentiment of the Chicano movement found expression in literature and the arts. In 1970 Richard Vasquez's *Chicano* (1970) told the story of the immigrant experience through the lives of three generations of a family. In *Barrio Boy* (1971), Ernesto Galarza shared the personal story of his family's move from Mexico. Corky Gonzales wove Mexican history and immigrant anguish into his moving poem "I Am Joaquin" (1967). The late 1960s and 1970s witnessed an explosion in Chicano journals, periodicals, and publishing houses.

Asian Americans

Dramatic increases in immigration following passage of the 1965 Immigration Reform Act contributed to a growing assertiveness among Asian Americans. In the twenty years following the 1965 act, the Asian population in the United States soared from 1 million to 5 million—nearly four times as many Asians entered the country during that period as had emigrated in the previous one hundred years. Before 1965 New York's Chinatown never had a population of more than ten thousand people; twenty years later it had become the home of one hundred thousand. During the same time period the Korean and Indian population in the United States jumped from ten thousand to more than five hundred thousand.

Unlike the impoverished and often illiterate laborers who had once flocked to American shores, many of the new Asian migrants came from middle-class backgrounds and had professional or technical skills. The educated middle class in such countries as India, the Philippines, and Korea realized that they could have better lives by finding employment in the United States. "Wages in Manila are barely enough to answer for my family's needs," said a Philippine immigrant. "I must go abroad to better my chances." By 1974 Asian immigrants made up nearly one of five practicing physicians in the United States.

Searching for an identity in a society that viewed race in terms of black and white, Asian Americans convinced the U.S. Census Bureau to list Asian as a racial category on the 1980 census form. At the same time, third-generation Japanese Americans, the Sansei, pressured Washington to establish a commission to investigate the internment of their parents during World War II. They also encouraged these parents, the Nisei, to speak out about their wartime experiences. In July 1980 the Commission on Wartime Relocation and Internment of Citizens recommended that the government issue a formal apology for the internment and provide $20,000 in compensation for each survivor. Congress accepted the recommendation and enacted it into law in 1988.

Challenging Gender Identities

The 1970s witnessed the flowering of two powerful movements that would challenge traditional notions of gender identity. Homosexuals organized to fight against discrimination based on sexual preference. Women's liberation emerged as the most powerful and influential social movement of the decade.

The Modern Gay-Rights Movement

Along with other groups, homosexuals challenged prevailing ideas about their place in society. While small gay-rights organizations such as the Mattachine Society and the Daughters of Bilitis had been fighting for civil rights for years, the modern gay-rights movement was born on June 27, 1969, when a group of Manhattan police officers raided the Stonewall Inn, a gay bar in the heart of Greenwich Village. Such raids, and the police abuse that frequently followed, were routine affairs. Not this time. As one reporter noted, "Limp wrists were forgotten. Beer cans and bottles were heaved at the windows and a rain of coins descended on the cops."

The Stonewall riot ignited a nationwide grass-roots "liberation" movement among gay men and women. Using confrontation tactics borrowed from the civil-rights movement and the rhetoric of revolution employed by the New Left, the gay-rights movement achieved a number of victories during the decade. The number of gay organizations in America grew from less than fifty to more than one thousand. In many large cities gays and lesbians created support networks, newspapers, bars, and travel clubs. In less than a decade, noted an observer,

American society had witnessed "an explosion of things gay." The gay-rights movement received a psychological boost in 1973 when the American Psychiatric Association reversed a century-old policy and stopped listing homosexuality as a mental disorder.

Though thirty-two states continued to designate homosexual practices as crimes, eighteen states eliminated sodomy laws that barred sexual acts between consenting adults. Many cities approved ordinances prohibiting job, credit, and other discrimination on the basis of sexual preferences. In Congress two dozen sponsors introduced an amendment to the Civil Rights Act of 1964 adding homosexuals to the list of groups that may not be discriminated against in public accommodations and employment. Many corporations enacted a policy of nondiscrimination on the basis of sexual orientation in hiring and promotion. In 1975 the San Francisco School Board voted unanimously to revise the school system's family-life curriculum to acknowledge homosexual lifestyles. "Gays felt some of the references reflected negatively on them," said one administrator. "They were right."

PRIMARY SOURCE

11.2 | *A Radical Manifesto, 1969*

The Stonewall riots radicalized many gay activists who saw a clear link between their cause and the plight of other oppressed groups in the United States. This "radical manifesto," issued in August 1969, captures the anger and frustration felt by many in the gay community. It also reveals their desire to build political alliances with other minority groups.

A Radical Manifesto—The Homophile Movement Must Be Radicalized! (August 28, 1969)

1) We see the persecution of homosexuality as part of a general attempt to oppress all minorities and keep them powerless. Our fate is linked with these minorities; if the detention camps are filled tomorrow with blacks, hippies, and other radicals, we will not escape that fate, all our attempts to dissociate ourselves
5 from them notwithstanding. A common struggle, however, will bring common triumph.

2) Therefore we declare our support as homosexuals or bisexuals for the struggles of the black, the feminist, the Spanish-American, the Indian, the Hippie, the Young, the Student, and other victims of oppression and prejudice.

10 3) We call upon these groups to lend us their support and encourage their presence with NACHO [the North American Conference of Homophile Organizations] and the homophile movement at large.

4) Our enemies, an implacable, repressive governmental system; much of organized religion, business, and medicine, will not be moved by appeasement or
15   appeals to reason and justice, but only by power and force.

5) We regard established heterosexual standards of morality as immoral and refuse to condone them by demanding an equality which is merely the common yoke of sexual repression.

6) We declare that homosexuals, as individuals and members of the greater
20   community, must develop homosexual ethics and esthetics independent of, and without reference to, the mores imposed upon heterosexuality.

7) We demand the removal of all restrictions on sex between consenting persons of any sex, of any orientation, of any age, anywhere, whether for money or not, and for the removal of all censorship.

25   8) We call upon the churches to sanction homosexual liaisons when called upon to do so by the parties concerned.

9) We call upon the homophile movement to be more honestly concerned with youth rather than trying to promote a mythical, non-existent "good public image."

30   10) The homophile movement must totally reject the insane war in Viet Nam and refuse to encourage complicity in the war and support of the war machine, which may well be turned against us. We oppose any attempts by the movement to obtain security clearances for homosexuals, since these contribute to the war machine.

35   11) The homophile movement must engage in continuous political struggle on all fronts.

12) We must open the eyes of homosexuals on this continent to the increasingly repressive nature of our society and to the realizations that Chicago may await us tomorrow.

Source: Donn Teal, excerpt from *The Gay Militants* (New York: St. Martin's Press). Copyright © 1971 Stein and Day. Copyright © 1995 St. Martin's Press. Reprinted by permission of Donn Teal.   ■ ■ ■

The Women's Movement

Each of these groups—African Americans, American Indians, Hispanics, Asian Americans, and homosexuals—initiated significant changes in American society during the 1970s. But it was the women's liberation movement that emerged as the largest and most powerful social movement of the decade. "There never has been a movement of social change that has affected so many people so quickly," said feminist Betty Friedan, whose book *The Feminine Mystique* (1963) had helped launch the movement. "The women's movement is everywhere—in sports, churches, offices, homes, languages. It has moved into society as a whole."

The women's movement divided over the proper strategy and goals for advancing their agenda in the 1970s. One group of feminists, led primarily by older professional women, sought to achieve change by working within the established political order. Formed in 1966, The National Organization for Women (NOW) best exemplified this reform impulse. NOW leaders Betty Friedan and African American Yale law professor Pauli Murray demanded an Equal Rights Amendment (ERA) to the constitution, which, if ratified by Congress, would legally abolish discrimination based on sex. They believed the amendment would also pave the way toward other benefits, including equal employment, maternity leave, child care, and the right to an abortion.

Many younger feminist leaders rejected NOW's moderate approach and advocating bolder measures. These women's liberationists, or "radical feminists," distrusted establishment political tactics and instead sought ways to change American culture through participatory democracy. Irreverent and eager to challenge prevailing beliefs, they used the tactics of mass protest, direct action, and political theater characteristic of other civil-rights struggles. For example, a number of radical feminists staged a protest at the 1968 Miss America beauty pageant in Atlantic City where they mockingly crowned a sheep "Miss America" and threw bras into a trash can.

Many feminists leaders were radicalized by their experiences working in the civil-rights movement in the 1960s, when many of their male counterparts treated them as second-class citizens. SDS and SNCC members Casey Hayden and Mary King likened their experiences to that of black slaves. "It needs to be made known that many women in the movement are not 'happy and contented' with their status," Mary King insisted. "It needs to be made known that much talent and experience are being wasted by this movement, when women are not given jobs commensurate with their abilities. It needs to be known that just as Negroes were the crucial factor in the economy of the cotton South, so too in SNCC, women are the crucial factor that keeps the movement running on a day-to-day basis." Hayden and King both decried the fact that women participants were relegated to roles as cooks, housekeepers, and secretaries. Many women also experienced pressure to engage in undesired sexual liaisons with movement leadership. The cumulative effect of such experiences was the radicalization of women who already considered themselves feminists.

Difference also emerged within the movement along racial lines. While some African American feminists joined predominately white feminist groups, many believed that their white counterparts underplayed the importance of race. Additionally, they criticized the civil-rights movement for failing to focus attention on problems of sexism. In 1973 nearly 400 black feminists founded the National Black Feminist Organization (NBFO). Women of color—including Puerto Rican women of the Young Lords, Native American women of the Women of All Red Nations (WARN), and African American women of the Black Panthers—played a leading role in the reproductive rights movement. These women fought for better access to birth control and safer abortions while resisting programs that forced women to accept sterilization in exchange for government welfare.

Legislating Change

The feminist movement won a number of impressive victories in the courts and legislatures during the 1970s. In 1972 Congress passed Title IX of the Higher Education Act, which banned discrimination "on the basis of sex" in "any education program or activity receiving federal financial assistance." The legislation set the stage for an explosion in women's athletics later in the decade.

Also in 1972 Congress passed and sent to the states a constitutional amendment banning discrimination on the basis of sex—the ERA. By the end of the year all fifty states had enacted legislation to prevent sex discrimination in employment. Federal and state laws protecting victims of domestic violence and rape were strengthened.

The women's movement helped precipitate a revolution in family law. As demands for divorce increased, many state legislatures liberalized their statues in an attempt to reduce the acrimony and shame associated with the divorce process. In 1970, California adopted the nation's first "no-fault" divorce law, which allowed a couple to initiate proceedings without first proving that someone was responsible for the breakup of the marriage. Within five years, all but five states adopted the principle of no-fault divorce.

The most dramatic change came in the area of reproductive rights. On January 22, 1973, the Supreme Court declared in the landmark case *Roe* v. *Wade* that a woman had a constitutional right to an abortion. Writing for the majority, Justice Lewis Blackmun asserted that the fourteenth amendment, which prohibited states from denying "liberty" to anyone without "due process," established a "right of privacy" that was "broad enough to encompass a woman's decision whether or not to terminate the pregnancy."

The court stated that during the first trimester, the decision to abort a fetus should be left to the discretion of a woman and her doctor. Over the next three months, up until the point of fetal viability, the state could establish some limits on the right to an abortion. In the final trimester, the government could prohibit an abortion except where necessary to preserve the mother's life or health.

Cultural Changes

There were also signs of change in American culture. At the grass roots, feminist organizations flourished: feminist bookstores, rape crisis and domestic violence centers, and chapters of NOW formed across the nation. A feminist magazine, *Ms.*, attracted a large national circulation. And the proportion of women entering professional and graduate schools rose substantially. By the 1980s, 25 percent of new graduates of law, medical, and business schools were women, up from only 5 percent in the late 1960s.

Opinion surveys recorded new attitudes toward gender roles. "Women's liberation has changed the lives of many Americans and the ways they look at family, job and sexual equality," *Reader's Digest* concluded in 1976. Over two-thirds of college women the magazine questioned agreed that "the idea that a woman's place is in the home is nonsense." During the 1970s the pollster Daniel Yankelovich reported a "wide and deep acceptance" of women's liberation. In 1970, 50 percent of college freshmen and 30 percent of women agreed that "the activities of married women are best confined to the home and the family." Five years later only 30 percent of men and less than 20 percent of women took that position."

Changing attitudes found expression in popular culture. Television viewers watched as the "perfect family" comedies of the 1950s and 1960s were replaced by new shows that dramatized the ambiguity of family and work. The *Mary Tyler Moore Show* featured an over-thirty career woman. Other popular television shows—Valerie Harper's *Rhoda* and Diana Riggs's *Diana*—presented strong, independent, and resourceful women. *Maude* starred a loud, opinionated feminist who decided to have an abortion in middle age. Male chauvinism was dealt a major blow in 1973 when fifty-five-year-old former Wimbledon tennis star Bobby Riggs, a self-avowed sexist, challenged the top woman's player, Billie Jean King, to a match. "You insist that top woman players provide a brand of tennis comparable to men's. I challenge you to prove it. I contend that you not only cannot beat a top male player, but that you can't beat me, a tired old man." Millions of Americans watched the match on television as King dismantled Riggs, winning in three straight sets. In 1976 journalist Barbara Walters broke through the glass ceiling at ABC, becoming the highest paid television anchor and the first woman to cohost the evening news.

Perhaps the most important accomplishment was the development of the women's health movement. What started as hippie "free clinics" in the 1960s soon grew into a national movement in the 1970s as female health activists disseminated biological knowledge, questioned doctors' control over reproductive decisions, and conducted "self-help gynecology" seminars. The publication of the popular *Our Bodies, Ourselves* (1973) marked an important shift in the women's movement. By emphasizing biological difference, the movement underscored the central paradox of postwar feminism: how to achieve equality while also honoring the difference between men and women.

Despite signs of progress, women still faced major discrimination in the workplace. In the 1970s, jobs were still typically classified as "men's" or "women's" work, and as a consequence over 80 percent of all women workers were clustered in 20 of the 420 occupations listed by the Census Bureau. "Women's" jobs—secretary, waitress, sales clerk—typically offered low pay, little security, and no chance for advancement. In those instances in which women did perform the same work as men, they received much lower wages. To compound these problems, unemployment rates among women consistently exceeded male averages by more than 20 percent.

This discrimination in the job market often had devastating consequences for women trying to live on their own. It was particularly hard on single women with children, who were increasingly numerous in the 1970s as divorce and out-of-wedlock births grew more common. During the 1970s, the number of women heading families with children increased by 72 percent. A large proportion of their households, as many as one-third, fell below the poverty line. By 1980, 66 percent of all adults whom the government classified as poor were women.

This new phenomenon, which sociologists called the "feminization of poverty," hit black women hardest of all. By 1980, one out of every three black children was born to a teenage mother, and 55 percent of all black babies were born out of wedlock. In inner-city ghettos, the figure often climbed above 70 percent, and two-thirds of all black families living in poverty were headed by women.

The Conservative Response

During times of uncertainty and change, Americans have looked to religion to provide a sense of stability. That was certainly the case in the 1970s and 1980s, which witnessed a dramatic increase in the number of self-identified evangelical Christians. The number of Americans who identified themselves as "born again" increased from 24 percent in 1963 to nearly 40 percent in 1978. By 1980, more than 45 million—one of every five Americans—considered themselves fundamentalists.

While they came from different faiths, they all experienced a "born again" conversion, believed in a literal interpretation of the Bible, and accepted Jesus Christ as their personal Savior. At a time when cultural values were in flux, religion provided them with a sense of certainty and clear guidelines of right and wrong. Religion provided an antidote to the "new values" that grew out of the 1960s.

Many fundamentalists were converted by television preachers who used mass media to preach a return to traditional values. The three most successful "televangelists"—Jerry Falwell, Pat Robertson, and Jim Bakker—reached an estimated 100 million Americans each week with fire and brimstone sermons about the evils of contemporary life. America, they preached, confronted a crisis of the spirit, brought on by the pervasive influence of "secular humanism," which stressed material well-being and personal gratification over religious conviction and devotion to traditional Christian values. In their mind, the federal government, and the liberals who staffed it, were responsible for America's moral decline. At the top of their agenda was overturning the 1962 Supreme Court's decision to ban prayer in the public schools (*Engel* v. *Vitale*) and the 1973 *Roe* v. *Wade* decision, which legalized abortion.

Religious Right ministers were as interested in winning votes as they were in saving souls. Falwell combined old time religion with the most sophisticated computer technology to target potential contributors. "Get them saved, baptized, and registered," Falwell advised his ministerial colleagues. In July 1979 he founded the Moral Majority, a group which lobbied on behalf of conservative causes. Within two years the group claimed 4 million members.

The Tax Revolt

Rising tax rates also increased anger toward government and fueled the conservative resurgence. Between 1960 and 1980, federal, state, and local taxes increased from less than 24 percent to more than 30 percent of the gross national product. The burden often fell heaviest on traditional Democratic constituencies—working-class families and elderly people on fixed incomes.

In addition, while taxes kept rising, Americans were losing faith in government and the way it spent tax dollars. Poll after poll showed a majority of Americans believed that government was wasteful and inefficient. The tax anger led to passage of Proposition 13 in California and its congressional cousin, the Kemp-Roth Tax Bill that called for slashing federal income taxes by one-third.

"Supply-side" conservatives believed that hefty cuts in corporate and personal tax rates would stimulate investment and encourage production and consumption. Unlike the Keynesian theory that had guided policymakers since the 1930s, supply-side advocates argued that tax policy should reward the suppliers of wealth and not the consumers. By lowering taxes on the wealthiest Americans, the government would provide an incentive for them to reinvest, creating new business and more jobs. Even though tax rates would be lower, revenues would actually increase, since more people would be paying taxes.

Neoconservatives

For most of the 1960s and early 1970s, liberals were able to control the national agenda. During the 1970s, conservative intellectuals began to dominate the public debate, ensuring that conservative ideas would receive respect and attention.

With funding from wealthy individuals and foundations, conservative think tanks produced mounds of studies advocating the need for smaller government and a return to traditional values. These new organizations provided an intellectual home to a number of prominent "neoconservatives," former liberals who had soured on government activism and who offered substantial intellectual ammunition to those seeking to reverse liberal "excesses."

A neoconservative, observed the social critic Irving Kristol, was a liberal who had been mugged by reality. Neoconservatives charged that many governmental programs of the sixties, designed to alleviate poverty and assist the working poor, had backfired. "Our efforts to deal with distress themselves increase distress," observed the sociologist Nathan Glazer.

If neoconservatives provided the intellectual scaffolding for the conservative movement, corporate America provided the muscle. During the 1970s, corporate America established a powerful lobbying presence in Washington to advance its agenda, which included not only antiregulatory goals but tax cuts as well.

Many corporations and trade associations opened Washington offices, hired Capitol Hill law firms, and retained legions of political consultants to keep track of pending legislation and to develop strategies for promoting favorable policies and killing those considered antibusiness. By 1980, nearly 500 corporations had Washington offices, up from 250 in 1970, and the number of lobbyists tripled. Trade associations opened national headquarters at a rate of one per week, increasing from 1200 to 1739 during the decade.

Corporate lobbyists took advantage of loopholes in the campaign finance system to fund incumbents and new candidates who supported their agenda. The proliferation of independent political action committees (PACs) allowed corporate interests to funnel millions of dollars to congressional candidates. There were 608 PACs operating when Congress passed campaign reform legislation in 1974. By 1977 the number had doubled to 1146, and continued to grow at 20 percent a year for the rest of the decade. In 1974, labor operated up to a third of existing PACs and accounted for half of all PAC spending. By 1982 business-related PACs were outspending labor in direct contributions to congressional campaigns by nearly three to one.

Cultural Crosscurrents

The 1970s experienced a bitter conflict over the legacy of the 1960s. On one side stood the champions of the youth culture who embraced the rights revolution; on the other side of the line were traditionalists who emphasized the importance of maintaining moral order and authority. While they fought over many issues, three were central to the conflict: the Equal Rights Amendment, busing to achieve racial integration, and gay rights.

The Battle over the Equal Rights Amendment

In 1972 Congress overwhelmingly approved the Equal Rights Amendment to the Constitution, which declared in simple but powerful language that "equality of rights shall not be denied or abridged . . . on account of sex." Within minutes after the amendment passed the Senate, Hawaii became the first to ratify it. Delaware, Nebraska, and New Hampshire ratified the next day, and on the third day Idaho and Iowa ratified. Twenty-four more states ratified in 1972 and early 1973. Throughout the ratification process polls showed that large majorities of the public supported the measure. While responses differed according to the wording of the question, the "average" survey found 57 percent for the ERA, 32 percent opposed, and 11 percent with no opinion.

But the ERA soon fell victim to the social politics of the 1970s and 1980s, as traditionalists tapped into public backlash against the rights revolution and the challenge to traditional gender roles, which the ERA represented. Support for the amendment, though broad, was not deep. Most Americans instinctively expressed support for the abstract notion of rights, even if they were unwilling to accept real changes in women's roles. In surveys more than two-thirds of people who supported the amendment thought that preschool children were likely to suffer if their mothers worked and believed married women should not hold jobs when jobs were scarce and their husbands could support them. Nearly one-half said they would not vote for a qualified woman for president.

The gap between support for rights and conservative attitudes about gender roles provided an opening to opponents of the amendment, who viewed it as a subversion of those roles. Especially for female opponents, the ERA challenged traditional perceptions of woman's proper place as homemaker. Traditionalists found a talented leader in Phyllis Schlafly, the "Sweetheart of the Silent Majority," who campaigned tirelessly against the ERA. Tapping into traditional views of womanhood, she complained that feminists had abandoned their God-given roles of wife and mother in favor of a radical political agenda that was "anti-family, anti-children, and pro-abortion." She charged that the ERA would promote lesbianism, require women to serve in combat roles in the military, and roll back protective legislation that housewives and female workers cherished.

PRIMARY SOURCE

11.3 | *The Power of the Positive Woman*
PHYLLIS SCHLAFLY

Not all women in the 1970s supported the feminist movement and passage of the Equal Rights Amendment. Phyllis Schlafly, a successful lawyer, conservative political activist, and mother of six, believed feminists were a radical fringe group that did not represent the views of most women. In her book *The Power of the Positive Woman*, published in 1977, Schlafly attacked modern feminism while underlining the virtues of traditional women's roles.

If man is targeted as the enemy, and the ultimate goal of women's liberation is independence from men and the avoidance of pregnancy and its consequences, then lesbianism is logically the highest form in the ritual of women's liberation.

The Positive Woman will never travel that dead-end road. It is self-evident
5   to the Positive Woman that the female body with its baby-producing organs was
not designed by a conspiracy of men but by the Divine Architect of the human
race. . . .

The Positive Woman looks upon her femaleness and her fertility as part of
her purpose, her potential, and her power. She rejoices that she has a capability
10 for creativity that men can never have. . . .

The women's liberationists are expending their time and energies erecting
a make-believe world in which they hypothesize that *if* schooling were gender-
free, and *if* the same money were spent on male and female sports programs,
and *if* women were permitted to compete on equal terms, *then* they would
15 prove themselves to be physically equal. Meanwhile, the Positive Woman
has put the ineradicable physical differences into her mental computer, pro-
grammed her plan of action, and is already on the way to personal achievement. . . .

Despite the claims of the women's liberation movement, there are countless
20 physical differences between men and women. . . . Males have a tendency to color
blindness. Only 5 percent of persons who get gout are female. Boys are born bigger. Women live longer in most countries of the world, not only in the United
States where we have a hard-driving competitive pace. Women excel in manual
dexterity, verbal skills, and memory recall. . . .

25 The differences between men and women are also emotional and psychological. Without woman's innate maternal instinct, the human race would have died
out centuries ago. . . . Even in the most primitive, uneducated societies, women
have always cared for their newborn babies. . . .

Why? Because caring for a baby serves the natural maternal need of a woman.
30 Although not nearly so total as the baby's need, the woman's need is nonetheless
real. . . .

The woman's liberation movement complains that traditional stereotyped
roles assume that women are "passive" and that men are "aggressive." The anom-
aly is that a woman's most fundamental emotional need is not passive at all, but
35 active. A woman naturally seeks to love affirmatively and to show that love in an
active way by caring for the object of her affections.

Source: Reprinted by permission of the author.   ■ ■ ■

The affirmation of traditional gender roles struck a responsive chord with
conservative men, but it also appealed to many working-class women who felt
estranged from the largely middle-class leadership of the feminist movement.
Homemakers viewed the amendment as another assault on their prestige by
upper-middle-class reformers who shared few of their values or experiences.
The cumulative weight of these objections doomed the ERA. On June 30,
1982, the deadline for ratifying the amendment passed with only thirty-five of
the required thirty-eight states having ratified: the Equal Rights Amendment
was dead.

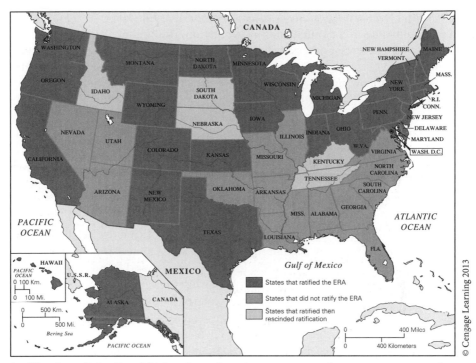

Ratification of the Equal Rights Amendment First proposed to Congress in 1923, the Equal Rights Amendment called for the equality of rights under the law regardless of sex. With the rise of the women's movement of the late 1960s, the amendment gained new life and passed the House in a 354–24 vote October 12, 1971, followed in 1972 by the Senate. Within one year, the women's organizations convinced thirty states to ratify, but then they began to run into stiff opposition from men and women who believed the amendment was too vague and would not protect traditional women's roles and who were fearful that women would then be eligible for the draft. Over the next six years, the momentum waned and five states rescinded their ratification, while another five ratified it. Despite a Congressional extension in 1978, the ERA failed to gain the three states it needed to pass and the amendment died July 1, 1982.

Busing

Ever since the famous *Brown* v. *Board of Education* decision in 1954, the Supreme Court had called for the desegregation of educational institutions. But it declined to specify remedies or insist on deadlines for implementation, and little progress occurred. Local school boards fiercely resisted local court orders and pleas from activists and parents. Faced with such determined resistance, liberals and civil-rights activists petitioned the Supreme Court to take a more forceful stand on the issue. In two unanimous cases, *Alexander* v. *Holmes County Board of Education*

(1969) and *Swann* v. *Charlotte-Mecklenburg Board of Education* (1971), the Supreme Court ordered a quick end to segregation, ruling that cities could be required to bus students if necessary to achieve integration. With the Supreme Court firmly behind busing as a remedy for school segregation, lower courts across the United States followed suit, ordering busing plans in numerous cities.

In 1974 federal judge Arthur Garrity condemned Boston's "systematic program of segregation" affecting the city's schools facilities and called for mandatory busing of seventeen thousand pupils to solve the problem. White residents in South Boston and Charlestown exploded in anger when informed of the plan. Former Congresswoman Louise Day Hicks sounded the alarm. "They shall not take our children from us," she thundered. Opponents created an organization, ROAR (Restore Our Alienated Rights), using as their emblem a large lion pawing a school bus. Busing touched many sensitive nerves. It tapped into deep racial fears and prejudice. "Yes, I'm a racist now," said a white man. "I weren't before that sick judge acted, but I am now. I don't want 'em in my neighborhood. I don't want 'em near my children."

But race alone did not explain the intensity of anger and fear. Class divisions exacerbated the issue as many working-class whites resented the affluent liberals who helped launch the plan but had the luxury of sending their children to private or suburban schools. Traditional distaste of an enlarged and arrogant national government, and of unelected judges, added an additional combustible element to the issue. Opponents of the plans viewed themselves as patriots fighting against the federal government. "I served in Korea, I served in Vietnam, and I'll serve in Charlotte if I need to," declared an antibusing activist. Underlying ROAR's hot words and sometimes violent acts was a sense of frustration and desperation of powerless people whose way of life seemed under siege. "We're frightened," said a ROAR founder. "We're locked in. People see their neighborhood threatened, and they're trapped there. What else could that mean but they'll fight back?"

Busing fractured the Democratic Party, turned working-class whites against government schemes for social improvement, and led to massive defections from urban public schools. In the 1974 decision *Milliken* v. *Bradley,* the Supreme Court prohibited the forced transfer of students between city and suburban schools. In many urban areas the decision accelerated "white flight" to the suburbs, leaving urban schools more segregated than they had been before busing. Between 1972 and 1976 nearly twenty thousand white students fled Boston's public school system for private schools or other cities. By 1976 minorities were a majority of Boston's public schools, making them, in the words of journalist J. Anthony Lukas, "the preserve of the black and the poor."

Anita Bryant and the Struggle over Gay Rights

In 1977 Miami's Dade County Council passed an ordinance that banned discrimination in employment and housing based on a person's "affectional or sexual preference." Those who opposed the ordinance immediately went to work to have it repealed and called on singer Anita Bryant to lead the resistance. As a Miss America runner-up, a popular singer billed as "the voice that refreshes," and the symbol of Florida orange juice, Anita Bryant had projected an image of devout wholesomeness for nearly two decades. As president of Save Our Children, she organized a drive that collected more than sixty-six thousand signatures on petitions to force a referendum on the issue. "This is not my battle, it's God's battle," she told a fundraising rally. "Before I yield to this insidious attack on God and His laws," Bryant declared, "I will lead such a crusade to stop it as this country has not seen before."

Besides her objections to homosexuality on religious grounds, Bryant charged that homosexuals preyed on innocent children. She referred to homosexuals as "human garbage" and contended that Miami's antidiscrimination law could protect the right to have "intercourse with beasts." She was often joined on stage at rallies by New Right ministers who preached that homosexuality violated both the laws of God and the laws of nature. "Homosexuality is a sin so rotten, so low, so dirty that even cats and dogs don't practice it," said one minister, concluding that passage of the ordinance "could be the end of the United States of America."

To many of the nation's 20 million homosexuals, the vote—the first of its kind in a major city—was a crucial test of whether the country was willing to extend civil-rights legislation to homosexuals. "Miami is our Selma," said one gay activist. After an intense and bitter campaign, Dade County voters overwhelmingly sided with Bryant, rejecting the ordinance. Even before the vote, Bryant announced that she would mount a national antihomosexuality campaign. Gay-rights leaders in a number of states vowed to fight her every step of the way. "We have lost a battle," admitted a Washington, D.C., human rights commissioner, "but we certainly have not lost the war."

The struggle over gay rights revealed the anguish of a nation attempting to come to terms with the American paradox. The 1970s witnessed an angry confrontation over the legacy of the 1960s. Inspired by the example of the early civil-rights struggle, many groups on the Left—women, Native Americans, homosexuals—embraced an "empowerment ethic," demanding that the nation live up to the American ideal of equal rights. While these groups achieved some important victories, their challenge to traditional values produced a powerful conservative backlash. Neoconservative intellectuals worried about the unintended consequences of reform, while the religious right reaffirmed deeply held values about gender roles. The political legacy of the 1960s remained unclear, but the cultural impact was distinct and dramatic: the ethic of self-fulfillment, which was so central to the counterculture of the 1960s, seeped into all aspects of 1970s culture.

SELECTED READINGS

▌ Bruce J. Schulman offers the best historical treatment of the decade in *The Seventies* (2001). David Frum offers a critical assessment of the social and cultural changes of the decade in *How We Got Here* (2000). Peter Carroll's *It*

Seemed Like Nothing Happened (1983) is a lively collection of anecdotes about the decade and its frustrations. Christopher Lasch's *The Culture of Narcissism* (1978) is an influential description of the Me Decade. *America in the Seventies* (2004), edited by David Farber and Beth Bailey, examines the 1970s as a transitional period. For disco, Alice Echols's *Hot Stuff* (2010) is valuable.

▮ In *The Declining Significance of Race* (1980), William J. Wilson describes the economic polarization of African American society. Douglas Glasgow's *The Black Underclass* (1980) charts the black economic decline of the 1970s. Nathan Glazer's *Affirmative Discrimination* (1975) details the controversy around affirmative action. J. Anthony Lukas's *Common Ground* (1985) is a moving account of the Boston busing crisis through the eyes of three families.

▮ Ernesto Vigil's *The Crusade for Justice* (1999) explains the development of the Chicano movement through the 1970s. Matt Meier and Feliciano Rivera explore the generational conflicts among Hispanics in *The Chicanos* (1972). *History of Immigration of Asian Americans* (1998), edited by Franklin Ng, contains essays that describe why increasing numbers of Asians migrated to the United States and their steps to create a new life. Paul Smith and Robert Warrior study the various Indian Movement actions, such as the takeovers at Alcatraz and Wounded Knee, in *Like a Hurricane* (1996). Editors Alvin Josephy, Joane Nagel, and Troy Johnson provide fifty primary documents that trace the American Indian activist movement in the last four decades in *Red Power* (2nd ed., 1999). Daniel Cobb's *Native Activism in Cold War America* (2008) places Red Power activism within a longer trend of Indian activism that grew out of the 1950s termination policy era.

▮ John D'Emilio's *Sexual Politics, Sexual Communities* (2nd ed., 1998) explores the formation of gay identity in the postwar years, and the history of the gay-rights movement is examined in Dudley Clendinen and Adam Nagourney's *Out for Good* (1999). Martin Duberman's *Stonewall* (1993) describes the birth of the modern gay liberation movement.

▮ Sara Evans describes how the women's liberation movement evolved from the civil-rights struggle in *Personal Politics* (1979). Kathleen Berkeley's *The Women's Liberation Movement in America* (1999) and Ruth Rosen's *The World Split Open* (2001) provide overviews of the women's movement. Susan Brownmiller's *In Our Time* (1999) describes the trials and triumphs of the women's movement by describing the work of some of the movement's lesser-known activists. Alice Echols explores radical feminism in *Daring to Be Bad* (1989). Susan Hartmann's *From Margin to Mainstream* (1989) has good material on economic discrimination by sex. Joel F. Handler's *We the Poor People* (1997) explores the feminization of poverty.

12 | *The Age of Limits, 1974–1980*

*I*n July 1979, faced with rising oil prices and plummeting public support, President Jimmy Carter scheduled a prime-time televised address to the nation. In a rare display of passion and eloquence, Carter gave a thirty-three-minute sermon that was unlike any speech ever given from the Oval Office. "This is not a message of happiness or reassurance," he declared, "but it is the truth and it is a warning." Convinced that the energy crisis was a symptom of a larger problem, Carter offered the nation his diagnosis of the "crisis of the American spirit." With a sharp voice and his characteristically flashing eyes, the president apologized for his own failures at leadership, confessing that "the gap between our citizens and our government has never been so wide." As a result, Americans had become pessimistic about the future and displayed "a growing disrespect for government and for churches and schools, the news media, and other institutions." The energy crisis, he sermonized, was a trial in which the security and the future of America were at stake. "Energy will be the immediate test of our ability to unite the nation," he said. "On the battlefield of energy, we can win for our nation a new confidence—and we can seize control of our common destiny."

Carter had successfully diagnosed the paradox confronting Americans in the 1970s. In the wake of Vietnam and Watergate, public faith in government declined at the same time that many groups looked to Washington for solutions to pressing social problems. Congress responded by attempting to make the government more responsive to the public will, but most of the reforms it enacted had the opposite impact. For the previous three decades economic growth had sustained American expectations of the future, but stagflation, a new and troubling combination of rising unemployment and soaring inflation, eroded the standard of living of millions of Americans and made them question whether they could pass on a better life to their children. Concern about limited resources also produced widespread fear of environmental disaster.

The solution to the urgent issue of energy required a united national response, but the nation had been deeply fractured by debates over Vietnam and race and proved incapable of forging a new consensus. President Carter seemed to understand the paradox, but neither he nor other public leaders offered convincing answers to the questions puzzling most Americans.

Discomfort Index   During the 1970s the United States experienced stagflation, the combination of rising inflation and increasing unemployment. During the 1976 presidential campaign Democrats developed the "discomfort" or "misery" index to measure the public impact of this destructive combination, and to attack Republican opponents for their poor management of the economy. In 1980, however, Republicans used the same index to highlight Jimmy Carter's economic mismanagement. *(Sources:* Economic Report of the President, 1999; Statistical Abstract of the United States, 1996*)*

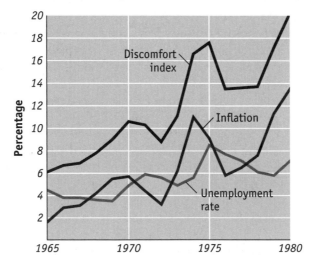

Watergate Legacies: The Diffusion of Power

The failure in Vietnam, the Johnson administration's duplicity in explaining it, and the exposure of Nixon's illegal behavior in the Watergate affair combined to erode public faith in the integrity of elected leaders. "All during Vietnam, the government lied to me," declared the journalist Richard Cohen. "All the time. Watergate didn't help matters any. More lies . . . I've been shaped, formed by lies." Pollster Daniel Yankelovich noted in 1977 that trust in government declined from 80 percent in the late 1950s to about 33 percent in 1976. More than 80 percent of the public expressed distrust in political leaders, 61 percent believed something was morally wrong with the country, while nearly 75 percent felt that they had no impact on Washington decision making.

The new skepticism found expression in the way the media dealt with political leaders. Reporters, believing they had been duped by Lyndon Johnson and Richard Nixon, developed a more assertive and confrontational style, challenging the official version of events. Inspired by the example of Watergate heroes Bob Woodward and Carl Bernstein, many journalists went in search of the next big scandal. "A lot of young reporters today are more likely to ask the right questions of the right people than before Watergate," observed an editor at the *New York Times*. Investigative reporting emerged as a major franchise in many newsrooms, organizing reporting teams and providing them with big budgets. The adversarial style, and the new emphasis on exposing corruption, contributed to growing public distrust of politicians and reinforced the notion that political leaders were corrupt.

In an effort to restore public trust, the nation's political leaders undertook a series of highly visible reforms. Most of the effort was directed at limiting the power of the presidency. In 1973 Congress passed the War Powers Act over President Nixon's veto. The act required a president to "consult with Congress" within forty-eight hours of committing American troops abroad and ordered him to withdraw them within sixty days unless Congress approved the mission. In addition, Congress enjoined the president from undertaking any military action in Vietnam after August 15, 1973.

On the domestic side Congress moved to increase its influence over domestic policy. The Budget and Impoundment Control Act in 1974 streamlined the budgeting process in Congress and created the Congressional Budget Office, which produced an independent analysis of the president's budget each year. Congress also expanded the personal staffs of individual senators and House members, enlarged committee staffs in both houses, and increased the research service of the Library of Congress. Congressional staffs, for example, increased by 41 percent between 1972 and 1978. These steps, though little noticed, represented a significant change in the relationship between the two branches. Congress acquired new capability to evaluate and challenge programs sought by presidents.

Increased staff also upset the balance of power in Congress. Since the staff increases were across the board, individual representatives were able to develop expertise and challenge the power of committee chairs.

Along with shifting power from the president to Congress and reforming the structure of Congress, legislators moved to limit the influence of money in politics. The Federal Election Campaign Act of 1974 placed caps on the amount of money that individuals could donate to political campaigns and provided some public funding for presidential campaigns. But loopholes in the act allowed new mechanisms of fundraising and donation that actually led to an increase in the flow of private money into elections. Political parties developed direct-mail techniques to solicit huge numbers of small donations that they funneled into important campaigns. Political action committees (PACs) proliferated and dispersed campaign funds.

The emergence of special interests further eroded the power of the political parties to forge consensus among competing factions. "The rise of special interests is directly related to the loss of trust that people have had in the traditional political institutions, parties specifically," noted the Republican pollster Richard Wirthlin. The turmoil of the 1960s, especially race riots and the Vietnam War, loosened the loyalties of many Democrats, while Watergate undermined the Republicans' claim to be the party of good government. Interest groups moved in to fill the void, but they had little interest in compromise and consensus. By taking uncompromising positions on sometimes emotional issues, they intentionally polarized debate. Many interest groups coalesced for the sole purpose of opposing an issue. "It's much easier to wage a campaign against something than for it," said a member of a right-wing group.

The Troubled Economy

The political system seemed stalemated at just the time that the nation desperately needed solutions to difficult economic problems. During the long postwar boom from 1947 to the mid-1960s, the United States enjoyed average annual productivity increases of 3.2 percent. From 1965 to 1973, however, productivity growth averaged only 2.4 percent annually. By the end of the decade, productivity was declining in absolute terms. As inflation exploded to nearly 10 percent, unemployment crept upward.

The nation's economic difficulties had many causes. First, the nation's expansion in the postwar era depended on the prodigious use of cheap energy. In the early 1970s, political turmoil in the Middle East led to dramatically higher oil prices and undermined the bedrock of this system. Between 1972 and 1979, the price of oil quintupled. Higher energy costs rippled through the economy. Inflation, which never exceeded 5 percent between 1955 and 1972, suddenly exploded to nearly 10 percent by the end of 1973.

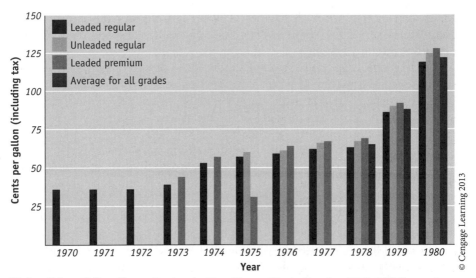

Rising Price of Gasoline   During the Yom Kippur War in October 1973, OPEC ceased exports of oil to the United States because of America's support of Israel. In the 1970s, the United States imported one-third of its oil, most of it from the Middle East, so this embargo created a severe shortage of oil-based products, such as gasoline and home heating oil. While the embargo was lifted in 1974, gasoline prices never returned to their earlier levels. A severe price spike in 1979 and 1980 was again the result of rising tensions in the Middle East, this time caused by the overthrow of the shah in Iran and the taking of American hostages in Lebanon.

Second, for the first time since the end of World War II, American business faced stiff competition from other countries. The industrial economies of western Europe and Japan, finally recovered from the war, began to win an increasing share of international trade. The surge in foreign competition offered consumers quality products at lower prices. But it also threatened jobs that had for years offered Americans high wages and dependable employment.

The decline of the American automobile industry provided a clear example of this trend. In the 1950s and 1960s, U.S. automakers had ruled the domestic market. In the 1970s, with gasoline prices soaring and buying power pinched by inflation, car buyers welcomed affordable, more fuel-efficient imports such as Japan's Toyota and Datsun. Detroit, geared toward producing bulky six-passenger sedans, failed to convert in time, and part of its market drifted away. By 1980, imports had grabbed 34 percent of the U.S. auto market.

These reverses assaulted Americans' optimistic faith in progress. For most of their history, Americans had believed that hard work and talent would be rewarded with upward mobility and greater economic opportunity. More, they had faith that the ingenuity of the American people and the continent's rich resources would lead to an ever-increasing prosperity for all. Americans, Alexis de Tocqueville wrote as early as 1835, "consider society as a body in a state of improvement." By 1979, however, 55 percent of all Americans believed that "next year will be worse than this year."

The Environmental Movement

The oil shock not only contributed to the nation's economic woes, it alerted many people to the possibility that the nation's prosperity had been built on an unsustainable base of limited resources. That belief contributed to a groundswell of concern for the environment.

The birth of the modern environmental movement dated to the publication in 1962 of marine biologist Rachel Carson's book *Silent Spring,* which documented evidence that the widely used insecticide DDT was killing birds, fish, and other animals that ate insects. Sufficiently concentrated, DDT also posed significant health risks to humans. In 1972 the government banned the sale of DDT.

Ironically, one of the nation's greatest technological achievements fed concern about the environment. In July 1969, *Apollo 11* astronaut Neil Armstrong lifted his left foot off the landing pad of his spacecraft and pressed it into the soft powdery surface of the moon's Sea of Tranquility. Over 1 billion people watched as Armstrong and fellow astronaut Buzz Aldrin planted an American flag and a plaque reading in part, "We came in peace for all mankind." The powerful images of earth, which seemed so small from space, underscored the limits of earth's natural resources and the need to preserve them. Those images helped inspire the first annual Earth Day celebration on April 22, 1970. Twenty million people gathered in local events across the country to hear speeches and see exhibits and demonstrations promoting environmental awareness.

Highly publicized disasters fueled public concern about the costs of a technological society. When people living in the Love Canal housing development near Niagara Falls, New York, reported abnormally high rates of illness, miscarriages, and birth defects, investigators learned the community had been built on top of an underground chemical waste disposal site. In March 1979, a frightening accident at the Three Mile Island nuclear power plant in Pennsylvania heightened public concern about the safety of nuclear power and led to calls for tighter regulation of the industry.

Uneasiness about the state of the environment persisted and found expression in the popular culture of the 1970s. In best-selling books, such as Hal Lindsey's *Late Great Planet Earth*, scientists were heard to predict the end of global supplies of oil and other natural resources. A popular movie, *The China Syndrome*, portrayed a fictitious nuclear power plant in which incompetence and greed threatened to lead to a nuclear meltdown. Others, such as *Soylent Green*, envisioned a world in which technological development and overpopulation had exhausted the earth's natural resources.

Nuclear Accident at Three Mile Island   Few Americans had ever heard of Three Mile Island, a nuclear energy plant built along the Susquehanna River in rural Pennsylvania, until March 28, 1979. On that day, cooling water accidentally escaped from the reactor core and the core started to melt, shooting radioactivity into the atmosphere. The governor ordered residents to remain in their homes, closed the schools, and encouraged pregnant women and families with small children to leave the area. The plant claimed to have the situation under control, but for several days the community's residents, along with the rest of America, waited anxiously. Five days after the accident, Jimmy and Rosalynn Carter toured the plant, calming the immediate fear of a complete core meltdown, but people were now more aware of the possibility of future accidents at the nation's nuclear power plants, and the intensity of the antinuclear movement increased. *(© J. Atlan/Corbis Sygma)*

A Time to Heal: The Brief Presidency of Gerald Ford

Gerald Ford did little to restore public confidence in the presidency. Faced with the delicate problem of succeeding Richard Nixon, Gerald Ford tried to present himself as a steady, sober leader whom the public could trust. With his friendly smile and reputation for honesty, Ford enjoyed wide respect. As he took the presidential oath of office on August 9, 1972, the sixty-one-year-old Ford announced that his top priority was to heal "the nation's wounds" and to restore a sense of confidence in government. Initially, the press hailed both the message and the messenger, finding down-to-earth Ford a refreshing break from imperious Nixon. "He's superbly average," observed *U.S. News and World Report*. "He's like Ike. He gives you an impression of solid dependability."

Within a month, however, Ford connected his administration to the Watergate scandal by granting Nixon "a full, free, and absolute pardon." Ford rightly believed that "it would [have] be[en] virtually impossible for me to direct public attention to anything else" if Nixon had been put on trial. "Public policy demanded that I put Nixon and Watergate behind us as quickly as possible." Although sound public policy, the decision to pardon Nixon produced a political maelstrom. Overnight Ford's approval ratings plunged from 71 to 50 percent.

PRIMARY SOURCE

12.1 | *Pardon of Richard Nixon*
GERALD FORD

When Gerald Ford became president upon the resignation of Nixon, he claimed he had no intention of pardoning Nixon, who still faced possible criminal charges. However, on September 8, 1974, Ford issued a pardon to Nixon, justifying his decision by saying it was to restore peace to a divided nation.

As a result of certain acts or omissions occurring before his resignation from the office of President, Richard Nixon has become liable to possible indictment and trial for offenses against the United States. Whether or not he shall be so prosecuted depends on findings of the appropriate grand jury and on the discretion of the authorized prosecutor. Should an indictment ensue, the accused
5 shall then be entitled to a fair trial by an impartial jury, as guaranteed to every individual by the Constitution.

It is believed that a trial of Richard Nixon, if it became necessary, could not fairly begin until a year or more has elapsed. In the meantime, the tranquility to which this nation has been restored by the events of recent weeks could be irrep-
10 arably lost by the prospects of bringing to trial a former President of the United States. The prospects of such trial will cause prolonged and divisive debate over the propriety of exposing to further punishment and degradation a man who has already paid the unprecedented penalty of relinquishing the highest elective office in the United States.

15 NOW, THEREFORE, I, Gerald R. Ford, President of the United States, pursuant to the pardon power conferred upon me by Article II, Section 2, of the Constitution, have granted and by these presents do grant a full, free, and absolute pardon unto Richard Nixon for all offenses against the United States which he, Richard Nixon, has committed or may have committed or taken part in dur-
20 ing the period from January 20, 1969, through August 9, 1974.

IN WITNESS WHEREOF, I have hereunto set my hand this 8th day of September in the year of our Lord nineteen hundred seventy-four, and of the independence of the United States of America the 199th.

Source: Proclamation of Pardon by Gerald R. Ford. ■ ■ ■

Ford had a hard time overcoming this poor start. His administration failed to develop a consistent approach to the economy. In his first month in office Ford faced an economy in steep decline: prices and unemployment continued to rise, but business was slowing and the gross national product was slipping. Initially Ford sided with conservatives, declared fighting inflation "domestic enemy number one," and called for budget cuts and a tax increase. But as unemployment jumped from 5.8 to 7 percent during the fall, and leading economic indicators signaled a steep recession, Ford switched gears and announced a tax cut to stimulate growth. The president's "flip-flop" on the economy and taxes contributed to a growing public perception that Ford was out of his depth in the White House.

Popular culture reinforced the image of Ford as an "amiable bumbler." Although he was an agile and athletic man, Ford tripped at the front door of the White House, fell on his hands and knees while debarking from a plane, and banged his head against an errant elevator gate. Every week many Americans tuned into *Saturday Night Live* to watch comedian Chevy Chase imitate the president's various pratfalls. Most critics saw a clear connection between Ford's physical aerobatics and his intellectual ability. "If he's so dumb, how come he's president?" Chase asked in one of his weekly skits.

On both foreign and domestic issues Ford had to contend with a Congress determined to assert its control over policy. Ford's plan for fiscal austerity also placed him on a collision course with Democrats, who controlled large majorities in both Houses. During his brief term in office Ford vetoed legislation calling for increased spending for federal aid to education and health care. When he refused to approve a federal bailout of New York City, the headline of the *New York Daily News* screamed, "Ford to City—Drop Dead."

In foreign policy Ford continued Nixon's internationalist course. Depending heavily on the advice of Kissinger, Ford traveled to Vladivostok in 1974 to negotiate a new nuclear arms treaty with the Soviets. The Strategic Arms Limitation Talks (SALT) II set equal ceilings on the delivery of strategic weapons. The following summer he signed the Helsinki Accords, which called for peaceful settlements of disputes and greater scientific and economic cooperation between the two countries. Both treaties ran into fierce opposition from conservatives and stalled in Congress.

Under attack from his right for appeasing the Soviets, and feeling the need to demonstrate American resolve following the fall of Saigon, Ford took a hard line when Cambodian rebels seized the U.S. merchant ship *Mayaguez* and held its crew hostage. "Let's look ferocious," Kissinger told the White House. Ignoring indications that the Cambodian government was looking for a peaceful solution to the crisis, the administration ordered a daring rescue mission, which resulted in the deaths of a handful of marines. The mission was a military disaster but a public relations coup for the president. The hostages, who had been moved to a different location, had already been released, but the nation applauded Ford's decisive action. "I am very proud of our country and our president today," said a congressman, echoing the feeling of his colleagues. The boost in the polls from the *Mayaguez* incident was short-lived: month after month of rising prices and higher unemployment sapped public support for the Ford presidency.

Jimmy Carter and the New Democrats

The downturn also forced a new generation of Democratic candidates to question the faith in expanded government that had guided a previous generation of liberal politicians. The most successful of the new breed of politician was former Georgia governor Jimmy Carter. Many observers saw Carter as a link between Great Society idealism and the economic realities of an age of limits. A Democrat with populist leanings, he was also an engineer with an instinctive aversion to spending and waste. "He's tight as a tick," declared his press secretary Jody Powell. Sensing the opportunity to capitalize on the Watergate affair and public distrust of Washington, Carter decided to run for president in 1976 by campaigning as an outsider who would clean up the mess in Washington.

Beginning his campaign with a name recognition of only 2 percent, Carter took advantage of Democratic Party reforms initiated after 1968 that increased the role of grass-roots activists in the selection process. Carter was able to roll over a number of better-known candidates on the way to a first-ballot victory at the convention. In an effort to reach out to the party's traditional power brokers, whom he had bypassed in the primaries, Carter selected Minnesota Senator Walter F. Mondale, a protégé of Hubert Humphrey, as his running mate.

Throughout the primary season Carter skillfully played to the public's conflicting mood. He combined biting attacks on the Washington establishment with uplifting sermons about spiritual renewal. A Democrat who thought like a Republican, Carter rejected social experimentation and instead emphasized the importance of social efficiency and prudent management of the nation's affairs. A deeply religious man and a self-described born-again Christian, he seemed to offer a religious salve for the nation's wounds, reassuring audiences that they deserved a government as "decent, honest, truthful, fair, compassionate, and as filled with love as our people are." Carter emphasized his rural roots and his lifelong distance from Washington, conveying a serene confidence in the relevance of old verities. There seemed to be nothing ailing America that could not be solved with a little more democracy. "It's time for the people to run the government," he declared.

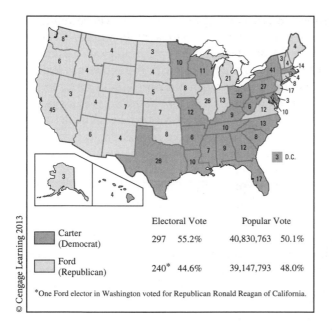

Electoral Vote   Popular Vote

Carter (Democrat)   297   55.2%   40,830,763   50.1%

Ford (Republican)   240*   44.6%   39,147,793   48.0%

*One Ford elector in Washington voted for Republican Ronald Reagan of California.

© Cengage Learning 2013

The Election of 1976 Ford's failure to solve the nation's economic problems led to doubts within his own Republican Party about his ability to lead the nation, while his opponent, Jimmy Carter of Georgia, emphasized the need for a moral president after years of political corruption unearthed by the Watergate investigations. Fallout from the Watergate era could also be seen in the low voter turnout for the election, as almost half of eligible voters, alienated by the scandal, failed to vote.

In August polls showed Carter leading President Ford by more than 30 percentage points. Not only was Ford burdened by his party's ties to Watergate and by his pardon of Nixon, but he also had to endure a bruising primary fight against conservative Ronald Reagan that left his image muddied and his party deeply split. By early October, however, Democratic mishaps and an effective Republican strategy had eliminated Carter's once-formidable lead. But the legacy of Watergate, continuing bad economic news, and his own lack of charisma were more than Ford could overcome.

On election night the Democrats won a narrow victory. Less than 2 percentage points separated the candidates in the popular vote—Carter won 40.8 million votes to Ford's 39.1 million. In the electoral college Carter defeated Ford 297 to 240. It was the narrowest electoral victory since 1916 when Woodrow Wilson defeated Charles Evans Hughes by 23 electoral votes. It was also one of the least compelling, to judge from the turnout. A smaller percentage of Americans voted in 1976 than in any election since 1948. The Democrats, however, maintained large majorities in Congress: a Senate margin of 62–38 and a House lead of 291–142.

The Democrats' Discontent

In clear contrast to his two Democratic predecessors, John F. Kennedy and Lyndon Johnson, who used their Inaugural Addresses as clarion calls of American greatness at home and abroad, Carter struck a tone of limits. "We have learned that 'more' is not necessarily 'better,' that even our great nation has its recognized limits, and that we can neither answer all questions nor solve all problems."

Carter sounded new themes, but he failed to develop a strategy for adjusting public expectations, whetted by years of prosperity, with the economic reality of an age of limits. The new president faced enormous obstacles in his effort to build a national consensus. His narrow electoral victory provided a shaky foundation for bold proposals. He presided over a party still torn by divisions over Vietnam and civil rights. A resurgent Congress eager to reassert its authority after Watergate, and a public grown cynical about Washington and angry about rising unemployment and high inflation, compounded his difficulties.

Carter began his presidency by raising spending, trying to put an end to the unemployment generated by Ford's fiscal and monetary restrictions. Unemployment did begin to come down, but only at the cost of another slow rise in inflation that ate into Americans' paychecks. By 1978, the inflation rate had soared to 9 percent, the third highest since 1945 and nearly three percentage points above administration predictions. In January 1979, a somber president lectured the nation about the need for fiscal restraint. In keeping with his theme, Carter submitted to Congress a "lean and austere" budget designed to reduce the federal deficit and reduce inflationary pressure. The liberal wing of the Democratic Party revolted, attacking Carter for sacrificing the poor on the altar of austerity.

Most vexing to the president's political fortunes was the gasoline shortage that plagued American consumers in early 1979. By May, gasoline lines in California ran as long as five hundred cars, and prices at the pump climbed about a dollar a gallon for the first time. "It's sort of like sex," explained one official. "Everybody's going to get all the gasoline they need, but they're damn sure not going to get all they want." Over the Fourth of July weekend, 90 percent of all gas stations in the New York City area were closed; 80 percent in Pennsylvania; 50 percent in Rhode Island. Polls showed overwhelming disapproval of Carter's handling of the economy.

In foreign policy, the president achieved a couple of notable successes. In December 1978, Carter completed the process initiated by Richard Nixon by formally recognizing the People's Republic of China. President Carter also convinced the Senate, in a very close vote, to ratify a treaty that promised to turn over the Canal Zone to Panama by the year 2000. Carter moved to identify the United States with black African nationalism and to end the "last vestiges of colonialism" in Zimbabwe/Rhodesia and Namibia. Carter chided white South African rulers for apartheid—an official system of segregating nonwhites and whites that included removals of blacks to designated homelands, discriminatory wages based on race, the denial of voting rights, absence of civil liberties, and arbitrary arrests for blacks.

For most of his four years in office, however, Carter struggled unsuccessfully to convince the American public that he could protect America's global interests from an aggressive Soviet Union. The memory of Vietnam haunted the

Carter administration's attempt to develop a coherent foreign policy. Since the beginning of the Cold War a commitment to global containment had characterized the Democratic Party's view of the world. Vietnam had called many of those assumptions into question. Unlike Munich, which forged a new consensus, Vietnam divided the party, polarized its leaders, and raised new questions about America's role in the world. The party of Lyndon Johnson, that expanded America's involvement in Vietnam, defended the military expansion, and opposed its withdrawal, was also the party of George McGovern, which cursed the war and called for American withdrawal. As the first postwar Democratic president, Carter had to pull together the polarized foreign policy establishment and create a coherent foreign policy.

Carter came to power promising to work for more amicable relations with the Soviet Union and to replace the Nixon-Kissinger commitment to realism with a concern for human rights. "We are now free of that inordinate fear of communism which once led us to embrace any dictator who joined us in our fear," Carter declared. He quickly opened a second round of arms limitations talks (SALT II) with the Soviet Union. One of the most complicated treaties ever negotiated, SALT II for the first time established numerical equality between the United States and the Soviet Union in total strategic nuclear delivery vehicles. But Carter was struggling to extend détente at a time when many Americans were questioning its benefits. Since Nixon and Kissinger had announced their aim of achieving détente, the Soviet Union had repeatedly made clear its continuing support for "liberation" struggles in the Third World. It ordered Cuba to send troops to potential allies in Africa and worked to win influence among Arab nations near the West's supply of oil.

1979: The Year of Crisis

In 1979 three events in the Middle East would have a dramatic impact on America's relationship with the world. First, in March 1979, Carter's persistence and vision produced the most notable success of his administration—the signing of the Camp David Accords. In 1977, Egyptian President Anwar Sadat had initiated a peace deal with Israel by making a dramatic trip to Jerusalem. However, Israel's prime minister, Menachem Begin, rejected Sadat's demand that Israel return the Golan Heights and the West Bank and that it provide a Palestinian homeland. Carter brought the two leaders together at the presidential retreat at Camp David, Maryland, in September 1978. After twelve days of secret negotiations, Carter announced that both Begin and Sadat, once bitter enemies, had accepted the outlines of a new framework for peace. The Camp David Accords, signed in March 1979, called for Egypt to recognize Israel's right to exist as a sovereign state and for Israel to return the Sinai Peninsula. The accords also called for Egypt, Israel, Jordan, and Palestinian representatives

Camp David Accords   Carter's greatest foreign policy achievement was his brokering of a historic peace between Israel and Egypt. In the Camp David Accords, signed by Egyptian President Anwar Sadat (*left*) and Israeli Prime Minister Menachem Begin, a framework for peace was established that ultimately led Israel to return all land in the Sinai in return for Egypt's recognition of the Israeli state. Though it did not solve the issue of Palestinian refugees, the Accords did lessen the tensions between the two countries and both men received the Nobel Peace Prize in 2002. (*Jimmy Carter Presidential Library*)

to seek a solution to the status of the West Bank and Gaza Strip, but little progress was made on the issue.

Second, revolutionaries ousted the pro-American regime of the shah of Iran, and Muslim fundamentalists loyal to religious leader Ayatollah Ruholla Khomeini gained control of the country. When Carter agreed to let the deposed shah come to the United States for cancer treatment, many Iranians took the act as a direct insult. On November 4, 1979, five hundred young Iranians occupied the American embassy and held fifty Americans hostage. Americans witnessed nightly serenades of "Death to America" from angry demonstrators, while the ailing, seventy-nine-year-old Ayatollah called the United States "the great Satan." "However the crisis ends," *Time* commented, "it seems likely to enhance the impression of American helplessness." With Carter unable to effect a release by threats or diplomacy, the hostages languished week after week, then month after month. In April Carter ordered an abortive rescue mission that resulted in the death of eight soldiers when two helicopters collided during a sandstorm in the desert. Burning helicopters in the desert symbolized America's inability to achieve even so limited an objective as freeing its citizens from the control of a third-rank nation.

Third, in December 1979, as the American hostages entered their eighth week of captivity, Soviet troops invaded neighboring Afghanistan, toppling that nation's bumbling puppet regime. The attack represented a bold military operation aimed at ending a tribal rebellion against the Marxist government. The invasion moved Soviet troops to within several hundred miles of the oil-rich and politically unstable Persian Gulf. Vowing to punish the Soviets for their intervention, Carter recalled the American ambassador from Moscow, put an end to SALT II talks with the Soviets, banned American athletes from participating in the Summer Olympics in Moscow, and imposed a politically risky grain embargo. More important, he supplied military aid to the Afghan *mujahideen*—a coalition of radical Islamic rebels from throughout the world who resisted the Soviet occupation.

Over time, the three events would polarize the region, feed the rise of Islamic radicalism, and present a serious threat to American global security. The Camp David Accords represented a major step in the development of moderate Arab regimes friendly to the United States and willing to live in peace with Israel. Yet the treaty also enraged the Arab militants who rejected Western influence in the region, opposed the state of Israel, and promised to overthrow the governments that made peace. Backing up their threats, Islamic militants assassinated Sadat in 1981. Militants were emboldened by the success of the Iranian revolution, which replaced a repressive pro-American regime with an Islamic government ruled by clerics. Finally, the Soviet invasion of Afghanistan served as a rallying cry for Islamic fundamentalists determined to expel the secular invaders. For a brief period, America and Islamic fundamentalists shared a common agenda. After the defeat of the Soviets and the end of the Cold War, however, the militants would focus their hostility on the world's only superpower: the United States. "It's all very far away from you in America, isn't it?" a rebel leader told an American reporter in 1983. "But it is not as far as you think."

The 1980 Presidential Campaign

Carter seemed helpless in the face of problems both at home and abroad. In late 1979, with inflation soaring into double digits, newly appointed Federal Reserve chairman Paul Volcker applied the monetary brakes. The nation's major banks responded by raising their prime interest rates, first to 13 percent and then to 14.5 percent. With the prime rate reaching all-time highs, the economy began its inevitable slowdown. In October the Dow Jones index of industrial stocks lost nearly one hundred points, auto sales dropped 23 percent compared to the previous year, and rising mortgage rates strangled the housing industry. Abroad the Soviet invasion of Afghanistan was raising fears that the USSR would strike at valuable Middle East oil supplies. Iranian militants continued to "hold America hostage," threatening to put their American captives on trial.

12.2 | *The Crisis of Confidence*
Jimmy Carter

As a result of major foreign and domestic problems, President Jimmy Carter's popularity ratings dropped below 30 percent by July 1979. Many American citizens, and some within Carter's own administration, questioned Carter's ability to lead. In a televised address on July 15, 1979, Carter responded to the nation's anxieties and malaise in a speech that examined the nation's "crisis of confidence."

Our people are losing that faith not only in government itself but in the ability as citizens to serve as the ultimate rulers and shapers of our democracy. As a people we know our past and we are proud of it. Our progress has been part of the living history of America, even the world. We always believed that we were part of a great movement of humanity itself called democracy, involved in the
5 search for freedom, and that belief has always strengthened us in our purpose. But just as we are losing our confidence in the future, we are also beginning to close the door on our past.

In a nation that was proud of hard work, strong families, close-knit communities, and our faith in God, too many of us now tend to worship self-indulgence
10 and consumption. Human identity is no longer defined by what one does, but by what one owns. But we've discovered that owning things and consuming things does not satisfy our longing for meaning. We've learned that piling up material goods cannot fill the emptiness of lives which have no confidence or purpose.

The symptoms of this crisis of the American spirit are all around us. For the
15 first time in the history of our country a majority of our people believe that the next five years will be worse than the past five years. Two-thirds of our people do not even vote. The productivity of American workers is actually dropping, and the willingness of Americans to save for the future has fallen below that of all other people in the Western world. As you know, there is a growing disrespect for
20 government and for churches and for schools, the news media, and other institutions. This is not a message of happiness or reassurance, but it is the truth and it is a warning.

These changes did not happen overnight. They've come upon us gradually over the last generation, years that were filled with shocks and tragedy. We were
25 sure that ours was a nation of the ballot, not the bullet, until the murders of John

Kennedy and Robert Kennedy and Martin Luther King Jr. We were taught that our armies were always invincible and our causes were always just, only to suffer the agony of Vietnam. We respected the presidency as a place of honor until the shock of Watergate. We remember when the phrase "sound as a dollar" was an
30 expression of absolute dependability, until ten years of inflation began to shrink our dollar and our savings. We believed that our nation's resources were limitless until 1973, when we had to face a growing dependence on foreign oil.

Often you see paralysis and stagnation and drift. You don't like it, and neither do I. What can we do? First of all, we must face the truth, and then we can change
35 our course. We simply must have faith in each other, faith in our ability to govern ourselves, and faith in the future of this nation. Restoring that faith and that confidence to America is now the most important task we face. It is a true challenge of this generation of Americans. . . .

Source: Address to the nation by President Jimmy Carter, July 15, 1979.　■ ■ ■

In the face of these crises, observers complained that Carter was aloof and arrogant, incapable of seizing control of the levers of power in Washington. His own party was in open revolt. With polls showing him leading the president by a 3–1 margin, Massachusetts Senator Edward Kennedy, the keeper of the flickering liberal flame, announced that he would challenge Carter for the Democratic nomination. Portraying Carter as a weak and ineffective leader who had abandoned the party's liberal tradition, Kennedy confidently declared, "The only thing that paralyzes us today is the myth that we cannot move."

The American people, however, instinctively rallied around the president during a time of international crisis. Carter watched his job approval rating double to 61 percent in January 1980—the sharpest one-month leap in forty-one years of polling. Capitalizing on his sudden surge of popularity, Carter played the role of national leader by standing above the partisan fray and refusing to campaign. As Kennedy's campaign wilted in the patriotic afterglow, Carter secured his party's nomination on the first ballot.

Believing the president's rise in the polls would be temporary, a revived Republican Party rallied around former Hollywood movie actor and successful two-term California Governor Ronald Reagan, who cruised to victory in the Republican primaries. An effective speaker and master of the media, Reagan articulated a simple but compelling message: love of country, fear of communism, and scorn of government. Reagan repudiated the traditional Republican economic doctrine of tight fiscal policy and balanced budgets and instead preached about the wonders of supply-side economics. Responding to fears that America's stature in the world was in decline, Reagan called for a muscular foreign policy, including huge increases in military spending. Reflecting the influence of the religious right, the GOP platform adopted a plank opposing abortion and the Equal Rights Amendment. In an overture to moderate Republicans, Reagan selected the genial George Bush, a vanquished primary foe and former Central Intelligence Agency head, as his running mate.

As the campaign moved into the final weeks, Carter and Reagan were dead-locked. The lone debate held a week before the election proved decisive. In his closing remarks Reagan focused public attention on Carter's responsibility for double-digit inflation, the hostages in Iran, and Soviet troops in Afghanistan. "Are you better off than you were four years ago?" he asked. "Is America as re-spected throughout the world as it was?"

On election day Reagan won 489 electoral votes to Carter's 49. In the popular vote the Republican challenger received 43.9 million votes (50.7 percent) to Carter's 35.5 million (41 percent). Carter became the first Democrat since Grover Cleveland in 1888, and the first incumbent since Herbert Hoover in 1932, to be voted out of the Oval Office. Independent candidate John Anderson, a Republican congressman who bolted his party claiming that it had been hijacked by conservatives, won only 5.7 million popular votes (6.6 percent). The Democrats, moreover, lost thirty-four House seats and lost control of the Senate as the Repub-licans gained twelve seats. Republicans controlled the upper house of Congress for the first time since the days of Dwight Eisenhower. Ominously, 48 percent of eligible voters did not cast ballots, the lowest voter turnout since 1948.

Reagan's rise to national prominence did, however, highlight the dramatic shift of political power from the more liberal Rust Belt, which extended from Massachusetts down to Delaware and across to Illinois and Michigan, to the conservative Sun Belt—the bottom half of the country extending from North Carolina to southern California. During the previous decade the Sun Belt had

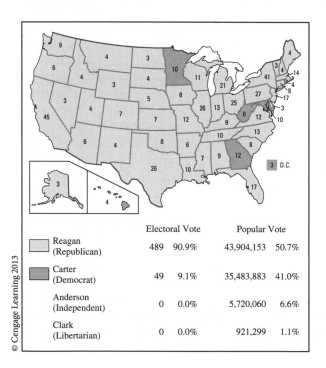

© Cengage Learning 2013

	Electoral Vote		Popular Vote	
Reagan (Republican)	489	90.9%	43,904,153	50.7%
Carter (Democrat)	49	9.1%	35,483,883	41.0%
Anderson (Independent)	0	0.0%	5,720,060	6.6%
Clark (Libertarian)	0	0.0%	921,299	1.1%

The Election of 1980 While Ronald Reagan won a landslide in the electoral college, the number of popular voters and nonvoters provides a much more complex pic-ture. Only 52.6 percent of eligible voters cast their bal-lots in the election, giving Reagan only 28 percent of the potential electorate and leading many to question why so many Americans chose not to vote.

State	1940	1960	1980	% Increase 1940–1980	% Increase 1960–1980
North Carolina	3,572	4,556	5,874	64.5	28.9
South Carolina	1,900	2,383	3,119	64.2	30.9
Georgia	3,124	3,943	5,464	75.0	38.6
Florida	1,897	4,952	9,740	413.4	96.7
Alabama	2,833	3,267	3,890	37.3	19.1
Mississippi	2,184	2,178	2,521	15.5	15.7
Tennessee	2,916	3,567	4,591	57.5	28.7
Louisiana	2,364	3,257	4,204	77.9	29.1
Arkansas	1,949	1,786	2,286	17.3	28.0
Oklahoma	2,336	2,328	3,025	29.5	29.9
Texas	6,415	9,580	14,228	121.8	48.5
New Mexico	532	951	1,300	144.8	36.7
Arizona	499	1,302	2,718	444.7	108.8
Southern Nevada[a]	16	127	461	2,781.2	263.0
Southern California[b]	3,841	9,399	13,803	259.4	46.9
Total	36,378	53,576	77,224	112.3	44.1
Northeast/Midwest	76,120	96,927	107,986	41.9	11.4
United States	132,165	179,323	226,505	71.4	26.3

[a] Clark County (Las Vegas SMSA)

[b] San Bernadino, Kern, San Luis Obispo, Santa Barbara, Los Angeles, Riverside, Orange, San Diego, Ventura, and Imperial counties

Sun Belt Population (in thousands), 1940–1980 With the application of air conditioning to American homes after World War II, parts of the country that experienced extreme heat in the summer, the South and Southwest especially, became more inhabitable. These regions, labeled the Sun Belt, were areas of the country that generally lacked strong labor unions and had an abundance of cheap land and labor, leading many corporations to relocate their northern industries. Workers also followed the expanding military industrial complex into the Sun Belt as defense contractors and military bases developed in the region. Different parts of the Sun Belt also experienced tremendous population growth due to the oil boom in the 1970s (Texas, Oklahoma, Louisiana), tourism (Florida and California), and Mexican immigration.

accounted for 90 percent of the nation's population growth and by 1980 claimed a majority of Americans. Just three states—California, Texas, and Florida— saw nearly 40 percent of the nation's population growth and controlled nearly 25 percent of the electoral votes needed to win the presidency. Polls showed that Sun Belt residents were more skeptical about federal power, more resentful of government regulation, and more anti-Soviet than the general voting public. Not surprisingly, the Republican ticket comprised a representative from California and one from Texas.

For many conservatives the 1980 election represented the inevitable triumph of Richard Nixon's conservative majority. "Like a great soaking wet shaggy dog, the Silent Majority—banished from the house during the Watergate storms—romped back into the nation's parlor this week and shook itself vigorously," observed the columnist William Safire. Reagan's message of economic and cultural conservatism appealed to Americans grown tired of social experiments and cynical about government power. The 1970s had dealt a number of body blows to American optimism at home and prestige abroad: the resignation of a president, the painful experience of a lost war, the trials of stagflation, and the humiliation of Americans held hostage in Iran. President Carter publicly questioned whether new social and international conditions required Americans to lower their expectations of the future. A majority of Americans, however, found Reagan's reassuring optimism about the future and his slashing attacks on government more appealing. The new president, however, was about to find himself trapped in the paradox of the nation's love/hate relationship with Washington.

SELECTED READINGS

▌ Arthur M. Schlesinger Jr. studies the growth of executive power that presaged Watergate in *The Imperial Presidency* (1973). Bob Woodward, one of the journalists who uncovered the Watergate conspiracy, analyzes the impact of that coverup on the five subsequent administrations in *Shadow* (1999). Essays examining the causes and consequences of America's erosion of faith in its government have been collected by David Robertson in *Loss of Confidence* (1998). Robert Heilbroner and Lester Thurow diagnose the economic ills of the 1970s in *Five Economic Challenges* (1983). John P. Hoerr's tale of America's declining steel industry, *And the Wolf Finally Came* (1988), demonstrates the nation's industrial decline during the decade.

▌ Rachel Carson's *Silent Spring* (1962) remains the eloquent first word of the environmental movement. Hal Rothman's *Saving the Planet* (2002) provides a good overview of the twentieth century environmental movement. J. Samuel Walker describes the nuclear power scare in *Three Mile Island* (2004), while Thomas Raymond Wellock looks at opposition to nuclear energy in California in *Critical Mass* (1998). Samuel P. Hays provides an overview of the movement in *Beauty, Health, and Permanence* (1987). Roderick Nash's *The Rights of Nature* (1989) outlines the environmentalist ethic.

▌ The failure of political leadership is the subject of Laura Kalman's *Right Star Rising* (2010). Douglas Brinkley provides a concise biographical portrait in *Gerald R. Ford* (2007). John Robert Greene studies the Ford administration in *The Presidency of Gerald R. Ford* (1995). Thomas M. DeFrank records Ford's reflections on his presidency in *Write it When I'm Gone* (2007). On the Carter presidency, see Charles Jones, *The Trusteeship Presidency* (1988); Burton Kaufman, *The Presidency of James Earl Carter, Jr.* (1993); and Gary

M. Fink and Hugh Davis Graham, *The Carter Presidency* (1998). Steven M. Gillon examines Carter and the Democratic Party in *The Democrats' Dilemma* (1992). Daniel Horowitz examines Carter's infamous "malaise" speech in *Jimmy Carter and the Energy Crisis of the 1970s* (2004).

▌ Gaddis Smith's readable *Morality, Reason, and Power* (1987) provides the best overview of Carter's erratic foreign policy. William Quandt describes the Egyptian-Israeli peace accord in *Camp David* (1986). Barry Rubin's *Paved with Good Intentions* (1980) covers America's relations with Iran, while David Farber offers the best account of the hostage crisis in *Taken Hostage* (2005).

13 The Reagan Presidency, 1981–1989

For almost three months before the opening of the 1984 Olympic Games in Los Angeles, the Olympic flame wound its way across the country, through small towns and big cities, country roads and freeways. The appearance of the torch in many areas touched off something resembling an old-fashioned Fourth of July parade. The sight of the runner entering town set church bells ringing and fire sirens blaring. In many communities, people who had waited for hours to see the flame, placed their right hands over their hearts and sang the national anthem. "When people see the torch, they relate it to patriotism," one runner observed. "There's a hunger for that in the land."

The torch ended its journey on July 28, when Gina Hemphill, granddaughter of Jesse Owens, the famed African American sprinter who starred in the 1936 Berlin Olympics, sprinted into the Los Angeles Coliseum. She ran a lap, then as the stadium shook with cheers, handed the torch to another African American, Rafer Johnson, the 1960 decathlon gold medalist, who ran up two long flights of stairs and ignited the Olympic flame that would burn throughout the games. It was left to President Ronald Reagan to make the opening official: "Celebrating the 23rd Olympiad of the modern era, I declare open the Olympic Games of Los Angeles."

The Olympics represented an international celebration of sport, but hosting the games stirred among Americans an outpouring of national pride and patriotism that no one had anticipated. With the Soviet Union boycotting the events in protest against American foreign policy, American athletes collected a record 83 gold medals. At times the colors of red, white, and blue seemed to overwhelm the main stadium as Americans waved flags and chanted: "U.S.A.! U.S.A.!"

The string of American victories thrilled an American audience in the grip of a resurgent nationalism that had swept the country since the election of Ronald Reagan. The new president came to office in 1981 riding a cultural backlash against the 1960s, a wave of frustration with a stagnant economy, declining prestige in the world, soaring inflation, and high taxes.

PRIMARY SOURCE

13.1 | *Inaugural Address*

RONALD REAGAN

Americans witnessed the opulence and style of Hollywood during the presidential inauguration of Ronald Reagan on January 20, 1981. Despite the show-biz atmosphere surrounding the inauguration, Reagan's speech demonstrated his political savvy as he promised "a new beginning" marked by a revised tax system and less government intervention.

The economic ills we suffer have come upon us over several decades. They will not go away in days, weeks, or months, but they will go away. They will go away because we as Americans have the capacity now, as we've had in the past, to do whatever needs to be done to preserve this last and greatest bastion of
5   freedom.

In this present crisis, government is not the solution to our problem; government is the problem. From time to time we've been tempted to believe that society has become too complex to be managed by self-rule, that government by an elite group is superior to government for, by, and of the people. Well, if no one
10 among us is capable of governing himself, then who among us has the capacity to govern someone else? All of us together, in and out of government, must bear the burden. The solutions we seek must be equitable, with no one group singled out to pay a higher price.

We hear much of special interest groups. Well, our concern must be for a
15 special interest group that has been too long neglected. It knows no sectional
boundaries or ethnic and racial divisions, and it crosses political party lines. It
is made up of men and women who raise our food, patrol our streets, man our
mines and factories, teach our children, keep our homes, and heal us when we're
sick—professionals, industrialists, shopkeepers, clerks, cabbies, and truck driv-
20 ers. They are, in short, "we the people," this breed called Americans.

Well, this administration's objective will be a healthy, vigorous, growing
economy that provides equal opportunities for all Americans, with no barriers
born of bigotry or discrimination. Putting America back to work means putting
all Americans back to work. Ending inflation means freeing all Americans from
25 the terror of runaway living costs. All must share in the productive work of this
"new beginning," and all must share in the bounty of a revived economy. With
the idealism and fair play which are the core of our system and our strength, we
can have a strong and prosperous America, at peace with itself and the world.

So, as we begin, let us take inventory. We are a nation that has a government—
30 not the other way around. And this makes us special among the nations of the
earth. Our government has no power except that granted it by the people. It is
time to check and reverse the growth of government, which shows signs of having grown beyond the consent of the governed.

It is my intention to curb the size and influence of the federal establishment
35 and to demand recognition of the distinction between the powers granted to the
federal government and those reserved to the states or to the people. All of us
need to be reminded that the federal government did not create the states; the
states created the federal government.

Now, so there will be no misunderstanding, it's not my intention to do away
40 with government. It is rather to make it work—work with us, not over us; to
stand by our side, not ride on our back. Government can and must provide opportunity, not smother it; foster productivity, not stifle it.

If we look to the answer as to why for so many years we achieved so much,
prospered as no other people on earth, it was because here in this land we un-
45 leashed the energy and individual genius of man to a greater extent than has ever
been done before. Freedom and the dignity of the individual have been more
available and assured here than in any other place on earth. The price for this freedom at times has been high, but we have never been unwilling to pay that price.

It is no coincidence that our present troubles parallel and are proportionate
50 to the intervention and intrusion in our lives that result from unnecessary and
excessive growth of government. It is time for us to realize that we're too great a
nation to limit ourselves to small dreams. We're not, as some would have us believe, doomed to an inevitable decline. I do not believe in a fate that will fall on us
no matter what we do. I do believe in a fate that will fall on us if we do nothing.
55 So, with all the creative energy at our command, let us begin an era of national
renewal. Let us renew our determination, our courage, and our strength. And let
us renew our faith and our hope. . . .

Source: The Public Papers of Ronald Reagan, January 1981

The postwar paradox shaped and defined both the Reagan administration and its legacy. At home the new president committed his administration to curbing the size and influence of the federal government by reducing spending and lightening what he called "our punitive tax burden." But his inability to reconcile the public's fears of encroaching federal power with its demand for government programs produced a massive budget deficit. Abroad Reagan spoke eloquently about the nation's commitment to freedom and liberty, but his administration, abandoning Carter's emphasis on human rights, often supported repressive regimes in the Third World. Finally, Reagan's style and leadership inspired the public imagination and raised expectations of government. By the end of his administration the public was placing even greater demands on government.

The Style and Substance of Ronald Reagan

The inaugural address, with its misty patriotism and unrestrained optimism, was vintage Reagan. Born in Dixon, Illinois, in 1911, Reagan graduated from Eureka College and worked briefly as a radio sports announcer before moving to California and signing a contract with Warner Brothers film studio in 1937. Over the next two decades he appeared in fifty-three movies but won little acclaim as an actor. The one exception was his role as George Gipp, Notre Dame's first all-American football player, in the 1940 classic *Knute Rockne, All American.* "Someday, when things are tough, maybe you can ask the boys to go in there and win just one for the Gipper," he pleads in a moving deathbed scene that brought tears to millions of eyes. As president Reagan would repeatedly invoke this phrase to rally the American people or galvanize the Republican faithful.

It was during the postwar years that Reagan underwent a political conversion from a New Deal Democrat of decidedly leftist leanings to a right-wing conservative. But in his youth, according to biographer Edmund Morris, he sought to become a member of the California branch of the American Communist Party. He suffered rejection, however, because leading figures in the party thought the $200-a-week actor was "a flake." Morris saw the conversion as a process involving both personal and political factors. On the personal side, there were the experiences of a near-fatal illness, the death of a child by Jane Wyman, Wyman's decision to divorce him, and his fading acting career. On the political side, there were his clash with communist elements within the Screen Actors Guild, and the growing belief that Joseph Stalin's Russia represented the same totalitarian threat as Adolf Hitler's Germany.

These overlapping emotional and ideological traumas shook Reagan to the core and forced him back to basic principles, which for him became a rock-ribbed belief in self-reliance and a conviction that government is "them" rather than "us." During the 1950s Reagan became the spokesman for General Electric, traveling everywhere by train because he was afraid to fly, speaking at plants across the country. He emerged from his travels a wealthy man with a practiced modesty, a set speech about limited government, and a muscular anticommunism that would remain the backbone of his message to the American people.

Reagan made his political debut during the 1964 presidential campaign when he delivered a moving tribute to Barry Goldwater. Columnist David Broder described the performance as the "most successful political debut since William Jennings Bryan electrified the 1896 Democratic Convention with his 'Cross of Gold' speech." Like Bryan's appeal for silver coinage, Reagan pitched an economic panacea. He called for the restoration of the supposed message of the nation's "Founding Fathers that outside of its legitimate functions, government does nothing as well or as economically as the private sector of the economy." The speech established Reagan's conservative credentials and launched his successful bid for governor of California in 1966. After two successful terms Reagan was ready for the national stage.

The portrait of Reagan that most often emerges from the memoirs written by members of his administration is of a president who was long on decency and determination and short on intellect. Even one of his favorite speechwriters, Peggy Noonan, who deeply admired the president, described his brain as "barren terrain." The release of his private letters after his death in 2004, however, reveal a far more sophisticated thinker. Over the course of a lifetime, Reagan penned over 5,000 letters. While many were short, sentimental notes to his wife and close friends, many others dealt with complicated public policy questions—arms control, welfare, government regulation, and the deficit. In his own hand, Reagan showed the mix of strong conviction, personal charm, and practical politics that made him so successful.

In Reagan's attempt to use the presidency as Theodore Roosevelt's "bully pulpit," his former career as a professional performer provided immense advantage. Not only did he have an acumen for rousing audiences, but he also could sense how a speech would appear on television. What animated Reagan was a public performance. On the stump as on television, Reagan was a distinctly nonthreatening individual. He never scolded a crowd; his style was always conversational, flavored with humorous and self-deprecating asides. His soft voice made every word fit the natural cadence of his speech. He read smoothly from the teleprompter, without miscue. Each gesture was practiced until it appeared genuine and spontaneous.

With his telegenic features and extensive experience in front of a camera, Reagan was ideally suited for politics in a media age. He appealed to values, invoked themes, and identified with myths that were embraced by most Americans. "With Reagan, facts don't determine the case," remarked the journalist Sydney Blumenthal. "Facts don't make his beliefs true. His beliefs give life to facts, which are parables tailored to have a moral." As biographer Garry Wills pointed out, Reagan's upbeat invocation of a simpler America appealed to millions of Americans who believed the same myths and enjoyed having them affirmed.

The Reagan Agenda

Reagan was going to need all of his charisma and skill if he was to succeed in lifting the nation's spirits in early 1981. The cost of living had increased by more than 12 percent in 1980, unemployment had risen to 7.4 percent, the prime lending rate was at an astonishing 20 percent, and the government was facing a projected budget deficit of $56 billion. The new administration also faced reminders of the nation's vulnerability around the world. Russian troops had swarmed over Afghanistan, moving closer to America's strategic oil supplies in the Middle East. Iranian militants had released the hostages after fourteen months of imprisonment, but relations with the former staunch and strategic ally remained tense. The turmoil took its toll on the nation's sense of self-confidence and eroded the public's faith in the president's ability to solve its problems. "The Presidency," noted *Newsweek,* "has in some measure defeated the last five men who have held it—and has persuaded some of the people who served them that it is in danger of becoming a game nobody can win."

At the outset the Reagan administration concentrated on reviving the slumping economy. The president's economic program consisted of three essential parts. First, embracing the supply-side doctrine of the New Right, Reagan requested a 30 percent reduction in both personal and corporate income taxes over three years. Tax cuts, the administration reasoned, would stimulate the economy by providing incentives for individuals and businesses to work, save, and invest. Second, he planned to cut government spending for domestic social programs. Third, he planned to use a tight monetary policy to squeeze inflation out of the economy. Taken together, these proposals would "revitalize economic growth, renew optimism and confidence and rekindle the nation's entrepreneurial instincts and creativity," Reagan said. "The benefits to the average American will be striking."

But before Reagan could implement his economic program, in late March 1981, a would-be assassin shot and seriously wounded the elderly president. A .22-caliber bullet ricocheted off the Presidential limousine, entered Reagan's chest under his left arm, and collapsed his lung. At the time, aides downplayed the extent of the president's wounds, but he came close to dying in the minutes after the shooting. The president lost more than half his blood, and doctors failed to adequately warm his transfusion plasma during a dramatic struggle to save his life.

Through the ordeal, Reagan showed courage and spirit. As he was wheeled into the operating room, he quipped to his wife, Nancy, "Honey, I forgot to duck." His behavior in adversity magnified his popularity and swayed Congress into accepting his economic plan. An ABC News-Washington Post survey indicated that the president's rating soared 11 points, to 73 per cent, immediately following the assassination attempt. "The bullet meant to kill him," observed *Newsweek,*

Assassination Attempt on President Ronald Reagan   On March 30, 1981, Reagan gave a speech to a building trades conference at the Washington Hilton. Just as he reached his limousine after the speech, 26-year-old John Hinckley Jr. opened fire on the president and his entourage. Of the six bullets Hinckley fired, one hit the president and entered his left lung; one hit Press Secretary James Brady (*third from the left*) in the forehead, permanently paralyzing him; one hit Secret Service agent Timothy McCarthy (*far right*) in the chest; and a fourth struck policeman Thomas Delahanty (*nearest the umbrella*) in the back. In 1982, a jury found Hinckley not guilty by reason of insanity and sentenced him to a mental facility. (© *AP/Wide World Photos*)

"made him a hero instead, floating above the contentions of politics and the vagaries of good news or bad."

In May dispirited Democrats joined Republicans in passing a budget resolution that called for deep cuts in many social programs and increased spending for the military. Casting the debate in stark ideological language, Reagan called on Democrats to support his program; those who did not would be defending the "failed policies of the past." In August Congress approved the administration's massive tax cut, providing for across-the-board reductions of 5 percent the first year and an additional 10 percent in each of the succeeding two years.

It was an impressive legislative achievement that earned Reagan the begrudging respect of his critics. "Mr. Reagan has established his goals faster, communicated a greater sense of economic urgency and come forward with more comprehensive proposals than any new president since the first 100 days of Franklin D. Roosevelt," observed the *New York Times*. In many ways, however, Reagan's economic policy failed to address the contradiction inherent in America's view of government. Since the New Deal Americans had come to expect the benefits of the modern welfare state without recognizing the legitimacy of government power. Reagan used the sense of economic emergency to tap into public disenchantment, but he avoided trimming the politically sensitive, middle-class entitlement programs—social security and Medicare—and instead cut programs that directly benefited the poor, such as food stamps, Aid to Families with Dependent Children, school lunches, housing assistance, and Medicaid.

While the public gave the president credit for pushing his legislative program through Congress, it blamed him for the inevitable slowdown that resulted from the Federal Reserve Board's tight money policies. Beginning in the final months of the Carter Administration, the nation's central bank started raising interest rates in an effort to squeeze inflation out of the economy. By limiting the amount of money in the economy, the Federal Reserve Board incited a recession by making it difficult for businesses to borrow and expand. By 1982 the recession forced some 10 million Americans out of work and the unemployment rate—9.5 percent—stood at its highest rate since 1941. "Main Street U.S.A. is in trouble," said a Senate Democrat looking forward to the 1982 midterm elections, "and they're going to turn to us." The president urged Congress and the American people to "stay the course," predicting that the economy would rebound in 1983. He was right: the gross national product (GNP) increased an impressive 4.3 percent, and unemployment declined to 8 percent.

Shrinking Washington

As a presidential candidate, Ronald Reagan pledged to shrink the scope of federal government by returning greater authority and responsibility to the states. He also pledged to take a tough line with organized labor. Anyone who thought that Reagan's tough talk was just bluster was disabused of that notion in August 1981, when members of the Professional Air Traffic Controllers union illegally went on strike. The president ordered the strikers to return to work in forty-eight hours or lose their jobs. Despite the potential hazards to air safety, he made good on his threat and barred the Federal Aviation Administration from rehiring any of the 11,400 fired controllers. His blunt and decisive action dealt a blow to organized labor, already reeling from declining membership, and emboldened the business community to get tough with unions.

He appointed to his cabinet conservatives determined to loosen federal regulation. His secretary of energy, James Edwards, a dentist and an ex-governor of South Carolina who favored unregulated development of nuclear power, planned to eliminate his own department. Secretary of Labor Raymond Donovan was a private construction contractor with few links to organized labor and an advocate of the elimination of several of the labor movement's most cherished federal work-safety regulations.

The most controversial of Reagan's administrators was Secretary of the Interior James G. Watt. Watt believed that after twenty-five years of federal land management it was time to return the use of government land to the public through the deregulation of natural resources. In his first official act as secretary he opened up California's coastline to offshore oil drilling and called a halt to future acquisitions of land for national parks. Under Watt's leadership the Interior Department opened federal lands to coal and timber production, narrowed the scope of the wilderness preserves, and sought to make 1 million offshore acres with oil potential available for drilling. Watt's policies and provocative public statements kept him in the middle of controversy until he finally resigned in 1983.

The turbulent history of the savings-and-loan (S&L) industry during the 1980s exemplified the dangers of the Reagan passion for deregulation. Since the depression, S&Ls (called thrifts) had been restricted to using investors' money for low-risk mortgage lending, while banks could offer checking accounts, trust services, and commercial and consumer loans. When interest rates soared in the 1970s, money bled out of the S&Ls and into higher-yielding money market accounts. Conservatives, arguing that deregulation was the key to saving the S&Ls and reviving the banking industry, loosened the rules governing S&L investments at the same time that they increased federal insurance on S&L deposits from $20,000 to $100,000. Flush with money from investors trying to turn a quick profit, many S&Ls made risky loans on malls, apartment complexes, and office towers. Opportunists such as Charles Keating, owner of Lincoln Savings, turned their thrifts into giant casinos, using federally insured deposits to bet on high-risk corporate takeovers and junk bonds. It was a game of blackjack that only the consumers could lose.

Instead of saving the S&Ls, the legislation provided thrift owners with an incentive to engage in high-risk activity. When regional economic conditions failed to meet expectations, hundreds of thrifts declared bankruptcy and turned to the Federal Savings and Loan Insurance Corporation (FSLIC) to bail them and their investors out. The rising number of failed thrifts ultimately resulted in the insolvency of FSLIC in 1986. Faced with a possible economic disaster, Congress responded in 1989 by creating the Resolution Trust Corporation. Eighty-one percent of the bailout costs fell to American taxpayers, who by 1995 had paid $123.8 billion.

Reagan Justice

As president, Reagan promised to appoint judges concerned with "protecting the rights of law-abiding citizens," defending "traditional values and the sanctity of human life," and maintaining "judicial restraint." Conservatives welcomed Reagan's efforts to realign the Supreme Court. In 1981 he appointed conservative Sandra Day O'Connor of Arizona as the first woman to serve on the high court.

When Chief Justice Warren Burger retired in 1986, Reagan elevated William Rehnquist, a Nixon appointee, to the chief justiceship and named to the vacancy the conservative Antonin Scalia, a federal judge who had taught at the University of Chicago Law School. Scalia soon emerged as a rigid advocate of presidential power.

In 1988, Reagan had sought to replace centrist Louis Powell with the conservative Robert Bork, but a coalition of civil rights and women's groups helped defeat the nomination. The seat was eventually filled by Anthony Kennedy, a federal appeals court judge from California.

The Reagan appointments tipped the balance of power on the Court, providing conservatives with a majority in many controversial decisions. Deciding most major cases by 5–4 margins, the Court ruled that under some circumstances police could submit as evidence confessions coerced from suspected criminals, and it curtailed the rights of immigrants to claim political asylum. In their most significant civil rights ruling (*Wards Cove* v. *Atonio*, 1987), the justices shifted the burden of proof from those accused of practicing discrimination to its victims. But the justices proved they were not always predictable. Justice O'Connor would occasionally side with the moderates in important cases. To the dismay of many conservatives the Court decided that burning the American flag was political speech protected by the Constitution.

The 1984 Presidential Campaign

The improving economy of 1983–84 revived Ronald Reagan's popularity. With polls showing the president enjoying a commanding lead against any potential Democratic opponent, many Republican strategists hoped for an electoral landslide that would herald Republican control of the White House for the rest of the century. The Reagan campaign strategy was simple: celebrate the president's identification with peace and prosperity, avoid a debate over specific issues, and identify his Democratic opponent with the "failed policies" of the Carter administration (high taxes, soaring inflation, and vacillating world leadership). Grand expectations were back in style.

Reagan's challenger, former Vice President Walter Mondale, had won his party's nomination after a bruising primary fight against civil-rights activist Jesse Jackson and Colorado Senator Gary Hart. Jackson, a former coworker of Martin Luther King, became the first African American to win substantial support in his bid to receive a major-party nomination. Mondale's challenge was to arouse the enthusiasm of the party's traditional constituencies—blacks, Jews, union members, urban residents—while pulling back into the party the "Reagan Democrats," the white middle class that had defected to the Republicans. As a first step in executing his strategy, Mondale tried to demonstrate that he was capable of bold leadership by selecting a woman vice-presidential candidate, former Congresswoman Geraldine Ferraro of New York City. A few weeks later, in his acceptance speech at the Democratic National Convention, Mondale tried to prove he was fiscally responsible by proposing to raise taxes to help reduce the deficit.

PRIMARY SOURCE

13.2 | *1984 Democratic Convention Speech*
MARIO CUOMO

New York Governor Mario Cuomo kicked off the Democratic convention with a fiery keynote address that contrasted Democratic and Republican values. He used the metaphor of "two cities" to capture the challenges confronting America and to highlight the different approaches between the two major parties.

Ten days ago, President Reagan admitted that although some people in this country seemed to be doing well nowadays, others were unhappy, even worried, about themselves, their families, and their futures. The President said that he didn't understand that fear. He said, "Why, this country is a shining city on a
5   hill." And the President is right. In many ways we are a shining city on a hill.

But the hard truth is that not everyone is sharing in this city's splendor and glory. A shining city is perhaps all the President sees from the portico of the White House and the veranda of his ranch, where everyone seems to be doing well. But there's another city; there's another part to the shining city; the part
10   where some people can't pay their mortgages, and most young people can't afford one; where students can't afford the education they need, and middle-class parents watch the dreams they hold for their children evaporate.

In this part of the city there are more poor than ever, more families in trouble, more and more people who need help but can't find it. Even worse: There are el-
15   derly people who tremble in the basements of the houses there. And there are people who sleep in the city streets, in the gutter, where the glitter doesn't show. There are ghettos where thousands of young people, without a job or an education, give their lives away to drug dealers every day. There is despair, Mr. President, in the faces that you don't see, in the places that you don't visit in your shining city.
20   In fact, Mr. President, this is a nation—Mr. President you ought to know that this nation is more a "Tale of Two Cities" than it is just a "Shining City on a Hill."

Maybe, maybe, Mr. President, if you visited some more places; maybe if you went to Appalachia where some people still live in sheds; maybe if you went to Lackawanna where thousands of unemployed steel workers wonder why we subsidized foreign
25   steel. Maybe—Maybe, Mr. President, if you stopped in at a shelter in Chicago and spoke to the homeless there; maybe, Mr. President, if you asked a woman who had

been denied the help she needed to feed her children because you said you needed the money for a tax break for a millionaire or for a missile we couldn't afford to use.

30 Maybe—Maybe, Mr. President. But I'm afraid not. Because the truth is, ladies and gentlemen, that this is how we were warned it would be. President Reagan told us from the very beginning that he believed in a kind of social Darwinism. Survival of the fittest. "Government can't do everything," we were told, so it should settle for taking care of the strong and hope that economic ambition and charity will do the rest. Make the rich richer, and what falls from the table will be enough for the middle

35 class and those who are trying desperately to work their way into the middle class.

You know, the Republicans called it "trickle-down" when Hoover tried it. Now they call it "supply side." But it's the same shining city for those relative few who are lucky enough to live in its good neighborhoods. But for the people who are excluded, for the people who are locked out, all they can do is stare from a

40 distance at that city's glimmering towers.

It's an old story. It's as old as our history. The difference between Democrats and Republicans has always been measured in courage and confidence. The Republicans—the Republicans believe that the wagon train will not make it to the frontier unless some of the old, some of the young, some of the weak are

45 left behind by the side of the trail. "The strong"—"The strong," they tell us, "will inherit the land."

We Democrats believe in something else. We Democrats believe that we can make it all the way with the whole family intact, and we have more than once. Ever since Franklin Roosevelt lifted himself from his wheelchair to lift this nation from

50 its knees—wagon train after wagon train—to new frontiers of education, housing, peace; the whole family aboard, constantly reaching out to extend and enlarge that family; lifting them up into the wagon on the way; blacks and Hispanics, and people of every ethnic group, and native Americans—all those struggling to build their families and claim some small share of America. For nearly 50 years we car-

55 ried them all to new levels of comfort, and security, and dignity, even affluence. And remember this, some of us in this room today are here only because this nation had that kind of confidence. And it would be wrong to forget that.

Source: Public Papers of Mario Cuomo, New York State Library   ■ ■ ■

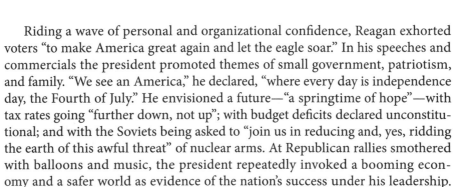

Riding a wave of personal and organizational confidence, Reagan exhorted voters "to make America great again and let the eagle soar." In his speeches and commercials the president promoted themes of small government, patriotism, and family. "We see an America," he declared, "where every day is independence day, the Fourth of July." He envisioned a future—"a springtime of hope"—with tax rates going "further down, not up"; with budget deficits declared unconstitutional; and with the Soviets being asked to "join us in reducing and, yes, ridding the earth of this awful threat" of nuclear arms. At Republican rallies smothered with balloons and music, the president repeatedly invoked a booming economy and a safer world as evidence of the nation's success under his leadership.

"The essence of the Ronald Reagan campaign," ABC reporter Sam Donaldson observed, "is a never-ending string of spectacular picture stories created for television and designed to place the president in the midst of wildly cheering, patriotic Americans. . . . God, patriotism, and Ronald Reagan, that's the essence this campaign is trying to project."

On election day voters returned Reagan to office with 58.8 percent of the vote and the biggest electoral college vote total in history—525. Mondale received 40.6 percent (37,577,185) of the popular vote and 13 electoral votes. Reagan swept the entire nation except for Minnesota and the District of Columbia. Rarely had America seen so all-encompassing a landslide. In every region, in every age group, in virtually every demographic slice of a heterogeneous nation, the message was clear: "Four More Years." Elderly voters, supposedly beset with fears about the dismantling of social security, gave 61 percent of their votes to the president. Women, for whom Geraldine Ferraro was portrayed as an irresistible symbol, backed Reagan by a 10-point margin. Voters under twenty-five gave 59 percent of their votes to the oldest president ever. The election, observed *Time* magazine, represented a collective "Thank You" to "a president who had made the country feel good about itself."

Reagan and the Cold War

Reinvigorating the traditional conviction that the United States had a mission to spread American values around the globe, the Reagan administration came to office determined to reassert American power. A classic Cold Warrior, Reagan saw the Soviets at the heart of every international dispute, from revolution in Central America to international terrorism in the Middle East. While the public generally applauded the president's tough rhetoric, it divided on the wisdom of his specific policies. Like previous postwar presidents, Reagan confronted the paradox of American power: public expectations of American influence often clashed with the reality of international power. Reagan proclaimed the United States a beacon of liberty and freedom around the world, but his excessive fear of communism led the administration to support repressive regimes that shared its opposition to Soviet power.

Most of the president's national security and foreign policy advisers— Secretary of State Alexander Haig, his successor George Shultz, Secretary of Defense Caspar Weinberger, National Security Adviser Richard Allen, and Ambassador to the United Nations Jeane Kirkpatrick—shared his exaggerated fear of Soviet power and his determination to assert American military might. To thwart the Soviets, Reagan called for the largest and most expensive peacetime military buildup in American history. "Defense is not a budget item," Ronald Reagan told his staff; "you spend what you need." Along with accelerating the development of existing weapons systems, both nuclear and conventional, the administration reincarnated programs canceled under Carter, including the trouble-plagued B-1 bomber and the controversial neutron bomb. By 1985 the Pentagon was spending more than $28 million every hour, seven days a week. Excluding veterans' affairs, the defense budget surged from $157 billion in 1981 to $273 billion in 1986. Corrected for inflation, the increases averaged nearly 7 percent a year.

While strengthening America's strategic arsenal, Reagan declared that the United States stood ready to support anticommunist regimes anywhere in the world. In the Middle East, the Philippines, Chile, South Korea, and Angola, the Reagan administration supported repressive governments if they stood strongly against communism. This approach to world politics was especially clear with regard to South Africa, where the system of apartheid, which brutally excluded nonwhites from basic rights, threatened to provoke civil war. Committed to working with the South African whites-only government, the administration abandoned Carter's efforts to force change and adopted a policy known as "constructive engagement." Reagan resisted all calls by liberal and human rights groups to join other countries in coercing the government of South Africa into dismantling apartheid. South Africa, he believed, was a bulwark against the spread of communism. Congress repudiated his policy in 1986, demanding that Reagan take bold steps, including the imposition of economic sanctions, against the South African government.

The New Arms Race

Reagan entered office with a deep-seated distaste for arms control. He was convinced that the United States had disarmed during the 1970s while the USSR had gained nuclear superiority. He planned to subject arms control to a period of "benign neglect" while the United States went about the business of "rearming."

Accordingly, Reagan took a tough position in negotiations with the Soviets. His hard-line positions angered the Kremlin, who grew increasingly distrustful of Reagan and his leading advisers. U.S.–Soviet relations were already tense when in September 1983, a Soviet interceptor aircraft shot down a Korean Airlines plane after it strayed into Soviet airspace on its flight from Anchorage to Seoul, killing all 269 on board. American intelligence suggested the tragedy was the result of confusion and incompetence on the part of Soviet military officials who believed the civilian airliner was a spy plane, but Reagan used the incident to bolster his contention that the USSR was an "evil empire." Moscow, angered by Reagan's moralistic condemnation and frustrated with the stalemate on arms control, feared the United States was preparing for war. For the first time since the Cuban missile crisis, Moscow sent a *Molinya* (Flash) message to its stations in Western capitals, telling its agents to secure staff and premises against imminent attack. "The international situation," declared Politburo member Grigory Romanov, "is white hot, thoroughly white hot."

Reagan's opposition to arms control and his tough Cold War rhetoric produced an unintended consequence: it revived the nascent peace movement. A nationwide poll in the spring of 1982 showed that 57 percent of the respondents favored an immediate freeze on the testing, production, and deployment of nuclear weapons.

The threat of global annihilation also seeped into the realm of popular culture. Americans crowded into movie theaters in 1983 to watch *War Games,* which showed a teenage computer hacker accidentally launching a nuclear war. (Computer: "Shall we play a game?" Teenager: "Let's play Thermonuclear War.") In 1984 over 100 million people anxiously watched a docudrama, *The Day After,* that portrayed the effects of nuclear war on Kansas.

Reagan tried to defuse the growing calls for arms limitation by proposing a space-based antiballistic-missile defensive shield that would use laser beams to destroy incoming missiles. Nicknamed "Star Wars" by the media, the Strategic Defense Initiative (SDI) reflected the administration's belief that improbable technological solutions could solve complex political problems. The administration's top military scientist, however, pointed out that the defensive system could be overcome by Soviet weapons unless it was coupled with an offensive arms control agreement. "With unconstrained proliferation" of Soviet warheads, he said, "no defensive system will work." Despite the criticism, the administration pushed forward, spending $17 billion on SDI between 1983 and 1989.

Ronnie and Mikhail

By 1984, however, a number of developments were pushing Moscow and Washington closer together. Claiming that the massive military buildup during his first three years in office allowed the United States to negotiate from a position of strength, Reagan called for a "constructive working relationship" with the Kremlin. At the same time, a new leader, who seemed readier than his predecessors to renew détente with the United States, assumed leadership in the Soviet Union. Mikhail Gorbachev, at fifty-four the youngest head of the Soviet Communist Party since Joseph Stalin, came to power determined to reform Soviet society. At home he advocated perestroika, or "restructuring," to relax government economic and social control. Abroad he advocated a new policy of glasnost, or "openness."

Hoping to avoid an expensive arms race, Gorbachev declared a moratorium on deployment of medium-range missiles in Europe and asked the United States to do the same. He began shifting government rubles away from the military, publicly assailed the failures of the socialist economy, and promised economic and political reform. For the rest of his tenure he made news practically every few months with another bold reform in the areas of perestroika, glasnost, and arms control. He made it clear he wanted out of Afghanistan, his country's Vietnam-like quagmire.

In a move that surprised liberals and angered conservatives, Reagan welcomed the Soviet initiatives and now expressed his support for new arms reductions talks. The result of these developments was a series of four Reagan-Gorbachev summits. In 1986 the two leaders met at Reykjavik, Iceland, and agreed on a first step toward cutting strategic nuclear forces in half. Gorbachev wanted to go further, calling for the complete elimination of all nuclear weapons, but he insisted that the United States also abandon SDI, something Reagan refused to do.

Reagan in Moscow   The thawing of Cold War tensions between the United States and the Soviet Union was evident in the signing of the Intermediate Nuclear Forces Treaty in December 1987, which eliminated intermediate-range nuclear missiles. This goodwill between the nations grew with Reagan's historic visit to Moscow in May 1988. Reagan and Mikhail Gorbachev toured Red Square and developed a cordial personal relationship. *(© AP/Wide World Photos)*

The following year the United States and the Soviet Union agreed to the INF treaty, which for the first time called for the destruction of existing missiles and allowed for onsite inspections to verify compliance. In December Gorbachev traveled to Washington to sign the treaty in a warm ceremony with Reagan. While in the United States, the Soviet leader announced a unilateral reduction in Soviet military forces.

By the time Reagan left office, he and his counterpart in the Kremlin had toasted each other as "Ronnie and Mikhail." Opinion polls reported Americans feeling friendlier toward the Soviet Union than at any time since the end of World War II. When a reporter asked Reagan in 1987 if he still thought the Soviet Union was an evil empire, he responded, "No, I was talking about another time, another era."

The Cold War in Central America

Before and during glasnost, Reagan's Cold War views shaped his approach to insurgencies in Latin America. Reagan believed Moscow was to blame for most of the trouble. For Reagan and his advisors, any leftist victory in Latin America would threaten the possibility of another Cuba that could serve as a staging ground for Soviet expansion in the Western hemisphere. The administration also worried that communist gains could produce a flood of political refugees who would pour over the U.S. border.

When a coalition of leftist guerrillas attempted to topple the government of El Salvador, Reagan provided the government with nearly five billion dollars of military and economic aid. The army used the arms to wage a campaign against civilians suspected of sympathizing with the rebels. In 1984, the moderate Jose Napoleon Duarte took control and opened talks with rebel leaders, but the bloody civil war continued.

In Nicaragua, President Carter had recognized the Marxist-led Sandinistas who overthrew dictator Anastasio Somoza in 1979. Reagan not only reversed Carter's policy but committed the United States to the Sandinistas' overthrow. Under Director William Casey, the CIA in 1982 organized, trained, and financed the contras, a ten-thousand-strong anti-Sandinista guerrilla army based in Honduras and Costa Rica.

In 1983, when a leftist government friendly with Cuba assumed power in the tiny island of Granada, Reagan ordered 6,000 marines to invade the island and install a pro-American government. The administration claimed the invasion was necessary to protect American students living on the island and to stop the construction of an air field that would serve Cuban and Soviet interests. World opinion condemned the invasion, but the successful military operation brought joy and pride to millions of Americans.

Fighting Terrorism

While seeking friendship and trade with Moscow, Washington confronted a new threat from well-organized terrorist groups. The threat of terrorism was greatest in the Middle East where, despite the Israeli–Egyptian treaty, peace proved elusive. In 1983, Israel attacked Palestine Liberation Organization (PLO) strongholds in southern Lebanon. The United States arranged for a withdrawal of both Israeli and PLO troops from Beirut, and sent two thousand marines into the region as part of an international peace-keeping force.

Because of America's close ties to Israel, radical Shiite Muslim groups hated having the marines on their soil. In October 1983, a Shiite terrorist drove a truck loaded with explosives into the lightly guarded U.S. barracks near the Beirut airport. The shattering blast killed 239 marines. Fifty French troops died in a related attack. Reagan responded by withdrawing the remaining marines. The bombing of the U.S. Marine barracks heralded a larger campaign of terror launched by groups linked to the PLO, to Iran's Hezbollah (Party of God), Syria's King Asad, and Libya's ruler, Muammar el-Qaddafi. Terrorists hijacked airplanes, attacked airports across Europe, and kidnapped nine Americans in Beirut.

In June 1985, American television captured the ordeal of the 135 passengers aboard TWA flight 847. Hijacked over Greece, they endured seventeen nightmarish days of captivity. A few months later, in October, PLO agents seized an Italian cruise ship, the *Achille Lauro,* and murdered a wheelchair-bound American passenger. In 1986, when Libyan agents were implicated in the bombing of a Berlin night club frequented by American soldiers, Reagan, calling Qaddafi the "mad dog of the Middle East," ordered a retaliatory air attack. The raid killed an estimated 37 Libyans, including Qaddafi's infant daughter.

Americans applauded the flexing of U.S. military muscle, but the cycle of terrorism escalated. In December 1988, a Pan Am jet en route from London to New York crashed near Lockerbie, Scotland, killing all 259 aboard, including numerous Americans. Investigators found evidence of a bomb hidden in the baggage section.

Iran-Contra Scandal

Having come to office on a groundswell of American outrage over the taking of American hostages, Reagan proudly emphasized his refusal to deal with terrorists.

While talking tough, Reagan was negotiating behind the scenes with Iran to secure the release of American hostages. The president approved a plan hatched by his National Security Advisor Robert McFarlane and CIA head William Casey to try and curry favor with the radical regime in Iran by selling them high-tech U.S. arms which they needed in their war against Iraq. The plot had an added twist: the United States overcharged Iran for the weapons and diverted the profits to fund the contras in Nicaragua. There was one big problem with the scheme—it was in clear violation of the Boland amendment, which expressly forbade aiding the contras.

The operation was carried out by NSC aide Oliver North, who used various middlemen to funnel millions of dollars illegally to the contras. The flow of money continued through the early autumn of 1986, when the plan began to unravel. On October 5, Nicaraguan soldiers shot down a U.S. cargo plane. The sole surviving crew member identified himself as a member of the CIA. A month later a Lebanese news magazine reported America's secret arms sales to Iran. Attorney General Edwin Meese announced on November 25 that his investigation had shown that some of the proceeds of arms sales to Iran had gone to the contras. While the administration denied that it had violated its own policy by offering incentives for the release of the hostages, Reagan appointed a three-person commission, led by former Senator John Tower, to look into the matter. The Tower Commission implicated several individuals in a covert operation to funnel money to the contras, but found no evidence of the president's culpability. However, they did acknowledge that Reagan's lack of direct management over his national security staff had allowed the diversion of funds to occur.

PRIMARY SOURCE

13.3 | *Iran-Contra Testimony*
OLIVER NORTH

In the summer of 1987 a joint congressional committee investigated the selling of weapons to Iran, despite the U.S. embargo, as well as the siphoning of these funds to aid the contras of Nicaragua. In July 1987, the person most directly involved in the deals, Lieutenant Colonel Oliver "Ollie" North, testified before the committee and admitted that such dealings had occurred.

It is also difficult to comprehend that my work at the NSC [National Security Council]—all of which was approved and carried out in the best interests of our country—has led to two massive parallel investigations staffed by over 200 people. It is mind-boggling to me that one of those investigations is criminal and
5   that some here have attempted to criminalize policy differences between coequal branches of government and the executive's conduct of foreign affairs.

I believe it is inevitable that the Congress will in the end blame the executive branch, but I suggest to you that it is the Congress which must accept at

least some of the blame in the Nicaraguan freedom fighters matter. Plain and
10 simple, the Congress is to blame because of the fickle, vacillating, unpredictable,
on-again, off-again policy toward the Nicaraguan Democratic Resistance—the
so-called Contras. I do not believe that the support of the Nicaraguan freedom
fighters can be treated as the passage of a budget. I suppose that if the budget
doesn't get passed on time again this year, it will be inevitably another extension
15 of another month or two. But the Contras, the Nicaraguan freedom fighters, are
people—living, breathing young men and women who have had to suffer a desperate struggle for liberty with sporadic and confusing support from the United
States of America.

Armies need food and consistent help. They need a flow of money, of arms,
20 clothing, and medical supplies. The Congress of the United States left soldiers
in the field unsupported and vulnerable to their communist enemies. When the
executive branch did everything possible within the law to prevent them from
being wiped out by Moscow's surrogates in Havana and Managua, you then had
this investigation to blame the problem on the executive branch. It does not make
25 sense to me.

In my opinion, these hearings have caused serious damage to our national
interest. Our adversaries laugh at us and our friends recoil in horror. I suppose it
would be one thing if the intelligence committees wanted to hear all this in private and thereafter pass laws which in the view of Congress make for better poli-
30 cies or better functioning government. But to hold them publicly for the whole
world to see strikes me as very harmful. Not only does it embarrass our friends
and allies with whom we have worked, many of whom have helped us in various
programs, but must also make them very wary of helping us again. . . .

Source: From Oliver North's Statement before a joint session of the Senate Select Committee on
Secret Military Assistance to Iran and the Nicaraguan Opposition and House Select Committee
to Investigate Covert Arms Transactions with Iran, July 9, 1987. ■ ■ ■

The scandal, which consumed Reagan's final two years in office, damaged
the president's reputation as an effective leader. A congressional committee
charged that the president had abdicated his "moral and legal responsibility
to take care that the laws be faithfully executed," but stopped short of accusing
him of intentionally breaking the law. Far more damaging was the report of
independent counsel Lawrence E. Walsh, who concluded that the White House
had successfully constructed a "firewall" to protect the president, allowing
lower-level officials—North along with NSC officials Robert McFarlane and John
Poindexter—to take the blame for an illegal policy approved by the president.
Walsh, however, never found conclusive evidence that linked Reagan directly to
the illegal activities. And although troubled by the Iran-contra affair, the public,
as with other scandals that plagued the Reagan administration, did not blame
the president himself. Polls showed declining support for the administration and
renewed questions about the president's casual leadership style, but Reagan remained immensely popular when he left office.

The Reagan Legacy

At a farewell party at the White House in January 1989, Reagan recited the data showing how much the country and the world had changed for the better during the 1980s, and he concluded, "All in all, I must say, not bad for a fellow who couldn't get his facts straight and worked four hours a day." Supporters argued that Reagan's economic policies produced a remarkable period of sustained growth. Between 1983 and 1990 unemployment fell to 5.2 percent, the economy grew by 33 percent, 19 million new jobs were created, and inflation remained stable at less than 4 percent. Conservatives spoke proudly of the "Reagan Revolution," which cut back the size of government, slashed taxes, and promoted economic growth.

Critics concede that Reagan steered public policy in a different direction, but they tend to focus on the underside of the administration's policies. His domestic policies imposed undue hardship on the poor and had little to do with the economic recovery. His income-tax cut proved illusory for all except the wealthiest Americans. By the end of Reagan's administration the average family was actually paying more in taxes than in 1980, thanks in large part to a sharp increase in social security taxes and hikes in state and local taxes. The GNP grew an average of 2.6 percent annually under Reagan, compared with 3 percent under Carter and an average of 3.4 percent under the previous four presidents.

The same polarized debate shapes discussion of Reagan's foreign policy. Reagan's supporters contend that his tough rhetoric and increased military spending not only pushed the Soviets to the bargaining table, but also forced them to accept American terms. Reagan's Star Wars proposal, by forcing the Russians to face the prospect of a crippling arms race, hastened the demise of the Soviet system. Critics challenge the notion that Reagan ended the Cold War: the Soviet Union, they assert, collapsed under the weight of America's bipartisan policy of containment, dating back to the Truman Doctrine and the Marshall Plan, and under the weight of communism's inherent instability.

It is difficult to reach conclusive answers on these questions. Until historians know more about the inner workings of Kremlin decision makers, it will be impossible to assess all the forces that contributed to Moscow's new openness to the West. It is fair to say, however, that Reagan was not as ideological as critics feared or as conservatives hoped. Certainly Reagan's strident anti-Soviet rhetoric and massive arms buildup intensified Cold War tensions. At the same time his lofty language of individual freedom inspired pro-democracy activists in Eastern Europe and helped expedite the breakup of the Soviet Empire. While many of his policies, especially those toward Latin America, overestimated Soviet influence and underplayed the role of local forces, Reagan also appreciated the need to soften his hard line with the Soviets by embracing Gorbachev and the new Soviet glasnost.

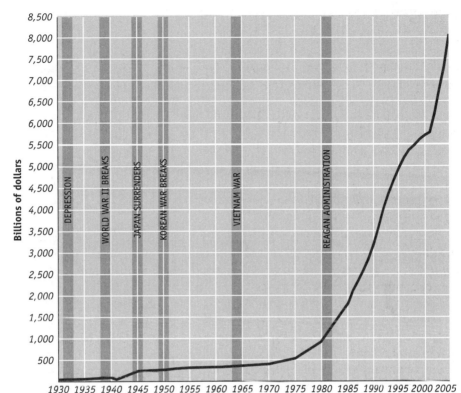

The National Debt, 1930–2005 Ending a trend of static or slightly rising national debt, the Reagan era saw the deficit more than triple from $908 billion in 1980 to $2.7 trillion at the end of 1989 as Congress and the president refused to raise taxes or cut popular programs. (*Sources:* Historical Statistics of the United States *and* Statistical Abstract of the United States, *relevant years; Council of Economic Advisors,* Economic Indicators)

While it is too early to reach a full assessment of Reagan's legacy, it is clear that he had a profound impact on American politics. Perhaps more than any political leader since Franklin Roosevelt, Reagan changed the nature of political debate in America and altered the competition between the two major parties. He pushed conservative ideas about smaller government and less regulation to the forefront of American politics. He energized the conservative movement and solidified its ties to the Republican party. At the same time, Reagan's skillful use of television changed the style of presidential leadership. Television forced politicians to articulate themes that could appeal to a broad spectrum of the electorate at the same time that it personalized politics by allowing leaders to bypass parties and build a direct relationship with voters. President Reagan was a master craftsman of the new technology. Leaving the details of governing to aides, Reagan concentrated on the symbolic aspects of his presidency. Using television to emphasize resilient themes of self-help, individualism, and limited government, he rarely discussed specific policies.

While Reagan restored respect for the presidency, he heightened expectations of what it could accomplish. Reagan's media savvy helped boost his personal popularity to record levels. Polls showed his approval rating at 68 percent in his final month in office—the highest ever recorded for a departing president. Reagan's appeal rubbed off on the rest of Washington. In 1980 only 22 percent of people polled said they could trust government "most of the time." After eight years of Republican rule the percentage had increased to 38 percent, and nearly 50 percent said they favored increased government spending. Reagan came to office preaching a message of limited government and individual initiative. The paradox was that his success over the next eight years increased public faith in government at the same time that his massive deficits crippled Washington's ability to respond to demands for greater services. It would be left to Reagan's successors to reconcile the contradiction.

SELECTED READINGS

▍ Gil Troy offers balanced accounts of the Reagan presidency in *Morning in America* (2005) and *The Reagan Revolution* (2009). Also valuable are Richard Reeves, *President Reagan* (2006) and Michael Schaller's *Ronald Reagan* (2010). *The Reagan Diaries* (2007), edited by Douglas Brinkley, provide insight into Reagan's thinking. Sean Wilentz tried to put Reagan and his presidency into historical perspective in *The Age of Reagan* (2008). Will Bunch provides insight and a critical look at the battle over Reagan's legacy in *Tear Down This Myth* (2009). In *Dutch* (1999), Edmund Morris, Reagan's authorized biographer, produces an idiosyncratic but useful portrait of the president. Lou Cannon's *President Reagan: The Role of a Lifetime* (rev. ed., 2000) stresses the theatricality in Reagan's presidency. For a vigorous conservative defense of Reagan and his presidency see two books by Steven F. Hayward: *The Age of Reagan: The Fall of the Old Liberal Order* (2001), and *The Age of Reagan: The Conservative Counterrevolution* (2010).

▍ Charles Murray outlines the major economic theories that informed Reagan's economic and social policies in *Losing Ground* (2nd ed., 1995). William Greider takes the Reagan economists to task in *The Education of David Stockman and Other Americans* (1982). Del Quentin Wilber provides a vivid account of the attempted assassination in *Rawhide Down* (2011).

▍ Richard Melanson argues in *Reconstructing Consensus* (1991) that the overarching foreign-policy goal of the Reagan administration was to rebuild the Cold War consensus destroyed during the Vietnam War. In *Reagan's War* (2002), Peter Schweizer argues that Reagan transformed American foreign policy by rejecting the defensive strategy of the Cold War. In *Buildup* (1992), Daniel Wirls stresses the importance of domestic politics in Reagan's foreign policy, and Frances Fitzgerald explains how Reagan spent billions for

Star Wars with public approval in *Way Out There in the Blue* (2000). Strobe Talbott surveys the escalation of the arms race in *Deadly Gambit* (1984). Jack Matlock provides an insider account of evolving U.S.–Soviet relations in *Reagan and Gorbachev* (2004).

▌ Broad introductions to Reagan's Central American policies include Walter LaFeber's *Inevitable Revolutions* (rev. ed., 1993); Kenneth Coleman and George Herring's *The Central American Crisis* (1985); and Cynthia Arnson's *Crossroads* (2nd ed., 1994). Robert Pastor surveys America's relations with Nicaragua in *Condemned to Repetition* (1987). David C. Wills examines Reagan's approach to terrorist threats in *The First War on Terrorism* (2004). The Nicaraguan operation fed directly into the Iran-contra scandal, which is covered by Bob Woodward's *Veil: The Secret Wars of the CIA* (1987).

14 Culture and Consumerism: 1980–1992

J erry Falwell, founder of the Moral Majority, believed that God instructed him to bring together "the good people of America" in a Christian crusade against pornography, sex education, and abortion. Abandoning traditional fundamentalist disdain for mainstream politics, Falwell decided in the late 1970s that it was no longer possible for Christians to stay out of politics. To spread the word, Falwell combined old-time religion with the most sophisticated computer technology, targeting potential contributors and lobbying for political candidates who shared his conservative views. "Get them saved, baptized, and registered," Falwell advised his ministerial colleagues.

Abandoning any pretense of nonpartisanship, Falwell became a regular visitor at the Reagan White House, prayed at Republican meetings, and helped draft the party's 1984 platform. He called Ronald Reagan and Vice President George Bush "God's chosen instrument for the regeneration of the country." With access to Washington, religious fundamentalists and other conservatives were strategically positioned to wage a war against social liberalism and secular humanism: to restore the moral authority of the family, reestablish appropriate gender roles, and reassert American nationalism.

The legacy of the 1960s was at the heart of the culture wars of the 1980s. The social turmoil of the 1960s exposed the tension between the nation's postwar faith in economic growth and its fidelity to traditional values. But prosperity helped produce a new middle class that challenged the existing morality, placing a new emphasis on self-fulfillment and personal gratification. The conflict between individual expression and moral righteousness, which had deep roots in the nation's past, found expression in the 1980s in battles over family values, abortion, gay rights, and immigration restriction. At the heart of the conflict were competing views of the meaning of American identity. Conservatives stressed cultural nationalism, emphasizing the existence of a singular American cultural tradition and a shared national identity. Many liberals, however, spoke a language of cultural diversity, highlighting the persistence of unique traditions, underscoring the importance of difference, and articulating a vision of a multicultural America.

While Americans engaged in an angry culture war over issues such as abortion, gay rights, and immigration, they formed a broad consensus in support of a new culture of consumerism. Everyone from the president to Hollywood producers to religious preachers praised the healing power of prosperity. After the slow-growing 1970s, expectations ran high that economic growth would end the scourge of poverty, guarantee opportunity to all citizens, and help bring Americans closer together. Once again, however, expectations clashed with social realities. In a classic example of the American paradox, the "culture of greed" that pervaded the decade produced a greater gap between rich and poor, increased the number of homeless and poor, and widened the racial divide in America.

PRIMARY SOURCE

14.1 | *Return to Traditional Religious Values*
JERRY FALWELL

The Reverend Jerry Falwell, recognizing the anxieties felt by many Americans who opposed the political and social changes of the 1960s and 1970s, founded the Moral Majority in 1979. In his 1980 work, *Listen, America!*, Falwell encouraged citizens to help him in his quest to return America to its moral traditions by transforming the political climate.

W e must reverse the trend America finds herself in today. Young people between the ages of twenty-five and forty have been born and reared in a different world than Americans of years past. The television set has been their primary baby-sitter. From the television set they have learned situation ethics
5 and immorality—they have learned a loss of respect for human life. They have learned to disrespect the family as God has established it. They have been educated in a public-school system that is permeated with secular humanism. They have been taught that the Bible is just another book of literature. They have been taught that there are no absolutes in our world today. They have been introduced
10 to the drug culture. They have been reared by the family and by the public school in a society that is greatly void of discipline and character-building. These same young people have been reared under the influence of a government that has taught them socialism and welfarism. They have been taught to believe that the world owes them a living whether they work or not.
15 I believe that America was built on integrity, on faith in God, and on hard work. I do not believe that anyone has ever been successful in life without being willing to add that last ingredient—diligence or hard work. We now have second- and third-generation welfare recipients. Welfare is not always wrong. There are those who do need welfare, but we have reared a generation that understands
20 neither the dignity nor the importance of work. . . .
There is no excuse for what is happening in our country. We must, from the highest office in the land right down to the shoe shine boy in the airport, have a return to biblical basics. If the Congress of our United States will take its stand on that which is right and wrong, and if our President, our judiciary system, and
25 our state and local leaders will take their stand on holy living, we can turn this country around.
I personally feel that the home and the family are still held in reverence by the vast majority of the American public. I believe there is still a vast number of Americans who love their country, are patriotic, and are willing to sacrifice for
30 her. I remember that time when it was positive to be patriotic, and as far as I am concerned, it still is. . . .
I believe that Americans want to see this country come back to basics, back to values, back to biblical morality, back to sensibility, and back to patriotism. Americans are looking for leadership and guidance. It is fair to ask the question,
35 "If 84 percent of the American people still believe in morality, why is America having such internal problems?" We must look for the answer to the highest places in every level of government. We have a lack of leadership in America. But Americans have been lax in voting in and out of office the right and the wrong people.
40 My responsibility as a preacher of the Gospel is one of influence, not of control, and that is the responsibility of each individual citizen. Through the ballot box Americans must provide for strong moral leadership at every level. If our

country will get back on the track in sensibility and moral sanity, the crises that I have herein mentioned will work out in the course of time and with God's
45 blessings.

It is now time to take a stand on certain moral issues, and we can only stand if we have leaders. We must stand against the Equal Rights Amendment, the feminist revolution, and the homosexual revolution. We must have a revival in this country. . . .
50 As a preacher of the Gospel, I not only believe in prayer and preaching, I also believe in good citizenship. If a labor union in America has the right to organize and improve its working conditions, then I believe that the churches and the pastors, the priests, and the rabbis of America have a responsibility, not just the right, to see to it that the moral climate and conscience of Americans is such that
55 this nation can be healed inwardly. If it is healed inwardly, then it will heal itself outwardly. . . .

The hope of reversing the trends of decay in our republic now lies with the Christian public in America. We cannot expect help from the liberals. They certainly are not going to call our nation back to righteousness and neither are the
60 pornographers, the smut peddlers, and those who are corrupting our youth. Moral Americans must be willing to put their reputations, their fortunes, and their very lives on the line for this great nation of ours. Would that we had the courage of our forefathers who knew the great responsibility that freedom carries with it. . . .
65 Our Founding Fathers separated church and state in function, but never intended to establish a government void of God. As is evidenced by our Constitution, good people in America must exert an influence and provide a conscience and climate of morality in which it is difficult to go wrong, not difficult for people to go right in America.
70 Americans must no longer linger in ignorance and apathy. We cannot be silent about the sins that are destroying this nation. The choice is ours. We must turn America around or prepare for inevitable destruction. I am listening to the sounds that threaten to take away our liberties in America. And I have listened to God's admonitions and His direction—the only hopes of saving America. Are
75 you listening too?

Source: Jerry Falwell, *Listen, America!*, copyright © 1980. Used by permission of Doubleday, a division of Random House, Inc. ■ ■ ■

The Politics of Family Values

Activist fundamentalists and evangelical Christians exerted increasing political influence throughout Reagan's two terms in office. Having played an influential role in the election of 1980, the Moral Majority again figured significantly in Reagan's landslide victory over Walter Mondale in 1984. By 1989, popular televangelists Jim and Tammy Faye Bakker, Jimmy Swaggert, Jerry Falwell, Pat Robertson, and Oral Roberts had launched over 1,300 religious radio stations and more than 330 Christian ministries on television. In addition to these enterprises, Christians boasted a billion-dollar book industry that offered instruction on how to be a better Christian, how to raise children, and how religion could cure an ailing nation.

The televangelists owed their success to their ability to combine all the elements that most characterized the Reagan era: money, morality, conservatism, entertainment, and religious and patriotic symbolism. But a less tangible, deeply embedded sense of anxiety infused the country's political culture and also fed into the revitalization of the New Christian Right. Politically active religious conservatives believed the root of America's social problems could be traced to the decline of the traditional family. Social changes over the previous few decades—an increased presence of women in the workforce, the heightened visibility of abortion and divorce, and the breakdown of the double standard for male and female behavior—had placed severe strain on the ideal two-parent family. During the 1980s, a rising divorce rate accompanied the soaring numbers of illegitimate births, which doubled between 1975 and 1986. By the middle of the decade, more than two-thirds of all young wives worked outside the home, whereas less than half did so in 1973.

Conservatives blamed social liberalism, inflation, and declining moral standards for such troubles. In 1987, the Reagan administration released a "White House Task Force Report on the Family," alleging that family life had been "frayed by the abrasive experiments of two liberal decades."

The pernicious influence of popular culture became a primary focal point of conservatives throughout the eighties. For many critics, liberals had transformed mass culture, which had helped mold reassuring images of consensus in the 1950s, into a subversive technology that eroded support for traditional values. Music, television, and film, they contended, emphasized sexual intimacy outside of marriage, violence, and profanity. "Television is undermining the Judeo-Christian values you hold dear and work hard to teach your children." Calling for a return to "traditional values," the religious right organized in local communities to challenge the teaching of evolution, ban books that ran counter to religious teachings, oppose sex education, and reinstate school prayer. Sparked in part by the highly publicized "textbook wars" in Kanawha County, West Virginia, during the mid to late 1970s, the censorship furor quickened during the eighties. One 1981 survey estimated that 20 percent of the country's school districts and 30 percent of school libraries had their literature and textbooks challenged. By 1985, the number of censorship efforts increased by 37 percent and included overt demonstrations in forty-six states.

Two of the most publicized court cases involving censorship erupted in Alabama and Tennessee. Led by Pat Robertson's National Legal Foundation, the evangelical plaintiffs claimed that Alabama's state board of education violated the establishment clause of the First Amendment by actively encouraging students to embrace "secular humanism," as a "religion" that contradicted Christian teachings. Meanwhile, in Tennessee, a federal judge considered the expulsion of students by the Hawkins County school district for refusing to read books they deemed "anti-Christian" to be a violation of their free exercise of religion. After initial victories in district courts, two circuit appeals courts overturned the earlier decisions. While liberals claimed a victory for diversity, ecumenism, and critical thinking, conservative evangelicals bemoaned the sanction of what they considered to be the teaching of evolution, feminism, socialism, and godless atheism.

But many liberals tried to redefine the debate over "family values" by focusing on economic issues—child care, tax credits for working families with children—that would lessen the burdens weighing on most Americans. They also preached about the importance of individual rights, and warned against unwarranted government intrusion into the lives of private citizens. In 1980, television producer Norman Lear founded the "People for the American Way" to provide a political counterweight to the New Right. "First and foremost among our shared values is a celebration of diversity and respect for the beliefs of others," he declared. People for the American Way entered the fray by providing the legal teams that represented the schools in both Alabama's and Tennessee's textbook wars.

Politics, no less than morality, shaped the debate over family values. Republican leaders used the family appeal to demonstrate compassion and rebut criticism that their party was only concerned with protecting the interests of the rich and powerful. "It's important to our party and our country that we talk as Republicans about the proper role for government to play in assisting families," declared a Republican governor. For Democrats eager to overcome the public perception that they catered to the poor and special interest groups, appeals to family issues allowed them to side with the struggles of the middle class. "The Democratic Party will be successful in recapturing the White House when it is successful in capturing the issue of family," noted a prominent Democrat.

The Politics of Abortion

Debates over family values turned inevitably into a clash over abortion. The legalization of abortion following the Supreme Court's decision in *Roe* v. *Wade* (1973) created a new and highly focused setting for confrontation by opponents: the hundreds of abortion clinics scattered throughout the United States, in shopping centers, office buildings, and residential neighborhoods. Initially, "prolife" organizers picketed and organized prayer vigils outside clinics. In January 1986, Randall Terry, age thirty, a born-again Christian, signaled the formalization of a more militant activism in the movement when he founded Operation Rescue. Over the next two years Terry organized tightly controlled blockades to prevent women from entering abortion clinics. "These acts of civil disobedience," he wrote, "are designed to save lives by preventing abortionists from entering their death chambers, and to dramatize for the American people the horrors of the abortion holocaust." Elsewhere demonstrators posed as patients, entered clinics, and then splattered red paint in waiting rooms, ignited stink bombs, or bound themselves to examining tables.

Even more frighteningly, the number of bomb threats and actual bombings at clinics soared. The Federal Bureau of Alcohol, Tobacco, and Firearms reported thirty bombings between May 1982 and January 1985. Three bombs ripped through Florida abortion clinics on Christmas morning 1984 and another in early January 1985. One of the people involved claimed that the bombings were "a gift to Jesus on his birthday."

The opponents of abortion and birth control found an ally in the White House. "I feel a great sense of solidarity with all of you," the President assured a crowd of antiabortion activists in 1985. In addition to providing verbal support to the cause of ending legal abortion, the president persuaded Congress to bar most public funding for birth control and to stop Medicare from funding abortions for poor women. An administration measure provided funding for religiously oriented "chastity clinics" where counselors advised teenage girls and women to "just say no" to avoid pregnancy.

The moral position of religious conservatives meshed with the political strategy of Republican operatives determined to use social issues to fracture the Democratic coalition. "There is a real feeling among blue-collar Catholics that the Democratic Party has been spending its time chasing women, blacks, and gays and ignoring everyone else," noted a Catholic writer. "Abortion serves as a symbol for that sense of abandonment as well as for the perception that traditional values are declining."

Among activists the debate over abortion revolved around different conceptions of motherhood. Abortion opponents believed in traditional sex roles and saw motherhood as a woman's highest mission in life. Viewing the conflict as a clash between "nurturance" and "selfish individualism," they considered abortion one more assault on the last bastion of human tenderness in a cold and uncaring world. "We've accepted abortion because we're a very materialistic society and there is less time for caring," observed an antiabortion activist in Fargo, North Dakota.

Prochoice activists, in contrast, believed that motherhood was only one of the many roles that women played. Only by addressing the gender inequalities that prevented women from competing equally against men, they argued, could American society support families. Feminists considered the option of having an abortion to be indispensable; as the responsibility for children devolved to women, so must the choice as to when to bear them. Along with supporting a host of political and economic reforms—paid parental leave, flexible hours, child-care facilities—feminists trumpeted the value of individual liberty over government interference. Observed Planned Parenthood President Faye Wattleton, "The fundamental principles of individual privacy are under the most serious assault since the days of McCarthyism."

Activists on both sides represented a small proportion of opinions, however. Polls showed a public torn between the extremes of the abortion debate: overwhelming opposition to an absolute ban on abortion but discomfort with an absolute right to abortion. The public debate, however, obscured opportunity for consensus as both sides used powerful symbols to rally support for their cause. In 1984 antiabortion activists produced a graphic videotape, *The Silent Scream,* which showed abortion "from the point of view of the unborn child." The film gained a wide audience after President Reagan endorsed it during the March for Life in January 1985. In response, prochoice advocates often displayed coat hangers—grim reminders of the illegal and unsafe abortions that had taken place before the Supreme Court ruling.

Class and religious beliefs served as the fault lines in the abortion debate. Polls showed that higher-income earners, people with a college degree, and the self-employed proved more likely to support a woman's right to choose. Only one-fourth of blacks and Latinos favored abortion, compared to more than one-third of Anglos. Surprisingly, women and men divided equally on the issue. But people who deemed religion as "very important" in their lives opposed abortion by an overwhelming 2–1 margin.

Debate over Abortion   As the Religious Right grew in political importance, so did the issue of a woman's right to an abortion, legalized by *Roe* v. *Wade.* Prolife organizations held rallies and protested in front of abortion clinics, emphasizing that abortion was a form of infanticide. Though prochoice advocates had the support of the courts, they continued to challenge the arguments made by prolife advocates, pressing a woman's right to choose, as seen in this battle of protest signs in front of an abortion clinic in Boston. *(© Evan Richman/ The Boston Globe)*

Surveys revealed a considerable regional variation on abortion issues. People along the Pacific coast and in New England favored the termination of pregnancies more than did other Americans. Smaller rural areas in the Deep South and Midwest registered markedly higher rates of opposition than the national average. Those who supported abortion rights often did not attend church services, lived near major metropolitan areas, and held liberal views on other family values issues such as gay rights. Those opposed to abortion more frequently expressed concern that the nation was in a state of moral decline, believed that a woman's place was in the home, and regularly attended religious services.

AIDS and the Struggle for Gay Rights

Perhaps with the exception of abortion, few subjects during the 1980s generated more raw emotion than homosexuality. The gay-rights movement, born at the Stonewall Inn in 1969, continued to gain momentum during the 1970s. Homosexuals flooded into cities such as San Francisco and New York and established a variety of support organizations. Between 1974 and 1978 more than twenty thousand homosexuals moved to San Francisco, many of them living in the city's Castro District. In response to the growing visibility of the gay community, a number of states repealed their sodomy statutes and a few enacted legislation preventing discrimination based on sexual orientation.

The movement took a tragic turn in 1981 when doctors in San Francisco and New York began reporting that young homosexual men were dying from a rare disease initially called Kaposi's sarcoma. As panic spread through the gay community, researchers at the Centers for Disease Control (CDC) discovered the villain: a deadly virus spread by bodily fluid that rendered the victim's immune system helpless against opportunistic infections. They renamed the mysterious disease Acquired Immune Deficiency Syndrome (AIDS).

Initially the majority of AIDS victims were homosexual men infected through sexual contact. During the 1970s many gay men associated freedom with sexual promiscuity. "The belief that was handed to me was that sex was liberating and more sex was more liberating," observed the activist Michael Callen. "[Being gay] was tied to the right to have sex." As the death toll mounted, gay leaders organized to educate the public and to pressure government to find a cure. In New York the Gay Men's Health Center spearheaded the effort, raising millions of dollars, offering services to the sick, and lobbying Washington. The Human Rights Campaign Fund, founded in 1980, raised millions of dollars to support gay-friendly politicians. The pressure produced tangible results. By the end of the decade 21 states and 130 municipalities offered gays and lesbians some form of legal protection against discrimination.

At the same time, radical groups such as the AIDS Coalition to Unleash Power, or ACT UP, founded in 1987 to protest a lack of commitment to finding a cure for AIDS, rattled politicians and drug companies with their colorful demonstrations. ACT UP's slogan, "Silence = Death," underscoring a pink triangle on black, became a trademark for late-1980s uncivil disobedience. Accompanied by chants such as "Out of the closets and into the streets!" its members picketed meetings of the Food and Drug Administration, disrupted Catholic Masses to protest church policies on AIDS, and chained themselves to the doors of major drug companies to protest high drug prices.

The AIDS crisis produced an outflow of gay literature and art. In 1987 the Names Project began sewing quilts for each victim who succumbed to AIDS. In a highly publicized event in 1992 the AIDS quilt—now incorporating thousands of individual panels—was unfolded in front of the Washington Monument. "It's a way for people to say, 'This person was here and won't be forgotten,'" said the quilt's creator. Hollywood addressed the crisis in a movie, *Longtime Companion* (1990), which followed eight gay men and one female friend through the history of the disease. Gay writers' works, such as Larry Kramer's *The Normal Heart* (1985) and journalist Randy Shilts's *And the Band Played On* (1987), raised public awareness about the disease and about gay life. Gay playwright Tony Kushner's drama *Angels in America* (1992) earned a Pulitzer Prize for its depiction of gay life in the 1980s.

Conservatives reacted with horror, viewing gay rights as unnatural, contrary to God's will, and hostile to the traditional family. The gay-rights movement represented "the most vicious attack on traditional family values that our society has seen in the history of our republic," declared a conservative congressman. White House adviser Pat Buchanan suggested that AIDS was God's revenge for violating natural law. "The poor homosexuals. They have declared war on nature and now nature is exacting an awful retribution."

The White House remained largely indifferent to the growing AIDS crisis. Scientists, including Surgeon General Dr. C. Everett Koop, urged Reagan to endorse a "safe-sex" program to combat AIDS. But the president, bowing to conservative pressure and personally uncomfortable dealing with questions of sexuality, shied away from personal involvement in the crisis. The administration barred the CDC from funding organizations that dealt explicitly with sex, homosexuality, or drug use. Not even the death of movie star and Reagan friend, Rock Hudson, in 1985 inspired the administration to make combating the disease a top priority.

Research on the AIDS epidemic continued even though the American people divided over the issue and the Reagan administration remained apprehensive. Dr. Mathilde Krim, who also contributed to the passage of the National Cancer Act of 1971, became an early advocate of consciousness-raising. In 1983 she founded the AIDS Medical Foundation and in 1985 merged it with the National AIDS Research Foundation in Los Angeles. The resulting American Foundation for AIDS Research played an integral role in lobbying for funds to

Reflecting on the AIDS Quilt on the Mall in Washington, D.C. The AIDS epidemic struck the city of San Francisco earlier than most of the nation's regions, and it was there that the idea for a tribute to those killed by the virus was born. In June 1987, friends and loved ones gathered to discuss ways to honor AIDS victims and provide a visual display that would force the nation to recognize the devastating effects of the disease on families and entire communities. The group decided to create quilt panels, each 3 feet by 6 feet in length, decorated with images that commemorated the lives of those whom they had lost. On October 11, 1987, organizers displayed the quilt for the first time on the national mall. At that time, there were nineteen hundred panels, but a subsequent four-month national tour of the quilt captured the attention of people across the country who began contributing their own panels. Parts of the quilt continued to tour the country and other nations as the AIDS death toll continued to rise and the number of panels submitted grew. In October 1996, the quilt stretched the entire length of the mall, providing an emotional example of the epidemic's human cost. *(© AP/ Wide World Photos)*

conduct research into the growing problem. Krim also led the effort to make homosexuality and AIDS a part of the public discourse and to discourage the stigmatization of the disease's victims.

Because of the painfully poor understanding of AIDS and the means through which it spread, most commentators defined the disease as a "homosexual problem." As this notion gained currency, a wave of reaction stemmed the liberalization of attitudes toward gays. In March 1986, the Supreme Court delivered a stunning 5–4 decision in *Bowers* v. *Hardwick* that upheld Georgia's antisodomy laws, which proscribed private homosexual acts between consenting adults. The decision dealt a devastating blow to gay rights. Chief Justice Warren Burger's concurring opinion demonstrated the deep-seated conflict over public and private morality. "To hold that the act of homosexual sodomy is somehow protected as a fundamental right," he averred, "would be to cast aside millennia of moral teaching." "Depriving individuals of the right to choose for themselves how to conduct their intimate relationships," Justice Harry Blackmun fired back in his dissenting opinion, "poses a far greater threat to the values most deeply [ingrained] in our Nation's history than tolerance of nonconformity could ever do." Only in 1996, with a 6–3 decision in *Romer* v. *Evans,* would the Supreme Court recognize the illegality of laws that discriminated against homosexuals. In 2003, the Supreme Court overturned the *Bowers* decision, declaring in *Lawrence* v. *State of Texas* that laws banning same-sex sodomy violated a person's right to privacy.

By the end of the 1980s the AIDS epidemic had spread far beyond gay men. Thanks to grass-roots organizing and public education, the number of new AIDS cases among homosexuals had stabilized. In 1987, 50 percent of the deaths from AIDS in the United States were among intravenous drug users and their sexual partners, a group that was 90 percent African American and Hispanic. Overall, blacks contracted human immunodeficiency virus (HIV), the precursor to AIDS, at a rate three times higher than whites. For Hispanics the infection rate exceeded that of whites by two times. An even more harrowing revelation came when researchers discovered that the disease also spread more rapidly among children than adults.

PRIMARY SOURCE

14.3 | *AIDS Testimony*
RYAN WHITE

Even though most of the early victims of AIDS were homosexuals and intravenous drug users, blood transfusions exposed thousands of hemophiliacs to the virus. On March 3, 1988, Ryan White, a hemophiliac diagnosed with HIV at age thirteen, braved the stigma society attached to the disease and testified before the Presidential Commission on AIDS, where he described the discrimination he faced as a carrier of the disease.

Thank you, commissioners. My name is Ryan White. I am sixteen years old. I have hemophilia, and I have AIDS. When I was three days old, the doctors told my parents I was a severe hemophiliac, meaning my blood does not

clot. Lucky for me, there was a product just approved by the Food and Drug
5 Administration. It was called Factor VIII, which contains the clotting agent
found in blood. . . .

Most recently my battle has been against AIDS and the discrimination surrounding it. On December 17, 1984, I had surgery to remove two inches of my
left lung due to pneumonia. After two hours of surgery, the doctors told my
10 mother I had AIDS. I contracted AIDS through my Factor VIII which is made
from blood. When I came out of surgery, I was on a respirator and had a tube in
my left lung. I spent Christmas and the next thirty days in the hospital. A lot of
my time was spent searching, thinking, and planning my life.

I came face to face with death at thirteen years old. I was diagnosed with
15 AIDS, a killer. Doctors told me I'm not contagious. Given six months to live and
being the fighter that I am, I set high goals for myself. It was my decision to live
a normal life, go to school, be with my friends, and enjoy day-to-day activities. It
was not going to be easy.

The school I was going to said they had no guidelines for a person with AIDS.
20 The school board, my teachers, and my principal voted to keep me out of the classroom . . . for fear of someone getting AIDS from me by casual contact. Rumors of
sneezing, kissing, tears, sweat, and saliva spreading AIDS caused people to panic.

We began a series of court battles for nine months, while I was attending
classes by telephone. Eventually, I won the right to attend school, but the preju-
25 dice was still there. Listening to medical facts was not enough. People wanted
100 percent guarantees. There are no 100 percent guarantees in life, but
concessions were made by Mom and me to help ease the fear. We decided to meet
everyone halfway—separate restrooms, no gym, separate drinking fountains,
disposable eating utensils—even though we knew AIDS was not spread through
30 casual contact. Nevertheless, parents of twenty students started their own school.
They were still not convinced.

Because of the lack of education on AIDS, discrimination, fear, panic, and lies
surrounded me: one, I became the target of Ryan White jokes; two, lies about me
35 biting people; three, spitting on vegetables and cookies; four, urinating on bathroom walls; five, some restaurants threw away my dishes; six, my school locker
was vandalized inside and folders were marked "fag" and other obscenities. I was
labeled a troublemaker, my mom an unfit mother, and I was not welcome anywhere. People would get up and leave so they would not have to sit anywhere
40 near me. Even at church, people would not shake my hand. . . .

It was difficult at times to handle, but I tried to ignore the injustice, because
I knew the people were wrong. My family and I held no hatred for those people, because we realized they were victims of their own ignorance. We had great
faith that, with patience, understanding, and education, my family and I could be
45 helpful in changing their minds and attitudes around.

My life is better now. At the end of the school year, my family and I decided to
move to Cicero, Indiana. We did a lot of hoping and praying that the community
would welcome us, and they did. For the first time in three years, we feel we have a
home, a supportive school, and lots of friends. The communities of Cicero, Atlanta,
50 Arcadia, and Noblesville, Indiana, are now what we call home. I'm feeling great.

I am a normal, happy teenager again. I have a learner's permit [to drive]. I attend sports functions and dances. My studies are important to me. I made the honor role just recently, with two A's and two B's. I'm just one of the kids, and all because the students at Hamilton Heights High School listened to the facts,
55 educated their parents and themselves, and believed in me. I believe in myself as I look forward to graduating from Hamilton Heights High School in 1991. Hamilton Heights High School is proof that AIDS education in schools works.

Source: Ryan White, excerpt from March 3, 1988, testimony before the Presidential Commission on AIDS. ■ ■ ■

The World Health Organization divided the AIDS epidemic into three distinct phases: the silent period (1970–1981), the initial discovery (1981–1985), and the worldwide mobilization (1985–). By 1992 HIV infected 12.9 million people worldwide, with most of its victims living in poorer nations that lacked the resources to mount effective campaigns to stem its spread. Sub-Saharan Africa, with 10 percent of the world's population, claimed 68 percent of the total HIV population (8.8 million). Scientists estimated that in sub-Saharan urban areas as many as 50 percent of all adults, including 20 percent of pregnant women, were infected—the vast majority through heterosexual contact.

American Racial Identities

Abortion, AIDS, and changing gender roles were not the only issues troubling Americans in the 1980s. The massive wave of immigrants that flooded American cities after 1965 raised new questions about the nation's racial and ethnic identity. "The nation is rapidly moving toward a multiethnic future," *Newsweek* reported in 1992. "Asians, Hispanics, Caribbean islanders, and many other immigrant groups compose a diverse and changing social mosaic that cannot be described by the old vocabulary of race relations."

The immigration rate of the 1980s eclipsed the previous high set during the century's first decade as the new immigrants, mostly from Asia, Central and South America, and the Caribbean, sought a new life in the United States. According to the Census Bureau, the nation absorbed 8.9 million legal immigrants—and, by most estimates, at least 2 million illegal ones—during the 1980s. By the early 1990s over 1 million new legal immigrants were arriving in the United States every year, accounting for almost one-half of U.S. population growth.

Most of these immigrants settled in large cities in a handful of states—New York, Illinois, and New Jersey, as well as Florida, Texas, and California. One of every three new immigrants entered the United States through California, making the nation's most populous state its unofficial Ellis Island. By 1990 the population of Los Angeles, the nation's second-largest city, was one-third foreign-born. Los Angeles was also home to the second-largest Spanish-speaking population (after Mexico City) on the North American continent. New York's foreign-born population also approached 35 percent of its total populace in 1990, a level the city had last reached in 1910.

Most Americans saw and heard daily reminders of the cultural impact of the new waves of immigrants. A complex chorus of foreign languages filled urban streets. In Miami 75 percent of residents spoke a language other than English at home. In kitchens across the country salsa replaced ketchup as America's favorite condiment. In music such Hispanic artists as Los Lobos, the Miami Sound Machine, and Lisa Lisa topped the billboards with hit songs. Many white artists tried assimilating new cultural impulses into their music. David Byrne injected Talking Heads music with African, Latin, and other rhythms. Peter Gabriel and Paul Simon found similar success with African rhythms.

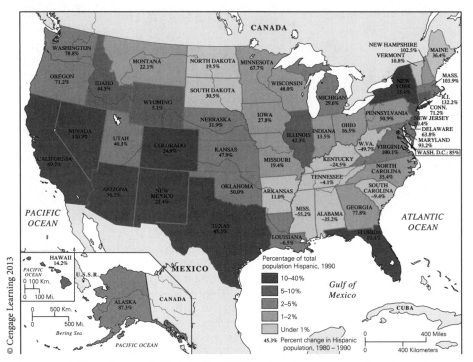

Growth of Hispanic Population in the 1980s For the first time in American history, the majority of immigrants came from countries outside of Europe. The Hispanic population claimed the largest percentage of new immigrants. This influx altered the social and cultural dynamics of cities and states across the nation, just as previous waves of immigration had done.

The new diversity provided fertile ground for bigotry. Blacks, Hispanics, and Asians often felt as much animosity toward each other as they did toward whites. In Florida, Hispanics and blacks, who had once considered themselves allies against the white power structure, battled each other for jobs and scarce resources. In many cities African American and Korean immigrants engaged in heated confrontations. At the root of the conflict, exacerbated by language and cultural differences, was resentment of Korean immigrants' success in running small businesses in economically depressed black neighborhoods. Acclaimed director Spike Lee captured this climate in satirical fashion in his movie *Do the Right Thing* (1989). A Korean shopkeeper in Brooklyn averts a confrontation with black residents of the neighborhood by shouting in desperation, "Me no white. Me no white. Me black."

Video of the Rodney King Beating   On March 3, 1991, Rodney King failed to stop when a Los Angeles police car signaled him to pull over, beginning a chase in which speeds reached an estimated 100 mph. When police finally stopped the car, they pulled King out and began beating him—according to the officers, because he showed signs that he might try to get off the ground and run. On the balcony of a building that faced the highway, George Holliday videotaped the incident. The next day Holliday gave the tape to an L.A. news station, which aired it. The video shows the police hitting King with their batons fifty-six times and kicking him six times—all within two minutes. King suffered eleven skull fractures, along with brain and kidney damage, yet officers, not knowing they had been recorded, failed to mention the injuries in their report. On May 15, four white officers identified in the video were charged with use of excessive force and assault with a deadly weapon, but were acquitted in April 1992. Later in the year, the officers were arraigned on federal charges, and two were convicted in 1993. (© *CNN/ Getty Images*)

The Los Angeles riots following the Rodney King trial in April 1992 were the most visible demonstration of this new tension. The riots commenced after a mostly white jury in a Los Angeles suburb acquitted four white police officers accused of savagely beating an African American motorist, Rodney King, after stopping him for a traffic violation. The jury arrived at the verdict despite the existence of a videotape showing the officers delivering numerous blows to a seemingly defenseless King.

Shortly after the verdicts were announced, African Americans in South-central Los Angeles erupted in the deadliest urban riot in over a century. They were soon joined by Latinos who were shocked by the verdict. As the violence unfolded, a unique pattern emerged: the riots were multiethnic, and they were not confined to a limited area. Latinos made up more than one-half of the first five thousand people arrested, and buildings from West Los Angeles to Koreatown and Santa Monica were burned. By the time the riots ended three days later, fifty-eight people lay dead, over eight hundred buildings had been destroyed, and thousands more had been damaged or looted.

The Backlash Against Multiculturalism

The riots intensified a simmering debate over the impact of immigration on American society. Many white Americans complained about new immigrants stealing jobs from native workers, worried about the cohesiveness of American culture, and questioned its ability to absorb and assimilate so many different cultural influences. "Is it really wise to allow the immigration of people who find it so difficult and painful to assimilate into the American majority?" asked conservative journalist Peter Brimelow. After years of debate on how to control illegal immigration, Congress in 1986 passed the Immigration Reform and Control Act. It offered legal status to undocumented aliens who had lived and worked in the United States but imposed fines on employers who hired new undocumented workers.

Critics also complained that immigrants imposed a heavy financial burden on local governments. On average immigrant-headed households included more school-age children than native households, were poorer, received more welfare, and, since they owned less property, paid less in taxes. Local governments provided many of the services immigrants needed, yet the federal government collected most of their tax dollars. By one estimate each illegal immigrant household in California consumed on average $1,178 more in public services than it contributed in taxes. When multiplied by the estimated 2 million undocumented aliens in the state, the figure amounted to a significant drain on public resources. If averaged out across the nation, the net burden would be much lower, between $166 and $226 per native household.

Fears about the swelling foreign-language populations produced a powerful "English-only" movement. In 1986 California spearheaded the drive for "English only" by voting overwhelmingly for a referendum outlawing bilingualism and defending "English as a unifying force in the United States." Representatives of Hispanic groups condemned the movement as "fundamentally racist in character," but before the end of the decade seventeen other states had joined California in passing English-only laws. "Language," *The Economist* noted, "symbolizes the United States' fear that the foreign body within its borders is growing too big ever to be digested."

The debate over American identity found expression on college campuses as students attempted to "increase sensitivity" to racial and cultural diversity in the university community. At Stanford reformers fought to change the Western Civilization curriculum, which they claimed presented a "male, Eurocentric" view of the world. Many universities accommodated the pressure to diversify by expanding the range of programs in disciplines such as Women's Studies, African American Studies, Hispanic Studies, and Gay Studies. In 1987 Allan Bloom led the conservative counterattack on changes in American higher education with his book *The Closing of the American Mind*. Subtitled *How Higher Education Has Failed Democracy and Impoverished the Souls of Today's Students,* the book asserted the primacy of "the great books" of Western civilization. "You can't talk about Chaucer without someone saying 'What's the woman's perspective?', 'What about the Third World perspective?' " he lamented. Bloom's volume remained at the top of the *New York Times* best-seller list for seven weeks, selling more than 1 million copies.

Are the Fears Justified?

Historical experience suggests that concerns about immigrants' failing to assimilate were misplaced; similar fears about past waves of immigrants proved unfounded. The public has always looked favorably on past generations of immigrants and unfavorably on contemporary migrants. In the nineteenth century Americans complained about the "lazy and hard-drinking Irish" who were "polluting" the cities; later waves of newcomers from Italy and Eastern Europe confronted similarly hostile attitudes. Over time, however, those groups became acculturated and now swell the mainstream that fears the addition of new migrants from Mexico, Iran, and Haiti. Strident affirmations of identity actually masked the degree to which ethnic differences grew less overt—higher education, consumerism, movies and television, professional sports, and popular culture worked to make Americans more alike, whatever their ethnic origins.

The rising rate of intermarriage between ethnic groups also suggested that ethnic differences were softening over time. In the 1980s more than 50 percent of all Japanese Americans, and 40 percent of Chinese Americans, married outside their ethnic group. As in the past, these relationships often resulted in families that blended cultural traditions. Weddings might incorporate symbolism and rituals from cultures of both the husband and the wife; children had the opportunity to develop fluency in two languages; the patterns of everyday life, from cuisine to entertainment, reflected the accommodation of two heritages. No matter what particular balance families struck, they reflected in microcosm the vitality of a dynamic American identity that drew its strength from diversity.

Greed Is Good

While Americans remained deeply divided over controversial social issues, they embraced a new culture of consumerism that celebrated wealth and prosperity. Ronald and Nancy Reagan epitomized the new money culture of the 1980s. They set the tone for the decade with a lavish inaugural celebration that included two nights of show-business performances, an $800,000 fireworks display, and nine inaugural balls. "Wealth is back in style," a journalist noted in 1981. "The Reagans are setting a lifestyle so different from the hide-it-under-a-bushel attitude of the Carters. The feeling now is that if you have it, why not enjoy it?"

The real nexus of the money culture, however, was Wall Street. Passage of the 1981 tax law, combined with the Reagan Justice Department's relaxed attitude toward enforcement of antitrust statutes, produced a "merger mania" on Wall Street. Between 1984 and 1987 Wall Street executed twenty-one mergers valued at over $1 billion each. The money culture created lucrative opportunities for the battalions of bankers, investors, and venture capitalists who made money out of money. Among the very highest rollers was Ivan Boesky, who worked eighteen-hour days behind a three hundred–line phone bank and made a fortune orchestrating merger deals. "Greed is all right," he told a cheering University of California at Berkeley Business School audience in 1986. "Everybody should be a little bit greedy."

Greed, however, soon landed Boesky in jail. In late 1986 he pleaded guilty to using confidential information about corporate takeovers to trade stocks illegally. In 1987 *Fortune* magazine named him "Crook of the Year." Boesky was far from the only lawbreaker. Between 1977 and 1989 Michael Milken raised more than $100 billion in funds for American business. In 1987 alone he earned more than $550 million in commissions. He later confessed to defrauding investors and rigging the bond market.

The emphasis on making money was a manifestation of the aging of the baby-boom generation—the 76 million men and women born from 1946 through 1964 who were entering high-earning, high-spending adulthood at the start of the 1980s. By mid-decade a new social category had emerged on the American scene. *Newsweek* magazine called 1984 "The Year of the Yuppie," an acronym for young urban professional. Yuppies aspired to become investment bankers, not social workers. "Much of the energy and optimism and passion of the '60s," *Newsweek* observed, "seems to have been turned inward, on lives, careers, apartments and dinners." As one observer noted, contrasting the difference between

Wall Street   Americans, fascinated with the accumulation of wealth in the eighties, saw Wall Street as the heart of the new money culture. Junk bond pioneers and corporate raiders like Michael Milken and Ivan Boesky personified the qualities Americans respected: they were aggressive risk-takers who succeeded in making quick profits which they spent to sustain their lavish lifestyles. *(© Ed Eckstein/CORBIS)*

two generations of young people, "Hippies were interested in karma; yuppies prefer cars."

No longer committed to social justice, yuppies opted for "networking." When college freshmen were asked in the late 1960s about personal goals, roughly 80 percent listed "develop[ing] a meaningful philosophy of life" and only about 40 percent listed being "well off financially." By 1985, 71 percent listed being well off financially and only 43 percent mentioned having a philosophy of life. Politically, yuppies blended an infatuation with wealth, conspicuous consumption, and economic conservatism with more liberal positions on social issues regarding the environment, abortion, and homosexuality. However, their first loyalty was to material comfort and social status. "The name of the game," declared *The Yuppie Handbook* (1984), "is the best—buying it, owning it, using it, eating it, wearing it, growing it, cooking it, driving it, doing whatever with it."

Even television preachers who pleaded for a return to traditional cultural values reinforced the message that wealth was a symbol of virtue. Their prosperity theology stressed that faith would bring both material gain and eternal salvation. "You sow it, God will grow it," Oral Roberts told his flock. In other words, God needed seed money in order to solve your problems. Robert Schuller called his church "a shopping center for God" and told audiences that "God wants you to succeed." Many of the preachers lived extravagant lifestyles with luxury houses, cars, and airplanes. Before being sent to prison for defrauding investors, Jim Bakker owned six houses, including one with gold-plated bathroom fixtures and an air-conditioned doghouse.

Popular writers fed the public's fascination with the excesses of wealth. In *People Like Us* (1988), Hollywood producer-turned-writer Dominick Dunne chronicled the status-crazed world of the superrich, where tycoons fight for party invitations, fly to Paris for lunch, and spend millions on the latest fashions. Jay McInerney's *Bright Lights, Big City* (1984) detailed the cocaine-snorting adventures of a pleasure-seeking yuppie who bounces from one Manhattan party to the next. Bret Easton Ellis's *Less than Zero* (1985) looked at the empty lives of Southern California's spoiled adolescents with money.

Television and movies reinforced the Reagan-era infatuation with wealth and status. *Dallas,* the most successful prime-time soap opera of the decade, chronicled the wealth, infidelities, and outrageous behavior of Texas oilman J. R. Ewing. Robin Leach's *Lifestyles of the Rich and Famous* took viewers on shopping trips along exclusive Rodeo Drive and into the homes of the wealthy before ending with Leach's trademark sign-off: "May you have caviar wishes and champagne dreams." In Oliver Stone's film *Wall Street* (1987), Michael Douglas, playing Gordon Gekko, a ruthless corporate raider who relies on inside information to make his deals, tells stockbrokers: "Greed, for lack of a better word, is good. Greed is right. Greed works."

Conservatives failed to appreciate the paradox of preaching traditional values while also celebrating the triumph of consumerism. The celebration of wealth often distorted national priorities, creating the self-satisfied and selfish society they cursed from the pulpit. African American theologian and social critic Cornel West expressed concern about the "unintended cultural consequences" of America's culture of wealth. He bemoaned "a spiritual impoverishment in which the dominant conception of the good life consists of gaining access to power, pleasure, and property, sometimes by any means." These manifestations of the market culture impinged on the influence of older civic institutions—families, places of worship, and local communities. "Is it a mere accident that nonmarket values like loyalty, commitment, service, care, concern—even tenderness—can hardly gain a secure foothold?" he asked.

The MTV Generation

Technological changes contributed to the culture of consumption by providing advertisers with new ways to reach high-spending consumers. Perhaps the most significant innovation was the widespread use of cable television. Over the decade cable television grew from a presence in less than 20 percent of homes to a place in 56.4 percent of television homes. At the beginning of the decade most households used an antenna to watch shows broadcast by the three major networks. By the end of the decade the average television household received more than twenty-seven channels. As viewers' choices grew, and the three broadcast networks lost their automatic grip on the audience, the spoils went increasingly to the programmer who could cater to a special interest and offer advertisers a small but well-targeted cluster of consumers.

At the cutting edge of this new TV environment, music television, known from the start as MTV, inspired a revolution in television broadcasting. "Ladies and Gentlemen," intoned a baritone voice at 12:01 AM on August 1, 1981, "Rock and roll!" MTV showed music videos around the clock, interrupted only by ads and bits of connective patter from "veejays." From the beginning MTV was designed to appeal to young adults with lots of disposable income. "It was meant to drive a 55-year-old person crazy," said chairman Tom Freston. But that was simply MTV's shrewd twist on the key selling strategy of the decade: "narrow casting," or "niche" marketing designed to "superserve" a narrowly defined viewer or reader or customer. In addition to MTV, networks pitched ads to children (Nickelodeon), to African Americans (Black Entertainment Television), to news junkies (CNN), and to women between ages eighteen and forty-nine (Lifetime). Viewers willing to subscribe to "pay" services that charged an extra fee could choose all-sports, all-weather, all-movies, all-Spanish, all-sex, and more.

The success of MTV and other forms of niche marketing contributed to the fragmentation of public culture. During the 1940s and 1950s many technological changes helped create a sense of community and a more national culture. The advent of television, with just three networks, combined with the burgeoning of long-distance telephone service, the construction of interstate highways, and the expansion of air travel, helped shrink distance and bring people closer together. Until the explosion in cable television and the proliferation of new networks, most of the viewing public watched the same television shows. As recently as the 1970s more than one-third of U.S. homes tuned in weekly to watch *All in the Family.* "Television in the old days made it a smaller community," said producer Norman Lear. In the 1980s, however, technology was transforming the "mass culture" into endless "niche cultures." With so many shows to choose from, the audience splintered into smaller subsets of viewers. Studies showed, for example, that blacks and whites watched completely different shows.

The Hourglass Society

The public focus on the money culture during the Reagan era obscured the social reality affecting most Americans. Society in the 1980s assumed the appearance of an hourglass: bulging on the extremes and thin in the middle. "There are more and more affluent people, and more and more poor people," said Martin Holler, a Methodist minister who ran a food bank in Wichita, Kansas. "More people who have much more than they have ever had, and more people with nothing."

The number of millionaires doubled during the decade. The net worth of the four hundred richest Americans nearly tripled. By the end of the decade the top 1 percent of families owned 42 percent of the net wealth of all U.S. families, including 60 percent of all corporate stock and 80 percent of all family-owned trusts. The richest 2.5 million people had nearly as much income as the 100 million Americans with the lowest incomes. Despite the continuing celebration of "people's capitalism," the percentage of American households owning at least one share of stock fell from 25 percent in 1977 to 19 percent in 1983, while the wealthiest 1 percent of all American households controlled nearly 60 percent of all corporate stock.

During a decade of ostentatious displays of wealth, the specter of an intractable poverty became the decade's quintessential paradox. Instead of bringing Americans closer together, the pursuit of profit divided the nation: rich and poor, city and suburb, black and white. The government classified about 26.1 million people as poor in 1979, 11.7 percent of the total population. By 1990 the number of poor had reached 33.6 million, or 13.5 percent of the country. The aggregate numbers masked a major transformation in the nature of poverty. Increased spending on programs such as social security and Medicare dramatically improved the lot of the elderly and handicapped. The bulk of the poorest segment of the population after 1980 therefore consisted of single mothers, young children, and young minority men with little education and few job skills.

A marked jump in out-of-wedlock births, which doubled between 1975 and 1986, and female-headed households, contributed to the feminization of poverty. By 1989 one of every four births in the United States was to an unwed woman. Many women also worked in the expanding service sector, which often paid little more than minimum wage. In 1988, 4.5 million American women worked full-time, but still lived below the poverty line.

The feminization of poverty was also disproportionately black. By the early 1990s, 26 percent of all children under eighteen lived with a single parent, with more than 60 percent of black children falling into that category. The rise in one-parent families contributed to an epidemic of child poverty. While child poverty had decreased from 27 to 15 percent between 1960 and 1974, it expanded to 21 percent by 1986. More than 40 percent of black and 38 percent of Hispanic children were poor.

By virtually any measure the problems of society's poorest worsened during the 1980s. High interest rates for construction coupled with tax law changes sharply cut commercial production of low-cost rental housing, leaving a shortage of affordable housing for low-income people. For many the only choice was the streets. At any given time during the decade, between 250,000 and 400,000 Americans were homeless. "Get off the subway in any American city," said the head of the National Coalition for Low Income Housing, "and you are stepping over people who live on the streets." Most of the homeless were unskilled workers, the chronically mentally ill, and women fleeing abusive spouses. Most had already been living in poverty before becoming homeless. When Reagan's budget measures reduced funds available for shelters for homeless people, cities and states could not respond to the crisis.

One homeless Vietnam veteran described the conditions in one of New York's homeless shelters as "rat infested, roach infested, drug infested, filth infested, garbage everywhere, and little children playing in the stairs. Innocent people, women, children," he continued, "boxed in by their misery."

Conditions on some of the nation's 278 Indian reservations, where half of the nation's estimated 1.5 million Native Americans lived, were just as grim. The unemployment rate on the Pine Ridge reservation in South Dakota averaged nearly 80 percent. Although four times the size of Rhode Island, Pine Ridge offered few commercial services—there were no banks, hardware stores, or clothing shops. The infant mortality rate ran five times the national average. By some estimates between 80 and 90 percent of the adult residents were alcoholics, and alcoholic-related diseases were the most common cause of death. Fifty percent of all crimes by adults on the reservation were linked to alcohol, but the Indian Health Service, the federal agency responsible for Indian health care, allocated only 3 percent of its budget to alcoholism treatment.

As some members of the middle class fell into poverty and others acquired wealth, the middle class shrank. According to some estimates, the middle class—families making between $20,000 and $60,000—dropped from 53 percent of the nation in 1973 to 49 percent in 1985. After doubling between 1947 and 1973, median family income stagnated. In 1985 the average middle-class family earned less money than it did in 1973. Hardest hit were younger families, who feared that the American dream of rising prosperity would pass them by.

The New Economy

The reasons for the growing disparity between wealth and poverty reflected deep currents of change in American society. Most of the new jobs created during the decade were lower-paying service jobs. By 1985 there were more people flipping hamburgers at McDonald's for minimum wage than working in steel manufacturing—one of the cornerstones of America's industrial might. Between 1979 and 1984 six of ten jobs added to the U.S. labor market paid $7,000 a year or less. Most were in the service sector, as home health-care attendants, salesclerks, food servers, janitors, or office clerks. Besides low pay, these jobs offered few pension or health-care benefits, were often part-time or temporary, and held out few opportunities for promotion.

In another classic case of unintended consequences, public and private efforts at urban renewal often exacerbated the problems of inner-city residents. In an attempt to revitalize crumbling downtown areas, city governments lured new high-tech industries to build office towers in areas where abandoned factories had once stood. In a parallel fashion, yuppies initiated a process of "gentrification," buying and renovating old homes in once-depressed neighborhoods. Federally subsidized expressways and commuter trains piped other highly educated workers into the city center during the day and out to bedroom communities at night. Together, these changes increased the cost of living in the cities, devastated the tax base that supported education and social services, and forced the poor into ever-smaller pockets of destitution.

Meanwhile, the marketplace underwent a process economists termed *globalization*. Rather than relying on domestic production for domestic consumption, American businesses more aggressively extended into the international market. Many domestic manufacturers moved their plants to underdeveloped countries in order to take advantage of the cheap labor they supplied. No less dramatic was the penetration of foreign goods in the American economy. Even as American corporations globalized, they found themselves challenged by an influx of foreign-manufactured goods. The United States began running exorbitant trade deficits in the 1970s as it imported more products than it exported. Japanese and German corporations bought out American industries, and the steel and automotive sectors suffered tremendous decline.

In the rural regions of the South and Midwest automation revolutionized farm labor. The era of the independent small producer had been in decline for decades. But the last vestiges of independent family-owned operations suffered even more as they failed to compete in an international market. During the 1980s, after several robust decades of growth, farm prices fell, land values depreciated, and real interest rates remained high. Farm income had been slashed to one-third its value in the years between 1980 and 1985. Bank foreclosures followed in the wake of many farm families' attempts to produce more by taking loans to invest in more seed, stock, fertilizer, equipment, and land. By mid-decade unemployment in the Midwest was twice that of the nation at large. In the wake of these disasters, corporations bought up the land, consolidated production, and introduced fewer labor-intensive production technologies.

Finally, during the decade the number of union members declined from 24 million to less than 20 million, a 16 percent drop at a time when the work force expanded by 20 percent. At their peak during World War II, unions had represented 35 percent of the work force; by 1990, however, unions represented only 16 percent of the nation's 100 million workers. The decline was the result of intense global competition, renewed anti-union activity by management, and declining public support for unions. More than 10 million industrial jobs, many of them unionized, were lost primarily due to lower-wage foreign competition. The decline of once-powerful unions contributed to lower pay and less job security for millions of American workers and the erosion of real income for many living in the middle class. When unions represented a larger portion of the work force, they put forward a larger social agenda that benefited union and nonunion workers, such as social security, occupational safety, and health care. By the end of the decade, however, opponents effectively painted union members as agents for special interests, thus minimizing their bargaining power.

While conditions restricted the opportunity for most people to make money, expenses for basic necessities soared during the decade. A typical family home in 1984 absorbed 44 percent of the median family's yearly income, compared with 21 percent in 1973. Buying the average-priced car cost twenty-three weeks of pay in 1988. Ten years earlier it had cost eighteen weeks of pay.

American Apartheid

The celebration of wealth reinforced the ideal of America as a classless society united by a common commitment to prosperity. The social reality, however, revealed a nation deeply divided by class and racial conflict. In 1968 the Kerner Commission, appointed by President Lyndon Johnson to study the causes of racial rioting, had warned that the country was moving toward a bifurcated society, one white, one black, and neither equal to the other. By 1990 African Americans were more segregated than they had been before the civil-rights struggles of the 1960s. The sociologist Douglas Massey used the term *hypersegregation* to describe the profound level of racial segregation existing in major metropolitan areas in the United States. The metropolitan areas he studied—Baltimore, Chicago, Gary, Cleveland, Detroit, Los Angeles, Milwaukee, Newark, Philadelphia, and St. Louis—contained roughly one-quarter of the African American population of the United States.

The dramatic movement of the white middle class from the central city to outlying suburbs exacerbated the growing physical disparity between the races. During the 1970s St. Louis, Cleveland, Pittsburgh, and Detroit lost more than 20 percent of their population. During the same period Philadelphia, Chicago, and New York City saw population drop by more than 10 percent. The movement of the white middle class to the suburbs accounted for much of the population loss. Between 1960 and 1990 the white population of New York fell by half. The jobs followed the middle class to the suburbs. Between 1947 and 1982 factory employment in Chicago declined 59 percent, but surrounding Cook County experienced a 131 percent increase.

While much of the nation prospered during the 1980s, inner-city neighborhoods fell deeper into poverty and despair. Suburbanization, and the complex of public transportation and highways that made it viable, left behind decaying urban centers populated by poor blacks and recent immigrants. By 1985, nearly 60 percent of all blacks in the United States lived in central cities of metropolitan areas, compared with 25 percent of all whites. In the urban centers of the Snow Belt—New York, Chicago, Detroit, Philadelphia, and Boston—77 percent of blacks lived in the city, but only 28 percent of whites. Poverty rates for inner cities soared from 12.7 to 19 percent during the decade. "In Chicago, there are neighborhoods where you can count up the number of bank branches and retailers that have closed up and five liquor stores have taken their place," observed a scholar. "You can clearly see neighborhoods shifting from working-class to hard-core poverty."

The physical distance between the races produced a growing trend toward racial segregation in the public schools. In 1954 when the Supreme Court issued its decision in *Brown,* one in ten public school students was nonwhite; by 1990 the figure was one in three. Between 1975 and 1990 the percentage of white students in Philadelphia public schools dropped from 32 to 23. "With more than 80 percent minority population, there's not much you can do," said a spokesman for New York City's public schools. The growth of Hispanic and Asian communities complicated the problem of desegregation. Urban classrooms in the 1980s, observed the *Boston Globe,* "are a sea of black and brown faces interrupted only by the occasional white child." Only the South, home of the highest proportion of blacks and site of the most ambitious desegregation plans, showed signs of progress.

Many black leaders now questioned their early enthusiasm for desegregation. They were frustrated over the slow pace of change and skeptical of the premise that blacks needed to attend school with whites to learn. Many civil-rights activists stressed the problem of class segregation: the white and black middle classes either moved to the suburbs or sent their children to private schools in the city. With the local tax base eroding, urban public schools lacked the resources to provide a quality education to their students. Numerous studies showed that minority schools were poorly equipped and had less experienced teachers, lower test scores, and a higher dropout rate.

Ironically, America's celebration of consumerism during the decade often masked the reality of deep cultural and class division. By focusing much of the public's attention on controversial social issues, the "culture wars" made it more difficult to build coalitions to tackle the widening class divisions in America. Many people hoped that the end of the Cold War would lead to a shift in national priorities, freeing up large sums of money previously allocated for defense for domestic priorities. Once again, however, those hopes were frustrated by events.

SELECTED READINGS

▮ William Martin's *With God on Our Side* (1996) describes the changing politics of the religious right. Clyde Wilcox studies the leaders of the religious right in *God's Warriors* (1992), while Burton Yale Pines looks at the cultural appeal of fundamentalism in *Back to Basics* (1982). Lisa McGirr roots the rise of conservatism in the fast-growing suburbs in *Suburban Warriors* (2002).

▮ Faye D. Ginsburg provides an insightful analysis of the abortion debate in *Contested Lives* (1998). N.E.H. Hull and Peter Hoffer offer a balanced history of the abortion debate in America in *Roe v. Wade* (2001). Rosalind Petchesky explains the philosophical and legal conflicts surrounding abortion in *Abortion and Women's Choice* (1990). Editor Rickie Solinger compiles a pro-rights look at the abortion debate from the 1950s through the 1990s in *Abortion Wars* (1998). A social history of the antiabortion campaign since the decision in *Roe* is provided by Kerry Jacoby in *Souls, Bodies, Spirits* (1998).

▮ Eric Marcus's *Making History: The Struggle for Gay and Lesbian Equal Rights* (1992) delivers a broad overview of the gay liberation movement. John Manuel Androite in *Victory Deferred* (1999) chronicles the impact of AIDS and the impact on the gay community as people stepped forward to protest government inaction. The growth of the gay community in San Francisco and the devastating effect of the AIDS epidemic are evoked through oral interviews collected by Benjamin Shepard in *White Nights and Ascending Shadows* (1997). Randy Shilts provides a firsthand view of the crisis in *And the Band Played On (2007)*.

▮ David Reimers's *Still the Golden Door* (2nd ed., 1994) is a good starting point for material on immigration. James Olson's *Equality Deferred* (2002) provides an overview of post-1945 immigration. Thomas Espenshade's *The Fourth Wave* (1985) describes the "New Asian" immigrants in California, while James Cockcroft's *Outlaws in the Promised Land* (1986) looks at the immigration experience of Hispanics. David Gutierrez examines how Mexican immigrants have defined their political and cultural identities in America in *Walls and Mirrors* (1995). Peter Brimelow's *Alien Nation* (1995) offers a pessimistic analysis of the new wave of immigration.

▮ Nancy Abelmann and John Lie examine the conflict between blacks and Koreans that led to significant damage to Korean American businesses in the L.A. riots in *Blue Dreams* (1995). The essays collected by Robert Gooding-Williams in *Reading Rodney King/Reading Urban Uprising* (1993) explore the connection between the Rodney King incident and the L.A. riots. James Delk's *Fires and Furies* (1995) chronicles how the riots unfolded.

▮ James Stewart's *Den of Thieves* is an account of the shady dealings in the financial markets during the 1980s. Connie Bruck's *The Predators' Ball* (1988) details the world of the junk bond traders. Nicolaus Mills's *Culture in an Age of Money* (1990) criticizes the influence of corporations and wealth on American culture during the 1980s. Barbara Ehrenreich studies the insecurities over wealth and status that preoccupied much of the middle class in her *Fear of Falling* (1989).

▮ Kevin Phillips attacks the growth of economic inequality in the 1980s in *The Politics of Rich and Poor* (1990). Thomas Edsall explains the political motivations for attacking the poor in *The New Politics of Inequality* (1984). Leslie Dunbar analyzes the impact of Reagan's economic policies on minorities in *Minority Report* (1984), while William Julius Wilson's *The Truly Disadvantaged* (1987) studies the effects of Reaganomics in the inner cities. The war on welfare is exposed in Michael Katz's *The Undeserving Poor* (1989). Nelson George's *Post-Soul Nation* (2005) focuses on cultural and political changes among African Americans in the 1980s.

15 *The End of the Cold War, 1988–1992*

Since construction in 1961, the Berlin Wall stood as a harsh physical emblem of the Cold War. The harrowing images of barbed wire and watchtowers, vast minefields, snarling patrol dogs, and well-armed sentries served as a stark reminder of a divided Berlin, of two Germanys, and of a world that separated East from West. But shortly after midnight on November 9, 1989, East Germany's communist government yielded to growing demands for freedom, and increased pressure from the reform-minded Soviet leader Mikhail Gorbachev, by opening the Berlin Wall, thereby symbolically raising the Iron Curtain and elevating hopes for an end to the Cold War.

Thousands of people on both sides of the wall gathered to celebrate the moment. "We are all Germans," the crowd shouted. People danced in the streets and cars honked their horns as hammer-wielding Berliners climbed atop the wall to pound away at its concrete surface. "I want to go across. We have waited for this so long," exclaimed a West Berlin resident who was fighting back tears. Jubilant Germans hung a banner on the wall: "Stalin is Dead, Europe lives." At Checkpoint Charlie, which separated the American and Soviet zones, small groups of Berliners walked across the white line that had divided East and West for forty years.

Fall of the Berlin Wall
1989 was the year of revolutions in Europe as Poland, Rumania, Czechoslovakia, and East Germany rebelled against communist rule. The most memorable act of tearing down the Iron Curtain came in Berlin where the wall that divided east and west came crashing down in November 1989. As Berliners from both sides of the divide celebrated, people poured freely through the opening for the first time in decades. (© *AP/Wide World Photos*)

The police made no attempt to stifle the celebrations or to block the movement from East to West. "They just let us go," said a shocked East Berlin woman as she set foot on western soil. "I can't believe it."

When he assumed the reins of power in 1989, George H. W. Bush confronted a world transformed by the dissolution of the Soviet Union and the end of the Cold War. The threat of a superpower conflict receded, but Iraq's Saddam Hussein reminded Americans that the post–Cold War world was not devoid of danger. While President Bush successfully rallied world opinion and American military might in the Gulf War, he failed to exercise similar leadership in confronting the American paradox of rising expectations. He faced a difficult problem: Ronald Reagan had bequeathed to his successor a federal government crippled by massive deficits and a public demanding increased spending on education, health, and the environment. Over the next four years Bush struggled to develop a consistent message that would satisfy public expectations of government without raising taxes. He failed. In 1992 the voters rejected Bush in favor of the tempered liberalism of Arkansas Governor Bill Clinton.

The Search for Reagan's Successor

Since the Twenty-second Amendment to the Constitution barred Reagan from seeking a third term, the GOP faced the difficult task of choosing a candidate who would continue his policies. The logical choice was George H. W. Bush, who had served as Reagan's loyal vice president for the previous eight years. Bush, however, was not conservative enough for many party members, who instead rallied around two formidable primary opponents: televangelist Pat Robertson and Kansas Senator Robert Dole. After a slow start Bush gathered both endorsements and votes in securing the nomination.

The son of a wealthy New England family, Bush joined the navy in 1942, earning the Distinguished Flying Cross after his plane was shot down in the South Pacific. Bush returned home after the war, graduated from Yale University, and moved to Midland, Texas, where he used family connections to make millions in the booming oil business. In 1964 he ran for the Senate as a "Goldwater Republican" who opposed the Civil Rights Act of 1964. He lost the election, but two years later, campaigning as a moderate, he earned a seat in Congress. Over the next few years he established his independence, voting for a controversial open-housing bill. "A man should not have a door slammed in his face because he is a Negro or speaks with a Latin American accent," he told a hostile white audience.

During the 1970s as conservatives were regaining a foothold in the party, Bush served in a number of appointive posts, including director of the Central Intelligence Agency (CIA). However, when he campaigned for the presidency in 1980, it was as a moderate; at one point he dismissed Reagan's recovery plan as "voodoo economics." Bush then spent the next eight years defending those same policies, often selling them to a skeptical Congress. "I'm for Mr. Reagan—blindly," he said in an awkward moment in 1984.

Bush faced a difficult political balancing act. Though Reagan remained as popular as ever, the same could not be said for the Republican Party or for the conservative ideas that had allowed him to gain power. In 1989 pollsters found that 55 percent of Americans believed the nation was on the "wrong track"; only 36 percent said it was on the "right track." By the end of the decade organized opposition to Reagan's antigovernment message showed new signs of life, complicating Bush's political task.

In his acceptance speech at the Republican convention in July 1988, Bush tried to articulate a message that would retain the loyalty of Reagan conservatives without alienating the growing number of moderates. In an effort to energize the party's conservative faithful, Bush promised to continue the fight against terrorism abroad and big government at home. The centerpiece of the speech was a dramatic and carefully scripted promise not to raise taxes. "Read my lips," he said. "No new taxes." The vice president also appealed to moderates by emphasizing his support for education and the environment. In a move that puzzled observers, and many of his closest advisers, Bush picked the untested and lightly regarded Dan Quayle, a conservative senator from Indiana, as his running mate.

The Democrats had a difficult time finding a nominee to challenge Bush. The party's front-runner, Colorado Senator Gary Hart, quit the race after reporters disclosed that he was having an extramarital affair. Michael Dukakis, the Greek American governor of Massachusetts, moved to fill the void created by Hart's absence. Dukakis faced a spirited challenge from African American civil-rights leader Jesse Jackson, who appealed to the party's traditional liberal base. Jackson won some important primaries, but in the end Dukakis's moderate message and well-oiled organization won more. Nominated at the Democratic convention in August, Dukakis tried to skirt the sensitive social issues that had divided the party since the 1960s by declaring that the campaign was about "competence, not ideology." To underscore his new centrist message, he chose conservative Texas Senator Lloyd Bentsen as his running mate.

The fall contest between Dukakis and Bush degenerated into one of the most negative campaigns in modern times. The Bush campaign concentrated on convincing the public that Dukakis was soft on crime, unpatriotic and weak on defense, and antagonistic to family values. Dukakis's membership in the American Civil Liberties Union (ACLU) became a device for highlighting the candidate's secularism, and the governor's opposition to requiring school children to recite the Pledge of Allegiance became shorthand for questioning Dukakis's patriotism.

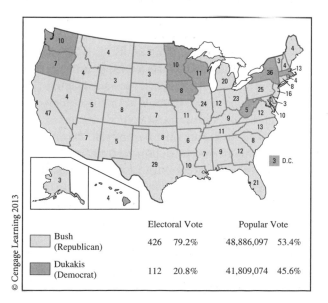

	Electoral Vote		Popular Vote	
Bush (Republican)	426	79.2%	48,886,097	53.4%
Dukakis (Democrat)	112	20.8%	41,809,074	45.6%

© Cengage Learning 2013

The Election of 1988

As vice president under Reagan, George H. W. Bush promised to continue the peace and prosperity he helped to create. At the same time he attacked his opponent, Massachusetts Governor Michael Dukakis, for releasing prisoners on furloughs, which left them free to commit more heinous crimes. For his part, Dukakis tried to reunite the divided Democratic Party, but he failed to win any key electoral states besides New York.

Bush's most effective advertisement told voters about Willie Horton, an African American who had raped a white woman while on leave from a Massachusetts prison while Dukakis was governor. "Dukakis furlough program," the announcer says as the camera shows hardened inmates streaming through a revolving door. Many escaped and "many are at large," he intones; now Dukakis "says he wants to do for America what he's done for Massachusetts." Dukakis responded defensively to these potent ideological charges. While Bush appealed to the values of the white middle class, Dukakis tried to connect to their pocketbooks. He traveled the country offering detailed proposals for student aid, health care, and a jobs program. By late October Gallup reported a "stunning turnaround" in the polls.

On election day Bush became the first sitting vice president since Martin Van Buren in 1836 to be elected directly to the presidency. Bush won 53.4 percent of the popular vote and carried forty states with 426 electoral votes. Dukakis won only ten states and the District of Columbia for a total of 112 electoral votes and 45.6 percent of the popular vote. The Democrats, however, managed to increase their margins in Congress, where they held an 89-vote advantage in the House and 56 of 100 seats in the Senate.

1989: The Year of Miracles

In 1989 as Bush was settling into office, a Polish shipyard electrician named Lech Walesa led the Solidarity trade union movement in a series of strikes that crippled Poland's Soviet-controlled government. Soviet leader Mikhail Gorbachev refused to use the military to quell the uprising, and he instructed the puppet regime to negotiate with the reformers. The result was an agreement to hold free elections in 1990—the first free elections in Poland in sixty-eight years. The winds of revolution blew rapidly from Poland to other Soviet-bloc countries. In Hungary reformers adopted a new constitution, called for elections, and disbanded the Communist party. In Czechoslovakia playwright and populist Václav Havel helped orchestrate a "velvet revolution" that resulted in the resignation of the Soviet-installed regime and free elections that carried Havel to the presidency. The most dramatic events were occurring in East Germany. On November 9 the Communist party announced that residents of East Berlin were free to leave the country. The Berlin Wall, the ultimate symbol of Cold War division, had suddenly been rendered irrelevant.

The revolutionary fervor was not confined to communist regimes in Eastern Europe but soon swept into the Soviet Union itself. The Baltic states—Estonia, Latvia, and Lithuania—had lived under Soviet rule since 1939 when Joseph Stalin seized control as part of the Nazi-Soviet pact. In December 1989, the Lithuanian Communist party formally broke ties with the Soviet Union. The following year Lithuania and Latvia declared their independence. Meanwhile, in March 1989, the Soviet Union held its first free elections since 1917. Hundreds of party officials went down in defeat.

All of these changes were too much for party hard-liners in the Soviet hierarchy; they staged a coup in August 1991. With Gorbachev held under house arrest, a defiant Boris Yeltsin, the newly elected chairman of the Russian parliament, thwarted the coup by rallying protesters and facing down the powerful Russian army. Gorbachev survived the failed coup, but Yeltsin emerged as the most powerful force for reform. By the end of the year Russia proclaimed its independence from Soviet control and, along with Ukraine and Byelorussia (now Belarus), formed the Commonwealth of Independent States. On Christmas Day 1991, a weary Gorbachev resigned as president of the Union of Soviet Socialist Republics that had ceased to exist.

Throughout the year the United States played the role of a cheering but cautious spectator. It found itself in an awkward position: since the beginning of the Cold War it had provided rhetorical support for prodemocracy movements in the Soviet bloc, but at the moment when the democracy movements were succeeding, U.S. leaders offered only tepid praise. Why? The administration wisely did not want to undermine relations with Gorbachev by appearing to exploit

Fall of the Iron Curtain, 1989–1992   To promote economic advancement at home, Soviet premier Mikhail Gorbachev understood the necessity of normalizing international relations. Promising more openness (*glasnost*) for Eastern Europe, Gorbachev announced in December 1988 that hundreds of thousands of Soviet troops would be pulled from the region and emphasized the need for each nation to form its own political ideology. After fifty years of repressive communist rule, Eastern Europeans saw this as a chance for complete independence. Poland initiated the change in June 1989 when the people rejected the Communist party in national elections. After Poland, the rest of Eastern Europe quickly followed suit. By early 1992, the movement for independence had consumed the former Soviet Union, leading to the creation of independent nations, loosely joined in the Commonwealth of Independent States.

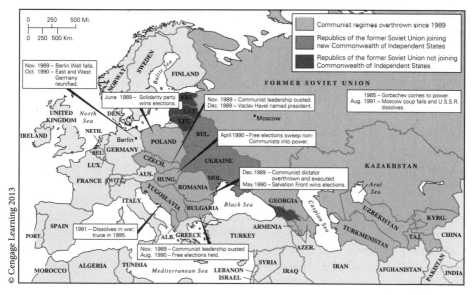

his troubles. Moreover, U.S. policymakers feared instability in the region. Who would control the powerful Soviet nuclear arsenal if the nation fragmented into a number of small, independent republics? "Whatever the course, however long the process took, and whatever its outcome," Bush later reflected, "I wanted to see stable, and above all peaceful, change."

The unraveling of the Soviet Union offered an opportunity to continue the progress in arms control that began in the final years of the Reagan administration. In 1989, Bush announced that it was time to "move beyond containment" by integrating the Soviet Union into "the community of nations." The two nations signed a series of arms control agreements that slashed their nuclear arsenals. Bush and Gorbachev signed agreements to open trade, expand cultural exchanges, and reduce chemical weapons. The Cold War was over.

The New World Order

President Bush declared that the end of the Cold War heralded a "new world order" in which the United States was the only superpower, the rule of law must govern relations between nations, and the powerful must protect the weak.

In some ways the optimism seemed justified. In a globe no longer dominated by Cold War confrontations, the prospect for resolving local disputes brightened. In South Africa, U.S.-imposed economic sanctions pressured newly elected President Frederik W. de Klerk to dismantle apartheid, by which whites had dominated the black majority for 42 years. Along with lifting the government's ban on antiapartheid organizations, de Klerk freed African National Conference Deputy President Nelson Mandela, 71, who was serving the twenty-seventh year of a life prison term.

In Latin America, the end of the Cold War coincided with the demise of a number of authoritarian regimes. In Chile, General Augusto Pinochet, the last military dictator in South America, turned over power to elected President Patricio Aylwin. In Brazil, Fernando Collor de Mello took office as the first directly elected president since a 1964 military coup. In Haiti, a leftist Roman Catholic priest, Father Jean-Bertrand Aristide, swept that nation's first fully free democratic election for president. Elsewhere in Latin America, shaky experiments in democracy showed signs of growing stability. In Nicaragua, newspaper publisher Violeta Barrios de Chamorro defeated Marxist President Daniel Ortega in a peaceful election, ending a decade of leftist Sandinista rule. In El Salvador, the moderate government and opposition leaders signed a peace treaty early in 1992.

The transfer of power in Latin America was not always peaceful. Convinced that Panamanian dictator General Manuel Noriega was the source of drug trade in the region, the administration decided to remove him from office. On December 20, 1989, more than twenty-two thousand U.S. troops, backed by gunships and fighter planes, invaded Panama in the largest military operation since the Vietnam War. After two days of intense fighting, Noriega's resistance crumbled and he sought asylum at the Vatican's diplomatic mission in Panama City. He later surrendered and was flown to the United States where he became the first former or current head of state to be convicted by an American jury.

The end of the Cold War also improved relations in the Middle East. No longer fearing Soviet influence in the region, and less concerned about offending its ally Israel, the United States applied pressure on both Palestinian head Yasir Arafat and Israeli leader Yitzhak Rabin to work toward stability. Secretary Baker engaged in a new round of shuttle diplomacy, traveling to the Mideast eight times in 1991 to arrange negotiations in 1992. After more than a year of secret discussions, Arafat and Rabin traveled to Washington in September 1993 to sign a declaration of principles that allowed for eventual Palestinian self-rule in the Gaza Strip and the West bank.

Only China seemed to buck the trend toward greater openness in the post-Cold War era. In 1989, the Chinese army brutally crushed a pro-democracy demonstration in Beijing's Tiananmen Square. The soldiers killed an estimated four to eight hundred young men and women. A wave of repression, arrests, and public executions followed.

The assault, covered extensively by American television, outraged the public and exposed an underlying tension in America's attitude toward the post-Cold War world: Should the United States emphasize its moral leadership by taking action against nations that failed to live up to American standards of human rights, or should it restrict itself to more practical questions of national security? Bush waffled on the question, leaving himself open to criticism on both the left and right.

War with Iraq

On August 2, 1990, elite Iraqi army troops smashed across the border of Kuwait and roared down a six-lane superhighway for Kuwait City 80 miles away. Iraqi leader Saddam Hussein justified the invasion by claiming that Kuwait had been illegally carved away from Iraq by British imperial agents in the 1920s. The justification masked a more pressing concern, however. Hussein had nearly bankrupted his country in his war with Iran and now needed Kuwait's huge oil reserves to pay the bills.

President Bush saw the invasion as a direct challenge to U.S. leadership in the post-Cold War world. "This must be reversed," he announced after learning of the attack. Over the next few months, in an impressive display of international diplomacy, Bush rallied world opinion against "Saddam." The United Nations Security Council passed resolutions to enforce economic sanctions against Iraq in an effort to force it out of Kuwait. In November, after Hussein showed no signs of retreat, the Security Council authorized use of force for the first time since the Korean War.

While rallying international opinion against Iraq, Bush confronted the difficult task of convincing the American people to go to war to expel Hussein from Kuwait. The administration faced an uphill battle. Polls showed that a majority of Americans opposed going to war. Most did not believe that American interests were at stake. "All that's happened is that one nasty little country invaded a littler but just as nasty country," declared an influential senator. In the end, Congress narrowly passed a resolution authorizing the use of force.

Armed with congressional approval and sustained by strong international support, the president started the war on January 16 with a massive and sustained air assault. On February 23, the Allies under the command of U.S. General H. Norman Schwarzkopf, launched a ground offensive that forced Iraqi forces out of Kuwait in less than 100 hours.

The victory produced an outpouring of patriotism and renewed faith in the military and its leaders that had been tarnished since Vietnam. It made heroes of military leaders, especially Schwarzkopf and Colin Powell, the first African American to serve as chairman of the Joint Chiefs of Staff. "By God, we've licked the Vietnam syndrome once and for all," Bush told a national television audience. The president reaped much of the credit for the operation. His approval rating shot to 89 percent—the highest ever recorded for a president.

The Gulf War   On January 16, 1991, Allied planes stationed at bases across the Middle East and ships in the Persian Gulf began a six-week air assault on missile and anti-aircraft targets in Iraq. On February 23, ground troops began pushing into Iraq and within three days of the ground assault's commencement Iraqi soldiers were in full retreat or surrender. The war resulted in the dismembering of the Iraqi army and the liberation of Kuwait, but left Saddam Hussein in power and did not protect the Kurds in the north.

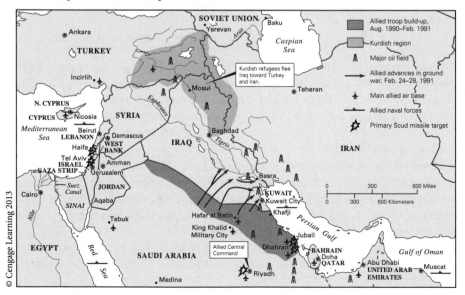

© Cengage Learning 2013

15.1 | *Congress Debates War or Peace with Iraq*

In January 1991, President Bush asked Congress to approve a joint resolution allowing the use of American troops to repel the Iraqi invasion of Kuwait. The three-day debate in Congress reflected the division among American citizens on the issue of American military intervention. Supporters of the resolution in Congress, most of them Republicans, argued that force had to be used to return peace to the region; Democrats insisted that economic sanctions, meant to punish Iraq until it left Kuwait, should be given more time to prove their effectiveness.

Voices in Favor of War with Iraq

(Representative Robert H. Michel, R-Ill.) I speak from the prejudice of being a combat veteran of World War II. And those of our generation know from bloody experience that unchecked aggression against a small nation is a prelude to an international disaster.

5 Saddam Hussein today has more planes and tanks and, frankly, men under arms, than Hitler had at the time when Prime Minister Chamberlain came back from Munich with that miserable piece of paper—peace in our time. I'll never forget that replay of that movie in my life.

And I have an obligation, I guess, coming from that generation, to transmit
10 those thoughts I had at the time to the younger generation who didn't experience what we did. Saddam Hussein not only invaded Kuwait, he occupied, terrorized, murdered civilians, systematically looted and turned a peaceful nation into a wasteland of horror. He seeks control over one of the world's vital resources, and he ultimately seeks to make himself the unchallenged anti-Western dictator of the
15 Mideast.

Either we stop him now, and stop him permanently, or we won't stop him at all.

(Senator Orrin G. Hatch, R-Utah) Unless Saddam Hussein believes that the threat of war is real, he will not budge. I think we've learned that. The only way to avoid war, in my opinion in this particular situation, is to be prepared to go to war and to show that our resolve is for real. . . . Our actions should be decisive.

20 *(Senator William V. Roth Jr., R-Del.)* One can only imagine what devastating consequence would fall should his dominance be allowed in the oil-rich Middle East. And this is the second reason why he must be stopped. When I speak of the danger that would result from his control of this region, I'm not talking about consequences to major oil companies—quite simply, I'm talking about jobs. I'm
25 talking about the raw material of human endeavor.

Oil runs the economy of the world. It fuels our factories, heats our homes. Carries our products from manufacture to market. It's as basic to the economy as water is to life. And the free trade of international supplies is critical, not only

30 for the industrial democracies, but the fragile third world nations that depend on
this precious resource even more than we do.

Any attempt to disrupt these supplies will send a devastating quake to these
economies, lengthening unemployment lines, boosting inflation in the industrial
democracies and crushing the economies of developing countries where day to
day existence depends on imported energy sources.

35 ### *Voices in Dissent*

(Senator George J. Mitchell, D-Maine) This is not a debate about whether force
should ever be used. No one proposes to rule out the use of force; we cannot and
should not rule it out. The question is should war be truly a last resort when all
other means fail or should we start with war, before other means have been fully
40 and fairly exhausted.

This is not a debate about American objectives in the current crisis. There
is broad agreement in the Senate that Iraq must fully and unconditionally withdraw its forces from Kuwait. The issue is how best to achieve that goal. Most
Americans and most members of Congress, myself included, supported the
45 President's initial decision to deploy American forces to Saudi Arabia to deter
further Iraqi aggression. We supported the President's effort in marshaling
international diplomatic pressure and the most comprehensive embargo in history against Iraq.

Despite the fact that his own policy of international economic sanctions was
50 having a significant effect upon the Iraqi economy, the President, without explanation, abandoned that approach and instead adopted a policy based first and
foremost upon the use of American military force. As a result, this country has
been placed on a course toward war. This has upset the balance of the President's
initial policy, the balance between resources and responsibility, between interest
55 and risk, between patience and strength.

(Senator Paul D. Wellstone, D-Minn.) I never thought that the first time I would have
an opportunity to speak in this chamber the topic would be such a grave topic—life
and death, whether or not to go to war, to ask America's men and women, so many
of them so young, to risk life and limb, to unleash a tremendous destructive power
60 on a foreign country and a far away people. This is the most momentous decision
that any political leader would ever have to make and decide we must.

And let no one doubt that the Congress has the responsibility to make this
decision. The Constitution is unambiguous on this point: Congress declares the
war, not the President.
65 The policies that I am afraid the Administration is pursuing, the rush to
war that I am afraid is so much of what is now happening in our country and
the world, will not create a new order, Mr. President, it will create a new world
disorder. What kind of victory will it be? What kind of victory will it be if we
unleash forces of fanaticism in the Middle East and a chronically unstable region
70 becomes even more unstable further jeopardizing Israel's security?

Some causes are worth fighting for. . . . This cause is not worth fighting for right now. We must stay the course with economic sanctions, continue

the pressure, continue the squeeze, move forward on the diplomatic front and Mr. President, we must not, we must not rush to war.

75 *(Senator Edward M. Kennedy, D-Mass.)* I urge the Senate to vote for peace, not war. Now is not the time for war. I reject the argument that says Congress must support the President, right or wrong. We have our own responsibility to do what is right, and I believe that war today is wrong.

War is not the only option left to us in the Persian Gulf. . . . Sanctions and
80 diplomacy may still achieve our objectives, and Congress has the responsibility to insure that all peaceful options are exhausted before resorting to war. . . .

Let there be no mistake about the cost of war. We have arrayed an impressive international coalition against Iraq, but when the bullets start flying, 90 percent of the casualties will be Americans. It is hardly a surprise
85 that so many other nations are willing to fight to the last American to achieve the goals of the United Nations. It is not their sons and daughters who will do the dying. . . .

Not a single American life should be sacrificed in a war for the price of oil. Not a single drop of American blood should be spilled because American automobiles burn too many drops of oil a mile; not a single American soldier should

Impact of War After Iraq's invasion of Kuwait on August 2, 1990, President Bush deployed more than 400,000 troops to Saudi Arabia in an attempt to force Iraq's withdrawal from its neighbor. Each American soldier sent to the Gulf left behind family and friends, as was the case with Army Specialist Hollie Vallance, seen here saying goodbye to her husband and seven-week-old daughter. *(© Allen Horne)*

85 lose his life in the Persian Gulf because America has no energy policy worthy of the name to reduce our dependence on foreign oil.

Source: The American Experiment: A History of the United States, 2nd ed., by Steven M. Gillon and Cathy D. Matson (Boston: Houghton Mifflin Company, 2006), 1297–1299. ■ ■ ■

Problems on the Home Front

Ironically, Bush's success in the Gulf War may have contributed to his political problems at home, which had begun soon after he took office. With the Cold War over, and with no clear foreign threat to distract them, Americans focused more attention on a stagnant economy. "We did not realize how much we had been leaning on the Berlin Wall until we tore it down," conceded one White House aide. While the president scored high marks for his adroit handling of the international scene, he never articulated a clear domestic agenda.

After only a few weeks in office Bush angered voters and enraged conservatives by disavowing his "no new taxes" pledge. In 1990 Bush agreed to a deficit-reduction compromise with congressional Democrats that included $133 billion in new taxes. Reversing the Reagan-era tax policies, the new legislation increased the top bracket from 27 percent to 31 percent, removed some exemptions used by high-income people, and increased "sin taxes" on cigarettes and alcohol. Most observers agreed with the decision to raise taxes, but few were convinced that Bush only learned after the election of the need to do so. The *New York Post*'s front page screamed the reaction—"READ MY LIPS: I LIED."

The deficit package failed to stem the fiscal hemorrhaging or stimulate the economy. The federal deficit continued its upward spiral to $290 billion in 1992, with forecasters predicting it would rise to $331 billion in 1993. While the gross national product increased at an anemic 2.2 percent, unemployment crept upward, housing starts dropped, and consumer confidence hit new lows. By 1992 Bush's approval rating sagged to 34 percent, with fewer than 20 percent of the public approving his handling of the economy. Voters clamored for the president to take decisive action to revive the ailing economy, but Bush and his advisers decided to take a hands-off approach. "I don't think it's the end of the world even if we have a recession," said Treasury Secretary Nicholas Brady. "We'll pull out of it again. No big deal."

Polls showed that Americans wanted more government involvement not only in economic matters but also in issues ranging from education to health care, but the president's hands were tied by the huge budget deficit. Bush did sign one meaningful piece of legislation—the Americans with Disabilities Act (1990), which prohibited discrimination against the 40 million Americans who from mental or physical disabilities.

Bush's handling of environmental issues underscored the difficult faced in trying to hold together a political coalition of moderates and conservatives during tough economic times. During the 1988 campaign Bush broke with Reagan's harsh approach to the environment, promising to be "the environmental president" who would champion tough new regulations to protect clean water and air and preserve public lands. Once in office, however, the president retreated when conservatives within the administration, led by Vice President Quayle, complained that new environmental initiatives would undermine American business competitiveness.

The debate sharpened in March 1989 when the giant oil tanker *Exxon Valdez* ran aground in Prince William Sound, Alaska, spilling 10.8 million gallons of crude oil that spoiled the pristine coastline and killed wildlife. Environmentalists called for an end to Alaskan oil drilling, but Bush disagreed, saying the oil production was essential to meet the nation's energy needs. In the Pacific Northwest environmentalists clashed with loggers and timber companies over whether to preserve the delicate ecosystems of old-growth forest and their endangered inhabitant—the northern spotted owl. Once again Bush sided with business interests, saying that maintaining jobs and profits was a higher priority. Environmentalists achieved a minor victory in 1990 when Bush signed a moderately progressive Clean Air Act, which forced gradual cutbacks on emissions from cars and power plants.

Many scientists were frustrated when the administration refused to join international efforts to control chlorofluorocarbon gases that eroded the Earth's ozone layer, to aid developing nations in developing alternative energy sources, and to slow the depletion of rain forests in South America and Asia. In 1992 the president attended a UN-sponsored "Earth Summit" in Rio de Janeiro, Brazil, but he refused to sign a sweeping, but nonbinding, resolution pledging the nation's support for biodiversity.

The 1992 Presidential Campaign

Already politically vulnerable because of the struggling economy and sinking job approval, Bush had to fend off a revolt of angry conservatives in the Republican primaries. As the election season opened, former Reagan speechwriter Patrick Buchanan scored a surprising victory in the Iowa caucus by attacking Bush as a captive of the Washington establishment who had lost touch with voters. The fiery conservative forced the president to endure a long primary season of punishing verbal assaults. Bush won all thirty-three primaries, but Buchanan took his challenge all the way to the Republican National Convention. The president secured the nomination, but not before Buchanan polarized the party and alienated many voters by calling for a "cultural war" in America.

Politically weaker than in 1988, Bush also faced a more formidable Democratic challenger in former Arkansas governor Bill Clinton. Born in 1946 in Hope, Arkansas, Clinton attended Georgetown University and went to Oxford on a Rhodes scholarship before returning to graduate from Yale Law School. In 1978, at the age of thirty-two, he won election as governor of Arkansas. A party moderate, Clinton appealed to fellow baby boomers by casting himself as a "new Democrat" who understood the concerns of the struggling middle class. Campaigning as a cultural conservative, he professed his support for capital punishment and promised to "end welfare as we know it," to make the streets safer and the schools better, and to provide "basic health care to all Americans." For traditional Democrats he offered a message of economic populism, promising to raise taxes on the wealthy and fight to preserve popular social programs.

A charismatic personality and spellbinding speaker, Clinton emerged as the front runner from a crowded pack of Democratic contenders. The road to the nomination, however, was strewn with difficult questions about marital infidelity and draft dodging. Throughout his public career Clinton had been shadowed by rumors and accusations of extramarital affairs. The issue came to the surface in 1992 when Gennifer Flowers announced that she had been Clinton's mistress for years—and produced taped phone conversations to prove it. In a televised interview with his wife, Hillary Rodham Clinton, at his side, Clinton acknowledged problems in their marriage but denied Flowers's charges. Reporters also questioned Clinton about conflicting statements concerning how he managed to avoid the draft during the Vietnam War and whether he had smoked marijuana as a student. According to his biographer David Maraniss, Clinton "played the draft like a chess player," managing to avoid both the army and the Reserve Officers' Training Corps. He was less adroit, however, at explaining his actions to reporters. Clinton's often evasive and unconvincing answers led to questions about whether he possessed the strength of character to be a good president.

The lingering doubts did not prevent him from winning the nomination earlier than any Democrat in more than two decades. At the party's convention in New York City, Clinton underscored the new Democrat theme by choosing fellow baby-boom southerner Al Gore, a senator from Tennessee, as his running mate. "There's a little Bubba in both of us," Clinton joked.

The fall race was complicated by the presence of an unpredictable third-party candidate, Texas billionaire Ross Perot. With a down-to-earth manner and a history of remarkable success in business, Perot tapped into public discontent with government and Washington by promising to balance the budget and cut the deficit. His position on most other issues remained a mystery, but by July he was leading both Clinton and Bush in the polls when he abruptly decided to leave the race. He returned just as unexpectedly in October, with only one month left, largely in the role of spoiler.

While Perot was on sabbatical from the campaign, Clinton moved to secure his followers and take the lead in the polls by focusing attention on the concerns of middle-class voters. He promised to "focus like a laser beam" on economic issues.

A sign hanging in his campaign office summed up the Democratic strategy: "It's the economy, stupid." Clinton also proved an effective and unconventional campaigner, chatting with young voters on MTV, taking calls on the popular *Larry King Show,* and playing the saxophone and discussing public policy with late-night talk-show host Arsenio Hall. While Clinton climbed in the polls, Bush floundered. His greatest successes had been in dealing with Iraq and Russia, but with the Cold War fading out of mind, the public showed little interest in foreign policy and instead directed its anger at the administration for the sluggish economy.

Voters rewarded Clinton on election night by giving him 43 percent of the popular vote, compared to 37.4 percent for Bush. Clinton's margin in the electoral college was far more decisive. He won thirty-one states and 370 electoral votes. The public registered its disenchantment with both parties by giving Perot a bigger share of the vote—18.9 percent—than it had any third-party candidate since Teddy Roosevelt scored 27.4 percent in 1912. The Democrats retained control of both houses of Congress. Voters sent six women to the Senate and forty-eight to the House of Representatives. California became the first state to elect two women senators—Barbara Boxer and Dianne Feinstein—and Illinois elected the first African American woman, Carol Moseley Braun, to the upper chamber. Observers triumphantly called 1992 "the year of the woman."

In the short run, although Republicans took credit for ending the Cold War, it was the Democrats who reaped the political benefits. The break-up of the Soviet Union removed anticommunism from among the arsenal of weapons conservatives had used to undermine support for Democrats. Diminished fear of Soviet power also shifted public attention away from international issues, where Bush

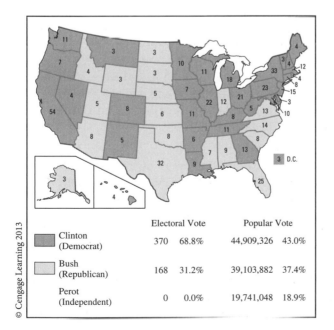

	Electoral Vote		Popular Vote	
Clinton (Democrat)	370	68.8%	44,909,326	43.0%
Bush (Republican)	168	31.2%	39,103,882	37.4%
Perot (Independent)	0	0.0%	19,741,048	18.9%

© Cengage Learning 2013

The Election of 1992

Despite America's victory in Operation Desert Storm, the stagnant economy hurt President George H. W. Bush's chances of reelection. His broken pledge not to raise taxes made him vulnerable to attacks by Democrat Bill Clinton who pledged to work for national health care, welfare reform, and a stronger economy. Dissatisfaction with Bush even spilled over into the third party of H. Ross Perot, who did not win any electoral votes in November but did gain 18.9 percent of the popular vote—the largest third party showing since the Bull Moose Party in 1912.

had strong credentials, and toward domestic problems, which favored Clinton. In the end, the Bush administration was trapped by the paradox of rising expectations and the reality of a crippling budget deficit. When Bush tried to reconcile the contradiction by raising taxes, he incurred the wrath of party conservatives, who accused him of abandoning the Reagan legacy. Bill Clinton and the Democrats pounced on the divided Republicans, but the question remained: Could the new administration square the circle of the American paradox?

SELECTED READINGS

▌ Bruce Buchanan's *Renewing Presidential Politics* (1996) covers the 1988 campaign. The first comprehensive history of the Bush administration is John Greene's *The Presidency of George Bush* (1999). Timothy Naftali offers a concise biographical portrait in *George H.W. Bush* (2007).

▌ There has been extensive material published on the end of the Cold War. Don Oberdorfer's *From the Cold War to a New Era* (1998) is a good introduction. Michael Meyer's *The Year That Changed the World* (2009), and Victor Sebestyen's *Revolution 1989* (2010) deliver powerful accounts of the events that led to the fall of the Soviet Union.

▌ George Bush and national security advisor Brent Scowcroft offer their views of foreign policy in *A World Transformed* (1999). The best overview of the first Gulf War can be found in Rick Atkinson's *Crusade* (1994). Edward Flanagan tells the story of Operation Just Cause in *Battle for Panama* (1994). Editors Ramon Myers, David Shambaugh, and Michel Oksenberg evaluate American policy toward China and Taiwan during the Bush and Clinton administrations in *Making China Policy* (2001).

▌ Charles Kolb describes the formidable political struggle Bush faced while trying to create his domestic agenda in *White House Daze* (1993). Editors Richard Himelfarb and Rosanna Perotti provide a reassessment of Bush's domestic policy in *Principles over Politics?* (2004). Arlene S. Skolnick's *Embattled Paradise* (1991) discusses the recession and budget crisis. Michael Meeropol's *Surrender* (1998) recounts how George Bush, and Bill Clinton after him, struggled to balance the budget.

▌ There have been several character studies of Bill Clinton. David Maraniss's *First in His Class* (1996) is the leading biography of the President. Also useful is Nigel Hamilton's *Bill Clinton: An American Journey* (2003). John Hohenberg's *The Bill Clinton Story* (1994) details the 1992 Democratic campaign.

16

The Clinton Presidency, 1993–2001

On January 7, 1999, a cold, drizzly day in Washington, Chief Justice of the Supreme Court William Rehnquist, dressed in gold-striped black robes, entered the majestic nineteenth-century Senate chamber. The room was hushed, the galleries were packed, and the one hundred senators were seated at rapt attention as the sergeant at arms opened the proceedings. "All persons are commanded to keep silence, on pain of imprisonment, while the House of Representatives is exhibiting to the Senate of the United States articles of impeachment against William Jefferson Clinton."

It was a historic event: the first impeachment trial of an elected U.S. president and only the second such trial in history. The House of Representatives had forwarded two charges against Clinton, the first two-term Democratic president since Franklin Roosevelt. The charges alleged that he had lied under oath and obstructed justice in an effort to hide his affair with Monica Lewinsky, a twenty-two-year-old former White House intern. Under the Constitution, if two-thirds of the Senate, or sixty-seven senators, voted for conviction on either of the two articles of impeachment, Clinton would be removed from office and Vice President Al Gore sworn in to replace him.

After days of listening to Republican prosecutors from the House and to the president's defense lawyers, the senators closed the doors, turned off the television cameras, and deliberated. At the end of the fourth day of closed-door meetings, the doors opened and curious onlookers packed the galleries and filled the aisles to hear the verdict. "Senators, how say you? Is the respondent, William Jefferson Clinton, guilty or not guilty?" Rehnquist asked after a clerk read the first charge of perjury. As the clerk called each senator's name, each stood to announce his or her verdict. Ten Republicans joined a united Democratic Party in declaring the president "not guilty," making the final count 45–55. On the obstruction of justice charge, five GOP senators crossed over, resulting in a 50–50 vote. Clinton "hereby is acquitted of the charges," the chief justice proclaimed.

A subdued Clinton emerged from the Oval Office two hours later to apologize to the American people: "I want to say again to the American people how profoundly sorry I am for what I said and did to trigger these events and the great burden they have imposed on the Congress and the American people." The president could take solace, however, from the fact that neither of the two articles of impeachment attracted even a simple majority of senators' votes, and both fell far short of the two-thirds majority needed to convict and expel the president.

The trial opened a window onto the conflicting social currents of post–Cold War America. Clinton came to office

Lewinsky Affair

After Clinton's confession of "a relationship with Ms. Lewinsky that was not appropriate," the House Judiciary Committee began its investigation of the affair. Meanwhile, the scandal set off a media frenzy as the affair became the most visible topic on news shows, the Internet, and in political cartoons. (*By permission of Mike Luckovich and Creators Syndicate, Inc.*)

attempting to construct a new vital center to respond to the American paradox. He planned to focus public expectations on incremental reforms, to preach the healing power of economic growth both at home and abroad, and to blur ideological lines by borrowing from both liberals and conservatives. But the president's personal behavior pushed the culture wars to the center of American politics. The scandal, kept alive by a steady diet of salacious details from the Internet and twenty-four-hour news programs, frustrated the president's supporters and emboldened his critics. Clinton remained personally popular throughout the scandal, but his actions helped to intensify partisan divisions, contribute to erosion of public faith in the institutions of government, and prevent him from creating an enduring political coalition.

The Clinton Agenda

As the first Democrat to occupy the White House in twelve years, Clinton set a new tone for his administration by calling for "a government that looks like America." True to his word, he appointed a number of women and minorities to top administration posts, including the first woman attorney general, Janet Reno.

Clinton fulfilled his promise to focus intensely on the economy. In February 1993, he submitted an ambitious economic plan to Congress calling for a combination of spending cuts and tax increases to reduce the deficit. Both liberals and conservatives took aim at the plan. Liberals objected because it contained only one ambitious new social program—a national service corps by which college students could pay off federal education loans through community work. Conservatives opposed the tax hikes, which raised the top rate from 31 to 36 percent. After months of haggling, most Democrats fell in line with the president's proposal and it passed the House by a one-vote margin. In an ominous warning of partisan confrontations to come, not a single House Republican voted for the Clinton program.

Even before he submitted his economic package to Congress, Clinton created a political firestorm by proposing to lift the long-standing ban on homosexuals in the military. During the campaign Clinton had lobbied aggressively for gay votes, and once in office he moved on a number of fronts to open opportunities for homosexuals. He ended the federal policy of treating gays as security risks and invited gay activists to the White House for the first time. But his proposal to end discrimination in the military angered the Pentagon and aroused conservative opposition. Months of acrimonious public debate forced Clinton to retreat and agree to an unworkable "don't ask, don't tell" policy that angered both gay-rights groups and conservatives. An uncomfortable and unworkable compromise, the "don"t ask; don"t tell" policy remained in effect until President Barack Obama repealed it in 2010.

After passage of his economic program, Clinton concentrated his energies on passing a complex health-care proposal. In 1993 more than 37 million Americans lacked medical insurance and millions more feared losing coverage. While coverage remained spotty, costs continued to escalate. Shortly after the election the president asked First Lady Hillary Rodham Clinton, an accomplished lawyer with liberal leanings, to set up a health-care task force. In October 1993, the administration unveiled its plan, which would guarantee Americans medical and dental coverage and an array of preventive services. The plan proposed to limit Medicare and Medicaid payments, cap premiums, and foster competition among providers.

Initially, polls showed a large majority of Americans in favor of the new plan and many prominent members of Congress welcomed the initiative. Five months later, however, the plan was dead. What happened? Business leaders and Republicans launched a successful campaign to convince the public that the plan was too costly and the president too liberal. A coalition of conservative opponents paid more than $15 million to air a series of devastating television commercials featuring "Harry and Louise," two ordinary Americans fearful of creeping government intervention in the health-care marketplace. But it was not just pressure from conservatives that killed the legislation. The plan was immensely complicated, running nearly 1,350 pages. It was also far too ambitious, especially given the president's slim victory, the Democrats' small majorities in Congress, and the public's lack of faith in government's ability to solve social problems.

More bad news followed the failure of the health-care proposal: Congress asked a special prosecutor to investigate whether the Clintons had been involved in financial wrongdoing stemming from a bad land deal in which they invested in the 1970s. The investigation into the "Whitewater" development venture in northern Arkansas focused on whether the Clintons had received favorable treatment and been forgiven loans after the failure of the project. Around the same time new reports surfaced that Arkansas state troopers had procured women for Clinton when he was governor. Together the questions over the land deal and the reports of womanizing tapped into larger public doubts about the president's character. By 1994 there were more news stories on Whitewater than on all facets of Clinton's domestic agenda combined.

The First Lady emerged as a lightning rod for conservatives. Hillary Clinton remained overwhelmingly popular among women, minority groups, and the rest of the traditional Democratic base. She wrote a popular book on children's issues, *It Takes a Village* (1996), and she impressed observers with her diplomatic skill and political savvy on solo travels to China, South Asia, South America, Bosnia, Greece, and Turkey. She also found herself at the center of White House controversies, from Whitewater to the failure of health-care reform. Within a few years her unfavorable rating jumped to nearly 40 percent, nearly 10 points above her favorable rating.

The failure of the health-reform package, controversy over the measure to allow gays in the military, and the drumbeat of charges over Whitewater eroded public support for the Clinton presidency. After two years in office Clinton had the lowest poll ratings of any president since Watergate. Energized Republicans, led by the Georgia congressman Newt Gingrich, pounced on the helpless Democrats in the 1994 midterm elections. Nearly three hundred Republican congressional candidates signed a ten-point Contract with America. Gingrich's goal was to nationalize the congressional election. Republicans had scored well in recent presidential elections, and contested for control of the Senate, but the Democrats' patronage power made it difficult to dislodge them from the House. By making each congressional race a referendum on Clinton, the Republicans hoped to tap into the conservative mood of the nation by transforming local races into referendums on national issues.

PRIMARY SOURCE

16.1 | *The Contract with America, 1994*

Seeking to reclaim power from Congressional Democrats in the 1994 midterm elections, Republicans created a comprehensive plan for improving America and winning voters. Written by House Republicans, specifically Georgia's Newt Gingrich and Texas's Dick Armey, the Contract with America stated the principles and intentions of Republicans in an election year and served as a foundation for legislation after their stunning November victory.

The Contract

As Republican Members of the House of Representatives and as citizens seeking to join that body, we propose not just to change its policies, but even more important, to restore the bonds of trust between the people and their elected representatives.

5   That is why, in this era of official evasion and posturing, we offer instead a detailed agenda for national renewal, a written commitment with no fine print.

This year's election offers the chance, after four decades of one-party control, to bring to the House a new majority that will transform the way Congress works. That historic change would be the end of government that is too big, too

10 intrusive, and too easy with the public's money. It can be the beginning of a Congress that respects the values and shares the faith of the American family.

Like Lincoln, our first Republican president, we intend to act "with firmness in the right, as God gives us to see the right." To restore accountability to Congress. To end its cycle of scandal and disgrace. To make us all proud again of

15 the way free people govern themselves.

On the first day of the 104th Congress, the new Republican majority will immediately pass the following major reforms, aimed at restoring the faith and trust of the American people in their government:

20

■ FIRST, require all laws that apply to the rest of the country also apply equally to the Congress;

■ SECOND, select a major, independent auditing firm to conduct a comprehensive audit of Congress for waste, fraud or abuse;

■ THIRD, cut the number of House committees, and cut committee staff by one-third;

25

■ FOURTH, limit the terms of all committee chairs;

■ FIFTH, ban the casting of proxy votes in committee;

■ SIXTH, require committee meetings to be open to the public;

■ SEVENTH, require a three-fifths majority vote to pass a tax increase;

■ EIGHTH, guarantee an honest accounting of our Federal Budget by implementing zero base-line budgeting.

30

Source: Rep. Newt Gingrich, Rep. Dick Armey, and the House Republicans, *The Contract with America,* 1994. Reprinted by permission of Republican National Committee.   ■ ■ ■

Republican Leaders of the House and Senate in 1994   The controversies that developed during Clinton's first two years in office revived the Republican Party and contributed to a sound rejection of Democrats in the 1994 elections. Republicans gained potent majorities in both houses. The new Speaker of the House, Newt Gingrich (*left*), saw the Republican victories as confirmation of the public's support for the party's campaign promises. During 1995 Gingrich, with the support of Senate majority leader Bob Dole (*right*), worked diligently to keep Republicans focused on the passage of the *Contract's* basic tenets into law. (*© Congressional Quarterly Photo/Scott Ferrell*)

On election day Republicans made major gains, seizing control of both houses for the first time in forty years and defeating thirty-five incumbent Democrats. "We got our butts kicked," said the chairman of the Democratic National Committee. The election solidified Republican dominance over the South. For the first time since Reconstruction, the Republicans controlled a majority of southern governorships, senators, and congressional seats. Southerners held most leadership positions in the party. The incoming speaker of the House, Newt Gingrich, hailed from Georgia, while the new Republican whip in the Senate, Trent Lott, was from Mississippi. In addition, the Grand Old Party controlled two southern state legislative houses—the North Carolina house and the Florida senate—for the first time since Reconstruction.

Moving to the Center

Clinton responded to the Republican triumph by moving to the center, professing liberal goals even as he co-opted Republican themes of small government and private initiative. By acting independently of both Republicans and Democrats, Clinton planned to occupy the high middle ground of American politics. Clinton adviser Dick Morris called the strategy "triangulation." The approach represented Clinton's response to the American paradox: he would give rhetorical support to public expectations of activist government, while also paying homage to public fears of federal power.

Clinton's first move was to accept the Republican goal of balancing the budget in ten years or less. "The era of Big Government is over," he announced in Reaganesque language. The president embraced other conservative proposals as well, including a crime bill that would put one hundred thousand new police on the streets and mandatory sentences for criminals convicted three times of felonies.

It was welfare reform, however, that was at the center of Clinton's new strategy. In 1996, he signed a welfare reform bill that eliminated the federal guarantee of welfare as an entitlement. The bill replaced welfare with a program that collapsed nearly forty federal programs, including Aid to Families with Dependent Children (AFDC), into five block grants to the states, giving the states authority to develop their own plans. The most striking provision of the new bill declared that the head of every family on assistance had to work within two years or the family would lose its benefits.

While promising to end welfare as it had been known, Clinton also pledged to "make work pay" by aiding the working poor. The administration's most important initiative, the earned-income tax credit, provided low-wage workers with cash bonuses of nearly $4,000. For someone leaving welfare for work, the program turned a job that paid $6.50 an hour into one that paid about $8.35 an hour. He also succeeded in promoting a series of smaller, often symbolic, initiatives aimed at middle-class Americans. The administration expanded the student loan program and streamlined procedures for gaining mortgage loans from the Federal Housing Administration. He successfully persuaded Congress to pass legislation requiring that manufacturers insert "V-chips" in televisions, thereby allowing parents to block violent or sexually explicit programming. Clinton brokered an agreement by the television industry to voluntarily devise a ratings system. The president opposed a constitutional amendment on school prayer but supported religious expression in schools. "He was saying yes and saying no at the same time," said a White House adviser. "He was stealing the center, creating the center."

While embracing Republican themes, the president also tried to stigmatize that party's leadership as extremists. Newly elected House Speaker Newt Gingrich played directly into Clinton's hands, misinterpreting the public mood: Americans wanted smaller government and lower taxes, but they did not want popular programs cut. Clinton understood the contradiction and exploited it, promising to cut the deficit and protect middle-class social programs. As part of an assault on the "welfare state," Republicans announced plans to cut projected spending on Medicare by $270 billion over five years. Gingrich shocked senior Americans who depended on the program by stating that Medicare should "wither on the vine." At the same time that he was attacking Medicare, Gingrich was pushing through Congress a tax cut for the wealthy.

When Clinton vetoed their budget and spending bills, the Republicans refused to pass the customary stopgap measures to keep the government operating. An angry public blamed the Republicans for the resulting shutdown of "nonessential" federal facilities and services. By March 1995, barely two months after Republicans took control of Congress, polls showed nearly six in ten Americans agreeing that Republicans "will go too far in helping the rich and cutting needed government services that benefit average Americans as well as the poor."

While moving to the right on many economic issues, the president adopted a more liberal stance on the environment. Many conservation groups had high hopes for the new administration: during the 1992 campaign Clinton had criticized George Bush's probusiness approach. Environmentalists expected the administration to fight for an energy tax hike, an upgrade of the Clean Water Act, the Endangered Species Act, and a renewal of the Superfund toxic waste cleanup law. For Clinton, however, the environment was a much lower priority than his plans for economic and health-care reform, so he refused to expend valuable political capital, and the measures failed to pass. In 1994 a conservation group gave the president a "D" grade for his work on the environment.

When the new Republican Congress threatened to "roll back" twenty-five years of bipartisan legislation, however, Clinton made protection of the environment a top priority. "The freedom to breathe clean air, drink safe water, pass a safe world to our children are liberties we dare not take for granted," he told audiences as he promised to veto any Republican attempts to weaken environmental regulations. Clinton found himself on the right side of public opinion. By 1995, 88 percent of the public considered the environment to be either "very important" or "one of the most important problems facing the country."

Winning a Second Term: The 1996 Campaign

By 1996 the president's effort to rebuild public support by co-opting Republican issues of welfare reform and balancing the budget had been remarkably successful. Aided by an expanding economy and declining unemployment, Clinton watched his job approval rating soar to over 60 percent—the highest rating of his presidency. Polls showed that many voters were willing to set aside concerns about Clinton's character in favor of their satisfaction with the humming economy—and their general perception that the country was headed in the right direction.

Republicans chose Kansas senator Robert Dole to challenge Clinton in the 1996 presidential contest. Dole, a seventy-three-year-old veteran of World War II and the oldest man ever to seek the presidency, failed to excite voters, despite a series of self-consciously dramatic gestures. In one of the most memorable campaign moments, Dole resigned from the Senate after three decades in Congress. He also put forth an ambitious 15 percent across-the-board tax-cut plan. In an effort to reach out to younger voters, he chose former Buffalo Bills quarterback and ex-congressman Jack Kemp as his running mate. When all else failed, Dole tried to exploit the "character" issue in the final weeks of the campaign. Nothing seemed to work.

Dole offered himself as a bridge to an older era of strong values and national pride. "Let me be the bridge to an America that only the unknowing call myth," he told cheering Republicans. Clinton countered, using the same metaphor, offering himself as a bridge "to the 21st century, wide enough and strong enough to take us to America's best days."

On election day Clinton became the first Democrat since Franklin Roosevelt to win a second term as president. Victories in thirty states and the District of Columbia gave him 375 electoral votes. Dole carried fourteen states, primarily in the solid Republican South and the mountain states of the West, with a combined 129 electoral votes. Ross Perot, the Texas billionaire who ran on the ticket of the Reform Party, finished a distant third, drawing roughly one-half of the 18.9 percent of the vote he had won in 1992. "They have affirmed our cause and told us to go forward," Clinton said of the voters. But the election hardly represented a clear mandate. Clinton failed to produce coattails for other Democrats as the Republicans retained control of the House and gained a few seats in the Senate. In a troublesome note on the character issue, more than one-half of all voters, even many who voted for him, told pollsters that the president was neither honest nor trustworthy.

The New Internationalism

As the first president elected after the end of the Cold War, Clinton faced a variety of new and complex questions. As the only remaining superpower, what relationship should the United States have to the rest of the world? Many Americans celebrated the end of the Cold War, viewing it as a victory for the American ideals of freedom and democracy. But how would the nation define its vital interests in the post–Cold War era? How would it balance its commitment to American ideals with the realities of global politics?

For all of the peril of the Cold War, it had provided policymakers with a framework, though often a narrow one, for interpreting world events and for calculating the national interest. The United States had a grand concept—containment—to guide its approach to the world. Without a grand strategy, the administration appeared to lurch from one international crisis to another.

The first occurred in the Horn of Africa, the northeast region of the continent, where many nations—Ethiopia, Sudan, and Somalia among them—had been suffering from drought, famine, and intermittent civil war. The situation grew grave in 1992 as fighting among rival factions threatened to cut off relief supplies to Somalia, leaving millions to starve. Pushed to respond by public reaction to television pictures of emaciated children, Bush had ordered nearly 30,000 troops to Somalia on a humanitarian mission to restore order and secure relief efforts. Initially, Operation Restore Hope succeeded, but before long the rival clans tired of the U.S. presence and began putting up resistance.

Clinton inherited a complex problem. U.S. troops could not guarantee the flow of supplies without fighting the clans, but engaging the rival factions risked getting America bogged down in a quagmire. Without seeking approval from Congress, Clinton left nearly 9,000 troops in Somalia and expanded their mission to include taking on the local clans. In October 1993, eighteen U.S. Army Rangers died in a bloody firefight with a gang of Somalis. A horrified nation watched television video of an American soldier being dragged through the streets of Mogadishu to the cheers of local crowds. The journalist David Halberstam called the incident "a major league CNN-era disaster." Clinton quickly retreated, withdrawing the remaining America forces. "Gosh, I miss the Cold War," Clinton remarked after learning that American soldiers had been killed.

The administration used the threat of military force more successfully closer to home in Haiti. In 1991 a band of military leaders overthrew the elected leader, Jean-Bertrand Aristide. The Clinton administration organized an international effort to restore Aristide, applying diplomatic pressure and convincing the United Nations to impose economic sanctions. The military regime showed no interest in giving up power voluntarily until Clinton decided to flex his military muscle, threatening to use the marines to expel the junta. With American warships looming off the coast, Haiti's military leaders backed down and allowed Aristide to return to power. The president learned, however, that there were limits to his power to transform foreign government. Old trouble spots, including the Middle East and Iraq, proved immune to economic incentives. In some countries economic assistance and the opening of markets failed to produce the expected reforms. Russia received enormous sums of international aid, but refused to phase out arms shipments to rogue nations. Many Third World nations suspiciously viewed globalization as a rich country's game where the rules were rigged to favor industrialized nations. In an age of globalization money could move around the globe with the flick of a few computer keys. The new international system transferred authority from local political leaders to a handful of powerful institutional investors.

Handshake Affirming the Oslo Accords   The Oslo Accords, officially known as the "Declaration of Principles," were the result of secret negotiations in Norway between Israel and the Palestine Liberation Organization (PLO) to try to create a foundation on which long-term peace between the two peoples could be established. Hosted by President Clinton, Israeli Prime Minister Yitzhak Rabin (*left*) and PLO Chairman Yasir Arafat (*right*) signed the accords at the White House on September 13, 1993, and concluded the ceremony with a handshake. The accords called for the removal of Israeli troops from the Gaza Strip and West Bank and required Arafat to renounce terrorism and diplomatically recognize Israel. The accords served as the basis for further negotiations through the rest of the nineties, despite intermittent resumption of violence in the region. (*© AP/Wide World Photos*)

Trouble Spots: Yugoslavia and Iraq

The end of the Cold War accelerated Yugoslavia's splintering into rival ethnic factions. For most of the Cold War era the strong leadership of Josip Broz Tito managed to balance the unstable coalition of Catholic Croatians, Eastern Orthodox Serbs, and Muslims that made up the Yugoslav nation. Tito's death in 1980, combined with the dissolution of the Soviet Union and the independence fever that swept through Eastern Europe, shattered the peace. In 1991 Yugoslavia's provinces of Slovenia, Croatia, and Bosnia-Herzegovina proclaimed their independence. The move infuriated the Serb-dominated federal government in Belgrade, headed by President Slobodan Milosevic. Determined to create a "Greater Serbia," Milosevic launched military attacks against Croats and Muslims living in areas dominated by ethnic Serbs. In Bosnia-Herzegovina Serbs shelled the capital of Sarajevo and murdered, raped, and imprisoned Muslims in a vicious campaign of "ethnic cleansing." By the end of 1992 more than 150,000 people had died.

The war produced confusion in Washington. Should the United States intervene? Were American national interests at stake in a conflict that was enormously complex and local, involving generations of ethnic rivalries? Any action also threatened the warm relations with Russia, which maintained close ties with the Serbs. Torn between a humanitarian desire to help and a public fearful of intervention, the administration waffled. The president sent confusing signals: "I will not let Sarajevo fall," he told Congress. Then he added, "Don't take that as an absolute."

The situation took a dramatic turn in February 1994, when a mortar shell exploded in Sarajevo's open market, killing sixty-eight people and injuring more than two hundred. A few days later the president delivered an ultimatum to the Serbs: either pull back all tanks and artillery from a 12.4-mile free zone around the city or risk assault from members of the North Atlantic Treaty Organization (NATO). Later that month NATO planes shot down Serb jets that violated the no-fly zone. It was the first time in the alliance's history that NATO planes had seen combat.

The exercise of force brought all the parties to the negotiating table in 1995. Under heavy pressure from the United States, the presidents of Bosnia, Croatia, and Serbia signed a peace agreement that solved territorial differences and brought an end to hostilities. As part of the agreement Clinton committed American troops to Bosnia as part of a multinational force to keep the peace. The move stirred up considerable controversy, especially among conservatives who opposed using American troops as part of a multinational force and who argued that American national security was not at stake. Clinton remained resolute. "We stood for peace in Bosnia," he told the nation in 1996.

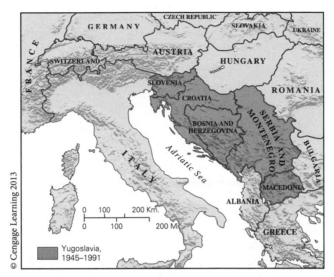

© Cengage Learning 2013

Division of Yugoslavia   By 1990, Yugoslavia suffered from a heavy foreign debt, inflation, and unemployment, but nothing was more divisive than the growing nationalism and ethnic conflict long suppressed by communist dictators who were swept out of office in 1989. In the spring of 1990, multiparty elections in Slovenia and Croatia resulted in the victory of parties that supported independence, and later the same year similar results occurred in Macedonia and Bosnia-Herzegovina elections. When Serbian leaders blocked the election of a Croatian to the federal presidency in June 1991, Croatia declared its independence, followed by the other three. Montenegro and Serbia joined together in April 1992 under the leadership of Serbian Slobodan Milosevic, who used his military to support ethnic cleansing and attempted to force the breakaway nations into accepting a resumption of a unified Yugoslavia, actions which led to international intervention in the region for the rest of the nineties.

Boxed in by NATO troops in Bosnia, Milosevic turned his war machine against the province of Kosovo, where ethnic Albanians were struggling for independence. When Serb troops embarked on another campaign of ethnic cleansing, this time in Kosovo, NATO tried to negotiate a peaceful settlement. The Albanian Kosovars reluctantly accepted the terms of an agreement that gave them political autonomy within Serbia. But the Serbs remained defiant, refusing to sign the treaty and stepping up their campaign against innocent civilians. In March 1999, the United States and the NATO allies decided to use force to challenge the Serbs. In the clearest statement of American policy in the region, President Clinton told a skeptical public that Kosovo represented a vital interest that the United States had to defend. Within hours U.S. warplanes, backed by cruise missiles and aircraft from other NATO allies, initiated a massive bombing campaign against the Serbs in Kosovo and Serbia itself. In May, after eighty days of intense bombardment that decimated the army and destroyed the country's fragile infrastructure, Milosevic relented to NATO demands and withdrew his forces from Kosovo.

In attempting to define American national interests in the post–Cold War world, the Clinton administration was forced to revisit the lingering threat posed by Saddam Hussein. Following his crushing defeat at the hands of the allies, the Bush administration assumed that opposition forces would mobilize to overthrow Hussein. Instead, the cagey leader emerged from defeat as powerful as ever, crushing potential adversaries, threatening to destabilize the region, and playing a game of cat and mouse with UN inspectors assigned to root out his secret stockpiles of chemical and nuclear weapons. When Hussein made threatening moves toward Kuwait in 1994, the Clinton administration deployed 54,000 troops and more warplanes to the gulf. Two years later U.S. air units struck Iraqi missile targets when Iraqi troops intensified their anti-insurgent operations in the northern part of the country.

As Hussein grew more intransigent, the U.S. position hardened. The change reflected the more hawkish views of Secretary of State Madeline Albright, who took over from the retiring Warren Christopher in 1997. Born a diplomat's daughter in Prague, Czechoslovakia, in 1937, she fled Nazi occupation with her family and spent most of World War II living in London. "Some people's historical context is Vietnam; mine is Munich," she told reporters. "For me, America truly is the indispensable nation." For Albright, Hussein seemed the reincarnation of Adolf Hitler, and she was determined not to go down the failed path of appeasement. When Hussein refused to cooperate with weapons inspectors, Albright urged the president to take dramatic action. In December 1998, the United States and Britain launched the largest bombardment of Iraq since the end of the Gulf War, unleashing cruise missiles as well as fighters and bombers. The U.S. military declared the attack a success, but Hussein remained defiant.

Free Trade and Open Markets

While uncertain about the use of military force in the post-Cold war era, the Clinton administration made economic policy a centerpiece of its approach to the world. The president described the United States as "a big corporation competing in the global marketplace."

In 1994, Clinton fought a tough legislative battle to win congressional approval of the North American Free Trade Agreement (NAFTA) negotiated during the Bush presidency. The agreement gradually abolished nearly all trade barriers between the United States, Mexico, and Canada. Later that year, Clinton won another key free trade battle when the administration convinced Congress to approve the General Agreement on Tariffs and Trade (GATT), which allowed the United States to participate in a new worldwide trade agreement.

While fighting for free trade in the hemisphere the administration fought to open new markets to American goods. The president created a new agency—the National Economic Council—to coordinate domestic and foreign economic policies. In 1994, the United States made its peace with Vietnam by lifting its trade embargo and normalizing relations. American companies, which had been barred from doing business in Southeast Asia, rushed into the country. Within hours of the announcement, Pepsi tried to get a jump start on its arch rival Coke by distributing over 40,000 free cans of its soft drink to the Vietnamese.

Russia remained a major worry for the administration. The transition from communism to capitalism left the Russian economy in shambles. A collapse in its domestic market would send shock waves around the world. To help prop up the Russian economy, the administration developed a $4.5 billion aid package to facilitate reform efforts and sustain Russia's currency, the ruble. At the same time, the administration worked closely with Russian counterparts to reduce stockpiles of nuclear weapons.

Impeachment and the Legacy of the 1960s

At the same time that Clinton was attacking Iraq, he was fighting a battle at home to keep his job as president. In December 1998, he became only the second president in U.S. history to be impeached by the House and, in January, tried in the Senate. The year-long drama that led up to the trial and consumed much of the nation's attention centered on an affair between Clinton and former White House intern Monica Lewinsky. When charges surfaced, a defiant president denied having had sexual relations with "that woman." After he made the same denials in a civil case, and to a grand jury, Kenneth Starr, the special prosecutor in the case, recommended that the president be impeached and removed from office for "high crimes and misdemeanors." To support his conclusion, he delivered a steamy report to the House detailing the affair and offering eleven potential grounds for impeachment.

PRIMARY SOURCE

16.2 | *Apology to the Nation*
BILL CLINTON

Threatened by a subpoena, Clinton appeared before Starr's grand jury, via closed circuit television, to answer questions concerning his testimony in the Paula Jones sexual harassment case and admit to an affair with Monica Lewinsky. That evening, August 17, 1998, Clinton addressed the national television audience concerning the affair. The speech Clinton ultimately gave was less apologetic than the original draft, leaving room for debate as to which version would have been more successful and less politically damaging.

Original Draft

My fellow Americans:

No one who is not in my position can understand the remorse I feel today. Since I was very young, I have had a profound reverence for this office I hold. I've been honored that you, the people, have entrusted it to me. I am proud of what
5 we have accomplished together.

But in this case, I have fallen short of what you should expect from a president. I have failed my own religious faith and values. I have let too many people down. I take full responsibility for my actions—for hurting my wife and daughter, for hurting Monica Lewinsky and her family, for hurting friends and staff, and for
10 hurting the country I love. None of this ever should have happened.

I never should have had any sexual contact with Monica Lewinsky, but I did. I should have acknowledged that I was wrong months ago, but I didn't. I thought I was shielding my family, but I know in the end, for Hillary and Chelsea, delay has only brought more pain. Their forgiveness and love, expressed so often as we
15 sat alone together this weekend, means more than I can ever say.

What I did was wrong—and there is no excuse for it. I do want to assure you, as I told the Grand Jury under oath, that I did nothing to obstruct this investigation.

Finally, I also want to apologize to all of you, my fellow citizens. I hope you
20 can find it in your heart to accept that apology. I pledge to you that I will make every effort of mind and spirit to earn your confidence again, to be worthy of this office, and to finish the work on which we have made such remarkable progress in the past six years.

God bless you, and good night.

25 ### Delivered Speech

Good evening.

This afternoon in this room, from this chair, I testified before the Office of Independent Counsel and the grand jury. I answered their questions truthfully, including questions about my private life—questions no American
30 citizen would ever want to answer. Still, I must take complete responsibility for all my actions, both public and private. And that is why I am speaking to you tonight.

As you know, in a deposition in January, I was asked questions about my relationship with Monica Lewinsky. While my answers were legally accurate, I did
35 not volunteer information. Indeed, I did have a relationship with Ms. Lewinsky that was not appropriate. In fact, it was wrong. It constituted a critical lapse in judgment and a personal failure on my part for which I am solely and completely responsible. But I told the grand jury today—and I say to you now—that at no time did I ask anyone to lie, to hide or destroy evidence, or to take any other
40 unlawful action.

I know that my public comments and my silence about this matter gave a false impression. I misled people, including even my wife. I deeply regret that. I can only tell you I was motivated by many factors. First, by a desire to protect myself from the embarrassment of my own conduct.

45   I was also very concerned about protecting my family. The fact that these questions were being asked in a politically inspired lawsuit, which has since been dismissed, was a consideration, too.

    In addition, I had real and serious concerns about an independent counsel investigation that began with private business dealings twenty years ago—

50 dealings, I might add, about which an independent federal agency found no evidence of any wrongdoing by me or my wife over two years ago. The independent counsel investigation moved on to my staff and friends, then into my private life. And now the investigation itself is under investigation.

    This has gone on too long, cost too much, and hurt too many innocent

55 people. Now, this matter is between me, the two people I love most—my wife and our daughter—and our God.

    I must put it right, and I am prepared to do whatever it takes to do so. Nothing is more important to me personally. But it is private, and I intend to reclaim my family life for my family. It's nobody's business but ours. Even presidents have

60 private lives. It is time to stop the pursuit of personal destruction and the prying into private lives and get on with our national life.

    Our country has been distracted by this matter for too long, and I take my responsibility for my part in all of this. That is all I can do. Now it is time—in fact, it is past time—to move on. We have important work to do, real opportunities to

65 seize, real problems to solve, real security matters to face.

    And so tonight, I ask you to turn away from the spectacle of the past seven months, to repair the fabric of our national discourse, and to return our attention to all the challenges and all the promise of the next American century.

    Thank you for watching, and good night.

Source: Address by President Bill Clinton, August 17, 1988 (original draft and delivered speech).

■ ■ ■

The reaction to the Starr Report exposed deep ideological and partisan divisions in Congress. The debate over impeachment transformed into a larger cultural war between liberals and conservatives over the legacy of the 1960s. Many conservatives viewed Clinton as a reflection of the moral laxity and self-indulgence of the baby-boom generation. "Why do you hate Clinton so much?" an interviewer asked a conservative. "Because," he responded, "he's a womanizing, Elvis-loving, non-inhaling, truth-shading, war-protesting, draft-dodging, abortion-protecting, gay-promoting, gun-hating baby boomer. That's why." For liberals, however, Clinton was being punished for continuing the liberal reforms of the 1960s, expanding the power of government, and challenging the establishment. "The president is guilty of being a populist leader who opened up government and access to power," thundered California Congresswoman Maxine Waters.

After weeks of public hearings the Judiciary Committee voted to send formal changes to the House, which in turn approved two charges—perjury and obstruction of justice—and sent them on to the Senate for trial. In 1999 the Senate rang in the New Year by putting the president on trial. Over the next few weeks the senators listened to often-repetitive charges and countercharges by the House prosecutors, also called managers, and the White House defense team. The thirteen prosecutors, all Republicans, had to convince Senators that the president's offenses were criminal and that they merited his removal from office. When the final votes were counted, the Senate failed to muster a majority on either count and fell far short of the constitutionally mandated two-thirds needed to convict the president.

The impeachment debate revealed that while most Americans were comforted by the rhetoric of traditional values, they were reluctant to impose on others the older standard of morality advocated by most conservatives. Instead of choosing between new rights and old values, the vast majority of Americans created a shield of privacy that allowed them to avoid passing judgment on questions of personal morality. Americans embraced a new faith in tolerance as a morally neutral middle ground. Polls showed that nearly 90 percent of Americans agreed that the country "would have many fewer problems if there were more emphasis on traditional family values." But nearly 70 percent agreed that "we should be more tolerant of people who choose to live according to their own moral standards, even if we think they are wrong."

In the end, everyone came out of the affair with tarnished reputations. The president enjoyed high job approval ratings throughout the investigation, but the public gave him low marks for honesty and integrity. The GOP's pugnaciously partisan pursuit of impeachment backfired. The Republicans lost a handful of congressional seats in the midterm 1998 elections. Republicans also appeared hypocritical when reports showed that some who condemned Clinton's behavior had checkered pasts of their own. Louisiana's Robert Livingston, for example, a harsh critic of the president's behavior whom Republicans chose to succeed Gingrich as House Speaker, was forced to resign his seat after confessing that he had "on occasion strayed from my marriage."

The media's obsession with the affair, and all its sordid details, came in for its share of criticism. There was a time when reporters did not think the private lives of presidents were relevant. Journalists kept silent about President John Kennedy's late-night trysts in the White House. The rules started to change in the 1970s when reporters exposed the relationship between powerful House Ways and Means Committee chairman Wilbur Mills (a Democrat from Arkansas) and stripper Fanne Foxe. In 1987 Gary Hart was forced to abandon his campaign for the presidency when journalists staked out his house and discovered him having an affair. By the time Monica Lewinsky entered the discussion, there seemed to be no rules. The advent of the Internet, twenty-four-hour cable television shows, and bombastic talk radio created new outlets for information. Congress posted on the Internet the Starr Report, which contained graphic

descriptions of semen-stained dresses, kinky acts with cigars, and c
Many Americans expressed alarm at the coarseness of the public discou.
news programs and talk shows that delved into the steamy sex escapade
high ratings.

The Clinton Legacy

Unprecedented prosperity helped Clinton weather the impeachment controversy. The Dow Jones Industrial Average soared from 3,241 when he took office in 1993 to over 10,000 by the time he left eight years later. The economy created 22.5 million new jobs, violent crime dropped by 30 percent, and teen pregnancies dipped 18 percent. The president's supporters insisted that he deserved some of the credit for the success, arguing that his 1993 budget plan, approved without a single Republican vote, created the foundation for the new economy.

It may be difficult to know whether Clinton deserved credit for the economy, but he certainly exercised a powerful influence on his own party. "He modernized the Democratic party for the information age," said a leading Democrat. "He made it competitive again in national politics, and it became a model for center-left parties all over the world." Polls showed that the public gave the Democrats the edge on economic growth, fiscal responsibility, and general fairness. He developed an approach that returned the white middle class to the party, forcing Democrats to shed their liberal skin. He often split with traditional Democrats on free-trade policies, welfare overhaul, and crime. He supported the death penalty and a balanced budget. "The Democratic Party brand used to stand for a lot of things—labor unions, big spenders, soft on crime," said an administration official. "Bill Clinton fundamentally repositioned the Democratic Party."

Clinton also managed to articulate a constructive view of government during conservative times. The president believed that before people would trust activist government, they first had to believe that government was under control. "Roosevelt saved capitalism from itself," Clinton told aides early in his administration. "Our mission is to save government from its own excesses so it can again be a progressive force." Compelled to deal with a Republican Congress, Clinton tried to use a smaller but still activist government to assist individuals to compete in the new economy. He increased funding for education, launched an initiative to broaden health care for uninsured children, and dramatically increased government spending for the working poor.

Even the president's detractors were forced to recognize his considerable political skills. He often outmaneuvered his opponents and frustrated his liberal allies by co-opting conservative positions on issues from crime to welfare. "I believe that Clinton is the best tactical politician, certainly of my lifetime," said his former nemesis House Speaker Newt Gingrich.

Clinton became the first president to contend with the relentless exposure of a competitive twenty-four-hour news cycle and the real-time universe of the Internet. His youth and style made the modern presidency more accessible and approachable. He answered questions on MTV about his underwear and talked about "causing pain" in his marriage. He blended Hollywood and government, blurring the boundaries between the public and private. In his role of celebrity-in-chief he invited the same scrutiny about his private life that Hollywood stars face. "At a time when people lost interest in big public questions, we've riveted our attention on the X-rated soap opera of the Clinton presidency," observed the scholar Michael Sandel.

The battle over Clinton's legacy symbolized the nation's continuing struggle with the cultural impact of the 1960s. Clinton may have forged a centrist coalition on policy, but his personal behavior produced a backlash on the issue of values. For many conservative Americans Clinton came to represent the worst that the 1960s generation had to offer. Ironically, his personal behavior angered and alienated the same middle-class voters to whom his policies were designed to appeal. Many of these voters opposed impeachment, but they wanted the president,

"Baby Boomers" Bill and Hillary Clinton   One of the reasons that both the President and the First Lady were so controversial was that many Americans viewed them as symbols of the baby-boom generation that came to maturity in the 1990s. Clinton won election as a centrist candidate and he often supported conservative legislation like welfare reform. But in style and temperament, both he and Hillary reflected the values of the sixties generation. Here, they enjoy one of the favorite activities of aging boomers: a morning jog.   *(© AP/Wide World Photos)*

and the party that supported him, punished for his reckless and irresponsible actions. They would get their chance at the ballot box in the 2000 presidential election.

SELECTED READINGS

▮ There have been several accounts of the Clinton presidency. Joe Klein's *The Natural* (2003) and John Harris's *The Survivor* (2005) are among the best. Former Clinton adviser George Stephanopoulos has written an insightful memoir, *All Too Human* (2000), and Clinton penned his memoir, *My Life*, in 2004. Hillary Clinton gives her unique perspective on events in the 1990s in *Living History* (2003). William Berman's *From the Center to the Edge* (2001) focuses on the origins and evolution of Clinton's programs and analyzes his successes and failures.

▮ Bob Woodward's *Agenda* (1994) is a detailed study of Clinton's first years in office. Gregory M. Herek's *Out in Force* (1996) chronicles the debate over homosexuals in the military. Jim McDougal's *Arkansas Mischief* (1998) explores the real-estate dealings and partisan wrangling that led to the Whitewater scandal.

▮ Charles Jones looks at Clinton's early initiatives that were thwarted by Congress and how Gingrich miscalculated Republican power in *Clinton and Congress* (1999). On the Clinton-Gingrich standoff, see Steven M. Gillon's *The Pact* (2008). *Washington Post* staff reporter Peter Baker presents a behind-the-scenes look at the events that led to impeachment hearings and the subsequent trial of the president in *The Breach* (2000). Marvin Kalb analyzes the media's role in the proceedings in *One Scandalous Story* (2001).

▮ David Halberstam's *War in a Time of Peace* (2001) analyzes the foreign policy of Bush and Clinton and how the end of the Cold War required changes in executive tasks. William Hyland examines the early failures of Clinton's foreign policy and his ability to learn from these mistakes and reinvent his policy in *Clinton's World* (1999). The American response in Somalia, Haiti, and Bosnia is described in Lester Brune's *The United States and Post–Cold War Interventions* (1999). The 1994 invasion of Haiti is the focus of Philippe Girard's *Clinton in Haiti* (2004). Wayne Bert outlines the struggle to create a policy concerning the Bosnian conflict in *The Reluctant Superpower* (1997). Daniel Byman and Matthew Waxman argue in *Confronting Iraq* (2000) that American pressure on Iraq has been successful in the years since the Gulf War. Thomas Lippman's *Madeleine Albright and the New American Diplomacy* (2000) analyzes Albright's struggle to redefine national security in an era of globalization, and in *Madam Secretary* (2003) Albright tells her own story.

17 The Prosperous Nineties

On August 23, 1995, Bill Gates, the often reclusive founder and chief executive officer (CEO) of computer software giant Microsoft, kicked off the sale of the much-anticipated Windows 95 software at a large party at the company's Redmond, Washington, headquarters. The party capped a worldwide megamarketing blitz for an $89 piece of software that Gates promised would help revolutionize the computer industry. Along with offering increased speed and a redesigned interface, the software included a controversial "bundling" of its Microsoft Network online service. "Microsoft is celebrating its 20th anniversary this year," Gates said to the crowd of two thousand five hundred people gathered under a packed circus tent and the thousands more watching by satellite hookup in forty-three cities around the world. "Its original vision for a computer on every desk and in every home is slowly coming true."

The highlight of the evening was a standup comedy routine between Gates and late-night-television host Jay Leno. "Windows 95 is so easy, even a talk-show host can figure it out," Gates said in an awkward attempt at humor. But it was Leno who stole the show, often poking fun at the multibillionaire Gates. "This man is so successful," Leno said, "his chauffeur is Ross Perot."

Afterward the crowd danced to the music of the Rolling Stones hit "Start Me Up," played with hundreds of helium-filled balloons, rode a miniature Ferris wheel, and sang an off-key version of "Auld Lang Syne."

The successful launch of Windows 95 made Gates the wealthiest man in the world at the same time that it spurred the computer revolution of the 1990s. The widespread use of personal computers (PCs) and the rise of the World Wide Web formed the foundation of a communications revolution that promised to transform American business and leisure. *The Economist* asserted that the Web represented "a change even more far-reaching than the harnessing of electrical power a century ago." This information society propelled the economy to new heights as high-tech firms produced a surge on Wall Street.

But neither the information society nor the burgeoning prosperity could resolve the American paradox. The new prosperity filled government coffers with added tax revenue, allowing both Washington and many states to balance their budgets after years of living in the red, but it failed to mend deep social divisions in America. The debate over popular culture, the persistence of racial conflict, and the rise of domestic terrorism revealed a wide gulf between American ideals and social realities. The paradox found full expression in the 2000 presidential election, which celebrated the fruits of prosperity while highlighting profound cultural differences.

The Computer Revolution and the Information Society

Changes in communications spearheaded the emergence of the global economy in the 1990s. The most dramatic development was the widespread use of the Internet. Scientists launched the first phase of the computer revolution in 1946 when they turned the switch to start up the mammoth Electronic Numerical Integrator and Calculator. This mainframe computer weighed 30 tons, filled an enormous room at the University of Pennsylvania, consumed 150,000 watts of power, and used 18,000 vacuum tubes. The machine required so much power it was rumored that when the scientists turned it on, the lights in the city of Philadelphia dimmed. Over the next twenty years businesses adopted mainframe computers to handle basic tasks such as automating payroll, billing, and inventory controls.

In the 1970s a diverse collection of tinkerers working in garages in the San Francisco Bay Area were responsible for the second phase of the computing revolution—the birth of the personal computer (PC). In 1977 two young entrepreneurs, Steve Wozniak and Steve Jobs, used a new microprocessor chip to assemble the first Apple II computer. This user-friendly and relatively inexpensive machine, composed of a keyboard and an external disk drive, would become the prototype of every desktop machine. By 1981 more than twenty thousand customers were using Apple II computers. The new product inspired fierce loyalty among its original buyers and had the opportunity to dominate the computer market. But Apple made a critical mistake: it refused to license its operating system, thus making it impossible for other computer makers and software writers to develop compatible systems. Apple was soon eclipsed by International Business Machines (IBM), which introduced its own PC in 1981. By 1985 the company had sold more than 6 million machines, primarily to its business customers.

Pressed by demand, IBM decided to outsource its operating system and its microprocessor. The decision was a bonanza for two young companies. One was Intel, a small Silicon Valley company that had created the first microprocessor, an integrated circuit that put the power of a mainframe on a single chip. The microchip was to the modern information economy what the combustion engine was to the earlier industrialization of society. The other company was Microsoft, founded by Bill Gates in 1975, which provided software for the PC. Since IBM used open architecture, Microsoft and Intel were able to provide the software and microprocessors to "Big Blue" as well as to the dozens of IBM "clones." As the PC market boomed during the 1980s and 1990s, Intel and Microsoft reaped enormous profits and their CEOs became international celebrities. In 1997 *Time* magazine selected Andrew Grove of Intel as its "Man of the Year." By that time Bill Gates had emerged as the wealthiest person and most recognizable businessman in the world.

The shift from the mainframe to the PC during the 1980s was made possible by tremendous advances in technology. For example, Intel built its Pentium microprocessor on a piece of silicon the size of a thumbnail. Two decades of steady increases in the capacity of microprocessors drove down prices and put tremendous computing power in the hands of the average citizen. With a PC, individuals could enhance and speed up their performance of personal and business tasks using word processors, spreadsheets, and personal databases. In 1983 *Time,* instead of naming its usual "Man of the Year," named the computer the "Machine of the Year." By the mid-1990s more than 90 percent of all businesses in the United States relied on the personal computer for essential functions. More than one-third of families had a PC at home. In 1995, for the first time, the amount of money spent on PCs exceeded that spent on televisions.

The Birth of the World Wide Web

The third phase of the computer revolution began with the birth of the Internet. Founded in the late 1960s by Defense Department scientists trying to develop a decentralized communications system that could survive a nuclear war, the

Internet created a set of standards, or protocols, that enabled thousands of independent computer networks to communicate. The real explosion in Internet use took place during the early 1990s with the development of the World Wide Web, whereby almost any user with a telephone line and a modem could log onto a worldwide computer communications network. By 1997 about 100 million people around the globe used the Internet; by 2000 that number had soared to 327 million, with Americans making up about 40 percent of total users.

The Web was the central character in a larger unfolding drama—the explosion in digital communications technology made it possible to convert text, sound, graphics, and moving images into coded digital messages. People could transmit those messages quickly and efficiently over wired and wireless networks. The Internet was the chief product of the new technology, but it was not alone. Cell phones, once a toy of the rich, became a standard feature in the workplace, as did fax machines and wireless modems.

"This is the Kitty Hawk era of electronic commerce," an Internet entrepreneur boasted. The Internet empowered individuals by putting vast amounts of unfiltered information at their fingertips. In medicine patients used the Internet to find out about new treatments, breaking the monopoly that physicians had once had on medical information. In business the sharing of electronic documents flattened hierarchies and gave lower-level employees access to huge amounts of information previously the purview of managers. Investors could bypass stockbrokers and plan retirement benefits online. By allowing people to communicate effortlessly across thousands of miles, the Internet gave rise to the "virtual corporation," in which employees and managers were located in different places. Politicians used the Internet to circumvent the traditional media and communicate their message directly to voters. In 1999 Republican Steve Forbes became the first presidential aspirant to announce his candidacy on the Internet. For millions of Americans the Web helped break down cultural and geographic borders by creating virtual communities of shared interests. America Online, the largest Internet provider in the United States, saw its membership soar to over 10 million by 1999. More than three-quarters of its subscribers used anonymous chat rooms to meet people with similar interests. People from all over the globe joined together in virtual town halls to discuss issues of mutual interest. Teenagers in San Diego could discuss music with peers in Boston and Washington; a senior citizen in Texas mourning the death of a loved one could commiserate with someone in Florida; a cancer patient in San Francisco could share treatment ideas with doctors in New York. In the early years of the twenty-first century weblogs, also known as blogs, allowed people to post pictures, biographies, diaries, and anything else on the Web. Blogs allowed anyone, generally free of charge, to communicate their personal views and life events with people around the globe, inextricably linking their daily existence to the virtual world of the Internet.

The technology also promised to reconfigure the consumer society, providing buyers with new options and increased power. Although mail-order catalogs had existed since the nineteenth century, a local merchant had the advantage of being the only store within driving range. Now with the Web, virtual stores were only seconds away, and they were open twenty-four hours a day. New virtual stores, such as amazon.com, grabbed a foothold in the book market by allowing customers to order books from the privacy of their homes. Three years after its launch, amazon.com had 2.25 million worldwide customers and sales that reached $350 million in 1999.

E-mail emerged as the most visible and commonly used feature of the new information society. By 1999 Americans sent 2.2 billion messages a day, compared with 293 million pieces of first-class mail. Nearly every college and university in the country provided some form of e-mail access for its faculty, staff, and students. Between 70 and 80 percent of university faculty used e-mail to communicate with their colleagues. E-mail changed the workplace, allowing employees to conduct business from the road and from home.

The information revolution raised new questions and forced Americans to confront old problems. How should government balance the right to free speech on the Web with parents' interest in limiting their children's exposure to indecent material? Religious and conservative groups pressured Congress to pass legislation that would limit access to the Web by banning indecent material. Libertarian and civil-liberty groups opposed any effort to limit the free flow of information. In 1996 Congress passed, and the president signed, the Communications Decency Act, which criminalized online communications that were "obscene, lewd, lascivious, filthy or indecent, with intent to annoy, abuse, threaten or harass another person." The Supreme Court ruled the law an unconstitutional infringement of freedom of speech, but Congress responded by passing a less restrictive law, the Child Online Protection Act (1998). The new legislation required all commercial websites—even those not in the pornography business—to use special services to protect children from material deemed "harmful to minors."

Many people also worried that the nation's reliance on computers would produce "technological segregation," aggravating the gap between the educational haves and have-nots. Households with incomes of $75,000 or above were twenty times more likely to use the Internet than were those with incomes of $20,000 or less. Whites were 39 percent more likely than African Americans, and 43 percent more likely than Hispanics, to have access to the Internet. "The digital divide is real, it is growing, and it is very divisive to the progress of the country," warned an observer.

A few critics pointed out that Internet chat rooms and customized newsgroups encouraged people to limit their exposure to like-minded people. Software, which allowed people to customize the information they received, resulted in what one journalist called "The Daily Me"—a personalized view of the world filtered to allow exposure only to individuals with similar interests and ideas. Though the Internet was in some ways very social, increasing people's capacity to form new bonds and social relations, it also limited the possibilities of debate and discussion of opposing points of view, breeding a high-tech form of social and intellectual isolation.

The Web also created new headaches for people trying to protect sensitive information. So-called hackers, ranging from curious teenagers to malicious governments, used their Internet expertise to gain access to privileged information. The issue of where to draw the line between consumer rights and creator's ownership in the digital age emerged in 1999 when Shawn Fanning, a nineteen-year-old student at Northeastern University, created "Napster," a program that allowed users to swap copyrighted music over the Internet. The recording industry sued, claiming that Napster facilitated music piracy. The heavy metal band Metallica called Napster an "insidious and ongoing thievery scheme." Napster fans retaliated, hacking the message "LEAVE NAPSTER ALONE" onto the band's website. In 2001 the courts sided with the recording industry, ordering Napster to bar copyrighted songs from its network.

A high-profile Justice Department suit against software giant Microsoft raised another troubling question: How relevant were the nation's century-old antitrust laws in dealing with the new digital economy? In 1997 the federal government and twenty state attorneys general claimed that Microsoft had unfairly limited competition by bundling its Internet browser with its popular Windows software. A defiant Microsoft rejected the government's charge. Claiming that its browser was an integrated part of its windows operating system, Microsoft contended that antiquated antitrust laws punished innovation and success in the digital age. In 2001, after a series of legal appeals, the two sides reached a compromise. The government dropped its charges in exchange for Microsoft's promise to allow Windows users access to the software of rival companies. A handful of states, however, refused to accept the compromise. "This agreement may not be good enough to protect consumers against misuse of monopoly, to prevent returns to violations of the law and to restore competition in this industry," said Connecticut Attorney General Richard Blumenthal.

Wall Street Boom

The surge in computer-related industry helped revive the U.S. economy during the 1990s. By the end of the decade the gross domestic product, discounted for inflation, was growing at an annual rate of 4 percent and unemployment had fallen to a quarter-century low of 4.7 percent. The output of goods or services per hour of work (known as productivity) had risen 2 percent, well above its historically slow annual growth trend of 1 percent since the early 1970s. All the while, inflation had fallen to less than 2 percent.

The information revolution was the cornerstone of the new prosperity, accounting for 45 percent of industrial growth. From 1987 to 1994 the U.S. software industry grew 117 percent in real terms, while the rest of the economy grew only 17 percent. By the end of the decade computer companies based in and around Silicon Valley possessed a market value of $450 billion. By comparison,

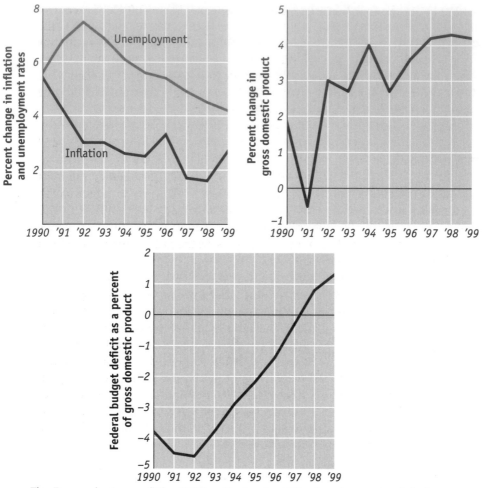

The Economic Boom of the 1990s   During the 1990s, Americans enjoyed the longest sustained period of economic growth since the end of the Second World War. Inflation remained steady, unemployment declined, and gross domestic product rose. Beginning in 1998, the government also had a rosier economic outlook as the federal budget managed a surplus. *(Sources: "News of the Week in Review,"* New York Times, *May 3, 1998, Copyright © 1998 by the New York Times Co. Reprinted by permission; Bureau of Labor Statistics,* Statistical Abstract of the United States, 1999; Economic Report of the President, 1999; *Bureau of Economic Analysis; Budget of the United States, 2001)*

the auto companies and suppliers of Detroit—the cornerstone of America's previous industrial revolution—were worth about $100 billion. The U.S. software industry accounted for three-fourths of the world market, and nine of the world's ten biggest software companies were located in the United States.

The nation watched as a new generation of computer moguls made millions from new inventions and rising stock prices. When *Forbes* magazine put together its 1990 list of the four hundred richest Americans, Microsoft chief executive Bill Gates was worth $2.5 billion. By 1998 he was worth $85 billion, equal to the wealth of at least one-third of the entire U.S. population. Much of his wealth was produced by the soaring price of Microsoft stock, which rose 38,000 percent between 1986 and 1998. By the end of the decade high-tech industry captains held most of the places on *Fortune's* list of wealthiest people. Of the first five, only one had not made his fortune in a computer-related field.

Wall Street was the most visible sign of the new prosperity. Between 1992 and 1998 the Dow Jones Industrial Average increased fourfold. The New York and NASDAQ Stock Exchanges added over $4 trillion in value—the largest single accumulation of wealth in history. The wealthiest Americans benefited the most from the rising price of stocks. Between 1990 and 1998 the average net worth of the four hundred wealthiest Americans climbed from $680 million to $1.8 billion. During the same time the average compensation for corporate CEOs rose from $1.9 million to $7.8 million, with most of the gain coming in the form of stock options.

In fact, the stock-market boom even reached the middle class. With the tide rising rapidly for more than a decade, stock assets accounted for a larger share of household wealth than ever before: 24.2 percent in mid-1998. Much of the growth resulted from the creation of mutual funds—large investment groups that bought shares in a variety of stocks and bonds to limit risk. In 1980 only 6 percent of U.S. households had mutual funds accounts for stocks or bonds. By 1997 the share had leaped to 37 percent, with a colossal pool of capital approaching $5 trillion. Most of the money for mutual funds came from special retirement funds—401(k) accounts—that allowed workers to have their contributions matched by employers. By 1998 more than 25 million workers had $1 trillion invested in their 401(k) accounts.

Globalization and Its Discontents

The new technologies and the stock-market boom were products of more open markets and reduced regulation. In 1990, $50 billion of private capital flowed into "emerging markets." By 1996 that figure had swelled to $336 billion.

The 1990s also witnessed a trend toward globalization in culture. By 1996 international sales of software and entertainment products totaled $60.2 billion, more than any other industry. The explosion in sales was spurred by the collapse of the Iron Curtain, rising prosperity, and the proliferation of TV sets, video-cassette recorders, stereos, personal computers, and satellite dishes. American corporations moved aggressively to tap into the new markets. The Blockbuster Entertainment video chain opened two thousand outlets in twenty-six foreign countries during the decade; Tower Records operated seventy stores in fifteen countries.

Foreigners were not only viewing and listening to U.S. culture—they were also eating American food, reading U.S. magazines, and wearing designer clothes produced in America. *Reader's Digest* circulated in nineteen languages; its forty-eight international editions, with a combined circulation of 28 million, dwarfed its U.S. circulation of 14.7 million. *Cosmopolitan* billed itself as the world's best-selling women's magazine, with international sales of 4.5 million from thirty-six foreign editions. Right behind it was *Playboy,* with sixteen international editions and a readership of 5 million. McDonald's restaurants were opening at a rate of six a day around the world. American fashion—baggy jeans and baseball caps—became the global teenage uniform. Globalization, an observer noted, had an "American face: It wears Mickey Mouse ears, it eats Big Macs, it drinks Coke or Pepsi and it does its computing on an IBM or Apple laptop, using Windows 98, with an Intel Pentium II processor and a network link from Cisco Systems."

There were clear winners and losers in the trend toward a global marketplace. Globalization widened the gap between the haves and have-nots in the world

McDonald's Goes to China American corporations expanded their overseas activities in the nineties, stretching into regions of the globe that just a few years earlier would have been off-limits to the United States because of the constraints of the Cold War. American goods poured into the Soviet Union after the collapse of communism and even became readily available in the communist stronghold of China. McDonald's, the epitome of America's passion for fast food, infiltrated the Chinese market with the opening of its first store in 1992 in Beijing. Serving American-style hamburgers as well as Chinese favorites, Mai Dan Lau (McDonald's in Chinese) proved so popular that by 1998 China had almost two hundred McDonald's, all sporting the golden arches in front. *(© Julia Waterlow; Eye Ubiquitous/CORBIS)*

economy. North America, the European Union, and Japan accounted for nearly 75 percent of all investment capital and 65 percent of world exports and global gross domestic product (GDP). As the historian David Reynolds has pointed out, two-thirds of the world's population accounted for only one-fifth of world trade and generated about 25 percent of GDP. Many places in the world also remained untouched by the communications revolution. In 1995 India averaged one phone line for every hundred people. While Americans wired their homes for cable television and Internet access, fewer than half the homes in India and Indonesia were wired for electricity.

The Rise of Osama bin Laden

During the 1990s, America's global dominance produced a backlash among Islamic fundamentalists who opposed continued U.S. military presence in the Middle East and rejected what they viewed as the corrupting influence of Western culture. The Islamic world was large and diverse, encompassing more than 1.2 billion Muslims living in 60 countries. A small number of militants, however, organized a campaign of terror against the symbols of American military and economic power.

In February 1993 five people died and more than one thousand were injured when a bomb exploded in New York City's World Trade Center. Federal agents traced the bombing to a group of radical Muslims in New York. American targets outside the United Sates also found themselves vulnerable to attack. In 1996 a truck bomb exploded next to a military barracks in Saudi Arabia, killing nineteen U.S. servicemen. Two years later, simultaneous bombs exploded in a crowded street in Nairobi, Kenya, and 450 miles away in front of the U.S. embassy in Tanzania. The bombs, said *Newsweek*, offered a dramatic but simple message: "Don't forget the world's superpower still has enemies, secret, violent and determined."

The chief suspect in these bombings was an extremist Saudi millionaire, Osama bin Laden, who called on Muslims to declare war against Americans. Crafting a public image in the Islamic world as the leader of a religious struggle on behalf of the poor and the dispossessed, bin Laden led a worldwide network of supporters known in Arabic as al Qaeda ("The Base"). Dubbed "Terror, Inc.," al Qaeda lacked a clear hierarchy, no lieutenants or generals, but maintained the sort of discipline found in well-trained armies. "It's a completely new phenomenon," said a British intelligence official. "You could call it disorganized-organized terrorism."

In 1990 when the United States sent troops to Saudi Arabia during the Gulf War, bin Laden denounced the "occupation" of the Arab Holy Land by "American crusader forces," which he described as "the latest and greatest aggression" against the Islamic world since the death of the prophet Muhammad in 632. In the Sudan, bin Laden financed several terrorist training camps and orchestrated attacks on

American interests, including the 1993 attack on the World Trade Center. By 1996, he was in Afghanistan, where he provided financial support to the radical Taliban leaders who were fighting against the more moderate Northern Alliance for control of the capital of Kabul.

With Afghanistan providing sanctuary, bin Laden escalated his attacks. In October 2000, the USS *Cole*, a destroyer making a refueling stop in Yemen, was nearly sunk when a small boat loaded with explosives slammed into its side. "The destroyer represented the capital of the West," bin Laden said, "and the small boat represented Mohammed."

From Wall Street to Main Street

The postwar paradox rested on the assumption that prosperity—produced with limited government intervention—would uplift the poor, provide the middle class with more leisure, and narrow the gap between rich and poor. "Rising tides would lift all boats" became a familiar refrain. The reality, however, proved more complicated. For one thing, the computer revolution seduced Americans into working longer hours. According to some estimates, the average American in the 1990s worked 164 more hours per year than in 1970—the equivalent of an additional month. One reason for the expanded hours was that technology virtually erased the boundaries between work and leisure, allowing employers to expect workers to be accessible and productive any hour, any day. A more compelling reason was that many people worked extra jobs to sustain their earning power. In 1979, 4.9 percent of U.S. workers reported working more than one job during the same workweek. By 1995 the percentage was up to 6.4 percent.

Virtually all of this increase occurred among women, who represented nearly half of all multiple-job holders. In many families both husband and wife were working full-time for wages. From 1969 to 1996 the proportion of full-time working wives in married households with children rose from 17 percent to 39 percent. Passage of the Family Medical Leave Act in 1993 made it easier for women to pursue both a career and a family by allowing eligible employees to take up to twelve weeks unpaid leave for the birth and care of a newborn without risk of losing their job. In households with no children the number of women in the labor force soared from 42 percent to 60 percent. An increase in the number of women holding college degrees allowed some to move into high-paying jobs. In 1970 only 11 percent of women between 25 and 64 had completed college; by 2004 that figure had swelled to 33 percent. Despite the improvement women failed to make significant gains in specialized and generally high-paying occupations in the sciences, law, engineering, and computer technology. In 2004, women made up 89 percent of all paralegals and legal assistants, but only 14 percent of architects and engineers.

Though American families were working more hours, they were not experiencing a significant increase in living standard. Between 1989 and 1998, for example, the bottom fifth of wage earners saw their average incomes grow less than 1 percent—an $85 rise—over a decade. In addition, despite low unemployment rates, the average hourly wage, $7.88, adjusted for inflation, had not increased in thirty years.

Nevertheless, many people benefited from the booming economy. The poor did not get poorer in the 1990s. Their family incomes rose slightly, the number below the poverty rate fell somewhat, and the average pay for low-wage jobs increased. Minorities, especially African Americans, showed real economic gains. In 1989, 30.8 percent of blacks qualified as poor. By 1997, 26.5 percent did. Moreover, incomes for African American households jumped 16.8 percent, or $3,600, between 1992 and 1999—nearly three times more than incomes for the nation as a whole. By 1998 a record 66.6 percent of households owned their own home and a large number of the new homeowners were members of minority groups and immigrants, groups traditionally shut out of the housing market.

While the poor were advancing by inches, the well-to-do were bounding ahead by miles. In 1990 a corporate CEO earned 85 times as much as the average factory worker; in 1997 he or she made 324 times more. The information society's demand

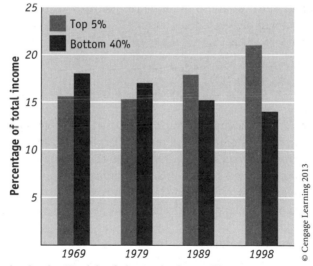

Growing Disparity in the Wealth of the Nation's Families After 1979, the yearly income of the wealthiest 5 percent of the nation's families grew rapidly, far outreaching the more modest progress in wealth experienced by the rest of the American population. While prices continued to rise in the 1980s and 1990s, wages for the poorest 20 percent remained stagnant, middle-income households saw an increase of 10 percent over the two decades, and the top 5 percent saw incomes that climbed an average of 150 percent in twenty years. By 1998, the gap between the top 5 percent and the poorest 20 percent was greater than at any time since the Great Depression.

for educated, high-tech workers contributed to the income gap. The new technology placed greater demands on people who worked with their heads, not their hands. The government classified six of every ten jobs created in the 1990s as managerial, professional, or technical. Most of the new job growth took place in industries, such as finance, engineering, data processing, consulting, and education, that employed a large number of college graduates. In 1990 college graduates earned 52 percent more than high-school graduates; in 1997 they earned 62 percent more.

By 1998 the combination of a healthy, growing economy, fiscal restraint, and the end of the Cold War had solved the budget crisis that had plagued Washington since the early Reagan years. Years of low inflation cut the government's cost of borrowing and held down spending on programs such as social security and Medicare. At the same time, the strong economy and stock market generated a rising tide of tax payments. In 1992 the annual deficit soared to $290 billion, an all-time high, leading politicians of both parties to warn that the United States was destined to leave its children a mountain of debt. By 1998 the federal government reported a $70 billion surplus for fiscal year 1998—the first in three decades—and projected a $4.4 trillion surplus over the next fifteen years.

Economists pointed out, however, that while the deficit had been eliminated, the United States still faced a mountain of debt, which was the cumulative amount of money the U.S. Treasury owed its creditors. As of 1999 the debt stood at $5.4 trillion, one-third of it owed to foreign investors. According to the Congressional Budget Office, 15.2 percent of all federal outlays were to pay interest on the debt, a total of $245 billion annually.

Social Tensions in the 1990s

During the 1990s, the struggle over American identity found expression in a number of angry debates. In 1991, President Bush replaced the retiring liberal justice Thurgood Marshall, the only African American on the Court, with Clarence Thomas, a black conservative federal judge who had once served as head of Reagan's Equal Employment Opportunity Commission (EEOC).

The nomination seemed certain until University of Oklahoma law professor Anita Hill stepped forward to charge that Thomas had sexually harassed her when he was her boss at the EEOC. Thomas, she claimed, had repeatedly asked her on dates, bragged about his sexual ability, and made explicit references to pornography. "On several occasions Thomas told me graphically of his own sexual prowess," she said.

Conservatives on the Senate committee successfully transformed Hill from victim to villain, characterizing her as part of a liberal conspiracy to sink the nomination. Although many wavering senators believed Hill's testimony and voted against Thomas, his nomination survived by a 52–48 vote—the narrowest margin for a Supreme Court nominee in the twentieth century.

But the public debate over Hill's charges raised awareness about sexual harassment in the workplace. By the 1990s, millions of women had moved into the workplace. In 1970, women made up only 42 percent of the workforce. By 1991, that number had grown to 57 percent. Polls showed that 40 percent of women said they had been sexually harassed, and 50 percent of men admitted to engaging in sexually aggressive behavior at work.

The hearings also inspired a younger generation of women activists to challenge older notions of gender identity. Shortly after the hearings, Rebecca Walker published an article in *Ms.* entitled "I am Third Wave." She argued that while the first wave won basic social and political rights in the nineteenth century, and the second wave, born during the 1960s, continued that struggle, it failed to address the concerns of younger feminists coming of age in the 1990s.

Critics charged that second-wave feminists focused too heavily on the concerns of upper-middle-class white women. The movement needed to account

Anita Hill at the Clarence Thomas Confirmation Hearing   When Thurgood Marshall announced he was retiring from the Supreme Court on June 27, 1991, President Bush immediately nominated federal appeals court judge Clarence Thomas, a conservative forty-three-year-old African American. At Thomas's Senate confirmation hearings, the expected opposition from civil-rights and liberal groups was overshadowed by the surprising accusations raised by one of Thomas's former subordinates at the EEOC, Anita Hill. Hill claimed Thomas sexually harassed her after she refused to see him socially. While the Senate confirmed Thomas in a 52–48 decision, Anita Hill's testimony made Americans aware of sexual harassment's impact on the workplace and led many to call for guidelines that defined proper behavior and speech in the office. *(© Bettmann/CORBIS)*

for the enormous diversity of gender identities. Women of color had a different set of priorities than white females. Gender identity also needed to take into account class differences. For example, many middle-class white women supported efforts to abolish welfare; poor women saw it as an assault on their livelihoods. The debate of gender identities mirrored the larger conversation about American identity. Women were grappling with the same question that confounded most Americans: How do you create a unified identity that also takes into account the enormous diversity of opinions and backgrounds?

PRIMARY SOURCE

17.1 | *Becoming the Third Wave*

Rebecca Walker's 1992 essay touched off a spirited debate about gender identity in the 1990s and the unfulfilled mission of the previous generation of feminists. Walker channeled the frustrations and desires of many young women coming of age in the 1990s.

I am not one of the people who sat transfixed before the television, watching the Senate hearings. I had classes to go to, papers to write, and frankly, the whole thing was too painful. A black man grilled by a panel of white men about his sexual deviance. A black woman claiming harassment and being discredited by
5 other women. . . . I could not bring myself to watch that sensationalized assault of the human spirit. To me, the hearings were not about determining whether or not Clarence Thomas did in fact harass Anita Hill. They were about checking and redefining the extent of women's credibility and power.

Can a woman's experience undermine a man's career? Can a woman's voice, a
10 woman's sense of self-worth and injustice, challenge a structure predicated upon the subjugation of our gender? Anita Hill's testimony threatened to do that and more. If Thomas had not been confirmed, every man in the United States would be at risk. For how many senators never told a sexist joke? How many men have not used their protected male privilege to thwart in some way the influence or
15 ideas of a woman colleague, friend, or relative?

For those whose sense of power is so obviously connected to the health and vigor of the penis, it would have been a metaphoric castration. Of course this is too great a threat.

While some may laud the whole spectacle for the consciousness it raised
20 around sexual harassment, its very real outcome is more informative. He was promoted. She was repudiated. Men were assured of the inviolability of their penis/power. Women were admonished to keep their experiences to themselves.

The backlash against U.S. women is real. As the misconception of equality between the sexes becomes more ubiquitous, so does the attempt to restrict the

25 boundaries of women's personal and political power. Thomas' confirmation, the ultimate rally of support for the male paradigm of harassment, sends a clear message to women: "Shut up! Even if you speak, we will not listen."

I will not be silenced.

I acknowledge the fact that we live under siege. I intend to fight back. I have

30 uncovered and unleashed more repressed anger than I thought possible. For the umpteenth time in my 22 years, I have been radicalized, politicized, shaken awake. I have come to voice again, and this time my voice is not conciliatory. The night after Thomas's confirmation I ask the man I am intimate with what he thinks of the whole mess. His concern is primarily with Thomas' propensity

35 to demolish civil rights and opportunities for people of color. I launch into a tirade. "When will progressive black men prioritize my rights and well-being? When will they stop talking so damn much about 'the race' as if it revolved exclusively around them?" He tells me I wear my emotions on my sleeve. I scream "I need to know, are you with me or are you going to help them try to

40 destroy me?"

A week later I am on a train to New York. A beautiful mother and daughter, both wearing green outfits, sit across the aisle from me. The little girl has tightly plaited braids. Her brown skin is glowing and smooth, her eyes bright as she chatters happily while looking out the window. Two men get on the train and sit

45 directly behind me, shaking my seat as they thud into place. I bury myself in *The Sound and the Fury*. Loudly they begin to talk about women. "Man, I fucked that bitch all night and then I never called her again." "Man, there's lots of girlies over there, you know that ho, live over there by Tyrone', Well, I snatched that shit up." The mother moves closer to her now quiet daughter. Looking at her small back

50 I can see that she is listening to the men. I am thinking of how I can transform the situation, of all the people in the car whose silence makes us complicit. Another large man gets on the train. After exchanging loud greetings with the two men, he sits next to me. He tells them he is going to Philadelphia to visit his wife and child. I am suckered into thinking that he is different. Then, "Man, there's a ton of

55 females in Philly, just waitin' for you to give'em some." I turn my head and allow the fire in my eyes to burn into him. He takes up two seats and has hands with huge swollen knuckles. I imagine the gold rings on his fingers slamming into my face. He senses something, "What's your name, sweetheart?" The other men lean forward over the seat.

60 My instinct kicks in, telling me to get out. "Since I see you all are not going to move, I will." I move to the first car. I am so angry that thoughts of murder, of physically retaliating against them, of separatism, engulf me. I am almost out of body, just shy of being pure force. I am sick of the way women are negated, violated, devalued, ignored. I am livid, unrelenting in my anger at those who invade

65 my space, who wish to take away my rights, who refuse to hear my voice. As the days pass, I push myself to figure out what it means to be a part of the Third Wave of feminism. I begin to realize that I owe it to myself, to my little sister on the train, to all of the daughters yet to be born, to push beyond my rage and articulate an agenda. After battling with ideas of separatism and militancy, I connect with my

70 own feelings of powerlessness. I realize that I must undergo a transformation if

I am truly committed to women's empowerment. My involvement must reach beyond my own voice in discussion, beyond voting, beyond reading feminist theory. My anger and awareness must translate into tangible action.

75   I am ready to decide, as my mother decided before me, to devote much of my energy to the history, health, and healing of women. Each of my choices will have to hold to my feminist standard of justice. To be a feminist is to integrate an ideology of equality and female empowerment into the very fiber of my life. It is to search for personal clarity in the midst of systemic destruction, to join in sisterhood with women when often we are divided, to understand power struc-
80   tures with the intention of challenging them. While this may sound simple, it is exactly the kind of stand that many of my peers are unwilling to take. So I write this as a plea to all women, especially the women of my generation: Let Thomas' confirmation serve to remind you, as it did me, that the fight is far from over. Let this dismissal of a woman's experience move you to anger. Turn that outrage
85   into political power. Do not vote for them unless they work for us. Do not have sex with them, do not break bread with them, do not nurture them if they don't prioritize our freedom to control our bodies and our lives.

I am not a postfeminism feminist. I am the Third Wave.

Source: Rebecca Walker, "Becoming the Third Wave," Reprinted by permission of MS. Magazine, © 1992.   ■ ■ ■

The Culture of Conspiracy

Despite Clinton's personal popularity, public distrust of government hardened during the 1990s. The explosion in the number of militia and patriot groups represented the most visible sign that some Americans harbored intense anger toward Washington.

Many like Timothy McVeigh were consumed by a paranoid hatred of the U.S. government. On April 19, 1995, McVeigh parked a rented Ryder truck packed with a mixture of ammonium nitrate and fuel oil in front of the Alfred P. Murrah Federal Building in Oklahoma City. At 9:02 AM the bomb exploded, and the blue-orange fireball ripped through the building, collapsing all nine floors on the building's north side. The blast killed 168 people, including nineteen children.

Many radical right-wing groups used the Internet to reach potential members and promote their paranoid fantasies. By 1999, more than 250 websites, chat rooms, and mailing lists promoted the radical-right cause. On the U.S. Militia site, arms-loving home shoppers could buy everything from explosives to computer mousepads to bumper stickers that said "Have You Cleaned Your Assault Weapon Today?"

Militia groups were but one manifestation of a larger culture of conspiracy. Surveys showed more than three-quarters of Americans believed President Kennedy was the victim of a massive conspiracy, not a crazed and lone gunman as a government investigation showed. Filmmaker Oliver Stone popularized the conspiracy theory in his blockbuster movie *JFK,* which speculated that Lyndon Johnson and the military backed the assassination.

Oklahoma City Memorial   On the fifth anniversary of the day Timothy McVeigh detonated a bomb in front of the Alfred P. Murrah Federal Building, the Oklahoma City Memorial was dedicated on the site of the tragedy. The memorial includes a reflecting pool, a
tree that survived the blast, and a museum dedicated to understanding terrorism. The most
moving scene at the memorial is that of the 168 empty chairs, each inscribed with the name
of a victim, which cover the ground where the building once stood. (© *Steve Liss/Time Life
Pictures/Getty Images*)

One of the most popular television shows of the decade, *The X-Files,* tapped
into the popular fascination with imagined conspiracies. The show featured two
FBI agents struggling to disentangle a giant government conspiracy involving
alien/human hybridization. "The truth is out there," the announcer intones.

Why the proliferation of conspiracy theories? Intense public mistrust of government and the media played a role. Real conspiracies in connection with Vietnam, Watergate, and Iran-Contra did little to boost public confidence and provided
cynics with ample evidence that Washington was capable of deceit. In addition,
the Internet provided virtual communities where people could find mutual support for theories. In the end, conspiracy theories abounded because they offered
simplistic and coherent explanations for complex and often incoherent events.

Race and American Justice

Sustained prosperity failed to bridge the gap between the races. The disparity in
world views between blacks and whites became clear during the murder trial of
former star football player O.J. Simpson, an African American, who was charged

...r of his ex-wife Nicole Brown Simpson and a friend, Ronald ...posh Beverly Hills home.

...televised trial, which lasted for nine months, transfixed the public, ...v life into struggling cable news shows and tabloid newspapers des-...tract an audience. Most experts found the evidence against Simpson ...ning. The jury of nine blacks, two whites, and one Hispanic, disagreed. ...ily a few hours of deliberation, they delivered a verdict of not guilty on all counts.

Polls showed that blacks and whites looked at the case through race-tinted glasses. By large majorities, African Americans believed in Simpson's inno-cence, convinced that the American justice system intentionally discriminated against minorities and that rogue cops often tilted the hand of justice. Their distrust of the police was so intense that even blacks who felt Simpson was guilty believed that much of the evidence was tainted. "They framed a guilty man," observed one writer. Nearly 75 percent of whites rejected the sugges-tion that race played a role in the investigation and prosecution, and assumed Simpson's guilt.

Perhaps the American system of justice was the final victim of the trial. Blacks and whites seemed to agree on one thing: there was a different justice for those who have money and those who do not.

The racial divide exposed by the Simpson case revealed itself in the continu-ing controversy over affirmative action. In November 1996, California voters, by a 54–46 percent margin, passed Proposition 209, a ballot initiative that banned any preference based on race and sex in determining college admissions, con-tracting, and employment by the state. Men overwhelmingly supported the ini-tiative (61 to 39 percent) while women disapproved (52 to 48 percent). Blacks and Latinos opposed it in large numbers.

As other states mimicked California, the nation engaged in an angry debate over racial preferences. Critics of affirmative action, some conservative blacks among them, contended that quotas undermined black morale, contributing to "an enlargement of self-doubt" by creating the perception that successful blacks could not earn their positions. Proponents continued to argue that affirmative action helped open the doors of opportunity for minorities and women, increas-ing their representation in the workforce.

Disillusioned with liberal remedies, many African Americans turned to black nationalism for answers. Membership in the Nation of Islam and other black Muslim groups swelled and Malcolm X reemerged as the decade's leading African American figure. Traditional African dress—colorful West African fabric, beads, and leather medallions with outlines of Africa—became popular in many black communities.

At the same time, Afrocentrism, which argued that black people possessed a distinctive set of cultural values and practices, became popular on some uni-versity campuses. Independent schools emphasizing an Afrocentric curriculum popped up in many major cities.

Hip-Hop Nation

The debate over new musical styles, especially hip-hop, among the young exposed racial tensions in America. Created by black artists on the mean streets of New York and Los Angeles, hip-hop used repetitive samples of other musical tracks as background for the rhythmic poetry of rap singers. "We're marketing black culture to white people," claimed rap artist Dr. Dre. In the past African American artists had softened their image to appeal to mainstream America. Hip-hop took a different approach, accentuating race and highlighting issues of the urban underclass. "Forget about watering down," claimed the cofounder of the group Public Enemy. "I think there's dehydration. Not only are we not going to add water, we're going to take water out." In 1998 rap surpassed country music as the nation's top-selling format. "Hip-hop is the rebellious voice of the youth," boasted rapper Jay-Z. "It's what people want to hear." By the end of the decade suburban whites purchased more than 70 percent of hip-hop albums.

Hip-hop was not only popular; it was also controversial. Its glorification of violence, relentless promotion of sex, and derogatory treatment of homosexuals and women appealed to many suburban white youth, but these same attitudes angered parents, the police, and many civic-minded groups. Police organizations complained about the song "Cop Killer," which included the lyrics "I'm 'bout to bust some shots off/I'm 'bout to dust some cops off" and the chant "Die, Die, Die, Pig, Die!"

Not all hip-hop artists promoted sex and violence. Artists such as DMX and Master P avoided controversy by writing songs that examined the pathologies of the black community but avoided encouraging social activism. Madison Avenue and Hollywood tried to tame hip-hop, making it less rebellious. Hollywood featured hip-hop artists Ice Cube, Queen Latifah, and Will Smith in movie releases. Designer Tommy Hilfiger turned an inner-city clothing style—oversized shirts and baggy, drooping pants—into a $1 billion business, and advertising firms used a toned-down version of rap to sell a number of products to young people.

Identity in a Multiracial America

Hispanics and Asians were dramatically altering a nation that had defined race in terms of black and white. Fueled by massive immigration and high birthrates, the nation's Hispanic population jumped by 38 percent during the decade, from 22.4 million to 35.3 million, while the overall population increased by only 9 percent. If the African American civil-rights slogan was "We shall overcome," claimed the editor of a bilingual magazine, the Latino motto will be "We shall overwhelm."

The growing numbers of Latinos caught the attention of business leaders and politicians. In 1995, American corporations led by Procter & Gamble, AT&T, and Sears spent more than $1 billion on Spanish-language advertising.

The concentration of Latino voters in a handful of key electoral states—New York, California, Texas, Illinois, and Florida—magnified their political power. Mobilized to political action during the 1990s by efforts in California to restrict immigrant rights, Latino voting jumped 27 percent between 1994 and 1998. During that same time period, the number of Latino office-holders statewide increased from 460 to 789.

Close proximity, and the constant movement between borders, produced a blend of Mexican and American cultures. Banda music, for example, which became a huge fad in Southern California in the 1990s, was an innovative mix of rock, salsa, country-western, and norteño—the traditional folk music of northern Mexico. The music was neither Mexican nor American, but rather a mixture of the two.

Many Dominican entrepreneurs owned bodegas (neighborhood grocery stores) in both New York City and Santo Domingo. They shipped merchandise back and forth, and often commuted between stores. Farm workers from Mexico traveled to the United States for the summer home-construction season in Texas and California, but worked the rest of the year closer to home.

By 2000, Asian Americans made up only 4 percent of the population, but they represented 5.4 percent of all college students, making them the only racial group whose percentage of students was above their proportion of the national population. One in four undergraduates at Stanford was Asian; one in five at Harvard, Northwestern, and the University of Pennsylvania. In California, where nearly 40 percent of Asians lived, they were the largest racial group among undergraduates at Berkeley, University of California at Los Angeles (UCLA), and UC Riverside.

Although they shared a common identity as minorities in America, blacks, Latinos, and Asians did not always agree on a common agenda. They collaborated on mutual interests, such as defending affirmative action, fighting against police brutality, and seeking more government spending on education.

But African Americans often opposed the efforts of Latinos to receive tax breaks for minority-owned businesses, or federal money to help students from disadvantaged backgrounds to attend college. Some blacks joined whites in opposing immigration, out of fear that immigrants would take away citizens' jobs.

In 1994, a narrow majority of black voters in California supported Proposition 187, which would have barred any sort of state assistance to illegal aliens. Many Hispanic leaders, in turn, complained that blacks were overrepresented in the federal government, where they made up 17 percent of the civil workforce, compared to 6 percent for Hispanics.

The Prosperity Paradox

By every statistical measure Americans were enjoying unprecedented prosperity in the 1990s. They were living in bigger homes, making more money, performing less hard labor, living longer, and enjoying more leisure time than ever before. Crime rates were down, the environment was cleaner, and the arms race had ended. The paradox, however, was that Americans were not feeling any better about their lives. "If we are doing so well why do we feel so bad," asked an observer. The "Prosperity Paradox," as the journalist Gregg Easterbrook called it, meant that "for every old problem solved, a new problem will always be created, meaning we should not expect a better life to improve happiness."

One of the biggest new problems created by the new prosperity was suburban sprawl. By the end of the decade the Sierra Club identified sprawl, defined as "low-density, automobile-dependent development," as the chief environmental problem facing the nation. Between 1992 and 1997 Americans developed about 3.2 million acres of open land every year, nearly double the rate during the 1980s. In 1920 there were about ten people living on every acre of land in America's cities and suburbs; by 1990 there were only four. The result was a human-made suburban landscape composed of strip malls and cookie-cutter residential areas. Sprawl eroded about 50 acres of valuable farmland every hour. "Where Old Macdonald had a farm, a hamburger joint now stands," noted *The Economist.*

One of the most annoying features of sprawl was traffic congestion. In 1990 Americans owned 180 million cars and light trucks. By 1997 the fleet was up to 200 million. With relatively few new roads to travel on, the extra cars inevitably caused more traffic jams. The expansion of stores, fast-food restaurants, and housing developments added to the congestion. Between 1982 and 2000 the U.S. population grew by 20 percent, but the amount of time Americans spent in traffic increased by a staggering 236 percent. Atlanta led the nation in the average distance its commuters traveled each day to work, 36.5 miles round-trip. Seattle residents spent an average of fifty-nine hours per year stuck in traffic, the sixth highest in the nation. "We moved to the suburbs to get lawns and a country setting," complained an environmentalist. "Now we find we are sitting in traffic going to work and going to get a quart of milk."

Ironically, the same technology that was knitting the nation closer together—cell phones, the Internet, automobiles—was also leaving many Americans feeling more isolated, less tied to their local communities. To illustrate the trend, the social scientist Robert Putnam pointed out that more Americans were "bowling alone." The number of bowling leagues dropped 40 percent between 1980 and 1995, even though the total number of bowlers in the United States increased by 10 percent. The problem went beyond the way Americans played sports and impacted nearly every aspect of modern life. Fewer Americans went to the polls to vote, participated in local community and civic groups, or were engaged in any organized activity outside the home. Prosperity provided Americans with the luxury of sitting passively at home watching hundreds of potential television stations and an endless number of websites. The result, however, was a loss of trust in public institutions, a decline in community spirit, and a growing sense of social isolation.

The 2000 Presidential Election

Prosperity and impeachment provided the backdrop to the first presidential election of the new millennium. The Democrats rallied around Vice President Al Gore, who promised to sustain the Clinton-era economic growth. In August at the party's convention in Los Angeles, Gore launched his "prosperity and progress" campaign, promising increased federal spending on health care, social security, and education. Striking a populist pose, Gore promised middle-class taxpayers that he would fight for "the people" and against "the powerful" special interests. Walking a political tightrope, Gore clung to Clinton's success while distancing himself from the president's scandals. "I stand here tonight as my own man," he told cheering delegates. As his running mate, Gore selected Joseph Lieberman, a centrist senator from Connecticut, who became the first Jewish American vice presidential candidate nominated by a major party.

Republican leaders, eager to win back the White House, threw their support and money behind Texas Governor George W. Bush, the oldest son of the former president. After stumbling in the primaries against Vietnam War hero Senator John McCain of Arizona, Bush regained his footing and captured his party's nomination. With federal coffers overflowing with revenue, Bush promised the nation "prosperity with a purpose." Calling for a "compassionate conservatism," the Republican nominee solidified his conservative base by advocating a massive tax cut while at the same time reaching out to independents with pledges to fund increased social spending for education and health care. Above all, he vowed to return honor and dignity to the White House. Ahead in the polls, and confident of victory, Bush chose the uncharismatic former Secretary of Defense Richard Cheney as his running mate.

Bush watched his once-sizable lead in the polls evaporate through the summer and fall. For the final two months of the campaign the two contestants remained locked in a tight race. Bush hammered away at the vice president's integrity, while Gore raised questions about Bush's stature and experience. Three presidential debates in October did little to break the logjam. Voters found Gore more knowledgeable on issues, but they felt that Bush appeared more relaxed and personable. While Gore and Bush battled each other, consumer advocate Ralph Nader, running on the Green party platform, mocked both candidates. Nader relished the role of spoiler, threatening to siphon enough votes in key states—California, Michigan, Oregon, and Washington—to deny Gore a victory.

On election night Gore clung to a small margin in the popular vote, but with Florida and its critical 25 electoral votes too close to call, the election remained deadlocked. After a series of counts and recounts, Florida's Republican secretary of state certified Bush the winner on November 27—more than two weeks after the election. But the campaign did not end there: Gore contested the results, claiming that many ballots remained uncounted or improperly counted, effectively disfranchising thousands of voters. Republicans accused Gore of trying to steal the election; Democrats attacked Republicans for thwarting the "will of the people." The nation braced for a constitutional crisis. On December 12, after weeks of legal maneuvering, a deeply divided Supreme Court ended the historic impasse. In a controversial 5–4 ruling in the case of *Bush* v. *Gore,* the justices blocked further manual recounts, which effectively named George Bush the winner. Bush became only the fourth president, and the first since 1888, to take office having lost the popular vote.

The election revealed that unprecedented prosperity had failed to mute deep social divisions in America. The public remained deeply troubled by the election outcome, the winner lacked a clear mandate, the Senate was split 50–50, and Republicans held only a razor-thin majority in the House. Included among the new class of senators was New York's Hillary Rodham Clinton, who became the only first lady in history to seek and win elective office.

The Election of 2000   Early on the evening of the election (November 7), most of the major media outlets proclaimed Al Gore and his running mate, Joseph Lieberman, winners in Florida, but as the night wore on and votes from the panhandle of the state trickled in, journalists had to recant. By morning, George Bush, if he held Florida, was the presidential victor, but his lead was so minimal that Gore did not publicly concede that he had lost the election. Questions concerning the Florida votes, especially the ballots discarded for improper marks, led to a month-long debate over whether the disputed ballots should be counted by hand, leaving the fate of the election undecided. On December 12, the Supreme Court ruled 5–4 against the manual recount and Gore accepted defeat, despite the fact that he had won the majority of popular votes.

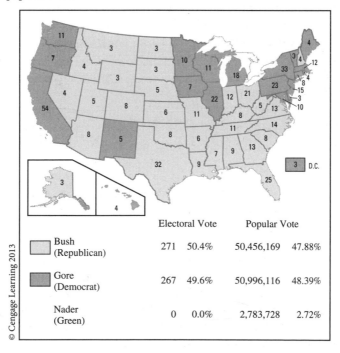

	Electoral Vote		Popular Vote	
Bush (Republican)	271	50.4%	50,456,169	47.88%
Gore (Democrat)	267	49.6%	50,996,116	48.39%
Nader (Green)	0	0.0%	2,783,728	2.72%

© Cengage Learning 2013

Analysis of voting results revealed a deeply divided nation. By region Democrats did well in urban areas; Republicans won majorities in suburban and rural areas. By race, African Americans gave 95 percent of their votes to Gore; whites preferred Bush. By gender, women favored Democrats; men leaned toward the Republicans. Finally, by religion, regular churchgoers voted Republican; infrequent churchgoers supported Democrats. The election revealed, observed the journalist Andrew Sullivan, "that America is currently two nations, as culturally and politically alien as they are geographically distinct."

SELECTED READINGS

▮ Arthur M. Schlesinger Jr.'s *The Disuniting of America* (1991) is a good discussion about the conflicts and tensions of 1990s American society. Robert Bellah et al. discuss the continuing presence of a national culture in *The Good Society* (1991). Haynes Johnson examines the prosperity of the decades as well as the culture's darker side in *The Best of Times* (2001). Alan S. Blinder and Janet L. Yellen analyze the economic lessons of the 1990s in *The Fabulous Decade* (2001).

▮ Michael Williams's *A History of Computing Technology* (1997) describes the development of the modern computer. In *The Politics of Cyberspace* (1997), Chris Toulouse and Timothy W. Luke explore the emerging information age. Art Wolinsky traces the development of the Internet as a communication tool from its military beginnings to its use in everyday life in *The History of the Internet and the World Wide Web* (1999).

▮ Harreel Rodgers discusses the impact on poverty as a result of changes in welfare laws in the late 1990s in *American Poverty in a New Era of Reform* (2000). Andres Duany, Jeff Speck, and Elizabeth Plater-Zyberk assess the impact of suburban sprawl on the economy, the environment, and society in *Suburban Nation* (2000).

▮ Popular culture in the 1990s has been exhaustively studied in popular books, though often without much historical perspective. Neal Gabler's *Life: The Movie* (1999) contains an excellent analysis of how entertainment has infiltrated and conquered reality. Gini Graham Scott explores the influence and impact of talk shows on society in *Can We Talk?* (1996). Lawrence M. Friedman's *The Horizontal Society* (1999) explores the democratization of modern popular culture.

▮ Richard J. Herrnstein and Charles Murray's *The Bell Curve* (1996), though still hotly debated, is emblematic of the debate over affirmative action. Editor Evelyn Hu-DeHart provides essays that examine the impact of globalization on recent Asian immigrants in *Across the Pacific* (1999). Robert Suro's *Strangers Among Us* (1998) investigates the history of the Latino community in America and the challenges its growth presents for the future.

Richard Abanes's *American Militias: Rebellion, Racism, and Religion* (1996) and Philip Lamy's *Millennium Rage* (1996) are both good introductions to the antigovernment groups of the 1990s.

▌ There is a small but growing body of literature on the impact of globalization. See, for example, two books by Thomas L. Friedman: *The Lexus and the Olive Tree* (1999) and *The World Is Flat* (2005). Also useful are Joseph Stiglitz, *Globalization and Its Critics* (2003) and *The Roaring Nineties* (2004); Michael Mandenbau, *The Ideas That Conquered the World* (2002); and Amy Chua, *World on Fire* (2004). Juliet B. Schor's *The Overworked American* (1993) and *The Overspent American* (1998) both study the impact of globalization on American workers. Jeffery Toobin offers the most balanced assessment of the disputed 2000 election in *Too Close to Call* (2002). The legal developments after the election are described by law professor Abner Greene in *Understanding the 2000 Election* (2001).

18 The Challenges of the New Century, 2001 to the Present

"**M**y fellow citizens, at this hour American and coalition forces are in the early stages of military operations to disarm Iraq, to free its people and to defend the world from grave danger," President George W. Bush told the nation in a televised broadcast on March 19, 2003. The announcement that the United States, and a small coalition "of the willing," was going to war followed months of failed diplomacy as the administration tried to convince the United Nations to support a resolution to remove Saddam Hussein from power. Secretary of State Colin Powell told the UN Security Council that the United States had overwhelming evidence that Saddam Hussein was harboring stockpiles of chemical and biological weapons in clear violation of past UN mandates. Iraq had "shown utter contempt for the United Nations and the opinion of the world" by refusing to cooperate with the inspection process, he said.

Most of America's closest allies remained skeptical of the U.S. claims that Hussein possessed weapons of mass destruction (WMD). They wanted to expand the inspection process to uncover clear evidence of Iraq's duplicity before using military force. French Foreign Minister Dominique de Villepin led the opposition. "The use of force against Iraq is not justified today," he declared. "There is an alternative to war, and that is to disarm Iraq through inspections." Secretary of State Powell responded for an administration still traumatized by the attacks on the World Trade Center and the Pentagon on September 11, 2001. "We cannot wait for one of these weapons [of mass destruction] to turn up in our cities. More inspections—I am sorry—are not the answer." On March 17, the administration, realizing its efforts to build an international coalition had failed, withdrew its resolution and gave Hussein forty-eight hours to leave the country. Two days later, Bush launched the attack and addressed the nation.

The debate over Iraq isolated the United States from Europe, exposing deep differences between the way Americans viewed their role in the world and the way most other nations saw the United States. "America is virtually alone," observed *Newsweek*. "Never will it have waged a war in such isolation. Never have so many of its allies been so firmly opposed to its policies." The Cold War had provided a common bond uniting America with Europe by a shared sense of threat from the Soviet Union. The breakup of the Soviet Union, the emergence of the United States as the world's sole superpower, and the rise of radical terrorist groups had rearranged the global order. It also exposed the paradox of American power in the post–Cold War era: never had the nation been more militarily powerful and yet so vulnerable and so isolated in the world.

September 11, 2001

At 8:45 AM a hijacked passenger jet, American Airlines Flight 11, crashed into the north tower of the World Trade Center. A few minutes later, a second hijacked airliner crashed into the south tower. The attacks on the World Trade Center were part of a well-coordinated terrorist assault on the symbols of American economic and military might. A third hijacked plane smashed into the western part of the Pentagon. A fourth plane, possibly headed to the Capitol building or the White House, crashed in a field in western Pennsylvania after passengers struggled with hijackers. Before nightfall, 2,813 civilians were dead, making it the bloodiest day on American soil since September 17, 1862, when 6,300 Union and Confederate soldiers were killed or mortally wounded in the Civil War battle of Antietam.

The repercussions spread across the nation. The government closed borders. Major skyscrapers and other potential terrorist targets were evacuated. Global financial markets plunged into chaos. "IT'S WAR!" screamed the headline of the *New York Daily News*. Many observers believed the threat of global terrorism would usher in a new era in international relations, reshuffling old alliances, and reaffirming others, in a struggle that would be as defining as the Cold War. "You recognize that something's changed forever in the way that the United States thinks about its security," observed national security adviser Condoleezza Rice.

The world community rallied around the United States in an unprecedented show of solidarity. In Germany, more than 200,000 people marched under the Brandenburg Gate to show their support. In London, Buckingham Palace played "The Star-Spangled Banner" during the ceremonial changing of the guards. The Paris-based *Le Monde* newspaper, often critical of American foreign policy, proclaimed: "We are all Americans now."

President Bush at Ground Zero   Three days after two planes crashed into the World Trade Towers, President George W. Bush visited Ground Zero, the eight-story-plus pile of rubble and debris that remained when the two towers and several surrounding buildings collapsed. Standing on a burned-out fire truck and using a bullhorn, Bush proclaimed to the crowd of rescue workers gathered near him, "I can hear you. The rest of the world hears you. And the people who knocked down these buildings will hear all of us soon." After his pronouncement, Bush comforted firefighter Bob Beckwith, seen here, while the crowd chanted "U.S.A., U.S.A!" *(© AP/Wide World Photos)*

On the evening of the attacks a shaken President Bush declared war on global terrorism. Intelligence experts suspected that only Saudi billionaire Osama bin Laden possessed the resources to pull off such a daring and complicated operation. The United States took aim at bin Laden and the radical Taliban government of Afghanistan, which provided a safe haven for his operations. In the weeks leading up to the actual military assault on Afghanistan, the administration built an impressive international coalition to bolster military action. As in the first Gulf War, the United States included a number of Arab states in its alliance to blunt bin Laden's effort to characterize the war as a battle between the Christian West and the Muslim East.

American military technology and air power proved no match for the poorly equipped Taliban fighters. On October 7 the United States and Britain launched a series of punishing air strikes using long-range bombers and cruise missiles. Weakened by the air campaign, the Taliban regime gave up the capital of Kabul to the opposition Northern Alliance forces in November. On December 6, Taliban forces surrendered the southern city of Kandahar, their last stronghold. Only pockets of Taliban forces continued to resist, launching hit-and-run attacks against Western troops. Many observers hailed the American campaign as "a masterpiece of military creativity and finesse," but it ended without the capture of Osama bin Laden or the leaders of the Taliban government.

PRIMARY SOURCE

Declaration of War on Terrorism

GEORGE W. BUSH

In a televised message on September 20, 2001, President Bush addressed the nation before a joint session of Congress and proclaimed war on terrorism in retaliation for the attacks on the World Trade Center Towers and the Pentagon.

On September the 11th, enemies of freedom committed an act of war against our country. Americans have known wars—but for the past 136 years, they have been wars on foreign soil, except for one Sunday in 1941. Americans have known the casualties of war—but not at the center of a great city on a peaceful
5 morning. Americans have known surprise attacks—but never before on thousands of civilians. All of this was brought upon us in a single day—and night fell on a different world, a world where freedom itself is under attack.

Americans have many questions tonight. Americans are asking: Who attacked our country? The evidence we have gathered all points to a collection of
10 loosely affiliated terrorist organizations known as al Qaeda. They are the same

murderers indicted for bombing American embassies in Tanzania and Kenya, and responsible for bombing the USS *Cole*.

Al Qaeda is to terror what the mafia is to crime. But its goal is not making money; its goal is remaking the world—and imposing its radical beliefs on
15   people everywhere.

The terrorists practice a fringe form of Islamic extremism that has been rejected by Muslim scholars and the vast majority of Muslim clerics—a fringe movement that perverts the peaceful teachings of Islam. The terrorists' directive commands them to kill Christians and Jews, to kill all Americans, and to make
20   no distinction among military and civilians, including women and children.

This group and its leader—a person named Osama bin Laden—are linked to many other organizations in different countries, including the Egyptian Islamic Jihad and the Islamic Movement of Uzbekistan. There are thousands of these terrorists in more than 60 countries. They are recruited from their own nations and
25   neighborhoods and brought to camps in places like Afghanistan, where they are trained in the tactics of terror. They are sent back to their homes or sent to hide in countries around the world to plot evil and destruction.

The leadership of al Qaeda has great influence in Afghanistan and supports the Taliban regime in controlling most of that country. In Afghanistan, we see al
30   Qaeda's vision for the world.

Afghanistan's people have been brutalized—many are starving and many have fled. Women are not allowed to attend school. You can be jailed for owning a television. Religion can be practiced only as their leaders dictate. A man can be jailed in Afghanistan if his beard is not long enough.
35   The United States respects the people of Afghanistan—after all, we are currently its largest source of humanitarian aid—but we condemn the Taliban regime. (Applause.) It is not only repressing its own people, it is threatening people everywhere by sponsoring and sheltering and supplying terrorists. By aiding and abetting murder, the Taliban regime is committing murder.
40   And tonight, the United States of America makes the following demands on the Taliban: Deliver to United States authorities all the leaders of al Qaeda who hide in your land. (Applause.) Release all foreign nationals, including American citizens, you have unjustly imprisoned. Protect foreign journalists, diplomats and aid workers in your country. Close immediately and permanently every terrorist
45   training camp in Afghanistan, and hand over every terrorist, and every person in their support structure, to appropriate authorities. (Applause.) Give the United States full access to terrorist training camps, so we can make sure they are no longer operating.

These demands are not open to negotiation or discussion. (Applause.) The
50   Taliban must act, and act immediately. They will hand over the terrorists, or they will share in their fate.

I also want to speak tonight directly to Muslims throughout the world. We respect your faith. It's practiced freely by many millions of Americans, and by millions more in countries that America counts as friends. Its teachings are good
55   and peaceful, and those who commit evil in the name of Allah blaspheme the name of Allah. (Applause.) The terrorists are traitors to their own faith, trying,

in effect, to hijack Islam itself. The enemy of America is not our many Muslim
friends; it is not our many Arab friends. Our enemy is a radical network of terrorists, and every government that supports them. (Applause.)

60   Our war on terror begins with al Qaeda, but it does not end there. It will not
end until every terrorist group of global reach has been found, stopped and
defeated. (Applause.)

    Americans are asking, why do they hate us? They hate what we see right here
in this chamber—a democratically elected government. Their leaders are self-

65 appointed. They hate our freedoms—our freedom of religion, our freedom of
speech, our freedom to vote and assemble and disagree with each other.

    These terrorists kill not merely to end lives, but to disrupt and end a way of
life. With every atrocity, they hope that America grows fearful, retreating from
the world and forsaking our friends. They stand against us, because we stand in

70 their way.

Source: Address to a Joint Session of Congress, Washington, D.C., September 20, 2001. ■ ■ ■

War with Iraq

Even while American troops were fighting in Afghanistan, the Bush administration began drawing up plans to send troops into Iraq. For the administration
terrorism had replaced communism as the new ideological and military threat to
American global interests in the post–Cold War era. They believed that new
threats from terrorist networks, and the states that sponsored them, required a
broader definition of American interests. "The greatest danger our nation faces
lies in the crossroads of radicalism and technology," the president declared in
September 2002. The proliferation of weapons of mass destruction—chemical,
biological, and nuclear—had rendered irrelevant Cold War concepts such as deterrence and containment. Since deterrence cannot work against those who "seek
martyrdom in death," the White House called for a new strategy of preemptive
strike. The United States would act decisively, and act alone if necessary, to eliminate potential threats.

On March 19, U.S. forces launched their "shock and awe" military campaign.
While cruise missiles and precision-guided bombs rained down on strategic
targets in Baghdad, more than 40,000 troops rolled into southern Iraq. Despite
encountering fierce resistance, U.S. troops moved into Baghdad on April 9.
On May 1, President Bush declared the end of "major combat operations" in Iraq,
but the guerrilla-style war intensified over the next few months. On December
13, American soldiers pulled a disoriented Saddam Hussein from a "spider's hole"
at a farm near his hometown of Tikrit, but his capture had little impact on the resistance. The administration discovered that maintaining the peace would prove
more difficult than winning the war. U.S. soldiers were subject to daily deadly

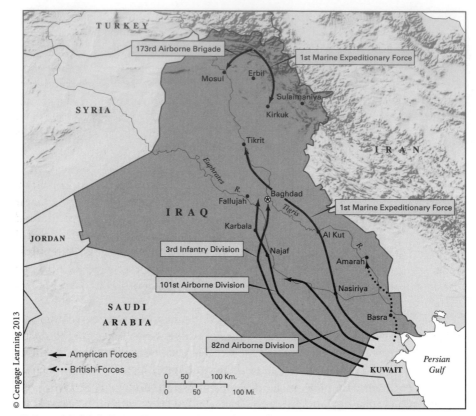

U.S. and British Troop Movements, March–April 2003   Operation Iraqi Freedom began
on March 19, 2003, with the launch of forty Tomahawk missiles from ships in the Persian Gulf
and Red Sea. While bombings continued, American and British forces began heading into
southern Iraq from bases in Kuwait on March 21, with American troops targeting Najaf and
Karbala on their way to Baghdad and the British moving on Basra and points along the Tigris
River. American and Turkish forces joined with Kurdish fighters in northern Iraq, targeting the
cities of Mosul and Kirkuk. On April 13, U.S. marines entered the city of Tikrit, the birthplace
of Saddam Hussein and the last major town not under the control of coalition forces.

attacks, while sabotage weakened the already crippled Iraqi infrastructure. Even
democratic elections in January 2005 did little to stem the violence. By May 2006
the war had claimed more than 2,400 American lives and left another 18,000
wounded. In April 2006, only 29 percent of Americans said the Iraq war was
worth fighting—down from 70 percent at the beginning of the effort.

Perhaps most damaging of all, the United States failed to uncover the promised stockpiles of chemical and biological weapons. In January 2004, former chief
U.S. weapons inspector David Kay told a Senate committee: "It turns out we were
all wrong." In response, the administration justified the war on humanitarian
grounds, claiming the United States had rid the world of a repressive tyrant and
laid the foundation for democracy in the Middle East.

The Paradox of Power

In 2004, the United States spent as much on defense as the rest of the world (191 countries) combined. According to a NATO official Europe was "a military pygmy" compared to the United States. The nation had never enjoyed a greater advantage in military power over either its allies or its potential adversaries. Yet rarely had Americans felt as weak, vulnerable, and isolated. Most of the world rejected the nation's justifications for war against Iraq. Europeans overwhelmingly disapproved: 87 percent in France, 85 percent in Germany, 83 percent in Russia, 79 percent in Spain, 76 percent in Italy, and 60 percent even in Britain, America's staunchest ally. While the United States believed the terrorist threat justified a unilateral approach, most Europeans emphasized the need to build coalitions by using existing international institutions. The new threat of global terrorism left Europe and the United States feeling insecure, but for different reasons. Americans felt vulnerable to another terrorist attack; Europeans, who had endured terrorist attacks of their own, worried about a unipolar world dominated by American military might.

The September 11 terrorist attacks also led to a major reordering of domestic priorities for the Bush administration. Having won election promising to shrink the Washington bureaucracy and limit government spending, Bush presided over an expansion of federal power unseen since the days of Lyndon Johnson's Great Society. Within the first few weeks of the crisis, the president approved $55 billion in federal spending, including a massive federal relief package for New York. The president abandoned traditional conservative faith in deregulation and orchestrated a federal bailout of the airlines. In June 2002, Bush called for the creation of a new Department of Homeland Security, which would include 169,000 employees from eight existing cabinet departments and a budget of $37.4 billion. The proposal represented the largest reorganization of the federal government since Harry Truman signed the National Security Act of 1947. In 2003, Bush added a new entitlement—prescription drug coverage—to Medicare. The new entitlement was expected to add at least $400 billion over the next decade.

In its first three years in office, the administration watched a $236 billion federal budget surplus transform into a $400 billion annual deficit. Overall government spending increased by 16 percent. Although post–September 11 defense needs accounted for much of the increase, domestic spending also grew by 11 percent. For the first time since World War II, federal spending per household topped $20,000.

Perhaps the greatest expansion of federal power came in law enforcement. The administration claimed that a network of "sleeper agents" was operating in the United States preparing a future attack. In the first few months after the attack, the FBI arrested over 1,000 suspects, moved them to unknown locations, and monitored their communications with their lawyers. Attorney General John Ashcroft said the policy was intended to stop inmates who had been involved in terrorism from passing messages to confederates through lawyers, their assistants, or translators. But critics asked how far the government would go in attempting to balance its need to protect the national welfare with its responsibility to protect civil liberties. A series of court decisions denied the government's efforts to detain terror suspects without filing formal charges or allowing them access to lawyers. "We call ourselves a nation of laws," a defense attorney said, "and the test of a nation of laws is whether it adheres to them in times of stress."

The administration appeared helpless, however, to tame the forces of globalization that produced a flood of white-collar jobs out of the United States. With the Internet and high-speed data networks increasing the speed and ease of communication over long distances, companies continued shipping "knowledge work" abroad. In 2003, Microsoft announced that it would invest $400 million in India over the next three years. That was in addition to the $750 million it was spending on outsourcing in China.

When combined with old-fashioned greed, globalization allowed rogue corporate managers to develop sophisticated methods for avoiding shareholder scrutiny. In many cases, they used the complexity of their worldwide operations to disguise their corrupt practices. In 2003, five companies—Enron, WorldCom, Tyco, Qwest, and Global Crossing—were charged with squandering a combined $460 billion in shareholder value.

While many Americans worried about job security, much of the nation was embroiled in a heated debate over gay rights. The controversy was ignited by a Massachusetts court decision that extended marriage rights to same-sex couples. At issue was a basic question of American identity: Could a minority be denied rights enjoyed by other Americans, and who—the courts, the states, or the federal government—should decide? Ironically, conservatives, who were traditionally skeptical of federal power, proposed a constitutional amendment that would define marriage as a union between a man and a woman. Liberals and gay rights supporters adopted the conservative states-rights mantra, while also claiming that the courts played a key role in the process. "It is fundamentally un-American for the tyranny of the majority to determine the rights of any minority," said a gay-rights supporter. "That's what this country was raised on. You don't have popularity contests about who is equal under the law."

2004 Presidential Election and Bush's Second Term

The war in Iraq provided the backdrop to the 2004 presidential contest. With polls showing strong support for his handling of foreign policy and the war on terrorism, President Bush campaigned as a wartime commander-in-chief, warning of dire consequences if the nation changed course. Hoping to neutralize the president's standing as a wartime leader, the Democrats nominated Massachusetts senator and decorated Vietnam War veteran John Kerry. More than 120 million people turned out on

2004 Presidential Debate Between John Kerry and George W. Bush The Democrats hoped that Kerry, a Massachusetts senator and Vietnam war hero, would neutralize President Bush's advantage as a wartime president. In this first of three debates, the discussion revolved around Iraq and homeland security, the key issues over which the campaign would be fought. Kerry seemed to waffle on whether the war with Iraq was necessary and never presented a convincing alternative to administration policy. *(Corbis)*

election day to cast ballots—the highest turnout since 1968. Bush won 51 percent of the popular vote and 286 electoral votes. Although not as razor-thin as the 2000 election, the results revealed continued geographical and ideological divisions. Bush won states in the South, the Great Plains, and the Mountain regions. Kerry swept states in the Northeast, North Central, and Pacific Coast region. The president faced the difficult task of uniting the country after a bitter and hard-fought campaign.

In his second term the president was burdened by the stalemate in Iraq and by charges that his administration badly mishandled the response to Hurricane Katrina. Early on the morning of August 29, 2005, Katrina—a category three storm packing sustained winds of 127 miles per hour—slammed into the southeast Louisiana coastline. The storm caused major damage throughout the Gulf region, but its greatest impact was in New Orleans, where the powerful storm surge smashed through the fragile system of concrete floodwalls that protect the city

Thousands of residents, many of them poor African Americans unable to evacuate the city, were trapped in the rising waters. Overwhelmed by the enormity of the crisis, local officials looked immediately to Washington for help, but the Bush administration was slow to respond. Many residents were trapped for days without food, water, or sanitation. A congressional investigation found that bureaucratic infighting and poor leadership contributed to the bungled relief effort. While President Bush's determined leadership had reassured the nation in the days following September 11, his shaky response to Katrina left many Americans wondering whether the government was prepared to handle future crises.

The public registered its dissatisfaction with the administration in the 2006 midterm election. Democrats gained 31 seats and took control of the House for the first time since 1994. They elected California's Nancy Pelosi as the first woman Speaker of the House. In the Senate, Democrats picked up 6 seats, giving them a small 51–49 voting majority over the Republican.

Meltdown on Wall Street

President Bush confronted another crisis in the final years of his presidency. After the attacks on September 11, the Federal Reserve Bank, which regulates the nation's money supply, had slashed the interest rate that it charges banks from 3.5 percent to one percent, its lowest level since the 1950s. The cheap financing produced a housing boom. Families took advantage of low mortgage rates to buy bigger homes and speculators bought properties to flip. Banks relaxed their standards, encouraging people with poor credit to take out risky subprime interest-only loans. By extending mortgages to unqualified lenders and accumulating large inventories of subprime securities, banks and other financial institutions took on enormous risks.

Those risks became public in 2007 as housing prices tumbled and many banks discovered the subprime mortgages they were holding had little value. Faced with the possibility of a collapse of the financial system, the federal government responded with unprecedented steps. The Federal Reserve bailed out Wall Street giant Bear Stearns and the insurance company American International Group (AIG). The Federal Reserve's decision not to aid another Wall Street firm, Lehman Brothers, sent shock waves through the international banking system. Global stock prices plummeted, many banks stopped lending money, and the world faced the prospect of a financial meltdown.

In September, the Bush administration proposed a $700 billion plan that would allow the government to buy bad assets from the nation's biggest banks. The goal was to restore confidence in major banks by removing liabilities from their balance sheets, allowing them to lend money and fuel economic growth. While Congress debated the radical proposal, stocks continued their precipitous fall. Unable to delay any longer, Congress, including many conservative Republicans, voted for the legislation. In a coordinated effort with other nations, the Federal Reserve slashed its interest rates to zero. While an economic catastrophe may have been avoided, the efforts failed to spur lending or restore confidence in the global markets. In November, the stock market hit its lowest level in a decade.

The Historic Election of 2008

The financial meltdown took place in the final weeks of the presidential election. The Republicans nominated 72-year old Arizona Senator John McCain. A Vietnam War hero, McCain had planned to campaign on his foreign policy and tough anti-terror credentials. Despite polls showing declining public support for the war in Iraq, McCain championed the administration's plan for a "surge" to quell insurgency before turning over the fighting to Iraqi fighting forces. Ironically, the surge succeeded in reducing American casualties, but it also allowed Americans to focus their attention on problems closer at home. McCain also had to contend with President Bush's low approval ratings, plummeting stock prices, and rising unemployment. Although he tried to distance himself from Bush, voters seemed determined to punish the president's party in November.

McCain tried to change the calculus of the race by choosing little-known Alaska Governor Sarah Palin as his running mate. While Palin energized social conservatives, she alienated just about everyone else, including key independent voters. Over time, the choice led some people to question McCain's judgment.

McCain also had to face a charismatic and energetic opponent in Illinois Senator Barack Obama, who defeated frontrunner Hillary Clinton for the Democratic nomination. At a time when Americans were longing for change, everything about Obama—his background, style, and message—established him as an agent of change.

Barack Hussein Obama Jr. was born August 4, 1961, in Honolulu. His parents, Ann Dunham, a white Kansas native, and his father, a black Kenyan, met as students at the University of Hawaii. After a divorce, his mother remarried and moved Barack to her second husband's home in Indonesia, where Obama lived for two years. He returned to Hawaii, where he was raised by his grandparents, before attending Columbia University and, later, Harvard Law School. He began his political career in 1997 as an Illinois state senator. In 2004, he won election to the United States Senate. After only two years in office he started campaigning for the presidency. Obama made "change" the central theme of his campaign, promising to end the war in Iraq, to allow Bush-era tax cuts to expire, and to pass a comprehensive health-care reform bill. The message resonated with traditional Democrats and independent voters, and especially among young people, who turned out in massive numbers to his campaign rallies.

Once again the legacy of the 1960s emerged as a campaign issue. Although Obama, born in 1961, was only a child during the tumultuous decade,

Republicans tried linking him to Bill Ayers, a Chicago neighbor who had been involved in violent anti-Vietnam War protests. The tactic failed to sway voters. Throughout the campaign Obama countered charges that he was unqualified by displaying a mastery of issues while projecting a steady, calm, and disciplined image. According to all the national polls, Obama emerged the winner of the three presidential debates between the two men.

On election day, Obama defeated McCain by 52.9 percent to 45.7 percent. The Democratic nominee took all 19 states John Kerry had won in 2004 plus another nine, including three in the Republican South. His electoral vote margin was even more impressive: 365–173. Democrats picked up 21 seats in the House and 8 in the Senate. Obama's election represented a historic moment for the nation. In the course of one generation, America went from denying basic rights to African Americans to electing one as president. "If there is anyone out there who doubts that America is a place where all things are possible; who still wonders if the dream of our Founders is alive in our time; who still questions the power of our democracy, tonight is your answer," Obama told followers after the election.

A Historic Inauguration   Shortly after noon on January 20, 2009, a smiling Barack Obama takes the oath of office as the 44th President of the United States and the first African-American elected to that office. *(MSgt Cecilio Ricardo/DefenseImagery.mil)*

The Obama Presidency

Concerns about the economy dominated the early months of the Obama administration. In 2009, Democrats passed a $787 billion spending bill designed to stimulate the economy. The bill passed the House with no Republican votes and with only three in the Senate. The administration also forced struggling General Motors and Chrysler into bankruptcy and then invested more than $60 billion in federal money to revive the ailing auto industry. The administration pushed through Congress tougher regulations on banks and a $75 billion program to help homeowners facing foreclosure. The measures likely stemmed the financial bleeding, but the recovery proved painfully slow. By 2010, unemployment passed 10 percent.

The administration juggled economic recovery with another major initiative—reform of the nation's health-care system. After months of negotiating, Congress passed an ambitious reform bill which prevented insurance companies from denying coverage to individuals with preexisting conditions. It also required all Americans to purchase insurance. Tackling another hot button issue, Obama also called for repeal of the military's "don't ask, don't tell" policy toward gays and lesbians in the armed forces. Although strongly opposed by conservatives, the Senate voted to repeal the eighteen-year-old ban, and the Pentagon implemented the new policy in July, 2011.

On foreign policy, Obama's policies reflected more continuity than change from the previous administration. He retained Bush secretary of defense Robert Gates, and while fulfilling his campaign promise to wind down the war in Iraq, he sent more troops to Afghanistan. The increase was necessary, he declared, "to stabilize a deteriorating situation in Afghanistan, which has not received the strategic attention, direction and resources it urgently requires." In May 2011, the administration achieved a major victory when a special forces team conducted a daring raid inside Pakistan and killed Osama bin Laden. Polls, however, showed that only 16 percent of Americans felt safer following bin Laden's death. Nearly 60 percent believed that his death increased the likelihood of a terrorist attack in the United States.

The burst of government activism proved too much for many Americans, who were angry about massive government spending, the bailouts of the big banks, and the growing national debt. Many critics gravitated toward the new "Tea Party," a loose coalition of largely white, middle-class Republicans who were determined to shrink the size of the federal government. The Republican Party channeled Tea Party anger into major gains in the 2010 midterm elections. On election night, Republicans picked up 63 seats and regained control of the House. After the election, Obama moved to the center, working with congressional Republicans to pass a deficit reduction plan as both sides positioned themselves for the 2012 presidential campaign.

The Evolving American Identity

The midterm election results revealed that Americans, even in the face of economic catastrophe, clung to traditional notions of limited government. At the same time, Obama's election in 2008, and the results of the 2010 census, underscored how American identity continued to evolve. By 2010, more than 9 million Americans self-identified as belonging to two or more race groups. The number who claimed they were both "black" and "white" grew by 134% from 2000 to 2010. Ironically, Obama was not counted as one of them. He identified himself as "black."

America was becoming more diverse as racial and ethnic minorities made up about 90 percent of the total U.S. growth since 2000. Because of declining birth rates, the non-Hispanic white share of the population dropped over the decade from 69 percent to roughly 64 percent. Hispanics alone accounted for more than half of the U.S. population increase. One of every six Americans identified as Hispanics. The Asian population also witnessed a dramatic increase, growing by 43 percent.

Americans also continued their migration to the Sun Belt. The growing populations of California, Texas, and the Mountain West in the west pushed the nation's mean center of population roughly 30 miles southwest to the village of Plato, Missouri. African Americans, who had migrated to northern cities earlier in the century, joined the movement south. They left Chicago and Detroit for the suburbs of Atlanta, Dallas, and Houston. The largest increase in Hispanic population also took place in the South, especially Alabama, Louisiana, North Carolina, and Louisiana.

While circumstances have changed since 1945, the nation continues to struggle with the same paradox that defined much of its history in the last century. Will popular attitudes toward government prove capable of reconciling the demands for greater services with the traditional fear of federal power? How will society adjust to the influence of its diverse population while maintaining its sense of common identity? Can the government protect the national interest abroad without sacrificing democracy at home? The answers to those questions may prove elusive, but Americans will continue their search for a better society. "The idea of the search is what holds us together," noted the historian Daniel Boorstin. "The quest is the enduring American experiment. The meaning is in the seeking."

Index

Note: Page numbers followed by *i* indicate illustrations.